A Social and Religious History of the Jews

In Three Volumes

VOLUME TWO

A
Social and Religious History of the Jews

BY

SALO WITTMAYER BARON

PROFESSOR OF JEWISH HISTORY, LITERATURE, AND
INSTITUTIONS, ON THE MILLER FOUNDATION
COLUMBIA UNIVERSITY

VOLUME TWO

NEW YORK : MORNINGSIDE HEIGHTS
COLUMBIA UNIVERSITY PRESS
1937

Copyright 1937
COLUMBIA UNIVERSITY PRESS
Published 1937

Printed in the United States of America.

CONTENTS

Abbreviations		vii
IX.	The Wanderer	3
X.	Within the Ghetto Walls	87
XI.	Emancipation	164
XII.	Nationalism	262
Epilogue		364

ABBREVIATIONS

Abhandlungen Chajes — Abhandlungen zur Erinnerung an Hirsch Perez Chajes. Vienna, 1933.
Abrahams Mem. Vol. — Jewish Studies in Memory of Israel Abrahams, By the Faculty and Visiting Teachers of the Jewish Institute of Religion. New York, 1927.
Ag.Ap. — Josephus' Against Apion.
AJSL — American Journal of Semitic Languages and Literatures.
Annual ASOR — Annual of the American Schools of Oriental Research.
Antt. — Josephus' Antiquities.
AO — Archiv für Orientforschung.
AR — Archiv für Religionswissenschaft.
ARN — Aboth de-Rabbi Nathan. Edited by S. Schechter.
AZ — Abodah Zarah.
b. — Babylonian Talmud.
Bar. — Baraita.
B.B. — Baba Batra.
Ber. — Berakot.
BJPES — Bulletin (*Yediot*) of the Jewish Palestine Exploration Society.
B.K. — Baba Kamah.
B.M. — Baba Mesiah.
Braude Jub. Vol. — Sepher ha-Yobel li-kebod Dr. Mordecai Zeeb Braude. Księga jubileuszowa ku czci Dra. Markusa Braudego (A Polish and a Hebrew section). Warsaw, 1931.
Bull. ASOR — Bulletin of the American Schools of Oriental Research.
Cant. r. — Midrash Rabbah to the Song of Songs, edited by S. Buber.
C. Th. — Theodosian Code.
Dubnow Festschrift — Festschrift zu Simon Dubnows siebzigstem Geburtstag. Edited by I. Elbogen, J. Meisl and M. Wischnitzer. Berlin, 1930.
EJ — Encyclopaedia Judaica, Vols. I-X. Berlin, 1928-35.
Festschrift Breslau — Festschrift zum 75-jährigen Bestehen des jüdisch-theologischen Seminars Fraenckelscher Stiftung. 2 vols., Breslau, 1929.
Festskrift Simonsen — Festskrift i anledning af Professor David Simonsens 70-aarige Fødselsdag. Copenhagen, 1923.
Freidus Mem. Vol. — Studies in Jewish Bibliography and Related Subjects in Memory of Abraham Solomon Freidus. New York, 1929.
Gen.r. — Bereshit rabbah (Midrash Rabbah to Genesis). Edited by J. Theodor and Ch. Albeck.
G.S. — Gesammelte Schriften.

ABBREVIATIONS

Guttmann Festschrift	Festschrift zum siebzigsten Geburtstage Jakob Guttmanns. Leipzig, 1915.
Hag.	Hagigah.
HTR	Harvard Theological Review.
HUCA	Hebrew Union College Annual.
Israel	La Rassegna mensile di Israel (New Series, if not otherwise stated).
j.	Palestinian Talmud (Jerushalmi).
JAOS	Journal of the American Oriental Society.
JB	JIWO Bleter, Vilna.
JBL	Journal of Biblical Literature.
JE	The Jewish Encyclopedia. 12 vols., New York, 1901-6.
JFF	Jüdische Familienforschung, Berlin.
JGJC	Jahrbuch für Geschichte der Juden in der Čechoslovakischen Republik.
JJLG	Jahrbuch der jüdisch-literarischen Gesellschaft in Frankfurt a.M.
JPOS	Journal of the Palestine Oriental Society.
JQR	Jewish Quarterly Review (New Series, if not otherwise stated).
JR	Journal of Religion.
JRAS	Journal of the Royal Asiatic Society.
JSSQ	Jewish Social Service Quarterly.
JTS	Journal of Theological Studies.
Jüdische Studien Wohlgemuth	Jüdische Studien Joseph Wohlgemuth zu seinem sechzigsten Geburtstage von Freunden und Schülern gewidmet. Frankfort, 1928.
JWS	Jüdische Wohlfahrtspflege und Sozialwissenschaft, Berlin.
KA	Korrespondenzblatt des Vereins zur Gründung und Erhaltung einer Akademie für die Wissenschaft des Judentums. Vols. I-IX, 1920-30.
Ket.	Ketubot.
Kidd.	Kiddushin.
Kohut Mem. Vol.	Jewish Studies in Memory of George A. Kohut. Edited by S. W. Baron and A. Marx, New York, 1935.
KS	Kirjath Sepher, Quarterly Bibliographical Review, Jerusalem.
Lam. r.	Midrash Rabbah to Lamentations. Edited by S. Buber.
M.	Mishnah.
MGWJ	Monatsschrift für Geschichte und Wissenschaft des Judentums.
Misc. JHSE	Miscellanies of the Jewish Historical Society in England.
MJ	Menorah Journal.
M.K.	Moed Katan.
MZ	Miesięcznik Żydowski.
Ned.	Nedarim.
PAAJR	Proceedings of the American Academy for Jewish Research.
PAJHS	Publications of the American Jewish Historical Society.

ABBREVIATIONS

PEFQS	Palestine Exploration Fund Quarterly Statement.
Pes.	Pesahim.
PG	J. P. Migne's Patrologiae cursus completus, series Graeca.
Philippson Festschrift	Beiträge zur Geschichte der deutschen Juden, Festschrift zum siebzigsten Geburtstage Martin Philippsons, Leipzig, 1916.
PJB	Palästina Jahrbuch.
PL	J. P. Migne's Patrologiae cursus completus, series Latina.
Poznanski Mem. Vol.	Livre d'hommage à la mémoire du Dr. Samuel Poznanski (1864-1921), offert par les amis et les compagnons du travail scientifique. Warsaw, 1929.
PWRE	Pauly-Wissowa-Kroll, Realencyclopädie der classischen Altertumswissenschaft.
r.	Midrash Rabbah.
RB	Revue biblique.
REJ	Revue des études juives.
R.H.	Rosh Hashanah.
RHPR	Revue d'histoire et de philosophie religieuses.
RHR	Revue d'histoire des religions.
RSR	Recherches des sciences religieuses.
Sanh.	Sanhedrin.
T.	Tosefta. Edited by M. S. Zuckermandel.
TJHSE	Transactions of the Jewish Historical Society in England.
TR	Theologische Rundschau.
TSK	Theologische Studien und Kritiken.
VSWG	Vierteljahrsschrift für Sozial- und Wirtschaftsgeschichte.
Yearbook CCAR	Yearbook of the Central Conference of American Rabbis.
Yeb.	Yebamot.
Yellin Jub. Vol.	Minhah le-David (Hebrew Essays in honor of David Yellin), Jerusalem, 1935.
ZAW	Zeitschrift für die alttestamentliche Wissenschaft und die Kunde des nachbiblischen Judentums.
ZDMG	Zeitschrift der deutschen morgenländischen Gesellschaft.
ZGJD	Zeitschrift für die Geschichte der Juden in Deutschland (New Series unless otherwise stated).
ZGJT	Zeitschrift für die Geschichte der Juden in der Tschechoslovakei.
ZMR	Zeitschrift für Missionskunde und Religionswissenschaft.
ZNW	Zeitschrift für die neutestamentliche Wissenschaft und die Kunde der älteren Kirche.

Volume Two

Notes, Bibliography, and Index to this work
will be found in Volume Three.

IX

THE WANDERER

IT was not in the East that the Judeo-Arabic spirit reached its highest fruition. In philosophy as well as in poetry, the greatest work of medieval Jewry was done in the smaller and weaker communities of the extreme West.

THE RISE OF SPANISH JEWRY

Spain and North Africa, which a tenth-century Arabian geographer deemed unworthy of inclusion in his description of the frontiers of the Islamic empire because they were merely "like the sleeve of a garment," were destined to become from that century on the intellectual and literary centers of the Arabic-speaking Jews. Ever since, Sephardic Jewry has remained in contact with the living currents of Islam. From the seventh to the twelfth century, and then again from the sixteenth century to the present, the overwhelming majority of Sephardic and oriental Jewry have lived under Muslim domination. During the intervening three centuries, a portion of that Jewry came under Christian rule and influence, but the impact of Islamic culture was felt deeply in all walks of Jewish life even then. Hardly a century after the Christian *reconquista* of Spain, moreover, reactionary tendencies began forcing more and more Jews back into the African and Asiatic provinces of Islam. In other words, Sephardic Jewry in the main continued to be a variety of the Judeo-Arabic group.

It was therefore natural that, when governmental toleration was withdrawn from the Jews of Spain and Portugal, the majority of the exiles should find their way into Muslim lands. Only an insignificant fraction turned to Christian countries, few reaching the hospitable regions of the Polish crown. Italy, the goal of many refugees, served for the most part merely as a halfway place. The sudden influx of the Sephardic Jewish masses into the Turkish possessions had all the aspects of a great home-coming. To be sure, Spanish culture had meanwhile deeply impressed itself upon this western offshoot of oriental Jewry. The Spanish language had become its mother tongue. That minority of Spanish and Portuguese Jewry which ultimately reached the shores of western Europe and America, could soon pride itself on memorable contributions to western economic, political and cultural developments (to mention only Spinoza, Ricardo and Disraeli). For the majority, however, the transition to eastern ways was comparatively easy. Where their infiltration was gradual and where they encountered deep-rooted Jewish-Arabic culture and speech, as in North Africa, they were speedily absorbed by the remnants of oriental Jewry. But wherever they arrived suddenly in large masses, and where the native language offered less resistance, their Castilian mother tongue, developing with its Hebraic and local ingredients into the so-called Ladino, came to dominate the entire Jewish community. This was especially true of the European provinces of the Ottoman Empire. Here the division of the conquered peoples into Greek and Slavonic-speaking elements, and the use of the Turkish tongue by the rulers, helped Ladino to maintain its predominance for centuries. The cultural supremacy of these western immigrants, moreover, enabled them to absorb with astonishing rapidity the aboriginal Jewish minority, weakened by the endless vicissitudes of Byzantine rule. Quickened by the dynamic force of rejuvenated Islam, there began among the Spanish refugees, almost immediately upon their arrival in the eastern harbors in the sixteenth century, an amazing cultural renaissance.[1]

TRANSMISSION OF EASTERN CULTURE

However, the intervening three centuries of Christian domination and the contact thus established between the Spanish outpost of western Christendom and the western branch of the Judeo-Arabic world, were of lasting import. Through the Jews of Spain — as well as through those of southern France and southern Italy, who had also had a short experience of Muslim rule — Latin Christianity received numerous impulses from the great culture of Islam. Even in the Carolingian age, the importation by the Jews of the superior products of the East had greatly contributed to raising the general material level of civilization, but now they brought still finer treasures of Eastern knowledge to the awakening semibarbarians of the West. They brought, moreover, not only the accumulated wisdom of millennia of oriental culture, but also much of the Graeco-Roman science and philosophy which had survived in the East.

Jewish influences were transmitted both through personal contacts and through literature. The importance of the personal element cannot easily be overrated. Arabs were not tolerated in most Christian territories, but Jews hailing from Arabian lands were freely admitted. Jewish physicians and synagogue officials, teachers and interpreters, as well as some of the traders and slave dealers, were often Hebrew and Arabic scholars. Whether merely traveling through western countries or permanently settled there, they spread certain rudiments of Arabian knowledge among the growing Christian intelligentsia of the age. No matter how much the Church insisted upon segregation of Jews from Christians — such legislation was still in its infancy — no water-tight walls could be erected against the penetration of ideas. Even personal relations between the Jews and the Catholic clergy could not be totally eliminated. Unfortunately, sources for the history of this personal transmission are, for obvious reasons, extremely scarce.

Much more is known about the Jewish contributions to the translation of Arabic works into Latin, with Hebrew often serving as an intermediary tongue. It is enough to recall the intellectual revolution about 1200 A.D., when Aristotelianism in its Arabian and especially Maimonidean and Averroistic form, began its triumphal march through Italy and France, England and Germany. A superficial comparison of the philosophic systems of the eleventh century with those of Albertus Magnus and his disciple, Thomas Aquinas, suffices to reveal the depth of the intellectual upheaval. When anti-Aristotelianism dared raise its head and when schoolmen in the Platonic tradition, like Duns Scotus, rejected the teachings of the Angelic Doctor, their most effective weapons had been supplied by the great Judeo-Arabic Platonist, Gabirol. It mattered little that the Scotch Franciscan, the most anti-Jewish of scholastics, was totally unaware, that, by invoking the authority of Avicebrol in support of his basic conception of the fundamental unity of matter in all creation, physical as well as spiritual, he was heavily leaning on a Jewish master. Eventually Averroism, with its acceptance of the eternality of the world and its rejection of the immortality of the individual soul, undermined the entire structure of medieval scholasticism and, through Ockham, opened many a gate which the medieval Church had vainly tried to keep shut. Averroism, although initiated by a non-Jewish Arab, found its main protagonists among the Jews of Spain and southern France. Today there seem to be more manuscript translations and commentaries on Averroës' works extant in Hebrew than in Latin, and perhaps even more than there are Arabic originals. Themistius, a famous ancient commentator of Aristotle, speaks to us, so to say, in the Hebraic tongue, two of his works having come down neither in the original Greek nor in an Arabic translation, but in a secondary version in Hebrew and a tertiary in Latin.

Judeo-Arabic influence upon medieval Europe was not limited to the field of philosophy alone. Although the impact of Arabic science cannot be traced back to a few great individuals, as in the case of philosophy (Maimonides and Gabirol, the Jews; and Avicenna, Al-Gazali and Averroës, the Arabs), it is precisely in the fields of mathematics, astronomy and medicine that the Western world is most deeply indebted to Arabian and Jewish culture. While opinions may differ as to the significance of medieval scholasticism for modern thought, there is no denying that in all scientific fields there is an unbroken line of evolution from Arabian science to that of our day. For centuries European science was little more than a transplanting of the results of Arabic investigations, and, however inferior these transplantations, they exercised an enduring influence upon the mind of Europe. Centuries after Arabic culture had spent its vital force, translations of Arabic works were still being consulted by the most distinguished European scientists.

Here Jews, including many converts to Islam and Christianity, whose Jewish birth can be detected only with great difficulty, were again both coworkers and mediators, original contributors as well as translators. Many a distinguished name still regarded as purely Muslim may, with the increase of our knowledge, turn out to be Jewish. It is hard to overestimate the revolution in European mathematical thinking in the twelfth century, for example, brought about by Avendeath's translations of Al-Khwarizmi. Not only were Arabic numerals here first introduced into Europe as external features of mathematics, but the whole method of approach was deeply affected. Avendeath, a professing or converted Jew, translated also the works of Mashaallah, an Arabic Jewish mathematician of the eighth century; while Plato of Tivoli, a native Christian, rendered into Latin a Hebrew treatise of his Spanish Jewish collaborator, Abraham bar Hiyya, known for centuries thereafter under the name of Savasorda. It was, indeed, Savasorda's geometry, translated by Plato in 1145, that first introduced Arabian trigonometry and mensuration to the West. The collected works (in Latin translation) of Isaac ben Solomon Israeli, a North African Jew of the ninth century, were regarded as medical classics by generations of European physicians. A professing Jew's (Farrachius') translation of the enormous *Liber continens* by Rhazes, the greatest Arabian physician; and a baptized Jew's (John of Capua's) Latin rendering of the *Hygiene* of Maimonides, were distinctive landmarks in the history of western medical science. The subsequent scientific achievements of the Jews themselves in southwestern Europe were merely a continuation of this trend. There were, for example, the two distinguished Jewish co-authors of the Alfonsine Tables, written in 1262-72, who were still wielding an important influence on astronomy in the days of Galileo and Kepler; there was Cresques of Majorca, who in 1375 produced the first world map, and in 1419 was summoned by Prince Henry the Navigator, of Portugal, to help establish a naval academy and astronomical observatory near Lisbon; there were Abraham Zacuto and his pupil Joseph Vecinho, with their memorable contributions in theory and practice to the discoveries of Columbus and Vasco da Gama. How instrumental the Hebrew language was in the development of sciences, can be judged by the fact that Gersonides, one of the most original of fourteenth-century thinkers and scientists, knowing neither Arabic nor Latin, could, by reading only Hebrew sources, familiarize himself with the state of philosophical, mathematical and astronomical scholarship of his day, and materially contribute to the advancement of each."[2]

Thus the intellectual center of gravity was gradually shifting to the Christian West. The dissolution of the caliphate, the state of permanent warfare, the invasions of the Turkish tribes, the growth of intolerance in religious and intellectual life, the Crusades, and the catastrophic Mongol invasions of the thirteenth century, combined to bring about a frightful decline of the economic, political and cultural power of the Arabic world. The rising West attracted more and more Jews, and the western settlements began to assume the leadership of world Jewry. It was the thirteenth century, the century of great transformations in European life, that witnessed the decisive transfer of the Jewish center from Islam to Christendom. The Christian reconquest of Spain coincident with the Mongol invasions of the East, decided the issue. But it must have been only a remnant of the Jewish people that was saved. Despite the astounding growth of Spanish, French and German Jewries, the people as a whole constituted at the end of the thirteenth century only a fraction of what it had been three centuries before. The three centuries that followed were merely a continuation of that prolonged numerical decline. Nevertheless, it was on the medieval European stage that the destinies of the entire people, for centuries to come, were to be shaped. Not the Byzantine Empire, that survival of classical antiquity, but the young and vigorous civilizations of the West offered the Jewish people the opportunity for their characteristic evolution.

ECONOMIC DECLINE

The decline in the status of the Jews during the age of the Crusades was clearly reflected in the constant shrinking of their economic basis. The prominent position they had occupied in international commerce in the days of the caliphate and the Carlovingian monarchs was no longer theirs. They had no chance of competing successfully with Italian traders, backed by the mighty fleets of the city republics of Amalfi, Venice and Genoa, who soon gained a virtual monopoly of the Mediterranean trade. As early as 945, the senate of Venice prohibited the transportation to the Orient of Jewish and other foreign merchants on Venetian vessels. Even before that time (932-36), Pietro Candiano, the Doge of Venice, in coöperation with the patriarch of Grado and the Venetian bishops, appealed to Emperor Henry I and the Archbishop of Mayence, forcibly to convert all Jews. Should they fail to do this, they ought at least to expel the Jews and to forbid them to touch with their "stained hands" the sign of the cross on any kind of merchandise. Neither were the other North Italian republics willing to tolerate Jews for any length of time. The figures recorded in the second half of the twelfth century by the famous traveler, Benjamin of Tudela, show that, while there was a considerable Jewish population in southern Italy, only a few families were to be found in the republics of the North. The decline in the purchasing power and productivity of the Muslim countries, moreover, made the importation of slaves unremunerative; at the same time, the Christianization of eastern Europe made the acquisition of Slavic bondsmen increasingly difficult. The decline of the Khazar Empire wiped out a Jewish stronghold in southeastern Europe. Although an extensive slave trade was plied along the shores of the Black Sea as late as the fifteenth century, the Jewish share in it was insignificant. Nor could the Jews enter the Baltic and the North Sea trade; most of the northern commercial cities, soon to be organized in the Hanseatic League, had long since closed their gates to Jewish settlers. Jewish traders were consequently limited more and more to local commerce in the towns of their settlement, or, at most, to transfers among neighboring continental countries.[3]

ELIMINATION FROM AGRICULTURE

At the same time, the alienation of the Jews from the soil made rapid progress. Whereas under Islamic domination Jews could be owners and tillers of land on the payment of a land tax, many forces combined to eliminate them from agriculture in Christian countries. Both the late Roman Empire and the Church forbade Jews to own Christian slaves; this constituted a severe handicap to the Jewish landlord. The progressive Christianization of eastern Europe affected the Jewish landowner, as well as the Jewish slave trader. The whole development of the feudal system in Europe, moreover, tended to make ownership of land the basis of all social and political life. He who possessed land possessed power. Under these circumstances, the insistent demand of the Church that infidels should have no political power over Christians, a policy which had already led to the exclusion of Jews from public office and military service in the Christian Roman Empire, was ominously extended to shut out Jews from ownership of most of the available land. The harsh measures of the seventh-century Visigoth kings were symptomatic of the uncertainty attaching to Jewish tenure of land. Sisebut's revocation of all grants to Jews made by his predecessors, and Egica's decree of "nationalization" of all Jewish landholdings which had at any time belonged to Christians, clearly revealed the fundamental trend.

Jewish landownership, however, faced many other than legal obstacles. The precariousness of Jewish life in the later Middle Ages, the frequent anti-Jewish riots, the numerous and sudden expulsions, necessarily made the possession of immovable property no unmixed blessing. The Jews expelled from French territories in 1306, for example, could not dispose of all their property in the limited time allowed them. Not until 1309 does a purchaser seem to have been found for certain rural holdings of Champagne Jewry. In Narbonne, in 1308, a Christian purchaser acquired fifty abandoned Jewish houses for £3,957, an amount so low as to provoke the ire of both the local viscount and the archbishop. To appease the former, the buyer handed over £5,000, two houses and a plot of ground; to the archbishop, he gave an unspecified sum. No wonder Jews often preferred to keep their wealth in money and jewels, so readily removable in emergencies.

Since Jews were not subject to the canonical tithe, the Church, which sometimes objected even to the acquisition of land by the tax-exempt clergy, had an active economic interest in detaching them from the land. Down to the thirteenth century, the more vigorous the Church became, the more effective was its opposition to Jewish ownership of land.

The combined influence of these forces led to a gradual estrangement of the Jews from agriculture, particularly where feudalism reigned supreme, as in France, Germany and England. To be sure, in France there was, near Narbonne, a *Terra Hebraeorum,* where Jewish seigneurs ruled over Jewish and Christian vassals; in Angevin England, a Jew named Isaac possessed two villages; and in 1289 Duke Albrecht of Austria gave a vineyard to one Isaac of Vienna. These were exceptions, however. On the other hand, in the Mediterranean countries, and in Poland and Silesia, the Jews long continued to own land. The Spanish kings were directly interested in maintaining Jewish landownership, as Jewish land, according to the prevailing theory that Jews and their property belonged to the king, was, in a sense, crown land. Inasmuch as, when a Jew or a Moor sold an estate to a Christian, the king lost his overlordship over it, special royal permission was required for such transactions. Carrying over large landholdings from the Islamic period, Jews are said to have owned one-third of all the land around Barcelona in the thirteenth century; no doubt the estimate is exaggerated, but it is significant. In Sicily, Frederick II encouraged the immigration of African Jews, to whom he gave crown lands to develop indigo plantations. Even in Spain and in Sicily, however, the growth of feudalism and of the Church's power adversely affected Jewish agriculture. The Cortes of Valladolid, in coöperation with King Sancho, passed a resolution in 1293 that thenceforth no land whatever should be transferred to Jews, and that estates taken over by Jewish creditors from insolvent Christian debtors should be sold to Christian purchasers within a year. Subsequent assemblies reiterated these demands with increasing vigor. Since Jewish landowners, belonging to a special taxpaying group, were exempted from district land taxes, local fiscal interests likewise played a part. The Cortes of Burgos, in 1345, complained that the acquisition of crown lands by Jews and priests diminished the treasury income, and thus indirectly swelled the burden of the Christian landlord.

The great expulsions put an end to Jewish participation in agricultural endeavors in western and central Europe. Even in Muslim countries and Poland, the Jews derived little advantage from the legal right to possess rural estates. Few became landowners, and fewer still tillers of the soil. Perhaps the sad experience of their forefathers in Germany and Spain taught them a lesson. The now-old habit of not living on the soil, the lure of quicker profits from commercial transactions, the desire of the government both in Poland and Turkey to have the Jews develop international trade, and the lack of personal attachment to a particular parcel of land, all contributed to reduce to the vanishing point the Jews' rôle in what was at the time the principal economic activity of all the world.

The influence of religion on Jewish social life contributed to bring this about. Although the severe biblical and tannaitic agricultural laws had been largely discarded or modified by talmudic legislation, there remained in the Jewish creed many obstacles to farming. The Jewish Sabbath, for example, imposed upon Jews abstention from work much more rigidly than did the Christian day of the Lord upon Gentile farmers. Beginning with the Council of Narbonne in 589, moreover, the Church demanded that Jews and their employees refrain from work in the fields on Sunday as well. The Jewish holidays, although well adapted to Palestinian agriculture, were not suited to the climatic conditions of Europe. Jews could perform many religious duties only in places of close settlement, which provided synagogues, schools, etc. Individual farms made this difficult, and, as time went on, Jewish villages, occasionally recorded in the early Middle Ages (such place names as Judendorf and Zydaczów still recall them), became scarcer. Thus the Jewish faith — in a sense true to its own spirit — combined with outward circumstances, deprived Jewry of the last vestiges of a territorial basis.

This does not mean that Jewish religious leaders consciously encouraged the abandonment of agriculture. Solomon Ishaki may have rationalized what appeared to him a wholly utopian rejection of worldly pursuits, ascribed by the legend to R. Simon b. Yohai, by explaining that those works "may be done by Gentiles, while the Holy One, blessed be He, distributes nourishment and profit to those who carry out his will" (*Commentary* on Shabbat 33 b). But, in practice, Jewish communities often granted tax exemptions to Jewish landowners, and such farsighted rabbis as Joseph Tob Elem of France in the eleventh century, and Meir of Rothenburg in the thirteenth, regarded it as praiseworthy to facilitate Jewish farming. Ritualistic requirements as to dairy products definitely encouraged Jewish dairy farmers. Eliezer ben Nathan went so far as to attempt to prevent Jews from selling land to Gentiles — a twelfth-century Jewish counterpart of the increasingly rigid prohibitions directed against Jewish acquisition of Christian land. But against overwhelming odds, all this proved of no avail.

Legislative prohibitions of Jewish landownership could be so applied as to include urban real estate. At first the Jews owned numerous houses in the cities in which they settled. They seem even to have introduced the construction of stone buildings into England. Whether due to the force of a tradition dating back to Palestine, where stone quarries are abundant, or to the sense of security given by stone walls, they erected stone structures which, looking like fortified castles, were soon generally copied. In the course of time, however, the Church and the burghers found it to their advantage to limit Jewish ownership of houses to the Jewish quarter, thus adding an incentive to Jewish territorial segregation. In Rome, after 1555, and in other cities, not even the ghetto houses belonged to the Jews.

Jewish participation in industrial enterprises also declined from century to century during the Middle Ages. At first the Jews, coming from the more advanced Muslim or Byzantine countries, rendered great services to the western European industry by introducing more efficient means of production. Even in the eastern Mediterranean, they had long been praised or envied as a people "endowed by grace divine with special gifts for handicrafts" (Cosmas Indicopleustes, in PG, LXXXVIII, 172). Among the Greek glassblowers in seventh-century France, it was a boast that they could produce glass of the type known as "Jewish glass." For centuries the greatest claim of the Jews to industrial distinction consisted in their artistic production of fine stuffs, some embroidered with gold and beautifully dyed by a complicated chemical process. As late as the thirteenth century, Frederick II, the most progressive European monarch of the age, called in Jewish manufacturers to build his great state monopolies of silk and dyed stuffs. In 1231 he conferred upon the Jews of Trani a monopoly for the purchase of raw silk, and its resale for the treasury at a profit of 33 percent. Likewise all dye houses in the kingdom were given to Jewish groups to manage. They naturally also gained thereby a considerable advantage over their Christian competitors in manufacturing finished products on their own account. Throughout the ages, Jews also excelled in various metal trades, especially in goldsmithery.

The Jews of Spain, Portugal, Sicily and southern France were industrial producers throughout the Middle Ages, and powerful Jewish artisan guilds successfully competed with

Christian guilds. The Jewish quarter of Saragossa, for example, had special streets of shoemakers, cutlers, tanners, saddlers and jewelers. The Jewish tailors' guild of Perpignan possessed its own hospital. The Jewish carpenters of Palermo were organized in a powerful league, whose president, Caschisi, distinguished himself in 1451 in the construction of the royal palace. When in 1492 the Jews were to be expelled from Sicily, the burghers remonstrated, fearing a general rise of prices and other economic disturbances. A list of Roman families, in the early sixteenth century, names many Jewish master artisans.

Except in Poland, Northern European Jewry was in a much inferior position. Backed by the municipal power, Christian guilds quickly acquired a monopoly of production and peremptorily excluded Jews from many branches. As long as their religion was tolerated, Jews were, as a rule, permitted to be butchers, bakers and tailors, because these crafts were connected with phases of their ritual. The biblical prohibition of *shaatnez* (mixing wool and linen together) thus helped salvage an important Jewish craft, and made possible the modern expansion of Jewish needle trades. Naturally, Jewish crafts were limited to the few countries of their more or less continuous settlement. Where expelled, even after readmission they were still less in a position to penetrate the strongly organized guilds.[4]

The development of the commercial guilds was equally prejudicial to Jewish trade. The increase of the power of the burghers in western and central Europe caused the suppression of the Jewish middleman, even in local commerce. Some cities, such as Trèves, Linz and Oldenburg, prohibited all Jewish commerce at an early date, while Nuremberg allowed Jews to engage exclusively in the horse and meat trades. The growing insecurity during the Crusades likewise militated against unhampered Jewish commercial activity. Toward the end of the Middle Ages, German and North Italian Jewry saw itself limited to a few branches of commerce, the most important being, as in the industrial pursuits, those serving the Jewish consumer.

Once more the Iberian Peninsula and Poland were notable exceptions. In Spain the royal power directly encouraged Jewish commerce. In some cities of Aragon, the kings forbade creditors to attach Jewish merchandise, displayed in the public bazaars, without special authorization. They went out of their way to protect Jewish merchants in their foreign relations. Certainly such hostile acts as the Aragonian prohibition of trade with Africa, in 1316 and 1326, severely hit Jewish commerce with Spain's closest neighbor. On the other hand, however, in 1270 James I granted special trading privileges to the Jews of Alexandria. In 1280, Pedro III sent letters to the Grand Master of the Knights Templars, to the consuls of Pisa and Venice, and to the Viceroy of Cyprus, defending his Jewish subjects against local acts of retortion for debts incurred by a Barcelona Jew. In Poland, where the cities were mostly founded and populated by a no less alien group, the German burghers, the aristocracy vied with the kings in extending facilities to Jewish commerce. The country's policy, dictated by the agrarian interests, fostered the exportation of agricultural, and the importation of industrial products, which was detrimental to the growth of the native (including Jewish) industry, but helped to expand international trade. Confronted by fewer legal obstacles than elsewhere, the Polish Jewish merchants effectively controlled many branches of that trade.

MONEY TRADE

The Jews of the rest of Europe, however, were more and more limited to one occupation, money lending. While in the earlier Middle Ages, "Jew" had become, even in legal terminology, a synonym for merchant (e.g., *Judei et ceteri mercatores* of the Raffelstädten toll ordinance of 906), from the twelfth century on, we find it increasingly identified with usurer. Even countries where the Jewish economic structure remained greatly diversified, did not escape this change. In Majorca, for example, where the Jews had been prominent merchants, shipowners, landlords and cattle raisers, they "converted a large and perhaps the larger part of their fortune into debts" (Royal edict of 1375 in F. Fita and G. Llabres, "Privilegios de los Hebreos," *Boletín de la R. Academia de la Historia,* XXXVI, 399 f.). Similarly in Toledo, during the twelfth and thirteenth centuries, no less than 54 documents in Arabic (of 1,175 published by C. A. González Palencia) speak of Jewish creditors, and only 3 of Jewish debtors (cf. F. Baer's review in *Tarbiz*, V, 235).

From the start, Jews possessed more available cash than their Christian competitors. Some of it they brought along from the East; some they realized from the sale of their landholdings. The high rate of interest, furthermore, helped them build large fortunes in a comparatively short time, provided there was no violent interference from outside. Church legislation, laying increasing stress upon the canonical prohibition of usury, fostered Jewish money lending. Although as late as the twelfth century the clergy was the most important group of money lenders in many European countries, and although, even later, Christians, with money to lend on interest, evaded the prohibition by subterfuge, still the Jews, being able to engage in this business openly and with legal protection, had the advantage over all competitors. Often Christian lords entrusted their cash to Jews to invest in profitable transactions. The kings, too, were vitally interested in the development of the Jewish money trade. It has frequently been pointed out that Jewish usury served as a sort of tax-collecting agency for the weak medieval state. Since rates of interest averaged between 33 1-3 and 43 1-3 percent annually (sometimes the law permitted charges as high as 86 2-3 percent, and once even 174 percent), capital could easily be doubled within two or three years. Frederick II, who attempted to limit the Jewish rate to 10 percent, himself paid more to Christian creditors. James I of Aragon set a legal maximum rate of 20 percent, but immediately exempted several Jewish communities. The government of Aragon, moreover, soon had to enlist the support of Jewish religious leaders, who threatened with excommunication transgressors of this law. When, in 1409, Ladislaus of Naples, at the instance of the burghers of Brindisi, allowed the Jews to charge 40 percent (raised in 1427 to 45 percent), this was hailed as a great relief for the poor citizens, who otherwise "would have been forced to sell their belongings at a very low price." Indeed, after the expulsion of the Jews in the following century, the Christian usurers demanded rates as high as 240 percent. It can be imagined how enormous Jewish fortunes (and those of other money lenders) would have become, had not their development been checked by expropriations.

The exchange of money and minting were connected with money lending. In the early Middle Ages the Jews performed truly pioneering services in this field. Charlemagne had a Jewish minter. During the eleventh and twelfth centuries Jewish minters in Poland, apparently because of their unfamiliarity with the Polish language, as yet hardly a literary medium, engraved Hebrew inscriptions on Polish coins. A number of Hebrew coins prepared by Jewish mint masters for Western German princes have likewise been preserved. The influence of these minters often extended into many other phases of fiscal administration, as illustrated by Schlom of Vienna, under the Babenbergs, truly a forerunner of the famous imperial "court Jews" in early modern times. It is hardly astonishing that avaricious or hard-pressed Jews abused their skill for the purpose of coin clipping on their own account, or for the benefit of their masters.

It must be borne in mind, on the other hand, that such important banking activities as receiving deposits and transferring money from country to country, were mainly in the hands of Christians. The insecurity of Jewish life was no inducement to a non-Jewish depositor to deposit money with a Jewish banker, except when he expected a large share of the profit. He went either to a church or to a monastery, which, like the ancient Babylonian and Greek temples, put the deposits under special religious safeguards; or else to one of the new Italian banks, such as the famous Banco di San Giorgio, founded in Genoa in 1148. The Lombards and Cahorsins, backed by the papal court, had an immense advantage over Jewish competitors in international transfer. While Jewish firms were not totally barred from the deposit and transfer business, their activities in these fields did not compare with money lending in significance.[5]

FEW PERIODS OF AFFLUENCE

The Jews had few periods of real affluence. Whenever they succeeded in accumulating treasures, the Christian princes sooner or later appropriated their fortunes for themselves. In ordinary years the taxes paid by Jews far exceeded their ratio in the population, and in years of stress taxation became almost expropriatory. There was a truly astounding variety of imposts, in addition to the usual head taxes which medieval Christendom inherited from the ancient and Muslim worlds. Property taxes, sometimes as high as 33 percent, were the most common means of speedily extracting large amounts of cash from the Jews. The number of "voluntary" and involuntary contributions is too large to be listed here. "Gifts" poured in at such a rate that, for example, in Perpignan an efficient tax collector succeeded within a few years in raising the revenue of the *demanda graciosa* from 2,000 to 14,000 solidi. Fines and tallages of all kinds were imposed upon entire Jewish communities to punish trangressions of a single member, or sometimes without any reason at all. The Jews of Angevin England had to contribute one-fourth of their chattels to the Crusade against Saladin, while the rest of the population paid only one-tenth. For the 100,000 marks' ransom of King Richard, the Jews were assessed 5,000 marks, and the entire city of London only 1,500. It has been estimated that in the twelfth century English Jewry, constituting one-quarter of one percent of the population, furnished fully 8 percent of the total income of the treasury. Similar conditions prevailed throughout medieval Europe. For example, when Alfonso IV needed money for a war against Granada in 1330, he imposed upon the Jews of his realm the enormous tax of 500,000 solidi. Not even wealthy Aragonese Jewry could meet its burden, and apparently compromised with the king for the sum of 340,000 solidi. On another occasion the prosperous Barcelona community, unable to meet its obligations to the king, had to borrow a large sum from French coreligionists, the king having expressly prohibited their contracting debts in Spain. The extraordinary tax imposed by Emperor Sigismund upon German Jewry, weakened by the aftermath of the Black Death and the growing anti-Jewish discrimination, yielded no less than 40,000 florins. In Rome, under the Counter-Reformatory popes, the Jewish fiscal burden rose in the brief span of thirty-two years (1636-68) from 1.62 to 5 percent of the available capital. The function of the Jews in the later Middle Ages has justly been compared to that of a sponge; during many years they sucked up much of the wealth of a country, only to be eventually squeezed dry by the government. "God be truly blessed," quite appropriately wrote Jacob ben Elijah, "who has enlarged our fortune, by means of which we can save our lives and those of our families and reduce to naught the evil designs of our enemy" (Letter, edited by Kobak, *Jeschurun,* VI, 17).[6]

Under these circumstances, the economy of the Jews in northern Europe became more and more uniform. They were largely money lenders, business, ecclesiastical or domestic employees of such, or else dependent on charity. The founders of German cities, such as Landshut and Kelheim in Bavaria (about 1180) and many northern Italian republics in the fifteenth century, expressly invited Jews to settle as money lenders and "to provide credit for the needy population." For this purpose a kind of international treaty (*condotta, capitoli*) was drawn up between various Italian city governments and groups of foreign Jews. When, however, it became possible to supply the Christian population with credit through the so-called *montes pietatis,* which, being charitable rather than profit-making institutions, did not violate canon law, the Jews became superfluous. The founder of the *montes* movement, San Bernardino da Feltre, went from town to town in Italy, urging their expulsion, frequently with immediate success. But wherever the Jews of central Europe survived the expulsions of the fifteenth and sixteenth centuries, it was due to a large extent to the importance of their money-lending activities. Inasmuch as only their religion assured them their privileged position in this field, it was paradoxically that religion which frequently saved the Jewish social group from extinction. But in the most important countries of Jewish life, such as Spain, southern Italy, Poland and Turkey, the Jewish masses could not subsist on the fruits of such rigidly restricted pursuits. Indeed, with the exception of agriculture, their economic activities were almost as diversified as those of the surrounding peoples. Medieval Jewry found its most typical expression, however, not in these countries, but in England, Germany, northern France and northern Italy.

At the same time, nowhere except in Spain did these Jewish bankers belong to the wealthiest groups. The riches of some early modern Amsterdam or German Jew should not blind us to the fact that these late exceptions were products of the new capitalistic age. Previously the most powerful Italian Jewish banking house, Da Pisa, commanded resources of approximately 100,000 florins only. The Peruzzi, a Florentine Christian house which went bankrupt in the thirteenth century, claimed uncollected assets owed by the king of England, amounting to 900,000 florins; the German contemporaries of the Da Pisas, the Fuggers, accumulated more than 4,000,000 thalers before they were forced to close by the refusal of Charles V to pay his debt. As a whole, the Jewish community in most countries belonged to the lower middle class, with a sprinkling of a few wealthier members and a considerable appendage of poor.[7]

NEW LEGAL STATUS

Economic developments helped to shape the political destinies of the people. The more limited their function in society became, the more restricted were their numbers and their rights. Where feudalism was strongest, society as a whole was dissolved into corporations, each with its own specific social and political function, with a corresponding specific legal status.

Each of the great estates represented such a corporation in public law, with special rights and duties. Everywhere the serfs, the majority of the population, constituted an enormous oppressed corporation with the least rights and the greatest obligations. The Jews belonged to the three upper estates, with relatively greater privileges and lesser duties.

The functions of military defense, administration and the upkeep of general culture were reserved to the estates of the nobility and the clergy. The position of the Jews resembled that of the burghers, whose chief function was to control the economic life of each country. The Jews, however, had to contribute proportionately larger amounts in taxes and public loans to the state treasury than the burgesses. For example, when the king of Aragon tried to impose a general war tax upon his Christian subjects in 1376, the representatives of the estates, at the Cortes of Monzon, replied that "in the past they used to serve in person in all wars, and only the Jewish and Moorish communities used to give money to the king" (Zurita y Castro, *Anales de Aragon,* Book X, Chap. 20; ed. Saragossa, Vol. II, 369 c).

In a warlike age, when spring was known as the season in which kings go to war, no section of the population could entirely escape the brunt. When a city was besieged by a foreign enemy, everyone, including the Jews, had to take up arms in its defense. In Cologne, for example, the entire task of defending the Porta Judaeorum in 1106 was entrusted by the city to the Jews. In such towns as Estella in Navarre, the Jews constructed their houses in such fashion as to help make the city's defenses impregnable. So often did the Jews of Germany become involved in military combats, that the great rabbinical authorities of the thirteenth century, Eleazar of Worms and Isaac Or Zarua of Vienna, permitted them to take up arms on the Sabbath day. In 1086, in the great battle of Zalaca against the Moors, so the legend runs, 40,000 Jewish soldiers fell.[8]

Although in general excluded from public offices, Jews were frequently employed as fiscal agents. Against this practice, the combined weight of tradition, ecclesiastical antagonism and competition of nobles and burghers, often proved of little avail. In the face of severe censure by popes and ecclesiastical councils, and of growing domestic opposition, many a hard-pressed Christian ruler persisted in employing Jewish tax collectors. Not only in Castile, but even in Aragon, where the rise of the burghers' power gradually eliminated the Jews from public employ, Jewish taxgatherers and fiscal agents were to be found to the very end. Abraham Senior, Isaac Abravanel and many others, were serving every branch of the royal treasury in 1492, the very year of the expulsion.

In the northern countries, the steady rise of the cities, accompanied by the economic decline of Jewry, necessarily led to a proportionate diminution of their fiscal contributions. The less useful the Jews were to the state, the lower, of course, their political standing fell. Before long the Christian burghers succeeded in persuading the rulers that they could entirely dispense with the Jews. Fiscal considerations thus frequently played a decisive part in the progressive decline of the Jews' political and legal status, and in their numerous expulsions.

The course of political development in western Christianity reinforced the corporate separation of the Jews. The primitive conquerors of western Germany, France and England imposed their own legal conceptions upon these former Roman provinces. The change from the territorial principle of Roman law to the Teuton personal principle, under which each member of a tribe carried his tribal law wherever he went, brought to the Jews both advantages and disadvantages. Jewish law, which had been respected, even in the last centuries of Roman domination, now governed exclusively the dealings among Jews. On the other hand, according to the conception of the early Teuton invaders, foreigners, as such, had no rights whatever, so long as they had no special protection from the local chieftain. This "law of aliens," common to all primitive races, had a special effect on the status of Jews in the early Middle Ages. Even later a survival of that law (*ius albinagii, droit d'aubaine,* etc.) made the king heir to all estates of foreigners dying in the land, regardless of whether or not they had legal heirs. Only special protection from the king enabled Jews and other aliens to avoid these disabilities.

JEWISH "SERFDOM"

This relationship between the king and the Jews contributed to the development of Jewish "serfdom." In all Christian countries, Jews gradually came to be regarded as royal "serfs." We find this legal terminology employed in Spain, France and England, as early as the twelfth century, but the most marked relations of this kind developed between the Holy Roman Emperor and the Jews. The Empire claimed an overlordship over its *servi camerae,* even beyond the boundaries of Germany. While records of the expression do not antedate Frederick II, the idea was much older. Two theories contested the rationalization of that institution. On the one hand, Thomas Aquinas, Innocent III and other churchmen declared the Jews to be the serfs of Christian princes, as a punishment for their participation in the crucifixion of Christ. While the Church derived therefrom a claim to overlordship over the Jews for itself, this justification of fiscal exploitation, so modified as to substitute Christian rulers for the Church as such, appeared plausible enough to princes outside the Holy Roman Empire. Referring to the overlords' right to tax the Jews or to expropriate them when necessary, Thomas argued that

the Church does not thereby commit an injustice. Since the Jews themselves are serfs of the Church, the Church can dispose of their possessions. [*Summa theol.*, II, 2, 10, 10.]

On the other hand, the Holy Roman Empire based a special claim to domination over the Jews on Titus' conquest of Palestine. Eike von Repgow and, more fully, the author of the *Schwabenspiegel* relate the story of how all Jews had become imperial slaves after the conquest of Jerusalem, and how, on the insistence of Josephus, Titus liberated them, except for a special tax. This was the origin of the annual taxes paid by Jews to the emperor. This theory of special imperial overlordship over the whole Jewish people was gaining ground. An Austrian chronicler tells us that the expulsion of the Jews from France in 1306, took place because the French king resented the alleged domination over the Jews of his rival, the emperor. How far the German rulers thought they were entitled to go, is indicated by a statement made by Charles IV in 1349 confirming that "he had given to the archbishop of Trèves the property of the Jews who had been slain in Alsace or elsewhere, or may be slain in the future, since the Jews and their property belong to the King and to the imperial Chamber" (J. F. Boehmer and A. Huber, *Regesta imperii,* VIII, 71, No. 869).[9]

The position of the Jews was, nevertheless, by no means unfavorable. Despite all high-sounding phrases, they were anything but serfs in the sense of villeins. They enjoyed freedom of motion. Richard the Lion-Hearted said in 1190, "Let them go whithersoever they will with all their chattels just like our own good and let no one keep them or prevent them" (Jacobs, *Jews of Angevin England,* p. 136), and the same conditions prevailed in other parts of Europe. Few princes felt bound to return foreign Jews to the domains of the "master" whence they had fled. The few treaties of extradition, concluded by neighboring princes in France, have all the earmarks of *bizarrerie*. The transfer of a few Jews from one master to another, often by sale or pawning as security for a loan, was never a transaction of civil law, but rather the renunciation by one prince in favor of another, of the revenue connected with the taxes on Jews. Emperor Charles IV, for example, transferred in 1348 the Jews of Worms, "with their persons and property and with all the uses and rights" connected with them to the city (Boehmer and Huber, *op. cit.,* VIII, 47, No. 529). But he did not hesitate a few years later (1353, 1355) to exercise jurisdiction over the admission of new Jews to settlement there. This at a time when landowners could sell their property by civil contract, and with it all peasants attached thereto. In Russia, down to the nineteenth century, every land transfer included the sale of "souls." In short, while the villeins — and a majority of the medieval European population was composed of villeins — were serfs of their masters in civil law, the Jews were the serfs of the kings in public law.

This distinction, although undoubtedly a simplification of a very complex state of affairs, was not outside the range of medieval jurisprudence. While in practice kings and emperors rarely drew a sharp line between their private estates and the royal domains, many jurists knew that such a distinction existed. Serfdom of the imperial chamber meant that Jews were serfs of the emperor *as such*. Lordship over them was inherited by the elected imperial successor, rather than by the legitimate heir of the private dynastic possessions. Undoubtedly, in some cases this relationship was somewhat obscured. In England and Spain, especially, where the centralized royal power blurred the dividing lines between public and private ownership, Jewish serfdom could easily appear in an exaggerated light. Involuntarily humorous, Bracton, the famous thirteenth-century jurist, wrote, "But a Jew cannot have anything of his own, because whatever he acquires he acquires not for himself but for the king, because they do not live for themselves but for others and so they acquire for others and not for themselves" (*De legibus,* edited by Twiss, VI, 51). But even for Bracton, these "others" were not private masters, but the king and Christian society at large.[10]

This was the basis of the close political relations between the Jews and the royal power, which in the long run were to prove a source of great difficulty for the weaker party. Sometimes they made the wrong choice between contenders for the throne, as when the Jews of Worms, in 1201, defended the city with "their own" arms against King Otto IV. More frequently, revolutionary forces, directed against the existing social order, form of government or individual monarch, struck at the Jews as the nearest and most defenseless representatives of the ruling power. Social uprisings of the peasantry often engulfed entire Jewish communities. The burghers, on political as well as economic grounds, tried either to eliminate the Jews or to wrest control over them from the kings. In western Europe, expulsion furnished the final solution. In Germany, the pages of the constitutional history of the Jews are marked first by the transfer of imperial power to local authorities, and then by numerous local expulsions. In Ratisbon, for instance, the respective rights of the emperor, the city, the bishop and the Bavarian duke, became a matter of such controversy that a visiting papal legate remarked, "there are many dogs for this one bone." As a rule, however, the kings tried to protect the Jews. After confidence in imperial protection had been shaken by the riots of 1096, Henry IV initiated a series of mutual treaties, beginning with the truce of Mayence (1102). In 1252, James I of Aragon wrote the city of Montpellier that "since the Jews are subjected to serfdom in almost all countries under Christian rule . . . we order all consuls of the city that they should not impose upon the Jews living there, now or in the future, any taxes or demands which would be prejudicial to our jurisdiction or dignity" (S. Kahn in *REJ,* XIX, 261 n. 2).

This alliance with the state, and even the mere sovereignty of the state, was accepted by the Jewish people with great reluctance. They regarded it as a necessary evil, a castigation inflicted upon them by God for the transgressions of their forefathers. They tenaciously clung to the theoretical sovereignty of their own people, tolerating the laws of the various kings only in so far as these did not conflict with the essentials of their own law. "The law of the kingdom is law" (*dina demalkuta dina*), long accepted by Diaspora Jewry as a *modus vivendi* in the face of conflicting powers, reflected, not wholehearted acceptance, but condescension toward the legislation of an alien state.

Notwithstanding local differences, the position of the Jews throughout western Christendom was largely uniform. There were no essential distinctions between the privileges granted them by the feudal lords and kings of France, Germany or England. This similarity far exceeded the well-known analogies between the medieval city custumals. The fundamental laws concerning the Jews in the various countries of eastern Europe, reveal the same uniformity. The privilege of Emperor Frederick II, of 1238, served as a model for the famous Austrian decree granted in 1244 by the last duke of the house of Babenberg, also named Frederick II. During the next two decades, this privilege was in turn adopted, with relatively minor modifications, by the kings of Hungary (1251), Bohemia and Moravia (1254), and by many dukes of Silesia and western Poland. The privilege of Boleslaw the Pious, of Kalisz (1264), which served as a basis for all later legislation concerning the Jews in Poland, is but an amplification of the Austrian decree of twenty years before. A similar privilege, granted by Vitold in 1388 and differing only in its details from the Polish edict, was the basic law of Lithuanian Jewry. When Poland and Lithuania were later permanently united under one king and grand duke, these fundamental laws determined the status of the then-leading Jewry in the world. One king after another, until the end of Polish independence, expressly or tacitly confirmed these privileges.

It may thus be said that the legal standing of the Jews was, as a rule, by no means unfavorable. Although, in the later Middle Ages, discriminatory laws piled up in western and central Europe from generation to generation, in essence the Jews still remained a privileged group, in most countries belonging to the privileged minority. True, their legal status was insecure. At best no king, according to medieval convictions, could bind his successors. Whenever a ruler died, the privileges of the Jews automatically expired, until renewed by his successors. Although this was the case with all laws, and though, as a matter of fact, renewals were always forthcoming, yet the Jews had to pay a considerable price for them, sometimes as high as one-third of all their property. In 1463, Albrecht III Achilles, Margrave of Brandenburg, solemnly declared that every new German king and emperor "may, according to old usage, either burn all the Jews or show them his mercy and, to save their lives, take the third penny of their property" (J. B. Koenig, *Annalen,* p. 48). No German emperor, however, ever seriously considered this alternative to the property tax.

Of course, the Jewish corporation had characteristics which distinguished it essentially from all other groups. Jews constituted a body apart, not only politically and legally, but, as we have seen, in an increasing degree economically as well. They were, in addition, a distinct religious and ethnic group. Their foreignness was obvious in all countries, particularly in those north of the Alps, where they were entirely segregated. It is no exaggeration to say that the Jews of Frankfort knew more about the life of their coreligionists in Cracow, Venice, Constantinople and Cairo, than they did about the life of their Christian neighbors outside the Jewish quarter. Christians knew still less of what was going on in the Jewish street of their town. So strange and mysterious did the life of the Jews appear to the Christian population that tales of an entirely untrustworthy character, accusations of the most incredible kind could circulate. Behind all popular misapprehensions loomed the conviction, legally restated as late as the eighteenth century by the sovereign court of Alsace, that "The Jew has no fixed domicile . . . he is condemned to perpetual wandering." [11]

THE "WANDERING JEW"

In these words is well epitomized the greatest transformation in the life of medieval Jewry. It was in medieval Europe that the Jew became the "Wandering Jew." Anti-Semitism had existed in one guise or another, wherever Jews lived in dispersion. In the Graeco-Roman, as well as in the Persian worlds, under the domination of the eastern as well as the western caliphs, there had frequently occurred bloody persecutions of Jews; and even legal attempts to eliminate or reduce this alien minority had not been wanting. But nowhere else than in medieval Europe did persecutions follow in such quick succession, assume such universal character, or have such lasting effects. Moreover, nowhere else did the practice of *expulsion* become such a prominent factor in the relations between Jew and Gentile. The Mazdakite persecution in Persia, the annihilation of the Jewish communities of northern Arabia by Mohammed and Omar, the pogroms of the Almohades in North Africa and Spain during the twelfth century, all doubtless caused much suffering to the Jewries of those countries; but nowhere was governmental policy so implacably and persistently bent upon placing before the Jews the alternative of giving up their faith or of leaving the country, as in certain Christian lands. In any case, apart from the transitory banishment of the Jews from Rome or Italy in 19 A.D., we hear of no outright decree of expulsion in the ancient world until Christianity became its dominant religion. It was left to Bishop

Cyril of Alexandria to introduce this means of adjusting Jewish-Christian relations, when about 415 he instigated the expulsion of the Jews from the city which had occupied such a glorious place in their history. His example was emulated by Justinian in 534, when he forced the Jews in the newly conquered district of Borion, in Africa, to adopt Christianity. Of prime importance were the decrees forcing either baptism or expulsion upon the Jewries of the entire Byzantine Empire, by Leo the Isaurian (723), Basil (about 875), and Romanus Lecapenus (about 930).

It is in western European Jewish history, however, that we find an unparalleled succession of expulsions, readmissions and enforced baptisms. Two particularly great waves of intolerance swept over medieval Europe. The first, rising during the seventh century almost without warning, engulfed the Jews of Visigothic Spain, the Frankish Empire and Langobard Italy. While it is possible that Sisebut, in 613, and again Chintila, with the coöperation of the Sixth Council of Toledo in 638, ordered the Jews only to be either baptized or banished, King Dagobert (instigated in 629, or more probably in 633-34, by Emperor Heraclius of Byzantium) seems not to have left them even this melancholy choice. In Italy, in 661, young King Perctarit simply decided to exterminate, at the point of the sword, all those who refused to embrace Christianity. These expulsions and enforced baptisms, if effectively carried out, would have practically put an end to Jewish settlement in Christian Europe.

After several centuries of comparative quiet, a new wave of intolerance, during the transition from the medieval to the modern period, threatened to submerge European Jewry. Beginning with the great banishment from England in 1290; through the expulsions of 1306, 1384 and 1396 from France (excepting papal Avignon), and of 1349 and 1360 from Hungary; and culminating in the exiles from Spain and Sicily in 1492, from Portugal in 1497, and from the kingdom of Naples and Sicily in 1509 and 1540, this wave uprooted thousands of thriving communities. Nontoleration of Jews became, for centuries, a corner stone in the religious policy of these leading European nations. In 1499 Spain decreed the death of all professing Jews, native or alien, thenceforth detected in the country, even though they expressed the wish to become Christians. During the same period, numerous regional and local expulsions from German and Italian territories eliminated many Jewish settlements from central Europe.[12]

Anti-Jewish mass demonstrations were the popular complements to the governmental decrees of expulsion, and bloody persecutions of Jews made their life eternally tragic, even in countries where the rulers had granted them toleration. Frequently arising from altogether insignificant incidents, such riots often spread with alarming celerity from province to province and from country to country. The march of the crusaders in 1096-97, with the concomitant wholesale massacres of Jewish communities from Rouen, in France, through the Rhineland, Bavaria, Bohemia, and down to Palestine, was a prelude to a great tragic epos of fire and blood. At least 4,000 Jews, if not twice or thrice that number, fell victims to the fanatical mob, many more escaping death only through baptism. Continental rulers during the Second Crusade (1146-47) kept the attacks against Jews within relatively narrow limits (Rameru, Carentan and Würzburg), and Frederick I, with an iron hand, preserved order throughout Germany during the Third Crusade (1189-90). During these later years, however, England suddenly plunged its Jewry into misery through massacres at York, London and other cities. These English pogroms were far overshadowed, numerically at least, by those of 1298, which swept over 140 Jewish communities in Bavaria and Austria; by the violent attacks of the Pastoureaux, who in 1320 destroyed 120 French communities; and by the so-called Armleder upheaval of 1337, which wiped out numerous Jewish communities in Alsace, Swabia, Bavaria, Austria, Bohemia and Moravia. With the coming of the inscrutable Black Death in 1348-49, panic seized the European peoples. Rumors of Jewish poisoning of wells were widespread, and the ensuing wave of pogroms throughout Germany, France and portions of Spain, led to the almost total extinction of some 300 Jewish communities. Even the large community of Saragossa is said to have been suddenly reduced to one-fifth of its former size.[13]

No western European country in the Middle Ages, except perhaps Italy, was spared some such general upheaval, which plunged the Jewries of a vast region into the depths of distress.

Spanish Jewry, which suffered from no extensive outbreak between the days of the Almohades and the year 1348, was startled when in 1391, Ferrand Martinez, the Queen Mother's confessor, proclaimed a holy war against it. Within a few months, the glorious Jewish communities of Seville, Cordova, Toledo, Burgos, Valencia, Barcelona and many others were annihilated. Poland, which, throughout the Middle Ages and in early modern times, prided herself on her tolerance, and which, indeed, had become the haven of refuge for harassed European Jewry, could not prevent the sudden outburst of anti-Jewish fury accompanying the Chmielnicki revolt in 1648. In comparison with these widespread pogrom movements, the local riots seem to be of less consequence. By their unceasing frequency and their enormous geographic extent, however, they had a cumulative effect, perhaps even more catastrophic than the larger upheavals.

The influence of the expulsions and pogroms upon the life of European Jewry was tremendous. Their political and economic standing, their social relationships with their Christian neighbors, their very culture and religion were profoundly affected. In no respect, however, was the effect more evident than in the increased emphasis upon the foreignness of the Jews. The Jewish people themselves became more and more conscious of their "exilic" existence. If their talmudic forefathers had already sounded the keynote of perennial complaints against persecutions, the medieval writers fill page after page with tearful descriptions of the tragic vicissitudes of their people. The words of the *Selihah*

> High above in Heaven's regions
> Far and wide in halls of learning,
> And where people meet together
> Be my sacrifices published;
> How my tender infants perished,
> How their tortures laid me prostrate;
> Learn to know their deeds of horror—
> We were crushed and rent asunder,
> Until corpse by corpse lay buried,
>
> [Quoted by L. Zunz, in his *Sufferings of the Jews during the Middle Ages*, p. 38.]

may be regarded as a leitmotif of a large body of historic, moralistic and poetic literature. In the overcharged atmosphere, the maddest as well as the most heroic impulses broke forth. On the one hand the age-old propensity for self-accusation took increasing delight in the vision of superhuman sufferings, since they seemed to offer such incontestable proof of Israel's own sinfulness. On the other hand, the finest spirits of medieval Jewry and, under their leadership, entire communities of ordinary Jews, reached heights of heroic self-sacrifice, unsurpassed by men of any race or creed—indeed, unrivaled in compass and duration. To "sanctify God's name" with one's life, to accept with joy painful death from the hands of a fanatic enemy, or preferably from those of a fellow sufferer, became an exalted merit, an achievement, often a much-coveted prize.

LACHRYMOSE CONCEPTION OF JEWISH HISTORY

The lachrymose conception of Jewish history, viewing the destinies of the Jews in the Diaspora as a sheer succession of miseries and persecutions, a conception from which Jewish historiography has not been able to free itself to this day, took in those years firm hold of the imagination of the people. Instead of quietly glorifying the achievements of the rabbis and teachers, as Sherira and Ibn Daud did, the new generations of historians outdid one another in passionate accounts of Israel's woes and sorrows. A classic expression of this conception was the work of the historian, Samuel Usque, who wrote the history of his people in terms of "Consolations"; while another, Joseph Hacohen, saw in it nothing but a tragic procession through a "valley of tears." Azariah de' Rossi, a solitary thinker in his day, investigated the past of his people in a more detached and serene mood; but he preferred the more ancient days, almost pointedly neglecting the recent past, to which most of his colleagues, both Jewish and Christian, devoted their attention.[14]

Equally baneful was the impact of these acts of intolerance upon the Christian mind. The more frequently Jews were seen abandoning their homes, bundles on their backs, for unknown destinations, the more deeply was the conception stamped on the mind of the masses that these "aliens" by race and religion were merely temporary sojourners. It mattered not that the Jews had admittedly been well established in the country long before the influx of the Goths, the Lombards, the Franks or the Normans. Once rooted in a territory, these latter arrogated to themselves the right of tolerating the Jews as strangers, on conditions imposed from above, or of altogether withdrawing tolerance and expelling them. Although innumerable legends were spun about the origin of certain Jewish communities, although monumental and documentary evidence existed or was manufactured to prove that the Jews of Spain, Bavaria, Narbonne and Prague had lived there long before the birth of Christ, and consequently had not taken any part in the crucifixion of Jesus, it was all of no avail. The widespread popular belief, nurtured by many Austrian historical accounts down to that of Fuhrmann, in 1738, that Jewish kings, margraves and tetrarchs had founded Stockerau 859 years and 9 months after the deluge, and afterwards Vienna and other Austrian cities, and that no less than 72 princes of Jewish extraction, known by name, had ruled over those territories before 201 B.C., did not prevent the expulsions of 1421 and 1670. The Jewish people became in Christian eyes more and more the eternal Ahasuerus, the Wandering Jew who cannot and must not find rest in his perpetual migrations. Old mythological concepts were revived and homiletically adorned to explain the strange phenomenon. Was not Abel the prototype of Jesus, the innocent son of man, whose offering was accepted by God, but who for this reason was slain by his older brother? It appeared only just that the new Cain, the Jewish people, should likewise be a "fugitive and a vagabond . . . in the earth" (Gen. 4:12). Distinguished by Cain's sign, circumcision, the Jews must constantly migrate from place to place, finding no permanent abode. This abstruse homiletical rationale did not appear at all abstruse to the medieval mind.[15]

RELIGIOUS AND ECONOMIC INTOLERANCE

Many complex forces were operative to bring about acts of intolerance and the mass psychology that went with them. Most obvious are the religious differences. In a period when religion was interwoven with the entire fabric of individual and national life and when the minds of men were bent upon uniformity, conformity and order, religious discrepancy was in itself a supreme offense. The representative leaders of the Church, to be sure, for reasons which will presently be discussed, consistently preached fundamental tolerance of the Jews. But at the same time they insisted upon the most rigid intolerance, both of heretical currents within Christianity, and of heathendom and Islam without. The popular mind was unable to make such fine distinctions. An early German Jewish chronicler thus quotes the crusaders: "Behold we are going on a long journey in search of the Holy Sepulcher and to take revenge on the Ishmaelites, and behold ye the Jews live among us whose forefathers have killed him and crucified him for no reason; let us revenge ourselves on them first and let us exterminate them as a nation and may the name of Israel be remembered no more, or else may they become as we are and may they profess our religion" (Historische Kommission für Geschichte der Juden in Deutschland, *Quellen zur Geschichte der Juden in Deutschland,* II, 1). Such reasoning had a tremendous appeal to the "common sense" of the man in the street. Should a few Jewish individuals be accused of trying to proselytize Christians, or merely of inducing a Jewish convert to Christianity to "relapse" into Judaism, the whole Jewish street would be sacked. In England, the alleged intrusion of Jews into Richard I's coronation ceremonies, from which they had been excluded *propter magicas artes,* served to provoke an outbreak of popular hatred. On another occasion, the ludicrous story that a single Jew broke into a Christian procession at Oxford, seized the crucifix, crushed it under foot and escaped (1268), had the same effect. Most widespread of all were accusations of alleged Jewish blasphemies against Christ and the Virgin, profanation of the Host and other Christian ritual objects, and poisoning of wells in order to contaminate and decimate the Christian population.

None of these, however, achieved the dubious prominence of the ritual murder accusation, that fateful intrusion of the darkest forces of folklore into the realm of history. This calumny, originally directed against Jews and Christians by the Graeco-Roman pagans and often repeated in the strife among the various Christian sects, had long been forgotten in western Europe. In the twelfth century it suddenly reappeared. In 1144 rumors spread in Norwich, England, that the Jews of the town "bought a Christian child before Easter and tortured him with all the tortures wherewith our Lord was tortured, and on Long Friday hanged him on a rood in hatred of our Lord, and afterwards buried him" (Jacobs, *op. cit.*, p. 19). In 1171 similar rumors brought about the immediate extinction of the entire Jewish community in Blois, in France. From that time on, this accusation, amplified by many a detail and especially by the allegation that the Jews need the blood of a Christian child to make unleavened bread for Passover, served as the most vigorous stimulus for popular hatred in the West. Notwithstanding its inherent absurdity, it captured the imagination and catered to the sadistic instincts of the masses. Certain vested interests, especially of monasteries which became pilgrimage centers through the possession of "relics" of a child-martyr, helped greatly to validate the popular belief in that source of martyrdom. Unceasing denials by Jews, and even by Jewish converts to Christianity, were as ineffective as had been similar protestations by early Christians. There is a strange irony in the fact that the French Christians should have so totally forgotten the phrase attributed to one of their early women martyrs, Byblis, "How could they eat their children, who may not eat blood even of creatures without reason!" (Eusebius, *Eccl. Hist.* V, 1.26). By the first half of the thirteenth century, the contagion had spread so far that both the emperor and the pope felt bound to intervene. Prompted by the blood accusation at Fulda in 1236, Frederick II called together lay and ecclesiastical dignitaries of the empire. Convinced of the Jewish abhorrence of blood, he sent "extraordinary ambassadors to all the kings of the West," to ask that converts experienced in Jewish law be sent to him. The decision of this tribunal was that the Bible, as well as the Talmud, insists that the Jews "must altogether beware of pollution with any blood whatever." Pope Innocent IV protested in 1247 against any such "thoughtless action" against the Jews, and in 1253 again forbade "that anyone should accuse them of using human blood in their ritual." All the papal, imperial and royal injunctions, repeated from generation to generation, proved of no avail, however, against the combined forces of popular suspicion and local profiteering.[16]

Apart from religious prejudice, economic factors, such as the competitive appetites of the Christian burghers, doubtless played a significant rôle. Even Jewish money lenders frequently found powerful Christian rivals, who, irked by the special Jewish privileges to engage in this trade, clamored for the total exclusion of Jews. In southern Italy, for instance, the Venetian and Florentine money changers were the most vociferous anti-Jewish agitators in the expulsion period. Even wealthy Spain, throughout the Middle Ages amply supplied with domestic credit, after 1492 fell a victim to the rapaciousness of the Italian and German bankers. In view of the prevailing exorbitant rates of interest, moreover, money lending became increasingly dangerous for the Jewish creditor and ruinous to the Christian debtor. One of the major complaints of the Spanish Christians, according to Ibn Verga, was that "the Jews have gnawed on us, confused us and taken away for usury even our cattle, so that we are unable to plough our fields" (*Shebet Yehudah,* edited by Wiener, p. 13). Sometimes the subjected masses revolted, not against the Jews as such, but against privileged groups in general, including the Jews. At times a peasant revolt, primarily directed against the landowning nobility, engulfed in its bloody procession one or another Jewish community. Even the "holy war" of 1391 in Spain, had many characteristics of a social revolt. For example, the farmers of Majorca, in arms against the central government, demanded that the Jews who had found refuge in governmental strongholds be either baptized or exterminated. The object obviously was the elimination of the Jews as a separate corporate body, with special political and economic privileges, and, as such, a permanent abetter of the royal power.

That religious fanaticism was often not the prime cause of such "direct actions," can easily be seen from the fact that next to the nobility and Jewry, the Catholic clergy suffered most. This is perfectly evident in the Chmielnicki revolt in 1648. The Ukrainian peasantry, differing in nationality, language and religion from the ruling class, directed its primarily social revolt against the Polish Catholic landowners and clergymen, as well as against the Jews, who had been their social and political allies. The subsequent pogrom movement of 1744, extending over a large area in White Russia and Lithuania, characteristically sprang from the widespread dissatisfaction of the masses with the administration of the ecclesiastical surplice fees. The administrators were the Jews, who had thereby immediate control over such intimate phases of peasant life as birth and baptism, wedding, and burial. Similarly, the revolting peasants in Alsace, in 1525, demanded bluntly, "Chastise the clerics and the Jews"; and their leaders gave out the instruction to the marchers, "Sack the Jews and the clerics." Indeed, Joseph of Rossheim with comparative ease persuaded these peasant leaders to spare the Jews. The Jews' relative disadvantage, compared to the nobility, arose from their general defenselessness. Although at the Bishop's Square in Mayence, in 1096, the Jews fought valiantly against the crusaders; and although, in 1648, the Polish Jews defended many a city against besieging Cossacks, they never had sufficient arms, and hardly ever any military training. Furthermore, they were scattered and easily exposed to the wrath of their neighbors. Unlike the Muslim minority, they could not threaten their assailants with retortion against the Christian minorities in other lands. On the contrary, even when in a position to deal a strong blow, their sense of solidarity with all Jewry often made them subordinate the destiny of an individual community to that of the whole people. The Jews in Tulczyn in 1648, for example, refrained from attacking treacherous fellow combatants among the noblemen; they chose to die instead, when their leader exhorted them: "we are in exile among the nations, if you lay hands upon the nobles, then all the kings of Christianity will hear of it and take revenge on all our brethren in the dispersion, God forbid" (Hannover, *Yeven mesulah*).[17]

The government, on the other hand, always tried to protect the lives of the Jews. Shocked by the pogroms of 1096-97, when imperial protection proved to be so ineffective, Henry IV began, from 1103 on, to mention the Jews specifically among defenseless groups, such as women and clergy, to whom truce was to be permanently extended by imperial treaty with the powerful lords. Emperor after emperor confirmed such guarantees. As the central authority progressively declined in Germany, the obligation of safeguarding the lives and property of the Jews was increasingly transferred to local or regional rulers. Even the urban patricians, many of whom must have resented Jewish economic competition, usually extended far-reaching protection to their Jewish neighbors. The influence of the precedent established during the First Crusade, a factor of prime importance in medieval life, was reinforced by the realization that mob violence, once unleashed against the lives and goods of Jews, would hardly respect those of wealthy Christians. In Spain, Sicily and England, where royal power retained its hold, the king remained the foremost natural protector of the Jews. In the more thoroughly feudalized France of the tenth to the thirteenth centuries, the protective functions were transferred to the regional vassals. Most independent, of course, were the sovereign Italian republics. Notwithstanding the great variety of hostile acts against the Jews, and the underlying lack of political balance in medieval Europe, one fact stands out clearly. In contrast to Czarist Russia, for example, no medieval government ever countenanced pogroms. When the government felt it could no longer protect the Jews and preserve order, the result was not a pogrom but an expulsion.

While there is no doubt that the personal greed of a monarch who, by expulsion, was enabled to appropriate all or a large part of the Jews' fortunes, was often the immediately decisive factor; and while religious prejudice and fanaticism undoubtedly played an enormous part in the agitation preceding each decree of banishment, neither motive offers a full explanation of a social phenomenon so widespread and so strikingly similar in all places and periods. Dagobert, Philip the Fair and Charles II of France, who were certainly no more pious than Louis le Debonnaire, ousted the Jews from France, while Charlemagne's son expressly invited them to settle with extensive privileges. Edward I of England, Ferdinand the Catholic of Spain, were neither more pious nor more greedy than were Henry III of England or James I of Aragon. But in 1290 the Jews were expelled from England, and in 1492 from Spain; while the crusaders, who reconquered Spain, treated the Jews very well, and Henry III's régime saw the greatest numerical and economic strength of medieval English Jewry. Both Edward I and Ferdinand the Catholic, attempting in the early years of their reigns to solve the question through mild measures, sometimes revealed a positively friendly attitude to their Jewish subjects. But Edward I, despairing of the effectiveness of the law of 1275, finally decided to cut the Gordian knot by eliminating the

Jews, while Ferdinand and Isabella, seeing that such measures as the Inquisition (established in 1478), the compulsory ghetto (1480), and expulsion from Andalusia (1483), did not solve the problem, embarked upon a policy of total exclusion. In fact, as late as 1491, they renewed for four years the contracts with some of their prominent Jewish tax farmers. It is easy to detect the immediate causes of these culminating decrees. In England there was, on the one hand, the outcry against Jewish usury; on the other, Pope Honorius IV's bull of 1286 denouncing widespread judaizing (a phenomenon whose very existence contradicts theories of universal hatred of the Jews). The spokesmen of the English people as a whole, moreover, were so desirous of getting rid of the Jews that they offered the king fully one-fifteenth of all English property to indemnify him for his loss of Jewish revenue. In Spain, antagonism to judaizing may have been primary; antagonism to usury, secondary. The position of the Jews was made additionally precarious, as they came to be suspected, not without reason, of encouraging the thousands of Marranos to adhere secretly to the Jewish faith. But the very existence of Marranos in the country cannot be explained wholly by religious or economic animosities.

LATENT NATIONALISM

Interwoven with all the underlying religious and economic conflicts, there was another force at work: the growing nationalisms of the European countries. While European nationalism in the contemporary sense is the product of developments of the last two centuries, its antecedents go back as far as the dissolution of the western Roman Empire. It is a matter of common knowledge that the development of the French, English and Spanish monarchies in the later Middle Ages was largely determined by their subjects' unity of "destiny and culture," and uniformity of speech and descent. No matter how strong the influence of the universal Church, no matter how wide the community of Christendom, these nations soon revealed in their political, literary and even religious lives, forces of nationalism, latent but vital. Even before the great revolutions of Protestantism, the Gallicanism of the Catholic Church in France, and especially the Hussite movement in Bohemia, marked stirrings of medieval nationalism in the field of religion.

Such unconscious nationalism affected the Jews most vitally. So many phenomena of their history, especially in Christian countries, can be accounted for on this basis alone, that the present author has ventured to formulate a historical law expressing this relation: the status of the Jews was most favorable in pure states of nationalities (*i.e.,* states in which several ethnic groups were included, none having the position of a dominant majority); least favorable in national states (*i.e.,* where state and nationality, in the ethnic sense, were more or less identical); and varying between the two extremes in states which included only part of a nationality. Up to the seventeenth century, this law was operative practically without exception. The reason is quite obvious. The state of many nationalities found the "foreignness" of the Jews less objectionable, since its major elements were ethnically differentiated among themselves. Such a state could even use the ubiquitous Jewish group as a link binding the disaffected elements in the population to the ruling authority. The kings, particularly, took advantage of the fact that the Jewish community was outside Christian society, to strengthen the centripetal forces in their realms, and thus prevent the dangerous growth of national solidarity. Examples of such pure states of multiple nationality were the early medieval states after the Teuton invasions; Muslim Spain from the eighth to the tenth centuries, as well as Christian Spain in the thirteenth century; the Carolingian Empire; early Angevin England; Poland, and Turkey. The more ethnically homogeneous these states grew through the process of mutual assimilation, the less favorable became the position of the Jews. Legal disabilities multiplied; disturbances of public order increased, both in volume and frequency, until they assumed the proportions of pogroms (obviously nothing but a disorderly move on the part of the populace to eliminate the Jews). Finally, when a state achieved complete homogeneity, there usually came the climax: a decree of banishment. The early national states of Spain, France and Lombardy in the seventh century tolerated the Jews no more than the newly centralized national states of England in 1290, of France in the fourteenth century, and of Spain and Portugal late in the fifteenth century. Medieval Italy and Germany, on the other hand, broken up into many sovereign or semisovereign states, each embracing only part of the whole Italian or German nationality, present a most variegated picture of exclusion and admission, of tolerance and intolerance, with intolerance gaining ground in the more purely national regions of northern and western Germany, and tolerance prevailing in the more mixed hereditary provinces of the Hapsburgs and in the Venetian Republic.[18]

CLOSE JUDEO-CHRISTIAN RELATIONS

It would be a mistake, however, to believe that hatred was the constant keynote of Judeo-Christian relations, even in Germany or Italy. It is in the nature of historical records to transmit to posterity the memory of extraordinary events, rather than of the ordinary flow of life. A community which lived in peace for decades may have given the medieval chronicler no motive to mention it, until a sudden outbreak of popular violence, lasting a few days, attracted widespread attention. Since modern historical treatment can no longer be satisfied with the enumeration of wars and diplomatic conflicts, the history of the Jewish people among the Gentiles, even in medieval Europe, must consist of much more than stories of sanguinary clashes or governmental expulsions. In fact, compared to the almost incessant wars which ravaged Europe in the late Middle Ages and early modern times, the pogroms, even of those most tragic three centuries from 1096 to 1391, were but sporadic outbreaks. No period of medieval Jewish martyrdom compares in bloodiness with such a century as the seventeenth, of which only twenty-one years passed without major international conflicts.

Normal relations between Jews and Christians were generally amicable, or at worst characterized by mild mutual suspicion. Particularly in the Mediterranean countries, social, economic and even intellectual interrelations were so intimate that for centuries church and state tried in vain to check what they regarded as overfriendly intercourse militating against their segregation policy. Even the Christian clergy were often associated with Jews in intellectual projects. In the darkest ages of Merovingian France, their convivial relations with Jews were so general as to draw the attention of many provincial synods. On the whole, social intercourse in Germany, northern France, England, Hungary and Poland was in normal years not much less frequent than that prevailing among burghers and nobles, or patricians and artisans.

Most pronounced, of course, were the economic relations. Even in the medieval ghetto, Jewish economic life was mainly built upon selling merchandise, or lending money to Gentiles. Often where Jews were permitted to own land, they cultivated it with the help of Christian laborers. Gregory I, while maintaining the prohibition of Jewish ownership of Christian slaves, allowed Jews to employ half-free Christian *coloni*. The more intensive Jewish industrial occupations necessarily led to the employment of Christian workingmen. The reiterated prohibitions of canon and civil law proved utterly ineffective in preventing the widespread employment by Jews of Christian domestic servants. On the other hand, Jews usually had to purchase from Christians the most essential household necessities, as well as raw materials for their trades. They frequently maintained special ritualistic supervisors in Christian dairy farms. Judah b. Samuel's *Book of the Pious* of the twelfth century refers to Jews as learning the bookbinding trade from Christian monks. In short, commercial interrelations were so intimate and deep that the Church felt it could easily impose certain regulations upon the Jews, merely by threatening to warn Christians to stay away from them.

Purely social relations, too, must have been very intimate at times. When we read in Juspa the Sexton's *Custumal* that in medieval Worms, a Jewish communal garden was maintained through the legacy of a Christian woman, who thus expressed her appreciation of the beautiful bridegroom's celebration during the Feast of the "Rejoicing over the Law" (quoted by A. Epstein in *Gedenkbuch David Kaufmann,* pp. 312 ff.); and that in 1484 a Palermitan Christian served as a functionary at a Jewish circumcision (for which he, as well as the father of the child, were fined), it becomes clear that social intercourse must have been extensive. Even the clergy could not avoid some sort of amicable relations with Jewish associates: they received instruction in Hebrew from Jewish teachers, lent money to Jews, borrowed money from them, and farmed out church revenue to them. As Guedemann points out, the ninth-century bishop, Arsenius of Orta, even wished to introduce the Jewish *tallit* into the Christian services. The Alba Bible, a Castilian translation of the Scriptures, produced in the fifteenth century by Moses Arragel conjointly with Christian clergymen on the order of Prior Louis de Guzman (published in 1920-22), affords a remarkable instance of intellectual coöperation at a time when the anti-Jewish feeling had risen to a very high pitch.

The inefficacy of legal segregation in preventing the growth of social ties between Jews and Gentiles, is strikingly revealed in the domain of sex relations, by their very nature so extremely personal and so largely immune from close social supervision. During the Italian Renaissance, the prevailing sexual licentiousness greatly facilitated such intimate relations between Jews and Gentiles. With the professional prostitutes, then mostly Christians, the Jews associated freely, being but rarely apprehended. Occasional criminal prosecutions shed a characteristic light. For instance, in Florence, during the fifteenth century, not less than thirty-seven out of eighty-five criminal proceedings directed against Jews, in which the reason for the indictment is known, were for such transgressions. In one case two Jewish bankers were heavily fined because they allowed their clerk to have an affair with a Christian girl. No wonder that a Jewish communal law, passed in 1314, protested against those Italian coreligionists "in whose eyes Gentile women were altogether permissible." Almost every contemporary Spanish Jewish chronicler remarks on the frequency of amorous ventures outside the fold. Zacuto, for example, poignantly explains the persecutions of 1391:

We have a tradition that they took Christian women into their houses until they became pregnant. Their children became Gentiles and afterwards were among the murderers of their fathers. [*Yuhasin,* edited by Filipowski, p. 225a.]

Ibn Verga repeats this accusation, adding that the Jews had cast their eyes upon the daughters of the land on account of the frequent friendly associations with Gentiles; and that Jews believed that intercourse with a Christian woman, punished by Jewish law by flagellation only, was prohibited in a lesser degree than such relationship with a Jewess. In fact, the

Portuguese Cortes, in 1482, complained that Jewish craftsmen, journeying through villages and employed by peasant families, seduced Christian women while the men were working in the fields.

More difficult to understand is the fact that there were even cases of intermarriage. Notwithstanding the severe penalties, as well as the refusal of either priest or rabbi to officiate at such a wedding, Jewish men seem often to have found means of marrying Christian women. This can be explained only in the light of the flexibility of medieval marriage laws. Neither medieval Judaism nor the Church until the Council of Trent required an ecclesiastical ceremony before a priest. Even the presence of ten adult male Jews at the recitation of the "bridegroom's benediction," although expected by law, was not indispensable (cf. Maimonides, *Mishneh Torah,* Ishshut X,6; and *Shulhan Aruk,* Eben ha-Ezer, LV,3; LXI,1 gloss). In fact, in respect to marriage, modern Jewish law merely incorporated the conditions set up by the modern state. Naturally, records of intermarriage are likewise more numerous in the Mediterranean countries than in those north of the Alps. In Spain, from the Visigothic period on, such cases are frequently mentioned. The great French rabbi, Moses of Coucy, for example, relates with great pride that in 1236 his sermons led many Spanish Jews to divorce their Christian wives. As late as 1714, the potters' guild of Lissa, in Poland, adopted a statutory prohibition against members marrying Jewesses. This prohibition is the more characteristic as it is aimed at unions between Christians and Jewesses, which, whether legitimate or illicit, were always less frequent than those between Jews and Christian women. Jewish objections to the former were so powerful that in one case two Spanish Jews slew their sister, who had become pregnant by a Christian. While this was an exceptional occurrence, the fact that a great rabbi, Asher b. Yehiel, permitted cutting off the nose of a Jewess involved in an affair with a Saracen, "in order that she become repellent to her paramours" (*Responsa,* 18,13), is proof enough of the double standard among the Jews in Spain.

Wherever Jews lived for a long period, their association with Gentiles was such that the local tongue became theirs and was carried by them to other lands when they left. The two well-known examples of Ladino and Yiddish indicate how far-reaching the intercourse between the Jewish and the Gentile populations in medieval Spain and Germany must have been. The Jews in Angevin England used as their mother tongue, French, the language in which they conversed with their noble and ecclesiastical compatriots. No wonder that many saw in such association a serious threat to the orthodoxy of the Christian population. It was at this point that the Church had to interfere.[19]

THE CHURCH AND THE JEWS

Through this kaleidoscopic pattern of the relations between the Jewish minority and the Gentile majorities, there runs one vivid thread: the attitude of the Church. This attitude was remarkably consistent, at least as far as the western Church was concerned. To understand it, one must bear in mind what was perhaps the most crucial distinction between eastern and western Christianity, namely, the relation of church to state. The orthodox Church has, from its beginning, been largely a state church. After the time of Constantine the Great, the Byzantine Empire overwhelmed the Church and made it subservient to its own needs. The emperor was its real head, the patriarch merely one of his appointed officers. Rightly, therefore, the Russian czar, as inheritor of the Byzantine emperor, continued to be the master of its destinies. The western Church was essentially international. After the dissolution of the western Roman Empire, it embraced numerous nationalities, organized in countless states under the feudal system of medieval Europe. For a while, the international Church tried to establish its political supremacy over the different nations. As long as it was opposed by another international power, the empire, the papacy was in the ascendancy politically. Only the rise of medieval nationalism, disrupting European unity, checked the expansion of the temporal power of the pope, and Europe finally reverted to the open or clandestine supremacy of state over church.

This internationalism of the Western Church helped to shape the destinies of the medieval Jew. Whereas the medieval state, as soon as it became nationally homogeneous, resented the existence of an ethnically alien body, the Church could be much more tolerant. Its usually farsighted and conservative policy was also less subject to momentary impulses. The economic and social functions of medieval Jewry, like those of the Church, were similar throughout Christendom, and largely irrelevant to regional interests and conflicts. The interstate Church and interstate Jewry were thus subtly congruous, amid the varying, regionally delimited careers of the European peoples.

Tradition played no minor part in this development. The origins of Christianity in Judaism, the descent of its founders from Jewish stock, have permanently influenced, both favorably and adversely, the relations between the two bodies. Had not Paul himself, with all his violent denunciations of the Jewish people, occasionally insisted upon some remnant of Israel's former glory? Following in his footsteps, the Church Fathers gradually evolved a definite policy and attitude. Although no longer Israel in the spirit, they proclaimed, the Jews were still Israel in the flesh. As such, the Jewish people still had a great function to perform; they served as living witnesses to the truth of the Christian tradition. Should anyone deny—and many did throughout the ages—the authenticity of the Gospel, the historicity of Jesus and the crucifixion, the Jews themselves, the enemies of Christianity, could testify to the Evangelic truth.

Thus [writes Thomas Aquinas], from the fact that the Jews observe their rites which, of old, foreshadowed the truth of the faith which we hold, there follows this good—that our very enemies bear witness to our faith, and that our faith is represented in a figure so to speak [*quasi in figura*]. For this reason they are tolerated in the observance of their rites. [*Summa theol.*, II, 2, 10, 11 transl. by the Fathers of the English Dominican Province.]

Therefore, the Jews were to be tolerated until the end of days, when all mankind, including the bodily descendants of Abraham, would have become converted to Christianity and the Jewish testimony would no longer be needed.

On the other hand, religious tolerance was not to extend to physical maintenance, beyond a very low level. The moment the Jews should become influential or dominant, their existence might become prejudicial to the vital interests of Christianity. Their influence might counteract all missionary efforts. Their different outlook might cause even faithful Christians to seek solutions for their religious problems other than those offered by the authoritative Church. The widespread heresies which accompanied the evolution of the Church almost from its beginning, kept it constantly on the alert. In short, to quote again the ancient myth, the new Cain on earth was to lead the life of a vagabond, but also "whosoever slayeth Cain, vengeance shall be taken on him sevenfold" (Gen. 4:15).

Behind these theological and mystic enunciations of the most distinguished Church Fathers and popes, of Jerome and Augustine, of Leo the Great and Gregory the Great, there loomed a stubborn reality. The Jews in the period of Constantine had remained a numerically and intellectually powerful group, which could not simply be decreed out of existence. To antagonize it to the extreme could hardly appear wise, at a time when the heathen masses were much more promising as objects of missionary activity, and when Judaism, having renounced proselytizing as a means of national aggrandizement, was a relatively innocuous bystander in that decisive struggle. The medieval Church, moreover, was so deeply ingrained with the spirit of Roman statehood that in its missionary work it turned to entire states, rather than to detached groups or individuals. Like Rome, the Church expanded by annexing one province after another, one tribe after another. This was the case in Germany, Bohemia, Poland, Scandinavia and east of the Baltic, the goal being often achieved through ruthless military as well as spiritual warfare. The nonpolitical entity of the Jewish people, long divorced from its state and territory, was, as such, beyond the reach of this type of propaganda. This policy, firmly established in the first millennium of expansion, was continued in the subsequent period of Christianity's concentrated attack upon the declining church-state of Islam.

Medieval canon jurists soon found the necessary rationalization: mankind as a whole is but the mystic body of Christ. In this *corpus Christi* are included not only Christians, but also infidels. In it, each corporate group, each *universitas,* has a special function, as of a special organ within a human body. The Jewish community, also a member of this universal body, must be maintained as such a *universitas* apart, with as much separation and segregation, and therefore as much self-government, as possible. This formula is the more remarkable, the more uncontested the general theory and practice of intolerance became in the Christian world.

The temporal power of the popes, and especially their sovereignty in the papal state, complicated the solutions which the Church sought of the Jewish question. The papal claim to overlordship over all Jews in the world, as voiced by Innocent III and Thomas Aquinas, might have had its chief practical bearing upon the Jewish subjects of Rome, through the fiscal policy of the pontifical treasury. But indirectly it had a tremendous effect upon the crystallization of the idea of Jewish "serfdom" throughout medieval Europe. When the Church, with a persistence which betrayed its great interest in the matter, demanded that Jews purchasing land from Christians continue to pay the customary tithe to the local parish, it might have wished merely to protect the acquired rights of the clergy. But when Innocent III, in 1205, upon learning that Castilian Jewry greatly increased its landholdings, speedily protested to the king of Castile that, through such proceeding, "the synagogue grows, while the Church diminishes and the handmaid is preferred to the free lady" (a variation from S. Grayzel's translation in his *Church and the Jews*, p. 113), the indirect effect necessarily was an increased opposition to the transfer of land from Christians to Jews.

Nevertheless, the principle of toleration prevailed within the confines of the papal state. Had this been like any other state, the Jewish inhabitants would have been expelled from Rome on more than one occasion, but as a matter of fact the Jews were allowed to remain in the capital of all western Christianity. For more than nineteen centuries since Emperor Tiberius permitted the Jews to reënter the city, they have lived in Rome, which thus harbors the oldest uninterrupted Jewish settlement in Europe. The somewhat dubious notice in the later Jewish chroniclers concerning Pope John XXI's intention, in 1321-22, of banishing the Jews, is indicative of the ease with which such a decree was obviated, rather than of a serious reversal of policy. Even when, under the impact of the Counter Reformation, two popes actually decided to expel the Jews from their realm,

Rome, Ancona and Avignon were expressly exempted. There was a profound difference, however, between the attitude of the central authorities, such as the papacy and the ecumenical councils, and that of the provincial clergy. The regional ecclesiastics of the different European countries were much more susceptible to the local temper than Rome, with its world orientation. French national sentiment eventually infused the French clergy with the ideas of Gallicanism. The Hussite and later Protestant movements roused a responsive echo in the clerical nationals of their followings. Similarly, each attempt of a national state to eliminate the Jews, found many protagonists among its ecclesiastical officers, who, under the impact of nationalist forces of exclusion, were prone to forget the Church's insistence on toleration. Even in a state of many nationalities, the local ecclesiastical powers were seldom its unqualified champions. They frequently felt obliged to counteract what they regarded as undue Jewish expansion. Numerous exceptions notwithstanding, it may be asserted that at least down to the middle of the sixteenth century, central agencies of the Church, as a rule, were more tolerant than the provincial clergy.[20]

THE PROBLEM OF CONVERSION

Toleration by the Church did not mean, of course, that no Jews should be converted to Christianity. But while pagans, Muslims and others might be Christianized at the point of the sword, with, according to many authorities, benefit to themselves as well as to the Church, Jews were not to be baptized forcibly. Gregory the Great renewed this prohibition of the Christian Roman Empire for medieval Christendom. Other Church teachers and popes likewise prohibited forcible conversion, Thomas finally uttering the memorable sentence, *quia credere voluntatis est* (*Summa theol.,* II,2,10,8). Even Vincente Ferrer, whose violent sermons were the source of great tribulations for Spanish Jewry during the fateful years 1391-1415, publicly protested against bloodshed as a means of propagating Christianity. On the other hand, in his interpretation of voluntary conversion, Gregory admitted all sorts of inducements. In two epistles, he advocated the use of tax reductions up to one-third as a legitimate means of attracting individual Jews, hoping that at least their children would be faithful Christians.

This principle of qualified tolerance was open to widely divergent interpretations in its details, however. What does forcible conversion mean? According to writers on both canon and civil law, the old Roman distinction between *vis absoluta* and *vis compulsiva* still carried weight. In a strict sense, therefore, force consisted only in sheer physical constraint. Such physical baptism without the consent of the baptized, was null and void. But was *vis compulsiva*, the compulsion under a serious threat, likewise to be deprecated? On this point opinions differed. A stricter interpretation excluded any threat other than that of loss of life. The Jews expelled from a country, and thus given the alternative of relinquishing their homes, suffering serious discomforts and sustaining economic losses, or embracing Christianity, were not classified as acting under such duress. Once even a pope (Leo VII) advised an archbishop to banish the Jews "with our authority, since we are not bound to keep company with the enemies of God" (937-39, Aronius, *Regesten*, No. 125). Indeed, all the medieval expulsions were based upon the assumption, implicit or explicit, that the Jews through baptism would automatically obtain the right to remain. None the less, the objections raised to expulsion were seldom, if ever, based upon the prohibition of forcible conversion.

Other interpretations arose out of the question as to the legal validity of accomplished facts. Was a Jew, who had undergone such forcible conversion, entitled to return afterwards to his former faith? In strict juridical argumentation, there could hardly be any doubt that, where willingness to be baptized was lacking, no baptism had taken place. Indeed, after the crusaders of 1096 had forcibly baptized large groups of Jews, particularly in Trèves and Rouen, the respective rulers, Emperor Henry IV and King William II, soon allowed these converts to become Jews again. In theory, too, Durandus of San Porciano, himself suspected of heretical proclivities, advocated leniency in such cases. More authoritatively, the Fourth Lateran Council (1215) spoke only of the "salutary compulsion," to be exercised against those who "by their own free judgment" had adopted Christianity. But more zealous jurists taught that the sacrament of baptism, if performed without physical violence, has an indelible character. "He who is violently drawn, through threats and entreaties, and in order to avoid damages accepts the sacrament of baptism, such an one . . . , so to say conditionally willing, although absolutely not willing, is to be compelled to observe the Christian faith," states the main medieval canon code (*Decret. Greg.*, III, 42, 3). Every later reversion to another creed was classified as full-fledged apostasy, punishable, according to both canon and secular law, by death.

Still another problem was that of the conversion of children, who theoretically had no valid will. Persons of fourteen or more had the right to choose their own faith. Canon law made a distinction only between children below and above seven. For those under seven, the will had to be supplied by the parents. In some cases, the desire of one grandparent for baptism was accepted in lieu of, or even against, the wish of the parents. A few jurists, however, searched for legal subterfuges to legitimize wholesale conversions of Jewish children. Vincent of Beauvais wished to see this right limited to the monarch, who, as overlord of the Jews, was master over all their belongings, including their children, but Duns Scotus eloquently pleaded for indiscriminate Christianization of Jewish youth. If credence is to be given to a Continental Jewish record, this theory was actually applied to thousands of children in England in 1290. Duns Scotus, of course, writing under the stimulus of English Jew-baiting during the expulsion period, had also championed forcible conversion of all Jewish adults, suggesting that the old prophecies might be respected by maintaining a few Jews on a distant island until the second coming of Christ.

When it came to action, the more tolerant legal maxims of the majority were often discarded. Once a child had been removed from the custody of its parents and brought into a monastery, the Christian authorities were very reluctant to give it up. Such cases occurred frequently, down to very recent times. The famous Mortara case, for example, arose from the confession of a Christian servant girl in Bologna that several years previously she had baptized the Jewish boy, Edgar Mortara, while he was sick. The child was immediately taken away from his parents, and the protests of the civilized world, including the Catholic Emperors

Francis Joseph and Napoleon III, proved of no avail. Pope Pius IX himself insisted upon the retention of the child and his Christian education. This was in the year 1858![21]

The means of persuading adults were many and varied. Under the guidance of the papal authorities, and especially after Nicholas IV's bull of 1278, there developed in Rome the custom, soon emulated by other cities, of preaching Christian sermons to Jewish audiences. The Jewish community was obliged by law to supply the necessary listeners. Increasingly minute legislation fixed the number of Jews required to be present, the frequency of attendance, and the sanctions against evasion. Moreover, the *domus conversorum* in London, the house of catechumens in Rome, and like institutions elsewhere were open to candidates for baptism. Here they found food and shelter, while receiving instruction in the fundamentals of the Christian religion. While many a hard-pressed Jew made fraudulent use of such opportunities, only to escape shortly before the final act of baptism, many others became and remained Christians. The baptismal ceremony was often a great social affair, with a dignitary of church or state as godfather. Nor did the Church withdraw its support from the faithful convert, whose financial welfare was entrusted to episcopal care. In a series of letters, Innocent III, in particular, reprimanded various leading churchmen for neglect of this duty.

If financial considerations thus tempered the missionary zeal of many an ecclesiastic, the fiscal interests of the state were even more directly involved in conversion. To influence the Christian government of ancient Rome to protect baptized Jews against disinheritance by enraged parents, was relatively easy for the Church. The medieval state, however, often felt that through the act of conversion, a person hitherto classified as a royal serf escaped the king's overlordship. In England, therefore, the king insisted that a convert's property be escheat to the royal treasury. Only shortly before the expulsion, in 1281, the exchequer was ready to compromise to the extent of obtaining only one-half the estate. In most other European countries, the convert was automatically disinherited. "Just as they have relinquished the law of their forefathers," stated the main privileges of German Jewry, "so did they abandon also their possessions" (Aronius,

Regesten, Nos. 170, 171, etc.). Even in Aragon, where James I won great praise from Innocent III for expressly permitting a baptized Jew or Muslim to retain all his property, there must have been many converts whose severance of relations with their Jewish families and friends proved expensive. It is hard to estimate the total number of Jews voluntarily converted during the Middle Ages. Certainly at times, and particularly in the Mediterranean countries, the number must have been quite considerable. In southern Italy during the thirteenth century, we have records of some 1,300 converts, 310 of whom lived in the city of Trani. In Saragossa, after the disastrous disputation of Tortosa in 1413-14, the community budget always reckoned with the possibility of diminished revenue on account of desertion. Judah the Pious frequently refers to voluntary apostates, even in steadfast German Jewry. But whatever the cumulative effects of these voluntary conversions, they were beyond doubt numerically insignificant as compared with mass Catholicization under duress.

LOW SOCIAL STANDING

The other fundamental principle, that of keeping the Jews in a low social position, likewise had several implications. The main objective being to stave off Jewish heretical influences, a wall had to be erected between Jews and Gentiles. Some Church Fathers, with unbridled hatred, stigmatized every association with Jews as a grave sin. For St. Ambrose, for example, "the very chatter with them is a great pollution" (PL, XVII, 618). According to Chrysostom, the Jews should be avoided like "a common pestilence and a disease of the entire world, since they are more savage than wolves" (*ibid.,* XLVIII, 871).

The provincial synods, particularly, outdid one another in erecting barriers between the two groups. Not only must Jews not employ Christian servants, because of questions both of heresy and prestige, but even relations based upon perfect equality were prohibited. Conviviality at meals was the more to be deprecated, since Jewish ritual law precluded Jewish participation in meals prepared by Christians. Behind the frequent prohibitions imposed upon Jewish butchers against selling to Christians the meat disqualified by their ritualistic experts, lay the idea that Christians would then appear to eat food not good enough for Jews. On the other hand, the prohibition of bathing together in public streams had as its motive the prevention of intimacy between the two groups. This prohibition, reënacted in medieval times, had been adopted as a general law for all Christendom, by the ecumenical council called *quinisextum* (Trullianum) in 692. It reappeared ironically in the edicts of Caliph Al-Hakim against Jews and Christians alike. It soon spread in the western countries. The city of Angers, for example, made the admission of Jews in the fourteenth century dependent on the express condition that they refrain from bathing in the river Main. The Church also forbade the summoning of Jewish physicians to the bedside of Christians. Their presence, particularly at the side of a dying man, might endanger his soul, since the defenseless patient is all too prone to follow a doctor's advice. The fact that so many Jews won great distinction in medical science and practice during the Middle Ages did not make them more welcome. On the contrary, widespread popular legends ascribed the powers of such healers, not to scientific training, but to black magic.

Of particular importance were prohibitions concerning intermarriage. Roman-Christian legislation had insisted upon the rigid segregation of the two groups in their family life. Since the days of the Council of Elvira (about 300 A.D.) the medieval Church, through its central as well as its local authorities, put increasingly vigorous sanctions upon such relationships. In order to prevent a state of affairs whereby "by error Christians should mix with Jewish or Saracen women, or Jews and Saracens with Christian women," the Fourth Lateran Council (1215) introduced the Jewish badge into the Catholic world at large. In contrast to marriage with a heretical or excommunicated Christian, which was classified as valid although performed in violation of a prohibitive impediment, marriage with a Jew was null and void. A prominent Italian jurist of the seventeenth century declared illicit intercourse with a Jewess to be a graver sin than such intercourse with a nun. The penalties for it, always severe, sometimes went, as in Emperor Constantine's decree of 339, to the extreme of capital punishment. Secular powers, especially municipalities, outdid the canon jurists in harshness.

For example, in 1267 the provincial synod of Breslau, presided over by the papal legate, Cardinal Guido, while adopting rigid measures to segregate Christians from Jews, was satisfied to levy a fine of ten marks on the Jewish male transgressor and to flagellate publicly and banish forever the Christian woman. About the same time, the municipal law of Prague (1269) unconditionally demanded capital punishment in the case of a married woman; and the compiler of one of the general German law books, the *Schwabenspiegel* (about 1275), stated without such qualification that "if a Christian fornicates with a Jewess, or a Jew with a Christian woman, they are both guilty of superharlotry and they should be put upon one another and burned to death" (Aronius, *Regesten,* Nos. 724, 737, 771). The local custumals of Teruel, in Aragon, and Cuenca, in Castile, a century earlier, likewise put such relations under the sanction of death by fire. As late as the seventeenth century we hear of the case of Jean Allard "who kept a Jewess in his home in Paris and had several children by her; he was convicted of Sodomy on account of this relation and burned together with his paramour, since 'coition with a Jewess is precisely the same as if a man should copulate with a dog'" (E. P. Evans, *Criminal Prosecution and Capital Punishment of Animals,* p. 153).

Characteristically, much less emphasis has been laid by Church and State on this prohibition in more recent times. It is hardly to be assumed that the Church has given up its antagonism to intermarriage. But the virulent denunciations of former ages lost much of their point, with the change in the social condition of the Jews. As long as they were superior both in culture and in economic standing to the large mass of the population—and this was the case in the earlier Middle Ages—there was great danger that intermarriage would result in the conversion of the Christian partner to Judaism, rather than in the baptism of the Jewish partner. In modern times, especially in the nineteenth century, experience taught that conversions to Christianity, as a result of mixed marriages, far outnumbered those to Judaism. The children of such marriages, moreover, were even more frequently raised in the Christian faith. The Church, therefore, had less urgent reasons to oppose actively what had become an effective missionary institution.

JUDAIZING ACTIVITIES

The fears of the Church were not altogether without foundation. To be sure, Judaism had long ceased to be a missionary religion, and reiterated accusations of direct Judaizing activities were a reflection, not so much of actual conditions, as of the Church's own missionary desires and perhaps of its bad conscience. None the less, the very presence of Jews within an otherwise homogeneous Christian society, easily became a contributory cause of the rise of heretical trends. The strange phenomenon of a religious group with a different way of life, one in some respects so repulsive, in others so fascinating, but always mysterious; a group, moreover, admittedly bearing the heritage of a formerly chosen people, necessarily aroused in many a thoughtful Christian meditations concerning the truth of the Christian dogmas; while in others it awakened uncontrollable superstitious fears. The closer the social relationships, and the higher the intellectual and economic position of the Jews, the greater the danger of Christians adopting some of their religious concepts and even practicing some of their rites. As far back as the fourth century, Chrysostom vigorously attacked those among his fellow Christians who believed that an oath taken in the synagogue was more valid, because subjected to severer sanctions, than one taken in church. The belief in the Jews' superior power of magic was no less widespread in the later Middle Ages. Nourished by the traditions of ancient magic, with its extensive use of Hebrew divine names, and strengthened through the Christian denunciations of "the Synagogue of Satan," the belief that the Jews were the dreadful allies of the devil took deep root. In the minds of profoundly religious persons, stirred to their depths by the problem of evil, the devil occupied a position second to none, not even to God himself. What wonder that the supposed children of the devil, endowed with satanic cleverness and superhuman powers, often fascinated them beyond control?

On the other hand, Jewish rationalism infected reasoning minds. Jewish criticism of Christian dogma and ritual, even when merely part of the defense of the Jewish creed against Christian attacks, was often vigorous and outspoken enough to perplex many of the more independent Christians. Moreover, were not the Jews recognized as experts in the interpretation of the Hebrew Old Testament, which, after all, constituted the larger part of the Christian Bible? In some cases, such as that of Nicholas of Lyra, the most learned Christian Hebraist of the fourteenth century, the acknowledgment of indebtedness to Jews did not lead to any doubts concerning the teachings of the Church. In fact, Lyra himself wrote two pamphlets against the Jews. But others could not quite so easily reconcile themselves to the extremely homiletical exegesis of the Church Fathers, once they had learned to read the Scriptures in the light of the rational commentary of Kimhi, or even of the mildly homiletical work of Rashi. For a time the Church flattered itself that, through the establishment of chairs for the study of Hebrew and the Old Testament at the Universities of Paris, Oxford, Bologna and Salamanca, it would give a new impetus to missionary activities amongst the Jews. But when this resolution of the Council of Vienne (1312) was carried into effect, it was discovered that the teachers of Hebrew themselves were not fully immune to heterodox influences. Within a century or two, it became proverbial that a good grammarian was a bad theologian. Even Erasmus looked with suspicion upon the Christian Hebraists of his age, and Luther, himself a Hebraist, accused others of "rabbinizing."

In addition to the growing interest in Hebrew studies, the awakened curiosity of the intellectual Christians in regard to philosophic and scientific problems, led to many contacts with Jews, which seemed prejudicial to the strict orthodoxy of both groups. In a period when Jews were being forced to listen to Christian sermons, Spanish aristocrats often flocked to the synagogue to hear the preachment of a famous Jewish rabbi and philosopher; and Venetian noblemen and friars went to listen to Leon of Modena. Before that time, the *Apostolical Constitutions* included a section forbidding Christians to enter a Jewish synagogue; and Agobard had complained that "foolish Christians assert that the Jews preach to them better than our priests" (*De insolentia Judaeorum,* Chap. V). But these contacts could as little be checked by legal segregation, as the influence of the Old Testament could be limited through the prohibition of reading it in vernacular translations, such as decreed by James I of

Aragon in 1233, when all bibles "in Romancio" were to be delivered to the bishops within eight days.

No wonder that the few sporadic missionary efforts on the part of the Jews were viewed by the Church with great alarm. In principle, Judaism no longer encouraged proselytizing of any kind. Yehudah Halevi, the most nationalist of medieval poets, particularly emphasized the inferiority of the proselyte. Nevertheless, there were converts to Judaism. An Oxford ecclesiastic or deacon, who fell in love with a Jewess and became converted to Judaism, was punished with death by fire in 1222, largely because of his ecclesiastical dignity. Not long before, an entire congregation of twenty-two proselytes is said to have lived in London—a large number, indeed, in a Jewish population of a few hundred families. They seem to have lived undisturbed, until the pogroms of 1189 exterminated them, with other Jews. Even in Germany and Poland, cases of conversions to Judaism occurred from time to time. The so-called memory book of Mayence, for instance, mentions seven men and three women who were proselyte-martyrs between 1264 and 1341. Among them appears a French proselyte, given the usual name Abraham, who before his conversion had been a superior of the "barefooted" friars. Polish public opinion was deeply stirred by the case of a woman proselyte, named Malcher, the wife of an alderman of the capital city of Cracow. Despite her fourscore years and her connections with the city elders, she was burnt at the stake in 1539, in a public auto-da-fé. The chronicler Bielski, reporting this event, cannot refrain from the admiring exclamation that she "went toward death as courageously as to a wedding" (*Kronika Polska,* VI, 58). But nothing could be more spectacular than the attempt of Abraham Abulafia, the kabbalistic pseudomessiah, to convert Pope Martin IV to Judaism!

On the whole, the flaming denunciations of Jewish proselytizing activities, as voiced in the famous papal bull, *Turbato Corde,* of Clement IV in 1267, and in those addressed to the French and English prelates by Honorius IV in 1286, doubtless were greatly exaggerated. Equally unjustified was, for example, the accusation hurled at the Polish Jews in 1539 that, utilizing the religious unrest accompanying the Reformation, they had circumcised numerous Christians and sent them off to Turkey to escape punishment. A royal investigation initiated on this score ended with the posting of a "bond" of 20,000 ducats by the Jews of Cracow.

More frequently still were the Jews blamed for the spread of heresies. The constant use of Old Testament quotations by the heretics in support of their arguments, furnished the substratum for these arraignments. With the rise of heretical mass movements, moreover, especially in southern France, it became customary for the warring camps to accuse each other of being Jews or Judaizers. The stigma attached to the Jewish name and the polemics against Judaism inherited from ancient times, helped to discredit anyone stamped a Judaizer. No wonder orthodox Catholics and heretics of all sorts indiscriminately employed this means of attack. Even such fervent opponents of the Old Testament as the Catharists, the inheritors of the ancient Marcionite ideas, were denounced as Judaizers. Once a link appeared to have been thus established between heresy and Judaism, it was natural to look for an explanation in the personal relations between individual heretics and Jews.[22]

THE INQUISITION

It was at this point that the Inquisition assumed jurisdiction over Jewish life. The workings of these ecclesiastical courts and their influence upon religious movements in Europe from the thirteenth century on, have been the subject of violent controversies from the time of their establishment. Their place in Jewish history has also generally been treated with partisan fervor, rather than with scientific objectivity.

A judicious weighing of all the evidence available to date must not depart from the fundamental fact that Jews as Jews were never subject to the jurisdiction of the Holy Office. Moreover, this was a self-imposed limitation on the part of the Church. Anyone familiar with the expansion of canon law in the Middle Ages, and with the deep inroads made by it into the most varied phases of secular life, will doubly appreciate the restraint of the Church in exempting, as a matter of principle, all infidels from its own jurisdiction. It arrogated to itself only the right of supervision over the relations between Jews and Christians, and of defense against

Jewish attacks on Christianity. Jews accused of trying to convert Christians to Judaism, of influencing them in a spirit inimical to the teachings of the authoritative Church, or of having publicly spoken or written disparagingly about Christianity, Jesus or the Virgin, were to be haled before the ecclesiastical court. Books written by Jews soon had to undergo Christian censorship, so that all writings prejudicial to the interests of the Church might be destroyed, or at least obnoxious passages therein might be eliminated. The great auto-da-fé of the Talmud in 1242 in Paris, as well as the preceding investigation of the papal commission convoked by Gregory IX, after an appeal to the kings and prelates of France, England, Castile, Aragon and Portugal, to seize the Hebrew books on a certain date, dramatized the canonical jurisdiction over this phase of Jewish life before the entire Christian world. The burning of many precious manuscripts of this and other Jewish classics is an irreparable loss for modern Jewish scholarship. But its direct influence upon the intellectual life of medieval Jewry itself was of far-reaching consequence only in so far as it strengthened the forces of segregation. It was not the Jews, then, who felt the brunt of the Inquisition. As long as they refrained from "blasphemies" or proselytizing they had little to fear from this quarter. The grand inquisitor, Nicholas Eymeric of Aragon, insisted that

the pope may also judge Jews, if they do something against their own law as well as in matters of moral behavior in so far as their own superiors fail to punish them. The same holds true if they invent heresies against their own religion.

But even he concluded that the pope might find it inadvisable to exercise this right, "either because he has no power or on account of the dangers or scandals which may arise therefrom" (*Directorium inquisitorum,* ed. Venice, f. 353 b). Similar sentiments with respect to papal jurisdiction over heretical rabbis, expressed by Jerome of Santa Fé, the main Christian debater at Tortosa, were but tactical moves. In Spain, where the Archbishop of Tarragona had obtained the right to appoint inquisitors as early as 1233, the ecclesiastical courts had long been comparatively inactive. Later it was the Spanish and Portuguese states which insisted upon the rigid surveillance of backsliding Jews, while the popes showed great reserve. The establishment of inquisitorial courts in Castile in 1478; the appointment of a supreme council for Castile and Leon, as well as the extension of the competence of this council over Aragon, including Catalonia and Valencia, in 1483; and the appointment of inquisitors on the Balearic Islands in 1489, all had to be wrung from the pope by difficult negotiations. Still greater efforts had to be made by the Portuguese government to obtain Rome's approval. Faced by the opposition of the unofficial envoy to the Holy See of the Portuguese Marranos, Duarte de Paz, who was well equipped to bribe papal officials, the negotiations took years. Not until 1547, half a century after the forcible conversion of Portuguese Jewry, was the Inquisition definitely established in Portugal; and thirty-two years more elapsed before the court acquired the power of confiscating the property of the condemned.

In southern France and southern Italy, on the other hand, where the Inquisition was in full operation during the thirteenth century, the state protected its Jews. Even Charles of Anjou, although deeply indebted to the Church, opposed the anti-Jewish activities of the inquisitor Bertrand Rocca in southern France, warning him in 1276 not to transgress his well circumscribed competences, and to leave the execution of sentences against Jews entirely to the secular powers. In the kingdom of Naples, the Inquisition was not entitled to open an investigation against a Jew without the coöperation of a secular jury and the royal captain, and in 1375 the Jews of entire provinces obtained the right of appeal to the royal courts against its decisions. There occurred, to be sure, cases in which professing Jews were condemned as accomplices of heretics. Rabbi Isaac Males of Toulouse, for instance, was burnt in 1278, because he had accepted a backsliding convert who wished to be buried in a Jewish cemetery. But such prosecutions were exceptional. It appears to have been a fact as well as a theory that Jews who never ceased professing Judaism were, on the whole, left undisturbed. The French Inquisition under Bernard Gui (1307-23) condemned 495 Albigenses, 127 other heretics and only 5 Judaizers, all either proselytes or backsliding Jews. In the fourteen years of activity of the Spanish Inquisition, from its reëstablishment in 1478 to the expulsion of the Jews from Spain, we hear of only one prosecution directed against a Jewish community, when the Jewry of Huesca was accused in 1489 of having readmitted *conversos* to the Jewish fold. It was precisely the inability of the inquisitorial courts to check Jewish influence on the *conversos* that served as the decisive argument for the "Catholic" monarchs in banishing the Jews from Spain. Where heresies flourished less and where there were no large bodies of Christians of Jewish descent, the influence of the Inquisition on Jewish life was negligible. German and Polish Jewry had few contacts with ecclesiastical courts, even at a time when the Hussite movement and later the Reformation made common the accusation of Judaizing. One may assert without much exaggeration that in so far as professing Jews (and Muslims) were tolerated at all, they were the only group in the European population beyond the direct reach of the Church and its administration of justice.[28]

MARRANOS

Only the Marranos gave the Inquisition a significant rôle in Jewish history. These Spanish Jews, who had adopted Christianity under the stress of riots or expulsions, were regarded by canon law as full-fledged Christians. Since they had had the alternative of leaving the country, no "absolute" force had been employed in their conversion. In Portugal, where the alternative was purely fictitious, at least children who were under fourteen in 1497 and, still more, those born after that time, could not be allowed to revert to their ancestral faith. Many Marranos, however, regarded the conversion as an act performed under duress, and tried to continue worshiping their Jewish God. The larger the number of such insincere converts, the greater was the zeal of the inquisitorial courts in stamping out by persuasion or force what they thought a most dangerous heresy. For centuries suspicion and recrimination poisoned all human relations on the Peninsula.

The Marranos became specifically an Iberian problem and, by virtue of the prolonged spectacular struggle of the Inquisition against them, a unique phenomenon in the history of Judaism. But Jews, coerced by outward pressure to adopt *en masse* a foreign creed while secretly adhering to Judaism, were to be found in many periods and under various civilizations. As early as the period following the expulsion of 19 A.D., there seem to have remained some such secret Jews in the city of Rome. This was also true in the Byzantine Empire, after the harsh persecutions of 723, 875 and 930; of Visigothic Spain, in the days of Sisebut and Chintila; of Apulia in the fourteenth century; of Almohadic North Africa and Spain during the twelfth century; and of Persia five hundred years later. As a rule, however, the officials of the dominant religion were satisfied with lip service from such neophytes. When, two generations after the intolerant decree of Leo the Isaurian, the Second Council of Nicaea in 787 forbade unreliable converts to attend church service, this lay but lightly on their conscience. In the expiring Visigothic kingdom, King Egica's orders that new Christians, when traveling, appear before a bishop or priest and produce evidence that they did not observe the Sabbath; and forbidding Christian merchants to engage in commerce with them unless satisfied that they could recite the Lord's Prayer and that they ate Christian food, were ineffectual attempts to cope with an extremely complex problem. It was left to the Spanish, and even more to the Portuguese, inquisitors to apply a procedure, refined to the last degree of efficiency and cruelty, to the new and numerous class of heretics of Jewish descent. Even so, the Inquisition was unable to stamp out all vestiges of this heresy. Although the last auto-da-fé of a Portuguese Marrano occurred as late as 1765, and although the Spanish inquisitorial court, after a temporary suspension during the era of the French Revolution, was again active until 1834, Marrano groups have survived until the present day. Distinguished from the rest of the population by race and mode of living, cherishing certain peculiar, though distorted, Jewish recollections, they are to be found today both on the Balearic Islands and in Portugal. Few adventures of twentieth-century travel rival in significance the alluring rediscovery of these stray sons of an ancient race, who have so long preserved remnants of old customs and ideas in the midst of a hostile environment.

The problem of the Marranos has ever since stimulated both scholarly research and popular imagination. Notwithstanding the tremendous amount of work done by Christian and Jewish scholars, many obscure points are still to be cleared up. Even the question of how many Spanish Marranos were burned, is open to such contradictory estimates as that of Rodrigo, the apologist of the Inquisition, who gives a total of 400; and that of Amador de los Rios, likewise an ardent Catholic, who estimates 28,500 for the first 45 years alone.[24] The nature of Marrano life, its secrecy, the bias of investigating prosecutors, the distortions of overzealous witnesses, the peculiarities of the inquisitorial procedure, all make it extremely difficult to establish the facts, even where documents have been thoroughly scrutinized. Moreover, masses of evidence, hidden in the libraries of monasteries and municipalities throughout Europe and America, still await examination.

Certain facts, however, are clear. For generations—and even today the same is partly true—Marranos mingled little with the general population. Endogamy was so prevalent that two centuries after the "expulsion," not less than 364 out of 625 Marranos, condemned by the Inquisition of Lisbon in the years 1683-1746, were of unadulterated Jewish descent. Indeed, many responsa written outside the Iberian Peninsula reveal these endogamous tendencies. Simon b. Solomon Duran in *Yakin u-Boaz,* for example, declares them to be "a generally recognized fact." This phenomenon is the more striking, since before 1492 free sexual relationships between full-fledged Jews and Christians of Spain were not uncommon. The popular reaction to the Neo-Christians had, indeed, all the characteristics of racial anti-Semitism. An anti-Jewish spokesman is quoted by Ibn Verga as saying:

It is of no use to your Majesty to pour holy water on Jews a῀ to call them Peter or Paul, while they adhere to their religion 1῀. Akiba or Tarphon. There is no advantage in their baptism except to make them overweening against the true Christians without fear, since outwardly they are accepted as Christians. The royal tribute, which they used to pay when they were Jews, they pay no more. Know, Sire, that Judaism is no doubt one of the incurable diseases. [*Shebet Yehudah,* p. 97.]

The author, apparently himself for ten years a Marrano, must have heard many such complaints, while in Portugal. Anti-Marrano riots, of which the nine days of street fighting in Toledo in 1467 are a typical example, were, if anything, more numerous in fifteenth-century Spain than attacks upon professing Jews. Not satisfied with the harsh regulations of the provincial council of Tortosa in 1429, and of the general council of Basel in 1434, as well as with a number of actual executions in these pre-Inquisition days, popular hatred clamored for the exclusion of all Neo-Christians from public office. Notwithstanding the firm opposition of the local clergy, a Toledan emergency court adopted, in 1449, a "statutory sentence" to the effect. Pope Nicholas V's reiterated condemnation of such evidently antimissionary measures found no echo among the unruly masses. Demands to distinguish the Marranos by a special badge, and to segregate them in a ghetto, were not infrequent. In 1562, the Portuguese bishops themselves advocated both measures. All the Chuetas ("swine," the synonym of Marranos) of Palma, in Majorca, were secluded in a street of their own. Not until 1782 did they obtain permission to reside outside this quarter, a permission of which few availed themselves until within recent years. In 1630, the students of the University of Coimbra, anticipating a commonplace method of modern academic anti-Semitism, attacked their Neo-Christian colleagues, prevented them from attending the lectures, and forced the authorities to close the university for a time. Again, "Half Neo-Christians," "Quarter Neo-Christians," etc., were socially much inferior to Spaniards of pure descent, whose *limpieza* was attested by special certificates of the Inquisition. Such publications as the *Green Book of Aragon,* which revealed the Jewish antecedents of many very prominent families, like the modern *Semi-Gothas,* increased rather than appeased popular resentment.

The economic implications of the Marrano problem were clearest in the first few generations, when the Marranos who, even as Jews, had belonged to the wealthier class still occupied a prominent position in peninsular economic life. When expulsion came, the poorer classes were readier to leave Spain than were those who had to abandon fortunes. Abraham Senior, official leader of Spanish Jewry and financial adviser to the crown, was, in adopting Christianity at the age of eighty, much more typical of the wealthy Jews than Don Isaac Abravanel, a comparatively recent arrival from Portugal, who led the majority of his coreligionists into exile. Naturally, when the confiscation of property became a salient feature of the Inquisitorial process, the great wealth of the Neo-Christians aroused the cupidity of the ecclesiastical judge and the secular power behind him. The fortune of a Diego de Susan, totaling 10,000,000 maravedis; or the wealth of the Portuguese Marranos as a whole, estimated early in the seventeenth century at 80,000,000 ducats, were no mean provocations to action. The Inquisition erected a beautiful palace for itself in Majorca from the proceeds of only one investigation, in 1678. Avarice thus joined fanaticism in these protracted persecutions.

On the other hand, the sense of solidarity, animating such persecuted groups, contributed to the success of many Marrano economic ventures. Their extensive coöperation, over a vast geographic area, was not limited to near relatives. The five brothers Lopez offer a notable illustration of such joint undertakings. They established, in the sixteenth century, five branches of one business firm in the five centers of Marranism: Lisbon, Toulouse, Bordeaux, Antwerp and London. No modern Masonic lodge, however mysterious its rites, can compare with the solidarity, even in economic endeavor, of this group, united by ethnic, social and religious bonds, facing constant common dangers, and bent upon the preservation of a tradition which it cherished above everything in the world. No wonder the Marrano community at times had at its disposal considerable funds for the bribing of officials in Rome and at home, and as late as 1605 could offer 2,000,000 ducats to the crown for the support of a papal amnesty.

There were, of course, many converts who broke away entirely. Some of them became the leading anti-Jewish agitators of the age. For example, Solomon Halevi's dazzling career as Paul of Santa Maria, who after a few years became Bishop of Burgos and a member of the Council of Regency in Castile, was really prejudicial to his former coreligionists. Not only did he write controversial tracts to combat Judaism, but he directly inspired the severe anti-Jewish legislation of 1412. His son and successor in his bishopric (an unusual phenomenon in a celibate priesthood) was one of the main instigators of the anti-Jewish enactments of the Council of Basel twenty-two years later. The more clandestine Marrano life became, the more it encouraged espionage and denunciation. Professing Jews had been able to combat it with legal means, often with capital punishment, but now it became a deadly weapon in the hands of inquisitors, who encouraged denunciations by wives of husbands, by children of parents, shielding the traitors behind an impenetrable secrecy. Even full-fledged Jews were enlisted to detect backsliding brethren. Failure to reveal such transgressions to the proper authorities constituted complicity in the crime. Even the spiritual forces of Judaism were invoked, and the rabbis were ordered to proclaim bans in the synagogue against those who concealed pertinent information. Although such bans were of dubious validity, since Nahshon Gaon had already openly taken a stand against those imposed under governmental pressure, the conscience of many a medieval Jew was torn, in a terrible dilemma.

Cases in which a group of Jews or Marranos, already established in a country, tried to keep away later arrivals for economic reasons, were not lacking in that or any other period of Jewish history. For example, the Jews of Algiers, in the fourteenth century, had to be severely reprimanded by the Arab governor as well as by their own rabbi (Isaac bar Sheshet), because, together with the native Arabs, they attempted to block Jewish immigration. They said they were prompted by fear that the prices of commodities would rise as a result of a sudden influx. On a similar occasion in Brazil, in 1637, three Neo-Christian signatures appeared on a petition to the Dutch governor-general, to expel the Jews. Such occurrences, however, served only to cement the unity of the honest and upright remnant.

MARRANO RELIGION

The difficulties of Marrano religious life are self-evident. In the fifteenth century, when many *conversos* were persons born and bred in the Jewish creed and when they could maintain living contact with professing Jews, their religion approximated true Judaism, within the limits imposed by the constant danger of exposure. But under the relentless impact of Christianity, syncretistic doctrinal formulations and rites, such as the concept of salvation through the Law of Moses and the worship of saints, assumed growing importance. New notions, often of accidental origin, began to replace the traditional ones in the minds of Marranos, who mistook them for genuine elements of the Jewish creed. Cut off from the living spring of Hebrew literature (to possess a rabbinic work was little short of suicidal), they had to interpret the Jewish part of the Christian Bible for themselves. Hence the great emphasis laid by them upon the apocryphal books, some of which had originated in the Hellenistic Diaspora, which, with its "Godfearing" appendage, had certain features analogous to crypto-Jewish experience. A passage in point, in the Epistle of Jeremy, offered them the consolation that worship of foreign gods would not count against them, so long as they remained in their hearts true to the God of Israel. Although we find no Jewish parallel to the casuistry of the Muslim teacher of Oran, who in 1503 gave to his former coreligionists in Andalusia detailed advice on reconciling outward Christian worship with an inner faith in the teachings of Mohammed, the Marranos were bound to devise many such reconciliations of their own. There were among them priests, monks and nuns entirely out of proportion to their number, and these were specially prone to invent syntheses. In the public autos-da-fé in Portugal in the years 1619-27, out of a total of only 231 persons no less than 44 nuns, 7 canons, 8 other clergymen and 2 professors of the university were condemned for Judaizing. A Venetian clergyman, in 1651, complained of the presence in his city of numerous Portuguese wearing their red hats as professing Jews, who had previously served as Christian ecclesiastics in their native country. Whether due to the greater security given by office, or to the higher average level of education, this crowding of the clerical professions was so conspicuous as to lead to curious mystifications. In a spurious responsum from Constantinople, the Jews of Toledo were advised to make their sons bishops and theologians, "in order that they destroy the Christian houses of worship." In another satire, circulated before the expulsion from Spain, appears a diploma supposedly issued by the king to a true Christian, permitting him to be a Marrano. As such, he would be entitled to cheat noblemen, to influence them to expropriate the peasants, to serve as a physician in order to kill Christians secretly and to take their women and so contaminate pure Christian blood. Above all, he could become a Christian cleric. Christian teachings, assimilated and spread by such Marranos, were reinforced by the prevailing lack of childhood memories of Jewish worship. Many a Neo-Christian father neglected to instruct his child in the tenets of the ancestral creed before the age of thirteen or even twenty, for fear of exposure by indiscretion. Marrano youths, thus deprived of the romantic appeal of certain Jewish ceremonies, had little power of resisting general environmental influences. In short, in the course of two or three generations, the departure from original Judaism was so considerable that seventeenth-century professing Jews began to regard Marranos as Gentiles, rather than as Jews.[25]

MARRANO INFLUENCE

The influence of the Marranos was felt far beyond the confines of the Iberian Peninsula. In fact, some of the most crucial developments in the history of the Jewish people in modern times were due to Neo-Christians living outside of Spain and Portugal. The modern Judaism of Holland, England, France, Hamburg and the New World owes its origin to a greater or lesser extent to Marrano refugees. On Queen Isabella's monument in Granada may still be read the name of Luis de Santangel, a Marrano, one of the main promoters of Columbus' expedition. Luis de Torres, a Marrano member of that expedition, is said to have been the first Spaniard to tread American soil. The Marrano share in the upbuilding of modern capitalism goes far beyond their numerical importance. Their great contribution to the rise of Christian Protestantism is still to be told in detail.

The influence of the Neo-Christians on the international relations of the sixteenth and seventeenth centuries can hardly be overestimated. Above all, the rise of the Ottoman Empire in the European scene opened new avenues to Marrano enterprise, political as well as economic. After the fall of Constantinople in 1453, the ancient link between Sephardic Jewry and Islam was reinforced by visionary preachments representing the rise of the new power as the coming of Antichrist. A century later a distinguished Jewish historian, Joseph Hacohen, interpreted the history of the world in terms of a permanent war between Turkey and France (or rather, the Franks), as the respective champions of Islam and Christianity. There is more than sheer oratory in the fiery tirade of John Capistrano, in 1453, against Jews, Hussites and Turks, who had joined forces against the pope and Christianity. A century later the Spanish ambassador in London reported rumors, blaming the Turkish invasion of Hungary upon Jews and heretics. A Jewish physician (formerly a Marrano?) at the court of the Sultan of Morocco prided himself on his great share in bringing about the defeat of the Portuguese army, which had invaded the country in 1578. While all this is more or less unauthenticated, there is no doubt that the Neo-Christians in Portugal and abroad lent strong support to Dom Antonio, the pretender to the throne, himself partly of Jewish descent.

Preëminent among such far-flung diplomatic ventures were the dazzling international careers of two members of the family Mendes, Don Joseph Nasi and Solomon ibn Yaish (Alvaro Mendes). The variegated activities of these two Jewish dukes (of Naxos and Mytilene) give an inkling of what influence the hatred of Spain and the Church, cherished by these Portuguese refugees, had upon the destinies of European nations. Don Joseph's skillful negotiations with Charles V and Queen Mary in Antwerp, until he had extricated himself and the fugitive widow Mendes from the clutches of this bigoted and ever-impecunious monarch, were a prelude to more ambitious political enterprises. A fracas with the king of France, on account of an unpaid debt, which ended in the seizure by the otherwise Francophile Turkish government of all French boats arriving in Egyptian harbors; an intervention to secure Polish neutrality, during the prolonged struggle between the Ottoman Empire and the Hapsburgs; the Turko-Venetian war; the exchange of sharp notes between the sultan and the pope and the support of the Netherlands revolt by Turkey, were the high lights of his career. In a correspondence extending over a period of twelve years, Sigismund August, the powerful king of Poland, addressed Don Joseph in flattering terms, such as "illustrious prince, our dear friend." Alvaro Mendes boasted of having prevented the conclusion of a truce between Spain and Turkey, which would have left England exposed to the undivided attack of the overwhelming Spanish forces. This information was speedily transmitted to Madrid by Bernardino de Mendoza, the Spanish ambassador to Paris, himself likewise styled a "Marrano." At the time of the Peace of Westphalia, the activities of the Dutch Jews of Portuguese descent reached far beyond the confines of Holland. In addition to helping co-religionists abroad, as by their attempt, in this case unsuccessful, to obtain the right of settlement for them in Belgium, their influence was often felt in the sphere of international politics in the Old and the New Worlds.[26]

RELIGIOUS CONTROVERSIES

While the Marranos fought for their Jewish mode of life in secret, professing Jews often struggled publicly in defense of their inherited creed. Much as the Church insisted upon the toleration of Jews, it was inherent in a universalistic and intrinsically intolerant creed to try all methods of persuasion to win them over. Moreover, from the days of the Church Fathers had come a tradition of denouncing Judaism, its theology and ritual, as a means of self-defense. What had been for early Christianity a prime necessity—to differentiate itself from its mother creed—was continued now by sheer force of habit. In many ways attacks against Judaism were reformulations of the Church's own position, rather than a serious offensive against the opponent. Up to the twelfth century, moreover, the imposing culture of Islam forced some Christian theologians to take up the defense of their creed, and especially of the dogma of the Trinity, which was widely used by Arabic polemists to impute polytheism to Christianity. It was natural that a polemic or apologetic treatise against Islam should simultaneously refer to Judasim in an equally polemic or apologetic vein. Much of the feeling of cultural inferiority in that early period, coupled with youthful exuberance and self-assertion, infused Christian polemical writings with a vindictiveness, maintained even when it was no longer warranted by real dangers from Jewish or Saracen quarters. Thomas Aquinas himself, usually a most circumspect writer, could not escape the expression of such venom in writing his polemical *Summa contra Gentiles,* much less in his pamphlet-letter *De regimine Judaeorum.*

The Jews did not remain silent. It is amazing to see in what a dignified and restrained, yet free and vigorous fashion, they fought back. In the Mediterranean countries, particularly, Jewish apologetics, steadily growing in volume, revealed a degree of courage on the Jewish side and of tolerance on the Christian side, not usually associated with the Middle Ages. There are few countries today that would tolerate the circulation of writings so critical of the fundamentals upon which society is built. Systematic Christian censorship was introduced comparatively late, and began to play havoc with Jewish apologetic literature only in an age when that literary *genre* had already lost its creative quality. Of course, before the introduction of printing, whatever the wish of the Church, the circulation of books put out by the process of manuscript copying could not be effectively controlled by any censor. It was comparatively late (1559) when the papacy gradually established its famous *index librorum prohibitorum,* a defensive rather than an offensive measure, since non-Christians were still allowed to read the prohibited books. Even in the more intolerant period of the Reformation and Counter Reformation, the *Strengthening of the Faith* of the Lithuanian Karaite, Isaac of Troki, aroused such widespread interest, in Christian society, that the work was translated into Latin, French, Spanish and German, almost immediately after its publication in 1681. The Church never suppressed the book, although its editor, Christian Wagenseil, had published it to show what subversive writings were current among the Jews. The only reaction was a crop of apologetic treatises by Christian theologians, anxious to counteract the deep impression left upon Christian minds by this work. It was, indeed, to furnish many a weapon to the anti-Church criticism of the writers of the French Enlightenment.

The literary medium was not used exclusively, however. Even more dramatic were the oral disputations, which sometimes assumed the character of grand public spectacles. From more or less amicable controversies, such as that witnessed by Alcuin in Pavia in the year 800, or that between the proctor of Westminster Abbey and a Jew born in Mayence in the eleventh century, these disputations soon developed into events of great consequence to both the disputants and the causes which they represented. The graphic description in William of Malmesbury's *Gesta,* of a disputation arranged by William II of England, however facetiously exaggerated, gives an inkling of what must have been at stake, even on the Christian side. According to this chronicler, the king aroused the Jews of London against our bishop to a contest because he, in joke indeed, I believe, said that if they conquered the Christians and confuted them with open argument he would join their sect. . . . And from this contest the Jews received nothing but confusion, though they often boasted that they had been conquered not by speech but by deeds. [Jacobs, *op. cit.,* p. 6.]

Much more serious was the disputation in Paris in 1240. Here the name appears to be a misnomer, and the defense of Judaism by the distinguished rabbis Yehiel of Paris, Moses of Coucy, and their associates had the characteristics of individual hearings before an inquisitorial court, rather than those of a public debate. The acrimony accompanying the proceedings, however, as well as the publication of the arguments on both sides, greatly embittered the relation between the French Jews and Christians. The valiant stand taken by these rabbis did not prevent the condemnation of the Talmud by the ecclesiastical court. That this was an ill-considered step, explicable only in the light of the Church's panicky fears in the face of the sudden growth of heresies, can be seen in the relaxation of these stringent antitalmudic measures after the end of the thirteenth century. It was in Spain, especially, that the ancient Latin predilection for *circenses* found expression in such creedal debates. On one occasion, King James I and his court, the dignitaries of the Church, the state and the city of Barcelona, listened for four days with bated breath to the dialectical clash between a professing and a baptized Jew. On the Christian side, Pablo Christiani used his more than ordinary attainments in Jewish studies to denounce the creed in which he had been born. His opponent, Nahmanides, far superior in learning and acumen, would have easily overpowered him, were it not in the nature of such disputations that they never convince anybody not previously of the same opinion. In the protracted disputation of Tortosa, which lasted from February, 1413, to November, 1414, only the combined pressure of king and pope, both of whom frequently attended the public sessions, succeeded in inducing several members of the large Jewish delegation to surrender. Still more fatal was the impression in the provinces, where undoubtedly exaggerated accounts of the weakness of the Jewish defense were circulated. Wives separated from husbands, children from parents, when many despaired of salvation in their inherited creed. But this outcome was the result of Spanish Jewry's general demoralization after the unexpected catastrophes of the preceding two decades, rather than of the effectiveness of this perfectly staged debate, which often degenerated from a regular "disputation" into a one-sided "information." On the whole, the innumerable stories of Jews converted to Christianity by means of disputations, usually accompanied by great miracles, are semblances of truth only in the sense that the Christian side, supported by political power and by the fear of capital punishment for apostasy, yielded even less frequently than the Jewish.

Disputations of this sort, consequently, were never popular with the Jews. Having long abandoned any missionary ambitions, they had very little to gain and very much to lose. Entire Jewish communities were endangered by the victory of their representatives, even more than by their defeat. The example of Nahmanides, whom the king tried to protect, but who, after the publication of his report on the disputation, had to leave Spain at the age of seventy, showed that his apprehensions at the outset had been justified. Even so, Pope Clement IV protested against the mild treatment of so outspoken an opponent. This incident may have provoked his bull, "Turbato Corde" of 1267, against the alleged Judaizing propaganda of western Jewry. No wonder that the Jews tried to avoid such religious disputations. To quote Solomon b. Moses of Rome: "I have, therefore, counselled my friends that, in order to escape the dangers of the time, they should refrain from discussing and debating matters of creed with Christians until the Spirit will rest upon us from above and all nations will invoke the name of the Lord and serve him shoulder to shoulder" (*Edut Adonai* in *Bet ha-Midrash,* I, 144; cf. Steinschneider, *Die hebräischen Handschriften . . . in München,* No. 312/8).

The unevenness of the battle could not escape the attention of the more judiciously minded Christians. The less impartial were at least impressed by the insignificant effects of such disputations, in regard to the expected mass conversions. The continued growth of heretical trends, moreover, and the influence of Judaizing tendencies upon the evolution of sectarian movements, although calling for a more aggressive public stand against Judaism, revealed the shortcomings as well as the dangers inherent in such public debates. Hence came

Thomas Aquinas' penetrating advice that disputations are to be avoided in countries where the uneducated masses are unaffected by doubts, since here they can do more harm than good. Only in regions where Jewish, heretical or pagan influences are deeply felt, should they be encouraged, "provided there be those who are equal and adapted to the task of confuting errors" (*Summa theol.*, II,2,10,7).

While the medieval polemists of both sides appear to have been, on the whole, competent and able, there were some extremely naïve and crude persons among them, and some who could not entirely conceal their insincerity. Even in the best there was often a typical lack of sophistication. Artificial arguments, with the help of such devices as the *gematria* (from a biblical word or phrase) were often deemed sufficient to confute an opponent—a double-edged sword, indeed, since with the help of the *gematria* anything could be proved (cf. Abraham ibn Ezra's remarks on Gen. 14:14). Christian and Jewish polemists, moreover, implicitly believed that the prevailing opinions of their age were of incontestable validity, and they freely criticized documents of the past solely from the viewpoint of medieval standards. A characteristic example is to be found in the lengthy twenty-fifth chapter of the third book of Joseph Albo's *Book of Principles;* Christian arguments against Judaism are here refuted, not as errors in approach, but as errors in fact.

This attitude itself underwent a curious evolution. The early polemical literature was filled with purely religious arguments. The Christians in general pursued the old tradition of the Church Fathers in attacking Judaism's "burden of the law" and its conception of the Messiah, and in trying to demonstrate the superiority of the New Testament over the Old. During the Middle Ages, however, new weapons were adapted from Jewish opponents of rabbinical Judaism. In the perennial controversies between the Karaites and the Rabbanites, much polemical material had been accumulated which Christian polemists, particularly those of Jewish origin, easily adapted to their own needs. Curious inconsistencies thus crept into anti-Jewish writings. Following the example of the Karaites, Petrus Alphonsi in his famous "Dialogue with Moses, the Jew" (namely with himself), as well as Nicholas Donin, Pablo Christiani, Abner of Burgos, Paul of Santa

Maria, Jerome of Santa Fé and others, accuse the Talmud of containing immoral teachings, and especially of breeding hatred against Christians and the Christian creed. Judah Hadassi's compilation of all the irate talmudic utterances concerning the Am ha-Ares found widespread emulation among Christian writers, down to Eisenmenger and his modern disciples. The ten bad commandments which Abner of Burgos contrasts with the good Ten Commandments in Judaism, appear much too closely related to the bad laws (*hukkim lo tobim*) enumerated by the Karaite, Salmon ben Yeruhim, in the tenth century to be merely an accidental repetition. As against the Karaite standpoint, however, the Catholic Church, with her own perennial emphasis on tradition, was hardly able consistently to pursue this line of attack against the Jewish tradition.

Since one of the major functions of Judaism in Christian society was, in the eyes of the Church, to bear witness to the authenticity of the New Testament records, it was only natural that the Talmud itself should be invoked time and again to furnish such evidence. On the one hand, the talmudic and post-talmudic Aggadah was attacked by Agobard and others as the source of contemptible teachings and, especially as containing highly objectionable anthropomorphisms. On the other hand, a brilliant mind like that of Abner of Burgos could not in his own fashion fail to perceive, through the crude cosmology of a *Sheur Komah,* reminiscences of ancient mysteries and gnostic teachings out of which had once arisen the Christian dogmas of the Incarnation and the Immaculate Conception.

Jewish apologists, while having a comparatively easy task in attacking the Trinitarian creed from the point of view of reason, were equally inconsistent when it came to the defense of their own beliefs. To be sure, it was not difficult to stand up for the Halakah, since it was admittedly derived from the divine law of the Pentateuch, whose abrogation by the preachment of Jesus Judaism never acknowledged. As to the Aggadah, however, uniformity was totally lacking. During the fateful disputation of Tortosa, for example, one-half of the Jewish delegation followed the more customary line of rejecting its authority and of declaring it an uncontrolled body of personal views, while the other half tried to defend it by allegorizing it away. Under the pressure of his debate with Christiani, even Nahmanides, otherwise its most reverent student, relinquished its defense before Christian public opinion.

In the course of time, these theological controversies were overshadowed by political and economic accusations and apologies. It is a far cry from the theological "refutations" of Judaism by the Abbot of Westminster about 1090, to the harsh denunciations of the Jewish people as a body of usurers by Bernardino da Feltre four hundred years later. The same change is revealed in the difference between Jacob ben Reuben's *Wars of the Lord* or Joseph b. Isaac Kimhi's *Book of the Covenant* (both composed in the twelfth century) with their main emphasis upon creedal distinctions; and the seventeenth-century writings of Simone Luzzatto and Menasseh ben Israel, which primarily stress Jewish contributions to European economy, religion and culture.

The most effective single argument against Judaism, voiced by both Muslim and Christian polemists, was the fact that the Jewish people was in exile, a persecuted minority among the nations. This seemed to indicate the inferior power of the Jewish God. Under one guise or another, this ancient ideology of Assyria and Egypt found its way into medieval writings. The Jewish answers were manifold. Suffering itself, some asserted, is a proof of the truth of one's convictions, rather than a sign of their futility. Is it not characteristic, argued Yehudah Halevi, that

Christians do not glory in kings, heroes and rich people, but in those who followed Jesus all the time before his faith had taken [...] wandered away, or hid themselves, or were killed wherever one of them was found, suffered disgrace and slaughter for the sake of their belief.... The light of God rests only upon the souls of the humble! [*Al-Khazari,* transl. by Hirschfeld, 4,22.]

In interpreting the Deutero-Isaianic prophecies of the suffering Messiah, Rashi seized the opportunity to explain that "all the nations will be forgiven through the sufferings of Israel" (*Commentary* on Isa. 53:4). In the fourteenth century Isaac Pulgar stressed the argument that a great rational creed cannot expect to appeal to the masses in the same degree as one in which miracle tales and material notions prevail. In other words, Judaism is the religion of the selected few, while Christianity and Islam are the creeds of the populace. Finally, Albo, writing *after* his disastrous experiences at Tortosa, invoked history to attest that for two thousand years before Moses all the nations worshiped idols, and yet everyone prospered in its own government. Even later, "the fact that Sennacherib and Nebuchadnezzar and Alexander were successful in ruling over Israel is no sign that their faith was better than that of Israel" (*Book of Principles,* edited by Husik III, 25, p. 228). Here Albo advanced a historical argument utilized by many Jewish apologists before and after him—the miracles recorded in the Old Testament. The fact that the revelation on Mt. Sinai was acknowledged by both Christians and Muslims, enabled Jewish writers to point out the unique character of the historical experience of Israel. At no other time in history, they declared, did God reveal himself before an entire people assembled in one place. Not through a messenger such as Jesus or Mohammed, but directly, the Lord spake to Israel during that unforgettable moment when he endowed them with his great mission. Afterwards, too, miracles happened to the nation of Israel as a whole, or to its prophetic spokesmen, in an unbroken succession, without parallel in any other faith. To quote Albo again:

the real proof of the truth of a faith is the continuity of miracles, such as we find in Israel when they lived on their own land. We do not find any such condition among the believers in Christianity or Mohammedanism. [*Ibid.*]

It was not in vain that history was invoked in the support of the historical creed!

Viewed as a whole, however, strictly polemic or apologetic endeavors, oral and literary, played a minor part in the intellectual evolution of both medieval Christianity and Judaism. Just as in Christian scholasticism the strictly apologetic part is secondary and helpful chiefly for formulating one's own position, so also Jewish apologetics, in comparison to legal and philosophic literature, occupy an inferior position. In the north, especially in northern France, England, Germany and Poland, apologetic literature never played any creative rôle. Even in the Mediterranean countries, where the closer social interrelations entailed certain dangers to Jewish survival, Jewish life was so consolidated as to need little direct defense.

Several centuries were to pass before the breaking up of Jewish seclusion in the era of the emancipation, exposed Judaism to such novel perils that, consciously or unconsciously, the apologetic tone invaded almost the entire realm of Jewish letters.[27]

MEDIEVAL MESSIANISM

Many a stormy session in public disputations and many a virulent chapter in polemical works, focused the world's attention on the Jewish doctrine of the Messiah. In more quiet periods, the messianic dogma remained the great eschatological dream in the life of the nation, as well as of the individual. While the longing for a return to the country of the forefathers and a liberation from foreign rule never died out completely, at such times it assumed the patient rhythm of waiting. But in periods of great stress, despair took the form of a violent "hastening" of the end. At each and every crisis, there appeared men of vision and great ambition, dreamers or fakers, who translated such longing into common action. These movements were limited neither to one country nor to one period. They were simply a correlative of life in the Diaspora, expressing the tenacious clinging to its national existence by a people unable to root itself firmly in foreign soil.

Thus throughout the Jewish dispersion, the Holy Land retained its elevated position as an ideal. In no period has the people as a whole given up its claim to Palestine. Only foreign force, used by the inscrutable will of God as an instrument for Israel's punishment, has temporarily deprived them of their fatherland, whose rightful masters they alone continue to be—this conviction held uncontested sway over the minds of medieval Jewry. Even in the early fourteenth century, at the height of prosperity of Spanish Jewry, Nissim Gerondi quoted, with full approval, the distinction drawn by a French predecessor between the validity of the royal enactments in the Diaspora and those in Palestine.

The talmudic principle, "the law of the Kingdom is law," applies only to a Gentile king [he says], because the country is his and he may warn the Jews that failure to fulfill his commandments would entail their expulsion. It does not apply to Israel's kings because all of Israel are co-partners in the land of Israel. [*Comment.* on Nedarim, 28 a.]

And Nahmanides, in interpreting Numbers 33:53, states, "In my opinion this is a positive commandment enjoining the Israelites to settle in the country and to inherit it because He gave it to them and they must not reject the inheritance of the Lord."

This acknowledgment of Palestine as the real homeland, had many practical effects. Some medieval rabbis upheld the ancient tradition that to dwell physically in Palestine is a great merit in itself. Nahmanides counted it among the 613 fundamental commandments of Jewish law. The prevailing view, doubtless fortified by the liberal grant of papal indulgences to prospective crusaders, was that to settle in Palestine expiates one's sins. Most rabbis agreed to maintain the talmudic law that when a man decides to emigrate to Palestine, his wife must follow him; in any case, she cannot demand divorce with full payment of the contractual amount, as she might in other changes of domicile to a new country. A son may go to Palestine against the commands of his parents. In accordance with this legal theory, numerous Jews throughout the Middle Ages, starting with the Rabbanite as well as Karaite "Mourners for Zion and Jerusalem," actually settled in the country. World Jewry, whether in Muslim or in Christian lands, regarded it as a great privilege to send charitable contributions to Palestine. When, about 1450, the Jerusalem community was in serious difficulties because of indebtedness, Italian Jewry assisted it with a large sum of money. As in antiquity, so also in the Middle Ages and in modern times, the pious (for instance, Paltiel, the Egyptian financier) wished their bodies to be interred in the holy soil. Voices raised against this custom, although supported by the Zohar, were ineffectual against the deep-rooted nostalgia of the entire people.

The Crusades added momentum to the longing for Palestine. For two centuries western Christendom bent all its united efforts to the redemption of the Holy Land, while the Muslim world waged a holy war against the invaders. Quite naturally the Jews, too, came under the spell of this extraordinary land. At a time when thousands of Christians took vows to participate in a Crusade and a multitude of others undertook pilgrimages, many European Jews also took the road to Palestine. While the spectacular journey, made in

1211, by three hundred French and English rabbis may have been provoked by oppression, or possibly—according to a recently advanced theory—timed to coincide with a synod convoked to pass judgment on the orthodoxy of Maimonides' writings, it was primarily an expression of the general irrepressible desire. Although in some ways reminiscent of the mass pilgrimages of the Christian clergy, especially that under the leadership of the Archbishop of Mayence in 1064, it seems to have had permanent settlement as its objective. At times the urge to go to Palestine was so strong that such western Jewish leaders as Hayyim ha-Cohen in the twelfth century, and Israel Isserlein in the fifteenth, felt prompted to issue a warning against the great dangers of travel by sea or land. The Portuguese fleet armed in 1318 to pillage Muslim and Jewish vessels and the Berber strongholds of piracy, certainly made the Mediterranean voyage extremely precarious. We even hear of a Jewish pirate in the sixteenth century. The zeal of new arrivals in Palestine was greatly dampened by the oppression of the corrupt local government (Christian as well as Turkish), the prevailing poverty, and the disorganization of the Jewish communities. In more quiet and prosperous periods, nevertheless, new settlers often sent out enthusiastic epistles about their new life, exhorting relatives and coreligionists to follow them.[28] Don Joseph Nasi and Solomon ibn Yaish went as far as to try to found in Tiberias a Jewish colony, to be settled by Jews from all over the world.

On slight provocation this longing for Palestine might assume the proportions of a messianic movement. Extraordinary events in the history of the surrounding nations, or plausible calendar computations based on biblical prophecies —especially the apocalyptic visions of Daniel—were sufficient to arouse popular hopes that redemption was at hand. On such occasions the pulse of the nation was quickened. Jews *en masse* began to prepare for the advent of the great day of the Lord. Many distributed their fortunes among the poor, while others gave up their homes and gathered around a leader who, they believed, was God's messenger. It is difficult to recapture the impression made upon the masses by such visionary preachments. The imagination of a people in distress was easily kindled to high frenzy by a pseudomessiah, himself frequently an enthusiastic psychopath. That a large number of sophisticated Bagdad Jews should gather with their wives and children upon the roof tops, expecting to be carried upon the wings of angels to the camp of their redeemer in distant Kurdistan sounds incredible, but this actually happened. The unsuccessful "flight" was a subject of ridicule among the Bagdad Arabs long after the event. In 1172 there appeared in the Yemen, one who preached that he was the forerunner of the Messiah. Asked by the Arab ruler to prove his mission by a miraculous sign, he unostentatiously offered to have his head cut off. Not even his tragic end could totally discourage some of his adherents, and for a long time they continued to hope that he would rise from the dust and help to redeem Israel.

There was an obvious contrast between the eastern armed uprisings and the western more or less visionary commotions, affecting the Jews' inner life rather than their external relations. In the East the proximity of Palestine and the relatively "normal" character of Jewish life operated to breed rather realistic efforts to reëstablish an independent Jewish state. The upheavals that shook Palestine during the last two centuries of Byzantine rule were not without a strain of *Realpolitik*. The Jews, revolting against Heraclius, succeeded in 614 in bringing Rome's archenemy, Persia, into the country, and only after fifteen years was the emperor able to reëstablish his reign and take bloody revenge on his erstwhile Jewish subjects. As late as the twelfth century David Alroy attempted to establish a Jewish kingdom in Kurdistan by force of arms, planning from there to lead all his coreligionists out of the dispersion. No similar movements are recorded anywhere in Europe. The messianic movement of the early eighth century, attached to the name of Serenus—if the story as narrated by Graetz and his successors on the basis of late and confused records is at all correct—was a mere reflection of the disappointment of Spanish Jewry, when their hopes of relief at the hands of the Muslim invaders from the desperate conditions of their life under the last Visigothic kings, proved illusory. In Maimonides' classical account of Jewish messianic movements after the rise of Islam, European Jewry begins to figure again about the year 1070. The unrest in Lyons (whose Jewish population of 10,000 families is grossly exaggerated in his *Epistle to Yemen*) was altogether local, however, and did not so much as attract the attention of contemporary Christian chroniclers. Not even the upheaval which came in the wake of the Crusades could stir warlike ambitions in the feeble Jewish minority of western lands.

European messianism later found expression beautifully, though in many ways grotesquely, in such men as Abraham Abulafia and Solomon Molko. Molko, a fascinating youth deeply imbued with the mysticism of the age, appeared before pope and emperor, hoping, by means of diplomacy and persuasion, to bring about armed intervention on behalf of a Jewish state in Palestine. The source of this idea, however, was the eastern Jew, David Reubeni, whose claim that he could marshal a large Jewish force against the Turks, provided Christendom would supply the necessary arms, was long seriously considered by the western monarchs. Unable to persuade Charles V, Molko chose to die at the stake in Mantua in 1532 rather than again become a Marrano; while Reubeni ended less conspicuously, but no less tragically, at Evora not long after. Oriental Jewry's messianic ventures culminated in the spectacular exhibition of Shabbetai Zebi. Its speedy and ignominious collapse showed that eastern messianism had spent its forces. The West, still more exhausted, produced in Jacob Frank little more than a charlatanesque distortion of Shabbetianism.

It is no mere accident that among the better known pseudomessiahs only two, Asher Laemmlein and Jacob Frank, were Ashkenazic Jews; and one, Frank, felt his call to messiahship only after a prolonged sojourn in Turkey. While the eastern uprisings, whether armed or unarmed, were mainly bent upon action and deliverance by deeds, the western Jews tried to accelerate the arrival of the redeemer only through fasting and increased piety. No wonder that in the East, from Abu Isa to Shabbetai Zebi, most of the pseudomessiahs were also founders of new sects, often greatly at variance with orthodox teachings and rites. In the western messianic activities (with the exception of the fantastic Frankist movement), the latent heterodox leanings were, as a rule, quite effectively concealed. At any rate, the ancient tradition concerning the abrogation of the Law after the advent of the Messiah, was never invoked.

This self-restraint might also have been a reaction to the

Christian emphasis upon this abrogation. Whatever bridges may have connected Christian mysticism and their cherished Kabbalah, these messiahs, essentially Jewish patriots, could not possibly identify themselves with the reign of Edom, as they now called Roman Catholicism. Nevertheless, the mere fear of the repercussions of such unrealized dreams upon Jews and Gentiles alike, was often enough to arouse the anger of the responsible Jewish leaders. The condemnation of Abulafia by the leading antirationalist Adret was no less harsh than Maimonides' *Epistle to Yemen*. Not even Jacob Mantino's unpleasant rôle in the persecution of Molko is wholly inexcusable, in the light of his apprehensions for the safety of the people.

It is amazing that all the perennial frustrations of the messianic movements, the constant apprehensions of the more far-sighted leaders, and the menace of Christian messianism, could not shatter the Jewish messianic hope. Belief in the final redemption had become so firmly integrated in the totality of Jewish religious experience, and so subtly interwoven with the deep yearning for a physical and spiritual homeland, as never to vanish altogether. The combined effect of all adverse conditions seems not to have been more than to bring about minor modifications of the messianic expectation, and of its position within Jewish theology.

Under Muslim domination the belief in the coming of the Messiah was generally assigned a place within the fundamental dogmas of the creed, whose denial was declared to be equivalent to the abandonment of Judaism. Hananel of Kairowan, for example, counted it among the four cardinal principles of the Jewish religion. Through Maimonides' authority, it is today one of the thirteen principal tenets of the religion, recited by orthodox Jews in their daily prayers. The wide compass of the Maimonidean belief in the "days of the Messiah" is best formulated in his own words,

> One must believe and regard it as true that the Messiah will come. One must not think that his coming will be postponed; if he delays his arrival, wait for him. One must not fix the date for, nor read into the Bible one's own opinions concerning the time of his coming. . . . One must believe that, in accordance with the predictions of all the prophets from Moses to Malachi, the Messiah will be more exalted and more honored than all the kings that ever existed. Whosoever harbors any doubts or whosoever lowers his dignity, such a one denies the Torah.

... It is a part of this tenet that Israel will have no king except one of the house of David and the progeny of Solomon. And he who opposes this dynasty denies the name of the Holy One, blessed be He, and the word of his prophets [*Commentary* on M. Sanh., 10, Principle 12].²⁹

In Christian countries, however, a more moderate attitude was adopted. Nahmanides, in the heat of the controversy with Christiani, declared that a Jew does not need the Messiah in order to be saved. On the contrary, since a holy life requires greater sacrifices under a Christian than under a Jewish king, the merits of a pious Jew increase in proportion to the obstacles he overcomes. In a more quiet mood, Crescas maintained that, while belief in the Messiah is binding upon every Jew, and disbelief is heresy, it is not one of the fundamental principles, "without which one cannot imagine the existence of the Torah" (*Or Adonai, fol.* 82b). This admission is the more remarkable, since it was Crescas who, against general theological opinion, elevated the future redeemer to a position superior to Moses. His disciple, Albo, in the critique of Maimonides' "Principles" to which he devoted his major work, also vigorously objected to counting among the indispensable principles of Judaism the messianic credo.

It is not a fundamental principle of the Law of Moses, as Maimonides thinks [he declared], for we can conceive of the existence of the Mosaic Law without it. It is a special principle of the religion of the Christians, for their religion cannot exist without it. [*Book of Principles,* I, 47.]

On the other hand, neither Albo, Crescas nor any other medieval Jew would have denied that, like creation *ex nihilo*, the messianic hope "is a dogma which it behooves every one professing Judaism to believe" (*ibid*). Even rationalists like Hayyim Galipapa, who interpreted all pertinent scriptural passages as referring to actual historical events rather than to a messianic future, agreed that the belief in the coming of the redeemer is firmly rooted in Jewish tradition. After all, what would have remained of dynamic historical Judaism, if this final goal of a purposeful evolution had been abandoned!³⁰

ESCAPE AND REALITY

The messianic hope greatly contributed to Jewish survival in medieval Europe, perhaps more so than in any other period of Jewish history. It helped illumine the road and lighten the burden of the Wandering Jew. Deprived not only of state and territory, but of any permanent abode whatsoever, he was the better able to accept the fate of an "alien" and frequently ill-treated guest, because he could, with implicit faith, look forward to the day when the redeemer would erect for him the state of all states, and root him again in the soil of his forefathers. Messianism, along with the other religious creeds and observances, all inseparably welded together with the ethnic tenacity of the people, overcame the endless vicissitudes of its sojourn in European Christendom.

That such an association was possible at all, depended largely on the Christian copartner. The Catholic Church had its full share, both in creating the adversities and in making possible the survival of Jewry in Christian lands. In the growing exclusion of the Jews from Christian society, in the increasing legal and economic disabilities, in the ever-deepening animosity and ill will between the two groups, the Church's teachings were the most decisive single factor. Paradoxically, the anti-Jewish animus of the Church became most effective in that domain of European life to which eventually the Church itself fell a victim, European nationalism. There have been nationalist trends, under one guise or another, throughout the history of mankind. But nowhere did nationalism acquire such exclusiveness in ideology and practice, as in Christian Europe under the indirect guidance of the western Church. Combining the intolerance inherent in every monotheistic creed with Roman implacability and ruthless perseverance, the Church evolved, through Augustine, a theory of intolerance unparalleled by any other religion in history. This intolerance, communicated to awakening European nationalism, became the force most inimical to medieval Jewry. On the other hand, the exception in favor of the Jews, established by the Church itself, greatly outweighed the influences of segregation and indirect complete exclusion. It may be asserted that, had it not been for the Catholic Church, the Jews would not have survived the Middle Ages in Christian Europe.

In defiance of this policy of limited toleration, semiconscious western nationalism succeeded in eliminating the Jews from most European countries. About 1550 there were no Jews lawfully resident in England or France, the Netherlands, Spain, Portugal, the Scandinavian countries, or Muscovy. All

Jewry in Christian lands was concentrated in Poland, a country of multiple nationality, and in certain more heterogeneous regions of Germany and Italy. Even when the large settlements under Muslim rule were added, the total number of Jews was rapidly declining to the lowest level in the history of the Diaspora.

This decline was wholly due to conversions, some voluntary, more of them forcible. Faced by pogroms and expulsions, many Jews joined the dominant religion, while others went in search of a new, temporary asylum. Unlike the Puritans, the Jews could not go out and found for themselves a new empire. Not having the backing of any state, totally lacking in political or military power, they could not have embarked upon any large-scale colonization, even if their aversion to statehood and their peculiar economic stratification had not precluded any such ambition. More like the French Huguenots, in the main an urban class of merchants and artisans, they applied for admission to the neighboring civilized countries.

Nevertheless, the widespread belief that Jewish life in medieval Europe consisted in an uninterrupted series of migrations and sufferings, of disabilities and degradation, is to be relegated to the realm of popular misconceptions. The Middle Ages were neither in themselves the dark ages they were once thought to have been; nor were they as dark for the Jews, in comparison with the rest of the population, as is still widely believed. The real clue to an understanding of the perplexing situation of the Jews will be found in the physical and spiritual structure of the medieval Jewish community within the larger frame of medieval Christendom.

X

WITHIN THE GHETTO WALLS

AMONG the numerous corporate bodies whose totality made up medieval society, the Jewish *universitas* had many unique features. In some ways part and parcel of the general social structure, in many others it appeared as an alien body outside the frame of every Christian nation. Christianity being the all-pervading force in medieval life, the Jews appeared in the eyes of their contemporaries as a socioreligious corporation apart from all others. The segregation of Jews found its highest expression inside the Jewish community. The life of each Jew was so thoroughly regulated by Jewish law; his actions so well supervised by his fellows, particularly the leaders of the community; his interests, religious and intellectual as well as social and economic, centered so much in the communal life—that developments in the outside world seemed to affect him comparatively little. Although changes in the world at large could not fail to penetrate the thickest ghetto walls, these influences worked slowly and imperceptibly. In appearance, Jewish life was purely Jewish. Thus the Jewish will to survive by clinging to the traditional mode of communal existence, coupled with the medieval corporate organization of society, facilitated the independent inner Jewish development. These two lines of evolution together built up a cultural and political body, with all the characteristics of a powerful state within the state.[1]

GHETTO AND BADGE

Territorial segregation in a ghetto was only one element of this largely self-sufficient life. Whether in a technical ghetto in which all Jews were forced to live, with Gentiles excluded, or in a ghetto in the nontechnical sense, *i.e.,* a Jewish quarter growing up freely, the separation was complete enough to make Jewish life an independent entity. In a sense, the technical ghetto was the less effective. The separation was most complete in the earlier centuries, when the Jews, like most other corporations, settled in a special Jewish street; when ancient traditions, as well as that of Muslim domination in Spain and Sicily, kept them apart; and when the Jews viewed permission to surround their street by a wall as a favor (such a privilege was granted them, for instance, in the famous decree of Bishop Huozman-Ruediger of Speyer in 1084). When, later, it became necessary to enact laws; and when, in particular, beginning in 1555 with the bull, *Cum nimis absurdum,* of Paul IV, the Counter Reformation in Italy established a series of technical ghettos—it was already too late. The Italian Jews of the seventeenth century had willy-nilly to maintain closer relations with the Gentiles than had their coreligionists in northern France or Germany before the enforcement.

The technical ghetto, however, remains the purest expression of the alien quality of Jewry within medieval Christendom. In oriental countries, partial or total segregation was a natural growth. The physiognomy of Bagdad was little altered by its three Jewish quarters. The motley of races and peoples, blending together while living apart from one another, was a natural aspect of the morphology of such an oriental metropolis. Twelfth-century Muslim sectarians, after fleeing from Cordova to Fez, settled in a specially assigned borough as a matter of course. A Jewish quarter in ancient Alexandria or Sardes, in medieval Cairo or Cordova, carried no connotation of inferiority. In fact, talmudic rabbis, and even more vigorously some Karaites, insisted upon separation on practical as well as ritualistic grounds.

As long as the Christian kings of Spain and Sicily retained such nontechnical ghettos (as recorded, for example, by Ibn Haukal in 967 for the city of Palermo), there was little friction. The decree of Infante Juan in 1369, demanding that certain Jews of Cervera return to the two districts which had been theirs, was issued after consultation with both the city elders and the heads of the Jewish community. But with the animosity growing out of the unholy war of 1391, came the erection of technical ghettos throughout the peninsula. In

Calatayud, in 1398, Jewish domicile among Christians was strictly prohibited, in order that "these dirty people should not infect the purity of the Christians through the vicinity of their habitation and in order that these men, putrefied through the sores of error and crime, should not corrupt the sanity of the pure Christian mind" (Baer, *Die Juden im christlichen Spanien*, I, 734 f.). In 1414 the inhabitants of Huesca attempted to relegate a newly created Jewish quarter to an out-of-the-way and unimproved location. In 1412 there was enacted in Portugal the first general law regulating ghetto life. Although adopted at the request of a nation-wide Jewish deputation, its main provisions were very harsh. A Jew found outside the ghetto after the first signal, was to be fined the enormous sum of 5,000 livres; after the second, 10,000 livres; and after the third, he was to be whipped through the streets. The German laws were comparatively mild, notwithstanding the bitter feeling ensuing from the events of 1348. The pact of 1362 between the archbishop and the city of Trèves, providing that no more than fifty Jews be allowed to live there, and that all but three gates of the Jewish street should be walled in; and the assignment of a new, enclosed quarter to the Frankfort Jews in 1462 (at the instigation of Emperor Frederick III), were no radical innovations. Even the erection, in 1516, of the famous Venetian Jewish quarter, from whose proximity to an iron foundry the name ghetto was probably derived, was preceded by long negotiations between the city and the Jews. Their spokesmen had previously suggested as a compromise the concentration of the Jews in Murano, the most fashionable suburban district. The segregation of the Jews of Cracow in Kazimierz and, to a certain extent, of those of Prague in the Josefstadt, led to the establishment of practically independent all-Jewish municipalities. It was only under the impact of the Counter Reformation that Paul IV initiated throughout Italy a series of conscious attempts to isolate the Jews, as a mark of degradation. The Jewish quarter of Rome remained secluded, until the Italian insurgents in 1870 wrested the city from papal control, and proclaimed her the capital of united, democratic Italy. In the grand duchy of Tuscany, this reactionary current led to the expulsion of the Jews, and their concentration in two specially constructed ghettoes in Florence and Siena. Characteristically, the Italian Jews were soon reconciled to their fate. In Verona and Mantua, the erection of the ghetto walls was long after celebrated by the local community in an annual festival modeled after Purim. As late as 1765, a Verona rabbi glorified the achievement and, invoking the authority of Aristotle and Maimonides, emphasized the great benefits of segregation.[2]

Many other methods of separation were taken over from the ancient world and Islam. Badges to distinguish Jews from non-Jews, and separate baths to prevent intimacy, were Byzantine and Muslim heritages improved upon by western legislators. While numerous distinguishing marks, forced on the "protected subjects" by Islamic rulers, found no imitation in the western countries (hardly anywhere in the West was horseback riding prohibited, and only in Crete, so close to Islamic lands, do we find houses labeled by special signs, such as wooden figures of the devil), such practices as were taken over, were much more rigidly applied. Stimulated by the example of southern Italy, Innocent III expressed a desire, as early as 1204, to mark out the Jews. Through the Fourth Lateran Council in 1215, he was able to impose this practice on all western countries. The argument that in this way the plea of ignorance would be removed, in cases of sexual intercourse between Jew and Gentile, furnished an easy, frequently reiterated excuse.

It was a century or two before the institution was firmly rooted. Although, under the powerful influence of Innocent III, England introduced the badge in 1217; and France (where sporadic cases of distinguishing marks for Jews are recorded even before 1215) speedily followed in 1219, the use of the badge seems not to have become general in the short period before the expulsions from these countries. In Spain, Italy and Germany, it found general acceptance only in the fifteenth century, when it was championed by the great philosopher Nicholas of Cusa, and the fanatical preacher John Capistrano, and when, on nine successive occasions, Venice reënacted the law requiring it. At the outset there was a great variety of regulations as to the form and color of the hat to be worn or the location of the special badges on the outer garment. In 1418 the Council of Salzburg, hardly aware that it had adopted an idea of Caliph Al-Hakim, suggested that Jewish women wear small bells as well as badges. The most prevalent distinguishing mark soon became the wheel; the color, yellow, the same as that decreed for Jews by the "Covenant of Omar." The use of such a wheel is recorded in the city of Augsburg in 1434. The decree of Ferdinand I, of 1551, for the Austrian provinces (reprinted in A. F. Pribram's *Urkunden*, I, 10 ff.), was typical of large portions of Europe. According to this law, Jews had to wear upon the left front side of the coat or dress a yellow wheel, two centimeters wide and eight centimeters in diameter. Any Jew found without this sign was to forfeit his wearing apparel and everything found upon him. Half of the fine was promised as a reward to the informer. A third offense subjected the guilty party to exile from all Austrian hereditary lands with his family.

Unlike the ghetto, the badge was deeply resented by the Jews. They combated, with all means at their disposal, this mark of degradation, which made of every Jew a target of attack, and which greatly hampered economic activity. In 1219 Spanish Jews threatened to leave the country, unless Ferdinand of Castile revoked the law, which he did, with the concurrence of the ecclesiastical authorities. A few decades later, Mordecai ben Joseph, of Avignon, was arrested for indignantly opposing the wearing of the badge. Large bribes were offered Paul IV and other popes for the revocation of this part of the edict. Physicians, scholars and financiers were often exempted, together with their families. Jews generally succeeded in obtaining exemptions for journeys, during which distinguishing marks would single them out for attack and abuse. As time went on, however, reluctant practice became second nature. Venetian rabbis long continued to officiate in an outlandish garb, increasingly sanctified by tradition; and before the Jews of Avignon could be induced to abandon the badge entirely, the French revolutionary government had to outlaw it under severe penalties.[3]

THE COMMUNITY AND ITS LAW

Within the material or legal ghetto walls, the Jewish community reigned supreme. It is hard to imagine today how much power rested in the hands of the communal leaders in medieval and early modern Europe. The law of the land affected Jews mainly with respect to their relations to the outside world. Whether or not public law fully recognized Jewish civil and criminal law, in most cases in which only Jews were involved Jewish law alone prevailed. As a matter of fact, most countries recognized the validity of Jewish law and the jurisdiction of the Jewish court not only in civil litigations, but even in minor criminal matters. King John's charter for English Jewry may be regarded as fairly typical of conditions throughout medieval Christendom. "Know that we have granted," the king decreed, "and by our present charter confirmed to our Jews in England that the breaches of right which shall occur among them, except such as pertain to our crown and service, as touching homicide, mayhem, deliberate assault, house-breaking, rape, larceny, arson and treasure-trove, be examined and amended among themselves according to their law, so that they may administer their own justice among themselves" (Rigg, *Select Pleas,* p. 2). Among the numerous Arabic documents preserved from medieval Toledo, not one is found in which two Jewish parties figure as signatories to a contract before a non-Jewish court. The rule adopted in the Balearic Islands after 1315, that Jews bring their lawsuits before the general court, was an exception.

Occasionally even cases involving capital punishment were left to the Jews themselves. The latter were especially interested in maintaining criminal jurisdiction over informers, who frequently caused considerable difficulty by denouncing communal leaders, or the community as a whole, to the government. So disastrous were the results of such accusations, often mendacious, that, building upon talmudic foundations, the Jews demanded capital punishment for the transgressors. Since informers, as a rule, were welcome instruments in the hands of potentates, helping them, at least to extort money from the Jewish community, the Jews could not always count upon the support of the state's courts in sentencing them. King Pedro's insistence that Solomon ibn Adret and Jonah Gerondi, the famous Spanish rabbis of the thirteenth century, sentence one such informer to death, is a very illuminating, but rare, example of a contrary attitude. Even in Poland, where the Jewish court had no right to inflict capital punishment, lynching, as an extralegal preventive, was encouraged by rabbinical authorities such as Solomon Luria (cf. *Yam shel*

Shelomoh, on Yeb. 10,2). As late as 1838, a Russian Jewish community, outraged by the treachery of one member, took the law into its own hands and executed the denouncer. Where the Jews had no authority to mete out the extreme penalty, other punishments were mutilation, *i.e.,* cutting off the informer's tongue (against which Solomon Luria and others vigorously protested), flagellation in the synagogue, and imprisonment. Jewish prisons are often mentioned in the responsa of Meir of Rothenburg, and one is still extant in the *Altneu* synagogue in Prague. In 1360 a royal French privilege empowered the Jews to banish one of their number, provided that the community indemnify the king with a hundred guilders for the loss of a taxpayer. Sometimes, however, the community had to bribe government officials to help carry out such an expulsion. Occasionally, even the assistance of other communities was invoked to suppress a powerful or crafty offender.

The extent of judicial autonomy varied in the different branches of judicature. The supremacy of the state was most pronounced in public law, a domain in which Jewish law had never reached the same degree of finality as in civil law, and where the necessity of adaptation to the varying systems of government retarded its development. In this respect more than in any other, the Jews acknowledged the state's sovereignty. Solomon ibn Adret drew the distinction along these lines, in a far-reaching decision as to when the law of the kingdom is supreme:

Know ye, that the sages had in mind only matters pertaining to royal authority, the laws of government, because just as we have a constitutional law, such as described by Samuel to Israel [I Sam. 8], so also have the other nations certain regulations concerning their mode of government. It is only to these that the sages referred by saying that their law is law. But the laws administered in the courts do not belong to the laws of government, the judges merely applying what they find in their law books. With any other interpretation [of this principle] you would abolish the laws of Israel, God forbid! [Cf. *Responsa,* VI, No. 254 and Karo, *Bet Joseph,* H.M. 26 end; Mordecai Yafeh, *Lebush Ir Shushan,* 26,4 repeats this definition almost verbatim in his own name; cf. also *ibid.,* 369,11.]

This did not mean that the Jews accepted each and every public law enactment, and especially the imposition of any amount of taxation, as legal. Mordecai ben Hillel Ashkenazi makes it clear that

> Since our taxes today have no limit and we have to pay as much as the ruler deems fit, and whosoever refuses to pay is liable to be executed or imprisoned and his property confiscated, these demands do not fall into the class of those in which "the law of the kingdom is law." They are simple robbery, like the case of the tax collector who knows no bounds, which the Mishnah lists with murder and pillage in the fourth chapter of Nedarim. [In fact, it is III,4.]

At the other extreme we find the fully autonomous, strictly religious law. Having decided to tolerate the Jews, the medieval world left them totally unhampered to work out methods for their own salvation. No medieval western monarch ever imitated the example of Justinian, who meddled with synagogue ritual and the study of Jewish law. Even the ecclesiastical court, as we have seen, refrained from intervening in internal Jewish affairs, unless called in by the Jews themselves. The right claimed by papal organs, to suppress Jewish heresies, was rarely and reluctantly exercised.

The legislation of the various states was mainly concerned with devising means of adjudicating quarrels arising between Jews and Christians. Through all medieval legislation runs the fundamental intention of extending to the Jews treatment as impartial and fair as possible. In most instances, courts sitting in judgment in such mixed cases were composed of an equal number of Jews and Gentiles. In others, special *judices Judaeorum* were appointed by the king or his direct representative. Thus the royal power sought to prevent such injustice to Jewish plaintiffs or defendants as might be feared from the ordinary local bodies. Occasionally a king leaned backward in his effort to be impartial, as when, for instance, he gave Lemberg Jewry the right to nominate for the office of such a "justice of the Jews," two Christian candidates, of whom the provincial governor was to appoint one.[4]

This spirit of fairness also permeates all laws concerning civil and criminal procedure. With minor exceptions, Jewish courts were allowed to map out freely their own course of action. Although couched in terms adapted from ecclesiastical usage, the privilege granted by the king of Aragon to the community of Huesca in 1390 is a striking illustration. The Jewish community is entitled, so the decree reads, to investigate every *malsin* (this Hebrew word for informer had long been naturalized in the Spanish tongue) by inquisitorial procedure at its own discretion. The judge may apply civil, canon or Jewish law; he may take minutes or dispense with them; he may accept or reject the testimony of witnesses; there is no appeal against his sentence. A Jew, seeking exemption from the jurisdiction of this court, is to be considered *ipso facto* an informer and liable to capital punishment by hanging. Royal officers must coöperate, on penalty of a fine of 500 solidi for refusal. While no such extreme regulations are found elsewhere, all legislation conceded expressly or tacitly the right of the Jewish judge to use exclusively Jewish formal as well as substantive law. In some countries a Jewish defendant was judged by his own law, even by mixed and Gentile courts. In one such case, Isaac bar Sheshet acted as adviser to a Spanish grandee; and in 1383, Pedro IV gave strict orders to the communities of Barcelona, Gerona, and Perpignan to prepare for him a Catalan translation of the Maimonidean Code for such use, "as speedily as possible if you want to retain our favor and escape our ire" (in A. Rubio y Lluch's *Documents per l'historia de la cultura catalana mig-eval,* I, 309, No. 338).

Jewish testimony was, as a rule, quite as valid as the testimony of Christians. Most legislators stipulated that no accused in mixed cases be condemned solely upon the deposition of witnesses of another creed. To prove a contention anywhere from one Christian and one Jewish witness to twelve Christian and twelve Jewish witnesses were required. Hai Gaon suspected the trustworthiness of writs issued by corrupted Muslim officials in small towns; and many medieval rabbis, especially in the earlier period, impugned the reliability of Christian court or notarial documents. But the validity of Jewish contracts was hardly doubted, even where, as in France and Portugal, Jewish notaries eventually lost the power to certify them. Indeed, special collections of Hebrew formularies were prepared in the so-called "Books of Deeds" of Saadia, Hai and Judah al-Barceloni. Numerous medieval Hebrew legal documents are still extant, including many from England and some sixty from Catalonia alone. The real-estate records of the Laurenz parish, in Cologne, incorporated Hebrew deeds with those in Latin and German. In England special royal chirograph offices were established in six or seven towns in 1194, as official registries of loans involving Jews and Christians; of course, the regulation did not apply where all contracting parties were Jewish.

Even the Jewish oath, *more judaico,* which provoked such widespread condemnation during the last century, had its origin, not in any conscious effort to degrade the Jewish litigant or witness but in an exaggerated emphasis upon the sanctity of the oath. The Jews themselves tried to surround the ceremony with such awe-inspiring features in order to discourage perjury. Abraham ben David of Posquières ruled that in order to remind the witness of the Day of Judgment, Jewish adjurations were to be administered in the synagogue with all lights extinguished and in front of a casket. The Christians went further. Apparently starting with the oath of abjuration taken by recent converts to Christianity, the Byzantine Empire evolved more and more elaborate formulae for the oath of professing Jews. One such formula is quoted in later sources from the *Book of the Prefect,* written in the tenth century. The institution spread to Western Christendom and East to the Islamic countries, where we find it well established in the thirteenth century. In Europe it was the more readily accepted, as the Teuton idea of an oath as an act of self-exposure to the wrath of the gods in the case of perjury had long before created a receptive mood. Entire phrases in the Jewish oath, from the brief Erfurt formula to that much amplified in the *Schwabenspiegel,* occur in early medieval references to the testimony of Teutons. In parts of Aragon, perhaps under combined Visigothic and Islamic influence, a formula containing the Ten Commandments and the endless list of curses in Deuteronomy 28:16-68 was long recited. The Jew had to repeat "I swear" after each Commandment, and "Amen" after each curse. Other, more obnoxious, ceremonies, such as standing on a sow hide or a three-legged stool, spread rapidly throughout the northern countries. Falling off the stool was punishable by a fine; repetition often entailed loss of the suit. Some such customs are recorded in the annals of Dortmund, Silesia, Hungary and Poland. In some communities the Jews were forced to swear bareheaded, by the ineffable name, Jehovah. In Breslau, in 1737, a woman was obliged to take the oath while wearing phylacteries. Such ridiculous exaggerations naturally discredited the whole institution. In the emancipation era, especially, it was denounced by Crémieux, Zunz and others as an extreme sign of degradation, which, indeed, it had become. Nevertheless, in 1827, the new Hannoverian code of legal procedure, published under the name of King George IV, restated the special formula, to be recited while facing the East. More than half a century after the formal emancipation in France, a revolutionary act by a rabbi was needed to eliminate this ugly ceremony from the courts. In the Middle Ages, however, the Jews seldom, if ever, protested against an institution whose intrinsic legitimacy in the contemporary situation they hardly doubted, and which, after all, touched only the periphery of their life.

On the whole, it was the Jewish court which seriously affected the ordinary flow of ghetto life. The obligation of the judge to set a hearing within from one to three days, was a great advantage. As in the proceedings of the Christian ecclesiastical courts, the elasticity of Jewish law and the all-pervading principle of equity contrasted favorably with the increasingly elaborate and technical procedure of the secular court. The fact that the revered rabbis and teachers who served as judges, were seldom, if ever, reproached for bribery, introduced an element of stability lacking in the case of a Jew before a Christian magistrate. Little wonder that Christians sometimes took advantage of the facilities of the Jewish court. As late as 1800, Derzhavin reported to the Czar numerous cases of Lithuanian and Ukrainian Christians, who repaired to Jewish judges.[5]

EDUCATION AND CHARITIES

If the general law of the country was of comparatively little importance in the everyday experience of the Jew, its intellectual and social life were still less so. Despite the complex social relations with non-Jews, the primary concern of every Jewish parent was to give his child a Jewish education. Educational activities, whether for children or adults, occupied a central position in the Jewish community, and in many special voluntary organizations. The efficiency of Jewish schools was rarely in doubt, and throughout the Middle Ages the educational level was far superior to that of their Gentile neighbors. For a long time, it may be asserted, almost all Jewish youths received a type of education roughly similar to that of the Christian clergy, until the Church, obviously building upon Jewish rather than Graeco-Roman foundations, gradually extended its educational facilities to lay pupils. Even under the much more democratic educational system of Islam, we hear, in 1565, the remarkable complaint of numerous "heretics" that "the Jews are a great deal better than we Muslims, for they fulfill the obligations due to the teachers of their children" (Ibn Hajar, quoted in *Enc. of Islam,* s.v. Madras).

In view of the diverse needs of the various social and geographic groups, there could be no educational uniformity throughout the Jewish world. Samuel Aboab's statement that "the Jewish people has various customs in regard to the method and scope of instruction" (*Zikronot,* 71 b), was as true of earlier periods as of the seventeenth century. In Spain the teachers usually received payment from the community, and the synod of Valladolid, in 1432, tried to introduce a special tax upon ritual meat and wine to maintain the local schools of Castile. In Germany and Poland, on the other hand, teachers were maintained only by the parents' fees; there often resulted incongruities in the age and preparation of the pupils. Perhaps the small size of the early German Jewish communities accounted for this deficient social control of education, and the later generations neglected it through sheer lack of tradition. Public schools for poor children (the so-called Talmud Torahs) were, however, often maintained by communities or special societies. Communal responsibility for higher education, although less clearly defined by law, was frequently more direct. Wherever a distinguished scholar attracted to his academy numerous students, the community deemed it a privilege to help maintain them. Meir of Rothenburg, for instance, had some seventeen pupils in his house. His disciple, Asher b. Yehiel, heading an academy in much richer Toledo, drew many more students from all parts of Europe, including distant Bohemia and Poland. The provincial statutes of Moravia provided that every community having thirty or more taxpaying members, ought to maintain a *yeshibah* with at least six advanced and six younger students. The itinerant students in medieval Germany were generally better cared for than the contemporary Christian "begging scholars," and became much less of a public nuisance. In 1564 David and Abraham Provençale, of Mantua, sent out a circular letter to all Italian communities, urging the establishment of a Jewish university.

The Jewish people developed an equally efficient system of meeting general and individual emergencies through charitable institutions, which were under rigid communal supervision, even when they were in part privately maintained. The original conception of *sedakah,* in biblical language the equivalent of justice but now meaning charity, lingered on, and the Jewish poor claimed support from the wealthier coreligionists as a right. In fact, Meir b. Baruch of Rothenburg unequivocally declared that "the poor have a positive claim upon the money coming from the tithe in accordance with a custom prevalent in the entire Diaspora" (*Responsa,* ed. Prague, No. 74). This, combined with the talmudic conception that the recipient of alms has enabled the donor to perform a good deed, made even the destitute beggar an upstanding, if not quite insolent, member of the community. Having inherited from the Orient a fear of the magic powers of a curse, wealthy Jews seldom faced an innocent poor man with equanimity. Most decisive, however, was the increasing lack of security, compelling all Jews to view charity as a sort of social insurance. Nobody could tell whether his accumulated fortune would not be destroyed overnight by a decree of the monarch or by pillage. Tomorrow he might himself take his place among the abject poor, dependent on the community. In some extraordinary cases, such as the Venetian Confraternity for the Redemption of Captives, the transition from business insurance to charity was altogether blurred. When that society levied a regular tax of one-fourth of one percent on all merchandise shipped to the Jews in the Levant, this was an indispensable safeguard against the evils of Mediterranean piracy. The idea of mutual responsibility, moreover, was deeply rooted in the religious conviction that "Jews are responsible for one another." As a result, charity was not only based upon voluntary individual contributions, which, the Jews prided themselves, proportionately far exceeded the donations of their non-Jewish neighbors, but a special tithe was expected to be set aside by every Jew for charitable purposes. In some communities the entire tithe was collected by force, if necessary. In others, the individual was permitted to select his or her object of charity in whole or in part. Various fines imposed by the Jewish court—for evasions of the prohibitions concerning interest on loans made to Jews, for refusal to appear before the court, etc.—swelled the charity fund. As retribution for minor transgressions, some Jews imposed eleemosynary payments upon themselves. For example, many took vows to pay a certain amount for charity after each card game, in order to check an inconquerable lust for gaming. In addition, the community at large assigned part of its budget to charity.

The modern conflict between private charity and state social insurance was partly obviated by the establishment of semi-private charitable organizations. One of the earliest and most widespread was the Hebrah Kadisha, a charitable burial society. Ancient in origin, it became firmly rooted in the thirteenth and fourteenth centuries, when we find it almost simultaneously in Huesca, in Spain (1323), and in Miltenberg, in western Germany (1326). Nissim Gerondi enumerated five societies in Perpignan about the middle of the century. Their number grew rapidly. In seventeenth-century Rome, there were not less than twenty-seven. The community always supervised them, even when it had no special power of confirming or rejecting officers, as, for instance, in Perpignan. In the final analysis, the community, as an institution of public law, took the chief responsibility for the care of the sick, the aged, orphans and destitute persons in general. Whatever drawbacks this system may have had, however large the communal debts became with the general economic decline of Jewry, it is apparently true that no Jew seems ever to have died of hunger while living in a Jewish community. This fact contrasts with Czarist Russia of the twentieth century, when in years of bad regional crops thousands of peasants died from starvation, while Russian grain was sold at low prices in London and Liverpool.[6]

The community played an important rôle, even in Jewish economic life. Its right to intervene in private enterprises, well established in the talmudic period, was strengthened by the general economic regimentation during the Middle Ages. As far as the Jews were concerned, the whole market police, the supervision over weights and measures, the fixing of maximum prices, and the demarcation of the rights of producers and consumers, were largely in the hands of the Jewish leaders.

Above all, the Jewish community was the chief tax-collecting agency for itself and for the state. The medieval state was too little organized to collect directly from individual taxpayers. Although most Jewish taxes were poll taxes, computed on the basis of population figures, payment was executed by the community at large, which had before allocated the amount among its members, according to wealth and income. Many of the poor, and especially those dependent on charity, were not assessed at all. Rabbis were exempted, both by Jewish law and by numerous state privileges, based on an analogy with the position of the Christian clergy. The state was thus deeply interested in the power of the community over its members, and tried to strengthen it by legislative measures.

To all these functions must be added the religious rôle of the community. Religion in general suffused all walks of public and private life, and the supervision of morals was an integral function of the community. There were often special officers, usually called *berurei aberot* (the supervisors over sins), for this purpose. Sumptuary laws against excessive luxury in dress and food, common in the later Middle Ages and early modern times, became especially important, as the community saw in them a means of stemming the tide of anti-Semitism, which often fed on envy, stimulated by the indulgence of Jewish women in jewelry and costly garments, or by expensive weddings and festivals.

The synagogue, in addition to being a house of worship, was the center of all Jewish social and communal life. Here was voiced the force of public opinion, so overwhelming in a small group restricted to a narrow street, and aware of the minutest details of one another's affairs. Every Jew regarded himself as responsible for the sins of all, and consequently as called upon to act. When the courts offered no redress, because a powerful individual had found means to intimidate the judge or because moral rather than legal issues were involved, the wronged could legally appeal to public opinion. In France, Germany and Poland, it became customary to exercise pressure upon recalcitrant Jews by "interrupting the prayers" and voicing grievances before the assembled congregation. Whether there are Palestinian or Babylonian antecedents for this practice is a matter of controversy, but the attempts of Gershom and Jacob Tam to limit such interruptions to evening prayers proved ineffective. Even they permitted the disturbance of morning prayers, should three suspensions of evening services be of no avail. The interruption of prayers is still common in eastern Europe, on the Sabbath and holiday mornings when the entire congregation is present. Should three interruptions have no effect, medieval law permitted a Jew to go further: he might stop short the prayers of the other congregations of the town. An unusual case of a Jewish "interdict" is recorded by Asher ben Yehiel: on one occasion a community closed the synagogue because its members were slow in paying their taxes.

EXCOMMUNICATION

In the last instance, the Jewish community had a peremptory means of enforcing its will—excommunication. Although the Jewish *herem* was rarely as severe as the dreaded Catholic excommunication *latae sententiae,* which became automatically active against the individual for certain transgressions against canon law, it made the excommunicated Jew an outcast within the community. Few men, no matter how wealthy or well educated, could withstand the mere threat of an anathema. Seventeenth-century Amsterdam was anything but a medieval city, and the case of Spinoza is by no means typical. As a rule, the community and its court obtained unconditional surrender by applying the various degrees of excommunication, the *nezifah* (reprimand over a period of seven days), the *niddui* (exclusion from divine services, etc., during thirty days), and finally the *herem* (extreme excommunication, without time limit). Their effectiveness was greatest where wise moderation prevailed, and where the synodal regulation, demanding full coöperation of the rabbi and the lay leaders in the issuance of bans, was strictly adhered to. Of Jacob of Moelln it was related, with evident approval, that throughout his life he was responsible for only one excommunication.

Excommunication could also be used for legislative and administrative purposes. The final effect of the famous "herem" of R. Gershom, outlawing polygamy, was to abrogate all pertinent talmudic and rabbinical laws. To be sure, the Sephardic communities never accepted that ban, and even Italy occasionally found means of evading it. At the time of publication, moreover, it seems to have been limited to the period ending in the year 5000 (1240 A.D.). Nevertheless, it has ever since remained unimpeachable for all Ashkenazic Jewry. Similarly, Gershom's enactments prohibiting the divorce of a woman against her will, and protecting the secrecy of letters, as well as the numerous synodal regulations of subsequent generations, generally issued under the sanction of excommunication, acquired the full validity of legislative acts. Among administrative bans, the most important are those directed against unrestricted competition, and the so-called *herem hayishub,* by virtue of which the community admitted or rejected newcomers. While Jacob Tam attempted to limit the exclusion to Jews who were too powerful, who denounced other Jews to Gentiles, or who refused to pay taxes, his grandfather Rashi and his successors, Eliezer ben Joel Halevi and Meir of Rothenburg, favored much wider communal discretionary powers. A publicly pronounced ban could also serve as a deterrent against theft, especially of synagogue paraphernalia. An old ban to this effect, issued by Abraham Maimuni, is still extant. A ban often served to discourage gaming with cards and dice, which in various periods enjoyed great popularity among both Jews and Gentiles. The Infante Juan twice extended to Jacob Xambell of Valencia the privilege of playing dice with Jews, Christians and Saracens, specifically exempting him from the contrary communal ban (1366, 1371).[7]

Inasmuch as disobedience was not merely a breach of the law but a grave sin against God, to whom nothing remains hidden, the power of the Jewish community over its members was enormous. Combining in itself many of the state's political, legislative, judicial, fiscal and police functions, with the religious, educational and charitable activities of the Church, all under the sanction of a divinely inspired law and under God's direct supervision, it reigned supreme over all domains of Jewish life. Indeed, it is hard to find any other commonwealth which enjoyed so dominant a position in the lives of its members.

At the same time, its government was generally democratic. Although through the ages Jewish communities had all sorts of constitutions, there was never any approach to monarchy, unless it be the exilarchate. The sovereignty of the people, in any case, was never contested; its only alternative was the sovereignty of God, whose power, however, was exercised through the people. Not even the rabbinical office, which about 1350 became a permanent salaried post uniting the rôles of judge, teacher and priest, had any charismatic character. The rabbi was subject to the general laws, as much as any layman. His rights and duties were those of every Jew. What superiority of position he might gain, was due to his personal eminence and the voluntary submission of others to his judgment. We find even extreme cases of "immediate democracy," when all communal officials were elected by lot. The community of Leghorn, especially, made many governmental experiments in the seventeenth and eighteenth centuries. As a rule, taxpayers only had electoral rights, which prevented Jews who received communal support from influencing elections in favor of their more generous patrons. This exclusion of an often substantial section helped make the community representative of the main body, which constituted a petty bourgeoisie. Not until recent centuries, when the community declined rapidly, did there develop a kind of aristocracy which seized the reins of government; then a few families began to rule the Jewish communities of Poland and Holland with an iron hand. Even in such vital communal decisions as the election of a new rabbi, voting was restricted to a small group of the wealthiest taxpayers and the few ordained *haberim*. In Germany, in the period of the court Jews, entire communities depended on the good will of their most privileged members.

CENTRAL AGENCIES

The power of the community was, of course, considerably increased by central institutions which were set up from time to time. In Muslim countries, exilarchs, *negidim* and *hahambashis* represented the Jews of a whole state. These Muslim traditions were powerful enough to perpetuate a chief rabbinate in Navarre and Portugal. In Portugal, especially, the chief rabbi supervised the administration of finances, justice and charity and the appointment of local rabbis and teachers, and was obliged to visit all Jewish communities annually. In Spain chief rabbis, at least of regions, were usual, capital punishment being reserved to the district court. Despite legitimate suspicions, reinforced by the general centrifugal trends in medieval Spain, that centralization might be abused by the government, Castilian and Aragonese Jewries from time to time acknowledged a leading Jew as their official representative to the crown. Toward the end of the fourteenth century, Hasdai Crescas, the philosopher, served in such official capacity for Aragon. The *rab de la corte* in Castile was often an unworthy, but influential politician, and as such denied all rabbinical authority by Adret and others. But sometimes, as in the case of Abraham Benveniste, the initiator and presiding officer of the synod of Valladolid, his prestige, strengthened by his official position, helped to unify for common action the diverse groups of Castilian Jewry. An attempt in 1354, however, to establish a central council for Aragon failed, because there was no persistent outside pressure.

In the north of Europe the oriental tradition was dim, and, since most communities had grown out of independent settlements, the Jews usually objected to the appointment of chief rabbis, whom they regarded as government agents, designed to strengthen royal control. Two or three decades before the final expulsion from France, Charles V appointed as chief rabbi Mattathiah ben Joseph Treves. But only the decision of the Spanish rabbis, Crescas and Profet, made in 1391, enabled Treves' son Johanan to hold the post, thus emphasizing Jewish independence in the choice of leaders. In Germany three successive attempts of fifteenth-century emperors, and one of Ferdinand I in 1559, to appoint chief rabbis for all German Jewry (Israel of Krems, Anselm of Cologne, Seligmann Oppenheimer of Bingen, and Jacob of Worms, were the nominees), proved of no avail against Jewish opposition. Israel of Krems, excommunicated by his fellow rabbis for accepting the appointment, speedily resigned. In Poland alone was a compromise reached between the crown and Jewry, which resulted in the eventual establishment of a Council (*Vaad*) for Three (later Four) Lands in Poland, and another for the Three (later Four and ultimately Five) Provinces in Lithuania. The two councils were of the highest importance in the life of all European Jewry. They dealt even with such minute questions as the rivalry of two Katzenellenbogen families, deciding that only the true descendants of Rabbi Meir of Padua were entitled to spell their names with a "b," while the others must write it with a "p." They issued ordinances regulating Jewish communal life and delimiting the rights of communal leaders as well as voters, and settled controversies between neighboring communities. In order to pacify the Polish nobles who served as tax farmers, the Polish Council in 1581 forbade the Jews to negotiate such contracts anywhere in western Poland. In 1676-1722, it pronounced bans on Shabbetai Zebi and his followers. Frequently both councils extended financial aid to stricken communities in Poland and abroad, and to individuals, especially authors, such as the celebrated preacher, Ephraim Lentshits, for the printing of their works. But perhaps their major function consisted in passing legal decisions and regulations which had wide authority, until the two councils were suppressed by the last Polish king in 1764.[8]

Jewish solidarity in all intellectual and social walks of life supported Jewish interterritorial cohesiveness. A catastrophe to the Jews of one country was felt by coreligionists all over the world as their own disaster. The organized attempt of Italian, Turkish and Dutch Jewry to release Polish Jewish captives, carried off by Tartars and Cossacks in 1648, was an instance of the social coöperation of world Jewry. The excommunication of the followers of Shabbetai Zebi, and the local struggle between Eibeschuetz and Emden, engaged the intellectual interests of wide circles. Certainly the Jewish people was then one single people, regardless of state boundaries and surrounding civilizations.[9]

RABBINIC SOCIAL PHILOSOPHY

This peculiar situation represents a climax in Jewish social and religious history. The emancipation from state and territory reached its highest peak. Everywhere in great measure separated from the soil economically, in many countries restricted to the money trade, the Jewish people led a life as remote from nature as can be imagined. Even in Spain, Poland and the Muslim countries, the Jews were far from being an agricultural population. The purest type of medieval Jews, found in Germany and northern Italy, was altogether urban, knowing nothing of nature. The very names of plants and animals, except the few of the household, lost their meaning to children and adults alike.[10]

The territorial state in which they happened to live, had

little significance for them. While adhering to the age-old principle of praying for the peace of the land, they could not fully identify themselves with states which merely tolerated them as aliens and which every so often cast them forth. Generally freed from military service, excluded from the administration, considered only a source of revenue, the Jews regarded the medieval state as no more than a place of temporary sojourn. Medieval Church theory opposed the mastery of man over man, as exemplified by the state. Despite Aquinas, however, the prevalent canonist conception was that the state, while the fruit of sin, also served as a remedy for sin. The Jewish mind, associating the idea of the foreign and hostile state with that of the Exile, saw in it likewise the fruit of sin, namely Israel's sin. In the opinion of the majority, however, it also had the capacity to purify and to compensate for their sins. This optimistic rationale of a reality, inescapable in any case, found a most eloquent spokesman in Halevi.

Disastrous wars caused the Jews to suffer with the rest of the population. Although some occasionally derived profit from commercial transactions with the contending armies, the people as a whole could not regard even victorious wars as a blessing. Hence the increased pacifism of medieval Jewry, which transcended even the ancient traditions. These half-patriotic, half-pacifist sentiments were well voiced by an Italian Jewish writer of the sixteenth century:

All the peoples of the world should know that as long as we, the remnant of Israel, live as strangers and sojourners in a land which is not ours, we are obliged, in accordance with the words of the prophets and the custom of our fathers which is law, to pray for the peace of the kingdom which rules over us. Especially at a time like this, when our sins have caused our dispersion to the four quarters of the world, we have also to invoke heaven to grant peace to the whole world, that no people should raise arms against another. [Azariah de' Rossi, *Meor Eynaim*, p. 446.]

Thus medieval Jewry, urbanized and demilitarized, progressed far indeed on the road of Pharisaic abandonment of the martial spirit permeating the Old Testament. On the other hand, the Church, starting with extreme Galilean pacifism, compromised first with warlike Rome and later with the medieval spirit of chivalry and the knightly conception of honor. Even in the medieval city where the Christian spirit was purest, the constant call to defense vitiated the sincerity of pacifist convictions. In a remarkable passage, Isserles, evidently referring to the ravages of the sixteenth-century wars of religion and unconsciously echoing Philo's arraignment of polytheism, wrote,

The numerous wars and conflicts befalling the world arise from differences of opinion. . . . Men become conscious of these differences, however, only on account of the images of worship they make, whereby it becomes evident to all that their creeds differ from one another. [*Torat ha-olah,* III, 38; referring also to Maimonides' *Guide,* III, 11.]

The need for solidarity, inherent in the life of a struggling minority, combined with the all-pervading theory of the equality of all Jews, to sharpen the sense of social responsibility. In theory and practice, the Jewish group recognized the superiority of communal over individual rights, to an even greater extent than did medieval Christendom. This served as a justification for innumerable regulations affecting economic enterprise. Talmudic ordinances against immoral commercial transactions, especially taking unfair advantage of ignorance or temporary pressure, were elaborated in great detail. Fair play between creditor and debtor, employer and employee, was emphasized ever more sharply. "He who delays paying wages to the wage earner," states Jacob b. Asher, "acts like one who sheds his blood and breaks five negative and one positive commandments" (*Tur,* H. M. 339). Full equality was to be safeguarded in the relations between master and servant, to the extent of both sharing exactly the same food, including wine. On the other hand, the employee must carry out his duties with scrupulous thoroughness. He must not halt in his work, even to return a greeting. Following talmudic precedent, medieval Jewish law regarded as null and void every commercial transaction in which the purchaser was overcharged, or in which the seller underrated the value of the merchandise to the extent of one-sixth of the just price. Realistically, however, the rabbis included overhead in calculating the just price, and also recognized the fluctuating character of market values. The Talmud expressly exempted transactions in slaves, deeds and land from these restrictions, and here we find a characteristic divergence among medieval rabbis. Alfasi and Maimonides, writing in a semicapitalistic Muslim environment, favored full freedom of price-fixing, in accordance with supply and demand; but the northern rabbis, Tam, Asheri and his son Jacob, annulled all contracts deviating from the just price by more than 50 percent. Because it involved an additional "desecration of the name" of God before the outside world, to cheat a Gentile was even more strictly prohibited than to cheat a Jew. True, nationalistic voices were heard sporadically asserting that conscious cheating, or at least taking advantage of an error, is permissible, should the Gentile be unaware of it, hence there being no such desecration to be feared. The majority of informed opinion countenanced no such evasions, however, which is the more remarkable, the more the double standard of morals in relation to one's own and to an outside group, prevailed in all walks of medieval life.

Under the impact of medievalism, the rabbis limited competition rigidly. Although perhaps of Arabian origin, the principle of *maarufia,* or the right of each merchant or artisan to a certain group of customers, flourished fully only in Europe north of the Alps. The old conflict between the rather capitalistically inclined Palestinian schools and the more feudal-minded Babylonian rabbis, was renewed in the medieval contrast between the Spaniards, Joseph ibn Migash, Meir Halevi and Joseph Karo, who favored the consumer, and the Franco-German jurists, who concentrated on the interests of the producer and distributor. This alignment reveals a striking reversal of the rôle of Spain, which usually adopted Babylonian patterns, and that of Ashkenazic Jewry, which, through Italy, was ordinarily open to the incursion of Palestinian customs and ideas. All agreed, however, that the manipulation of prices by withdrawing grain from the market, was to be punished by flagellation. The community, as well as the artisan and merchant guilds, was entitled to set obligatory maximum or minimum prices, and to fix working hours. Heavy fines were imposed upon the lawbreaker. Characteristically the stability of social conditions was taken so much for granted that, as in the case of Yehiel, father of Asheri, in the thirteenth century, and of two Cairo Jews in 1564, families often concluded compacts of "perpetual" friendship.

Despite all this, the basic insecurity of Jewish life militated against a purely static conception of life. No rabbi has ever gone to the extreme of believing in an unchangeable society, a conception underlying all early medieval and, to a certain extent, even the Thomistic social philosophy. The dissatisfaction of medieval Jewry with existing conditions naturally stimulated a desire for change. The nature of the Jewish religion, perhaps also a national characteristic, with its crucial messianic doctrine oriented forward, rather than toward the past, steadily nourished the hope for a better future. Maimonides undoubtedly struck the keynote of medieval Jewish optimism when, in reformulating the talmudic injunction to the prospective proselyte, he contrasted the eternity of Israel with the ephemerality of other nations:

If thou seest Israel suffering in this world, it is for the sake of the future good, for they cannot receive much well-being in this world as do the other nations, because they may become haughty, err and lose the reward of the hereafter. . . . However, the Holy One, blessed be He, does not bring upon them too severe punishment, lest they completely disappear. But the other nations vanish, while they last forever. [*Mishneh Torah,* Issure Biah 14, 4-5; cf. also S. W. Baron's remarks in "The Historical Outlook of Maimonides," *PAAJR,* VI, 103 ff.]

Life was consequently cherished as a supreme value in itself. Long before foreign interference, Jewish law had practically wiped out capital punishment. Maimonides summarized talmudic law very well in stating that no circumstantial evidence suffices for a serious conviction, and that capital punishment must not be inflicted upon a criminal, when all the judges vote for it, without the redeeming feature of a dissenting minority. The Jews certainly never applied torture to obtain a confession in lieu of other evidence of crime. Suicide was greatly discouraged. The care of a sick person, even if hopelessly ill, was regarded as one of the highest duties of a Jew. Individual tenacity of life was, after all, the best guarantee for the survival of the people.

Charity was a focal point in Jewish life. For the righting of inequalities of nature or of social status, rabbinic ethics combined social control with the expression of individual sympathy. Even the Jews who were supported by public charity were obliged to contribute a farthing to the alleviation of human misery. National pride barred the acceptance of support from strangers.

If a Gentile king or dignitary send money to Jewish charities, for the sake of peace one ought not to return it to him. One should merely distribute it secretly among the Gentile poor. [*Tur,* H. M. 254.]

On the other hand, Gentiles should always be included in acts of mercy. Rashi, without much ado, pointed out that Christians knew they were supported by Jewish charities; and an eighteenth-century apologist stated, without fear of contradiction, that "all our books are full of injunctions concerning charity without difference of nationality" (J. D. Eisenstein, *Ozar Wikkuhim,* p. 179). The constructive type of charity (e.g., the extension of a loan to enable a man to work) was particularly extolled. On the other hand, the poor must accept any kind of work, rather than become a burden to society. These moral injunctions, largely derived from the Talmud, were invested with the full force of law by the medieval codifiers, who always saw in social justice a source of social equilibrium. In fact, rabbinic theory declared *sedakah* to be higher than any other positive commandment, since its omission may at times be the equivalent of bloodshed. Meir of Rothenburg, when asked whether a donation for the synagogue was to be preferred to one for charitable purposes, decided in favor of the latter. Two centuries later Jacob Moelln severely scolded overzealous worshipers who diverted the charitable tithe to the purchase of candles for synagogue services. It is to be noted that the amount of support granted to a destitute person was to be measured by his accustomed needs, rather than by any objective standards.

These needs were, as a rule, very moderate. Moderation in personal expenditure was often prescribed by law or communal ordinance. Although, under foreign domination, money had become increasingly the Jews' basis of subsistence, the rabbis tried to discourage its excessive evaluation. Typical of rabbinic theory is Saadia's polemic against those who emphasize the importance of, and the power attached to, its possession. "I have looked into their words and I have seen that the best thing in money is when it comes to one without exertion and fatigue; but whosoever seeks to obtain it, gets it really through hardships, constant thinking and nervousness, through sleepless nights and trials in daytime" (*Beliefs and Opinions,* Section X). On the other hand, Saadia himself approved love of money to the extent of man's efforts to preserve what God had given him. In another connection, he argued physiologically that a man who constantly lives on coarse food, becomes coarse by nature, so that the subtleties of wisdom escape him. From another angle, Joseph ibn Kaspi enjoined his young son,

> Pay no regard to money, for true wealth consists only of a sufficiency of bread to eat and raiment to wear. Why weary thyself to gain much silver, when neither thou nor any other could equal the vast store accumulated by the great mountain in our native city, l'Argentière, even though that mountain is but a soulless heap? [I. Abrahams, *Hebrew Ethical Wills*, I, 145.]

Like the medieval canonists, however, who abandoned the early ideal of poverty, Judaism, with the exception of certain ascetic branches, did not regard poverty as desirable in itself.

Neither was medieval Judaism affected by the celibate tendencies of the Church. Ancient Pharisaism having peremptorily rejected the Essenian and Pauline denunciation of sex, medieval Jewry encouraged marriage with all the means at its disposal. Following the Talmud, it demanded that every man marry by his eighteenth birthday. Jacob ben Asher declared it especially meritorious to marry at thirteen. Girls, particularly, were often given in marriage at the age of twelve. To explain this patent disregard of a talmudic prohibition, a Franco-German scholar reasoned,

> Today the Exile increases from day to day. If one is able to give a dowry to his daughter now [he should do so]. Later he may be without means and his daughter may remain an old maid forever. [*Tosafot* Kidd. 41 a.]

Asheri decreed that a bachelor of twenty may be forced to marry by the court. Although no such action is recorded, public opinion sufficed to make confirmed bachelors a rare phenomenon in the ghetto. Despite the talmudic permission to those devoting their life to learning, to postpone their matrimonial ties indefinitely, we know of no distinguished medieval rabbi who lived as a celibate for any length of time. In fact, as late as 1741, Jonathan Eibeschuetz refused the title *Morenu* to Mendelssohn because "it is against the general custom to confer the honor, *Morenu*, upon a bachelor" (cf. his letter of recommendation published by J. L. Jeiteles in "A Fine Recommendation," *Kerem Hemed*, III,224 f.). Monasticism made little impression upon medieval Jewry.

Marriage was, however, only a means to an end. Every Jew was obliged to attempt to have at least one son and one daughter. In the polygamous period, when the first wife proved barren, it was permissible to take a second. After the ban of Gershom, sporadic voices argued that sometimes in such circumstances divorce might be more cruel than bigamy. The prevailing opinion was, however, that after ten years of childless marriage, a Jew should divorce his wife and take another, in order to have progeny. Although the courts rarely exercised direct pressure (a fact recognized by Profet and invested with the validity of a binding custom practiced "for many generations" by Isserles in his gloss to *Shulhan Aruk,* E.H. 1,3), many a ghetto tragedy occurred because of this. Such emphasis upon procreation was a natural complement to an ethnic religion, based upon and aiming at the preservation of the people.

The eugenic ideals of rabbinic theory were often interfered with by economic and social forces. As in the higher strata of medieval Christendom, marriage increasingly became a deliberate affair, based upon calculation rather than physical or mental attraction. Although the rabbis tried to discourage the marriage of a young man to an old woman for the sake of money, they did not dare interfere when it actually occurred. They sometimes legislated against parental interference with young people's marrying persons of their own choice, but in practice parents selected the prospective mate; often the bridal couple met for the first time at the wedding. If matrimonial happiness seems, nevertheless, to have been more prevalent in the ghetto than today, this was due to the less complicated structure of life, to a moderate subservience and a kind of heroism in medieval woman, to the influence of morality upon family life, and, perhaps most of all, to the early average age of marriage. The young boy might not have known his fiancée before wedlock, but, as a rule, he neither met nor desired any other woman. He soon loved in his wife the only woman he really knew. Surrounded by numerous children, burdened with constant worries over the support of a large family, and subjected to the rigid supervision of his fellow Jews, he seldom had the wish or opportunity for romantic escapades.

Rabbis and philosophers, without being prudes themselves, preached erotic self-control as well as decency in speech. Following ancient practice, Maimonides and his successors quite freely discussed the intimate relationships between men and women in so far as they had legal or ethical bearing. But Albo shuddered at the thought of a community of women, as preached by Plato. "Plato made a grievous mistake," he declared, "advocating the unbecoming as though it were becoming" (*Book of Principles,* I, 8,3, p. 82). In Italy, to be sure, the prevalent laxity in literature had some influence upon Jewish writers. But Immanuel of Rome, the alleged friend of Dante, who often satirized women as outspokenly as did Boccaccio, was an exception in medieval Jewish letters. The reaction against him is best illustrated by Karo's summary dismissal.

Books of poetry and fiction of a profane nature and erotic writings such as the Book of Immanuel and also books of adventures must not be read on Sabbath. Even on week days they are forbidden, because their reading is like sitting "in the seat of the scornful" [Ps. 1:1]. It is also a violation of the prohibition "turn ye not unto the idols" [Lev. 19:4] which means that you must not turn to the products of your imagination [a reference to a statement of R. Hanin, Shabbat, 149 a]. As to the erotic writings one should also consider that they excite the evil spirit [lust], and he who composes or copies them and, more so, he who prints them causes the multitude to sin [*Shulhan Aruk,* O. H. 307, 16].

Similarly mixed dancing was frowned upon. The "dancing houses," maintained even by many northern communities, were thrown open, as a rule, to wedding parties in which men and women danced separately. After trying with much sophistry to interpret away biblical references to heterosexual diversions, Solomon Luria declared that one must not recite the customary benediction "in whose dwelling there is joy" at a wedding at which men and women are sitting together, "because at that hour there is no joy before the Holy One, blessed be He, in his dwelling" (*Yam shel Shelomoh,* on Gittin I,18). In the new regulations adopted by the Prague community in 1552, evidently under the instigation of the puritanical preacher, Ephraim Lentshits, most paragraphs dealt with feminine morality. Not only were prostitutes banished from the Jewish quarter, but women peddlers were forbidden to enter alone houses of Christians, and young girls were told not to stroll about in the evening, even in groups of two or three. These regulations, composed with the usual homiletical effusiveness of typical guardians of morals, resounded from every pulpit in town for several months in succession. While there was much hypocrisy in all these matters of sex, one must bear in mind that this moral restraint was commanded primarily as an act of religious discipline. Secondarily, however, there was constant apprehension lest sexual laxity dissolve the bonds of communal life and divert the energies from the study of the law.

Within the family, while the supremacy of the father was uncontested, the position of the woman was little short of enviable as compared with that of her Christian contemporary. She may not have been celebrated by minstrels and troubadours, but she was the equal partner of her husband in joy and in sorrow, and often the responsible manager of business and household. Glueckel of Hameln best typifies such a Jewish wife. The husband frequently devoted all his time to study, thus earning for himself and his spouse a place in the world to come. The Jewish codifiers and ethical writers unceasingly preached, to attentive ears, family peace, mutual respect and devotion.

The duties of parents in giving children a proper education, physically and mentally, until they could support themselves, were also well defined. On the other hand, the rabbis never tired of repeating the obligation of children to honor their parents. Later codifiers quote approvingly Maimonides' restatement of talmudic injunctions, that "even if a man be dressed in gorgeous attire and sit at the head of an assembly, and there come his father and mother and tear his dress and knock him on his head and spit in his face, he must not insult them but must remain silent" (*Mishneh Torah,* Mamrim VI,7). In practice, of course, such exaggerations carried little weight. In fact, no less a man than Meir of Rothenburg (or was it Meir Abulafia?) did not wish to see his father, once he had achieved greatness. In general, the golden mean was here, too, the rule of behavior.

High above the father towered the scholar. Codifiers and popular philosophers tirelessly emphasized the supreme value of scholarship and the general obligation to revere a scholar. A son who feels that he can receive better instruction from a teacher other than his father, may disobey his father and follow his own inclination. Faced by the alternative of following a prominent teacher or his father, a man must give precedence to the teacher. Judah b. Samuel in his *Book of the Pious,* however, added the significant reservation that this law holds true only in so far as tuition fees to the instructor were not paid by the father. Innumerable practical benefits were bestowed by Jewish law upon scholars as a class. They were exempt from all taxation by state or community, except for obligatory contributions to communal expenditure for necessities of life, such as digging wells. Maimonides and Karo quote with approval Joseph ibn Migash's decision to free a scholarly owner of gardens and orchards from payment of thousands of guilders of taxes due the government, although even the poorest were subjected to this tax. Another medieval rabbi declared that, in case of conflict, a scholar might put under the ban a recalcitrant community; on the other hand, communal excommunication of tax evaders had no application to scholars, even when they were specifically mentioned. Since medieval scholars derived their livelihood largely from business, especially before the days of the professional rabbi, Jewish law was bent upon granting them as many commercial privileges as possible. Maimonides and Asheri repeated without reservation the talmudic postulate that a scholar should be enabled to dispose of all his stock before anyone else. More realistically, Nahmanides, followed by Karo, decided that such law is applicable only in case there are no non-Jewish competitors. Wherever Jews had a monopoly of a branch of commerce, preference was to be given to the scholar in its exploitation. Busy merchants were excused for failing to devote time to study, if they turned some of the profits over to scholars or, still better, if they made a scholar a silent partner.[11]

Encompassing the entirety of human relations, rabbinic theory thus sought to achieve equilibrium between classes and groups, as well as between the individual and society. This equilibrium consisted largely in the establishment of an aristocracy of learning, accessible to everyone; and in the diversion of personal energies and ambitions into mental channels. Intellectual interests were again focused on talmudic learning and tradition. The social philosophy of the rabbis optimistically disregarded the existing wretchedness of Jewish life, positing marriage, property and work; and rationalizing human life for the purposes of this world and the hereafter.

Thus it was more "modern" and nearer to the capitalistic view of society than even the Catholic doctrine as revised by Thomas and the canon jurists. On the other hand, its insistence upon social control, social justice and political equality was strongly socialistic. Carrying over the memorable synthesis of semicapitalist Rome and semifeudal Persia, achieved in the Babylonian Talmud, rabbinic economic and social philosophy was, as a whole, more "advanced" than contemporary Christian thought down to the Reformation. The ability of the Jews to maintain the ancient structure intact in the medieval environment was thus due to the combined forces of tradition, progressive urbanization, concentration in the "higher" economic pursuits, and increasing segregation and autonomy.[12]

Rabbinic social philosophy doubtless strengthened the solidarity so necessary to the people's struggle for survival. The Jewish people managed for so long without state and territory because of the idealizing legal system and the reality of Jewish communal life. Through these forces the Jews developed substitutes: instead of their own country, they possessed quarters of their own in most European and oriental cities; failing to establish their own state, they created in the "community" a quasi state, more powerful than any of the surrounding genuine states. Beyond all state boundaries, they established commercial, social and intellectual interrelations, which gave rise to a feeling of solidarity more real than those existing in many a political body. All this was artificial, but so necessary as to be intrinsically true and real. Scattered throughout the world, the Jewish people thus embodied, more clearly than ever before, the teachings of the Jewish religion.

MEDIEVAL HALAKAH

In so far as the religious life of the Jews can be discussed in isolation from the complicated structure which it permeated, it must be said that here, too, the Middle Ages were a period of highest development. Of course, distinctions must be drawn between countries of Jewish mass settlement and those with sparse and scattered communities. Along the Mediterranean, a diversified intellectual life corresponded to the variety of occupations, but even there Jewish law remained the foundation of Jewish life. It is no mere chance that the Babylonian Halakah, growing out of a society in many ways feudalistic, spread its tentacles most easily in northern France and Germany, where feudalism was supreme and Jewish corporate life purest. Despite dividing centuries and distances, the dialectical elaborations of the French and German Tosafists were of the same lineage as the "dialectics of Abbaye and Raba." Although Spanish and Italian Jewry produced such distinguished teachers of all Israel as Alfasi, Isaiah of Trani, Maimonides and Adret, they never ascended these heights in talmudic speculation. Isaac Alfasi's fame at first spread more rapidly throughout the Jewish world than that of Gershom and Rashi. Not only did Spanish rabbis and those of southern France of subsequent generations bow to his authority, when, for instance, Abraham b. David of Posquières expostulates against contradicting the master in certain details, although "I should have closed my eyes and shut my mouth and followed him to the right or to the left, without turning aside" (*Temim Deim,* 238); but the northern Tosafist, Isaac the Elder, extolled his work, "which none were able to compose unless the *Shekina* [the divine spirit] rested upon him" (quoted by Menahem ben Zerah, *Sedah la-derek,* Intro.). At the same time Ibn Daud, in his *Book of Tradition,* did not mention Rashi, and spoke of Jacob Tam merely from hearsay. But soon the superiority of the Franco-German schools with respect to pure dialectics became more marked. Maimonides, complimenting his Provençal correspondents, foretold that the future of Jewish learning lay in France. As the Christian crusaders recaptured one Spanish province after another, the chief leaders of Jewish learning in the Iberian Peninsula began to acknowledge the primacy of their northern colleagues. Nahmanides, for instance, spoke with the highest reverence of the French sages, who "teach and instruct us in all hidden things" (Intro., *Kuntres dine de-garme*); and Isaac b. Sheshet Profet paraphrased the biblical verse to read: "for from France shall go forth the Torah and the word of the Lord from Germany" (*Responsa* No. 376). To be sure, the Spanish and Provençal rabbis were more systematic. They were the chief codifiers and systematizers of the Talmud, the authors of talmudic handbooks and treatises on methodology (Samuel ha-Nagid, Menahem ha-Meiri, Jeshua Halevi, and Isaac Campanton). But the Talmud itself was by no means systematic, and, however valuable for pedagogical purposes, every attempt at systematization and methodical treatment was bound to be both too simple and final to preserve the essence of the talmudic mode of thinking. The northern rabbis, occasionally emulating the systematic method of their Spanish colleagues (Samson of Chinon, etc.), but for the most part heaping dialectical queries and answers in the Talmud's own sequence, were truer to its spirit, the eternal flow of tradition and discussion, than were their Mediterranean brethren.

Of course, the appreciation of the two types of scholarship was frequently determined by individual temper or regional bias. Israel Bruna, for example, taught that in a practical decision a judge is to follow a clean-cut interpretation of a talmudic source, rather than a dialectical derivation; but he insisted, nevertheless, that "the rabbinate depends chiefly on dialectics [*pilpul*]." On the other hand, his contemporary, Joseph Kolon, a Frenchman living in Italy, acknowledged the great relative value of the speculative method, but firmly claimed that "there is more proof for the assumption that the main function of the rabbinate depends on erudition than that it hinges on dialectical acumen" (*Responsa,* No.167). The southern rabbis, even after 1492, followed the lead of their Spanish predecessors. Moses Alashkar and others extolled, especially, the merits of the Maimonidean code, and even Karo adopted as a yardstick for his own decisions the agreement or disagreement of the "three pillars," Alfasi, Maimonides and Asheri. Even Asheri, though of northern origin, reflected in many ways the Halakah of his adopted fatherland, Spain. This Sephardic accent of Karo's codification, although buttressed in his *House of Joseph* by innumerable quotations from Ashkenazic sources, caused widespread resentment among the northern rabbis; and Luria, Isserles, and Yafeh increasingly reiterated, in all possible variations, Profet's flattering epigram concerning Franco-German superiority. Nevertheless, these provincial quarrels and preferences affected very little the fundamental unity of medieval Halakah.

Even the northern continuators of talmudic tradition found that life forced many new adjustments on them. After all, a millennium of history could not be overlooked, any more than could a crucial change in geographic environment. However insulated the Jewish street might be from the rest of the French or German town, however wide and adequate the self-government of the Jews, there arose conditions so novel that they had to be coped with anew by Jewish law. Often enough, reinterpretation of the old law sufficed. But often new regulations, or so-called *takkanot,* were essential. These were proclaimed, either individually, by a distinguished rabbi, or, more frequently, by a collective decision of many, in one of the frequent synods. Northern scholarship actually began with such innovations through the famous excommunications of Gershom, "the light of the Exile."

Neither did his disciples in the following generations overlook realities, when many such deviations were called for. To mention only one typical example: the main occupation of the Jews having become money lending, the old biblical and talmudic characterizations of the charging of any interest whatever as usury and as a violation of six different commandments, were felt to be serious handicaps. The Babylonian Talmud, reflecting the conditions of a settled and diversified Jewry, demanded that even to Gentiles loans be granted without any charge, though preferably not at all. An exception was made only in favor of a money lender who depended on this income for a livelihood (*kede hayyav*). The European scholars could no longer draw such fine distinctions. Ethically the author of the *Book of the Pious* may still oppose charging interest to Gentiles, "if one can make a living from the fields" (Section 808), but even he does not venture to state this in terms of legal prohibition. More radically, the medieval rabbis soon had to find a legal opening for profitable banking transactions between Jews. Applying a widespread method of evading canon law among the Christians, the rabbis gradually established the principle of *heter iska* (the permission of commercial interest), based upon the legal fiction that the money lender, though ostensibly charging interest, is really a silent partner in the profits of the borrower. The rabbis here merely followed the example of Antonino of Florence and Bernardin of Siena, who, under the impact of the incipient Italian commercial revolution, legalized lending at interest to Christian creditors through this subterfuge. Pious Jews of eastern Europe, in signing bills of exchange carrying interest, still jot in a corner the four Hebrew letters constituting an abbreviation of *al sad heter iska* (on the basis of *heter iska*). Of course, gratuitous loans were often made to fellow Jews in emergencies. Special Jewish charitable organizations arose, whose sole task was the meeting of such needs. But even where no serious risk was involved, no moneyed individual could be expected to lend large portions of his capital, now the chief source of income, without making a charge.

Such changes and modifications were made in almost all branches of Jewish law. A deep transformation took place, even in the court of justice which had to administer the law. In most civil and minor criminal cases, it was no longer three laymen who sat in judgment, as in the tannaitic age, but, through progressive changes, a professional rabbinical court.

Even more than in the geonic age, custom was the main creative force of law. As Jewish life became more diverse in the various lands, local usages, also more and more diversified, assumed the character of binding laws. Asher ben Yehiel was generally self-reliant enough to contradict the geonim and Ahai of Shabha, and to make a decision against the combined authority of Alfasi, Maimonides and Isaac the Elder, on the ground that "Jephthah in his generation is like Samuel in his." But he hesitated to change a custom which he regarded as faulty, without finding some slight talmudic support. His contemporary, Adret, stated succinctly: "we must not discard a tradition held by our old womenfolk even in the face of six hundred thousand proofs to the contrary" (quoted in his name, by Moses Teitelbaum, *Heshib Mosheh* to O.H. 13). Such unwritten laws were reinforced through the influence of Teuton law, where local usage also had a validity superior to the general law of the country (*Landrecht bricht Reichsrecht*), a principle, also accepted in the main by the *Siete Partidas* for Spain and by Gratian for canon law. Of course, Christian and Jewish leaders realized that they could not recognize every custom which might have had its origin in accident, ignorance or superstition. Even those rabbis who sang the praise of the customary in high superlatives, had to reject numerous "erroneous customs" or "foolish customs." But they wisely refrained from drawing a sharp logical line, and preferred leaving acceptance or rejection to the somewhat arbitrary decision of the leaders of each generation.

Examples of widespread customs at variance with talmudic law, are too numerous to be cited. To the most interesting belong the pilgrimages to the graves of great scholars and saints, which had originated in the East under Gentile influence. Notwithstanding the protests of the rabbis, this custom, which at once struck the cords of piety and superstition, could never be wholly eradicated. Mohammed is said to have cursed the Jews because they converted the graves of their prophets into places of worship. In the Middle Ages this sophisticated remnant of ancestor worship was amplified by another custom, likewise with talmudic antecedents, when families began to compete for the honor of burying deceased relatives near the sepulcher of a great man. When Meir of Rothenburg's body was retained for fourteen years by the emperor, in order to extract money from the Jewish communities, one Suesskind Alexander Wimpfen of Frankfort obtained it for interment in the Jewish cemetery of Worms, on deposit of a large sum, his reward being a burial place near that of the celebrated rabbi. Ironically, it was precisely Meir of Rothenburg who denounced pilgrimages to the graves of the saints, more vigorously than any other medieval teacher.

Another unwritten law of old was to cover the head during prayers, as a sign of reverence for God. In the Orient, this custom was part of general etiquette. In fact, Maimonides compared the reverence for God to that for the earthly king, on this basis. In Europe, however, it had become a token of reverence to uncover the head, and apparently in medieval France the Jews prayed in this fashion. The oriental custom had become deeply ingrained, however, and to this day orthodox Jews avoid uncovering their heads, especially while uttering prayers or benedictions.

As in the days of the Talmud, most conscious adaptations were made through an interpretive extension of traditions, rather than by bold deviations. There was, no doubt, serious danger that the noncanonical talmudic text would be altered to suit the needs of the moment, as an easy expedient. The medieval disregard for textual correctness is notorious. Glaring mistakes of copyists, as well as conscious interpolations or omissions made with theoretical or practical bias, were uncritically accepted. There existed no legal, and hardly any moral, copyright to protect literary property from such damaging interference. Moreover, Christian and Jewish writers alike often bodily lifted extensive passages from older works. Sometimes they went to the extreme of plagiarizing entire sections of a book, as was done in 1372 by Isaac di Lattes in his *Kiryat Sepher* with Menahem ha-Meiri's introduction to *Bet ha-behirah*. Occasional rebukes, such as Nahmanides' biting remark on a supposedly original idea of Abraham b. David, "His words are identical with those of Rashi and he has added nothing but the praise which he has showered upon them" (*Lekutot*, fol. 3b, to Ber. 50 a), had slight effect. This freedom in disposing of the works of others is illustrated by Eliezer of Metz, who, finding an erroneous statement, or what he thought to be an erroneous statement, in his copy of Jacob Tam's *Sepher ha-Yashar*, deleted it altogether. The prevalent scarcity of manuscripts forced many scholars to depend upon their memory, the reliability of their quotations naturally leaving much to be desired. Under these circumstances, the apprehension grew that, should similar negligence prevail with respect to the Talmud, the various groups of Jewry would soon possess widely differing texts, this being liable to destroy the uniformity of Jewish law. For this reason, Gershom expressly prohibited any kind of textual amendment in the Talmud; while Maimonides and Abraham b. David, in harmony for once, referred to a kind of gentleman's agreement among Jewish scholars the world over, to preserve the talmudic text unchanged. Only after the invention of printing, when the Hebrew presses, beginning in 1475, placed an increasing number of uniform copies in the hands of the reading public, was the great concern over the possible divergences of the available texts partly allayed. At that time leading talmudists, such as Solomon Luria and Joel Sirkes, ventured to compose marginal annotations, suggesting more correct readings in the Talmud. So many of Luria's suggestions in the original edition of his *Hokmat Shelomoh* are said to have been incorporated in the talmudic text especially by the printers of the famous Amsterdam edition that they published only the remaining, considerably shortened, part of the work.[18]

Even in the Middle Ages proper, however, the shackles imposed by this text were not felt to be severe. Its adaptation to life was greatly facilitated, both by its bulk and by the varieties of opinion recorded in it. The medieval scholars could, by a dialectical interpretation, deduce from the Talmud almost anything they wanted. In fact, Jacob Tam, echoed by Nahmanides, boasted that

> even if the Talmud states in one connection that a man is guilty and in another that he is free, I can well explain the divergence. Even more easily can I answer other questions. [*Sepher ha-Yashar,* ed. Vienna, 78 b.]

Naturally, such dialectical processes lent themselves to grave abuses. As time passed, the *pilpul* often became a purely intellectual game, altogether divorced from reality. Such was the case when a rabbi, from whose copy of the Talmud, it is said, a few pages were missing, undertook to explain the continuity of the discussion. Little wonder that such exaggerations evoked harsh condemnations and ridicule. The celebrated rabbi, Loew ben Bezalel of Prague, around whom folk imagination spun many a beautiful tale, advised students to prefer a game of chess. But in essence the *pilpul* had great pedagogic value and, properly used, helped mold the mind of the medieval Jew to think in the unadulterated talmudic idiom.

The *pilpul*, employed with moderation, was the most conspicuous vehicle of the adjustment of law to life. To counteract the overwhelming power of tradition, the duty was imposed upon every individual to investigate the law in the original sources. Not only did the philosopher, Bahya, advise intelligent men to use their own judgment, so that traditional commandments would also be clarified by reason, but even a halakist of the rank of Zedekiah b. Abraham insisted that he who relies solely upon the authority of codes, responsa or custom, "has not fulfilled his duty" (*Shibbole ha-leket,* Intro.). Even after the publication of Karo's, Isserles' and Yafeh's standard codes, Meir of Lublin emphatically declared:

> It is not my way, when it comes to a legal decision, to place great reliance in such works [*Shulhan Aruk,* and *Lebush*], which are like brief unintelligible summaries causing many to err so that, alas, they permit the forbidden, discharge the guilty or vice versa. [*Responsa* No. 135.]

It is understandable, nevertheless, that the less independent or courageous a rabbi was, the readier he was to lean upon a recognized authority, rather than to decide according to his own light. In ritual law, especially, the temptation to avoid responsibility, by following the more rigid interpretation of a predecessor or by deciding every doubtful issue in the stricter sense, was great. True, rabbinical social philosophy militated against undiscriminating severity and "the Torah is merciful in regard to Jewish money," and "a large loss," are frequent refrains in rabbinical literature, to explain more lenient views. Asheri, especially, was very emphatic in insisting that every attempt at interdicting the use of anything must be supported by unequivocal proofs (*Responsa*, 2,17). But the tendency to heap one restriction upon another became more irresistible as the range of social activities narrowed. Joseph Kolon, paraphrasing a well-known rule in the Talmud, succeeded in reversing it completely by stating that "the force of the rigid interpretation is stronger than that of the lenient" (*Responsa* No. 37). In the eighteenth century, Shneur Zalman, of Ljosna, was able, without doing violence to the facts, to declare that "the entire oral law is to multiply restrictions and minutiae of scribal interpretations in the positive and negative commandments" (*Likkute Torah* on va-Ethanan, ed. Vilna, 19 a).

As in the geonic age, the chief media of jurisprudence remained the codification, the halakic exegesis of the Talmud, and the setting of a judicial precedent by a responsum. Partly in imitation of European custumals, central European rabbis of the fifteenth century added collections of local customs, as a summary of the past and a guide for the future. Subsequent to Maimonides, codifiers were less ambitious. They attempted to systematize the steadily increasing bulk of knowledge and juridical detail only in so far as it had a bearing upon practical questions. Such were, in the first place, the great systematic codes: Jacob ben Asher's *Arbaah Turim* (*The Four Pillars*), Joseph Karo's *Shulhan Aruk* (*The Table Prepared*), Mordecai Yafeh's *Lebushim* (*Vestments*) and Shneur Zalman's *Shulhan Aruk*. Detailed investigations into the 613 commandments in all their ramifications, such as Moses ben Jacob of Coucy's so-called *Great Book of Precepts*, and Isaac ben Joseph of Corbeil's *Short Book of Precepts*;

or collections of local customs, such as Jacob of Moelln's *Custumal,* were among the other significant compilations of a large body of rabbinical law. In the exegetical field, whole treatises, apparently containing nothing but comments on older sources, frequently served the purpose of law-finding, rather than of pure exposition. For example, the *Tosafot* and still more the halakic commentaries (like those of Adret, Yom Tob b. Abraham and Mordecai b. Hillel), were written chiefly in order to establish the law.

Medieval responsa differed profoundly from the geonic. No longer backed by the authority of an official academy, each decision rested entirely on its own merits. Only the fame of an individual rabbi, which often spread over all the Jewish world, could make of his decision an authoritative source for the further development of law. The number of inquiries likewise depended on his reputation. According to the historian, David Conforte, Solomon ibn Adret wrote more than six thousand such replies. The seven volumes hitherto published, which could easily be amplified through the available manuscript material, contain only half that number. This amazing output far exceeds the total number of the responsa, both genuine and apocryphal, attributed to even the centenarian, Hai Gaon.

It is amazing to see how little external prestige mattered, and how often rabbis of the largest and wealthiest communities bent their heads before the superior learning of some remote teacher, serving a smaller congregation. When Karo, Isserles and Yafeh almost simultaneously undertook to recodify Jewish law, they did so, not by virtue of any superior office, but because they felt the need of eliminating perplexities. Isserles and Yafeh, residing in Cracow and Venice respectively, upon learning that the distinguished Palestinian author of the *House of Joseph* and the *Double Desire,* contemplated compiling a brief code, immediately postponed their own work until after its publication. On one occasion, in fact, Isserles forced his community to accept a regulation of Karo which conflicted with his own opinion. Karo's authority to issue a ban on an individual in Carpentras was as little contested as was his and his colleague's decision in the controversy over the boycott of Ancona. If the moderate attitude of the Italian rabbinate in regard to de Rossi's work eventually prevailed, this was due less to separatist tendencies than to Karo's intervening death. In fact, medieval Jewry, as a whole, revealed an astounding measure of both sound popular instinct and intellectual discernment, in the recognition it granted to self-appointed leaders in this field. Examined in retrospect, few halakic authorities seem to have earned unmerited popularity. That such discipline should have prevailed amid so much freedom is really remarkable. What a contrast to the imposture and fraud which occasionally played such an important part in some of the uncontrolled kabbalistic practices and messianic movements!

The study of the law overshadowed all other intellectual activities, the Bible itself being largely neglected. It frequently became a coöperative endeavor, when entire congregations assigned to their members the various tracts of the Talmud, so that the entire work could be completed within a year. Shneur Zalman enthusiastically proclaimed this form of adult education as the duty of every congregation in Israel. The talmudic regulation that everyone devote one-third of his time to the study of the Bible, and two-thirds to that of the Mishnah and Talmud, was generally disregarded. The rabbis strained their ingenuity to explain away this educational requirement. Meir Halevi said:

The minds of the former generations were more open, and they were able to comprehend the Mishnah and Talmud by devoting to them only two-thirds of their days, whereas we must be satisfied with our childhood recollections in regard to Scripture, and hope that the rest of our lives prove sufficient for the Mishnah and Talmud. [This statement was quoted with approval by Yeruham and Karo; cf. *Tur, Y.D.* 246.]

On the other hand, Jacob Tam simply reiterated the ancient equivocation of Natronai Gaon and others, that the Babylonian Talmud, containing such a mixture of biblical, mishnaic and talmudic elements, is a satisfactory substitute for all required readings. The result was that a seventeenth-century Frankfort author could write, without too much exaggeration, that in his day there were many rabbis who had never seen the Bible (S. Assaf, *Mekorot le-toledot ha-hinnuk,* I, 80). No wonder German rabbis knew so little Hebrew, and were extremely clumsy in confiding to writing the "depth of their ideas." In some countries, such as Italy, the burning of the Talmud left more time for the study of the Bible and grammar. But even there and in Spain, the study of the law was paramount. Adret could find no fuller justification for a Jewish judiciary than the additional stimulus it gave to the study of the civil and criminal aspects of talmudic jurisprudence. A characteristic inversion, indeed! Not law for the sake of justice, but justice for the sake of law! Similarly, economic endeavor was frequently justified on the ground that otherwise "one would become impoverished and unable to study the Torah" (Mordecai Yafeh, *Lebush ha-tekelet*, 156,1).[14]

WESTERN SCHOLASTICISM

Though the Halakah was the chief interest of the Jews, it was not their only one. The Mediterranean countries, with their greater largesse of life, invited all to broader avenues of thought. As usual the wealthier strata of society tried to formulate religion through rationalistic philosophy, on the one hand, and through mysticism on the other. In the fourteenth century Jewish scholasticism had another period of efflorescence in Spain and southern France, before suddenly vanishing as a motivating force. It was increasingly replaced by the mystic lore of the Kabbalah.

Jewish rationalist philosophy in Christian lands was essentially a hangover from the Islamic period. Scholasticism certainly filled a need among the Jews under the domination of Islam, as it did generally in Arabic and Christian life; but this was much less so in the case of European Jewry. Had it not been for the impact of Judeo-Arabic philosophy, it appears, even Spanish and Provençal Jewry would never have created anything but at best pale imitations of contemporary Christian thought. Indeed, in Ashkenazic Jewish circles, the examples of Albertus Magnus, Duns Scotus and Ockham had hardly any repercussions.

While the Arabs dominated the peninsula, the Jews, even in the Christian parts (Halevi, for example), wrote their philosophy in Arabic. Later Spanish and French Jewry had to find a new medium. Latin rarely appealed to them, perhaps because it was the sacred tongue of the Church, perhaps also because so many Latin scholastic treatises owed their origin to an Arabic or Hebrew prototype. It was only in

Italy at the height of humanism, that Elijah Delmedigo wrote philosophical treatises in that language. To satisfy the new demand, Jewish scholars, mostly with Arabic antecedents, succeeded in creating, within an amazingly short time, a new Hebrew philosophic terminology, undoubtedly an accomplishment of prime magnitude. Once more translation became the foremost vehicle of linguistic creativity. Just as the Byzantine Karaites (Tobiah, the Translator, etc.) felt the need of acquainting their Balkan brethren with some Judeo-Arabic writings in Hebrew translation, so Provençal Jewry, but to a much greater extent, transmitted in a Hebrew garb the philosophic, scientific and juridical heritage of Arabic-speaking Jewry to their European coreligionists. The Ibn Tibbon family, particularly, furnished the most eminent translators. Although at first somewhat clumsy and precise, rather than elegant, these translations were from the outset better than the early Arabic renditions from Greek and Syriac, which had been almost unintelligible to a native Arab. As fast as installments were shipped from Fustat to Provence, Samuel ibn Tibbon translated Maimonides' *Guide,* completing the work in 1204, shortly before the death of the author. Provençal Jewry commissioned the poet, Judah Alharizi, to translate Maimonides' commentary on the Mishnah, to which work the poet soon added a new version of the *Guide.* He excelled Ibn Tibbon in smoothness of style, but was far less accurate. Within a century, however, the philosophic and kabbalistic writers developed a scientific Hebrew style, which combined great elasticity with precision. It is enough to compare the original writings of Gersonides and Ibn Latif with the translations of the Tibbonides to see the rapidity of the adaptation. Those works of oriental and Spanish scholars which, for some reason or other, found no Hebrew translator, soon ceased to be living links in the literary evolution of the people.

Besides the problem of linguistic adjustment, Provençal and Spanish thinkers encountered difficulties from the growing force of antirationalism. A measure of religious skepticism and ritualistic liberalism survived the downfall of the Moors for a time. If we may believe such conservatives as Moses of Coucy and Adret, tens of thousands of Jews neglected ceremonial laws, concentrating, not on literal application, but on trying to find their inner meaning. There also arose rationalist philosophers, such as Isaac Albalag, who ventured to take over some of Averroës' radical teachings concerning the eternity of the world and the twofold truth. This compromise, ascribing independent validity to contradictory religious creeds and scientific findings, was here, as elsewhere, only a poor disguise for agnosticism. Even those who remained true to the Maimonidean tradition, tried to reconcile, in one fashion or another, the teachings of the master with the Averroist reformulation of Aristotelianism. Samuel ibn Tibbon himself assiduously translated a few minor tractates of Ibn Roshd. Shem Tob ibn Falakera and Moses Narboni commented on the *Guide* in a critical vein, the latter, especially, often giving precedence to the doctrines of the Arab thinker. He and Jacob Anatoli, who enjoyed close personal contacts with Emperor Frederick II and the Christian sages assembled at the court of Naples, were also open to the influences of Christian Averroism.

The antirationalist forces, however, were incomparably stronger. Stimulated by the Church's antiheretical reaction, many Provençal rabbis began attacking rationalist philosophy in the person of its most influential spokesman. Beginning with the sharp attacks of Meir Abulafia, Samson of Sens, and Solomon of Montpellier in the early 1200's, the anti-Maimonidean controversy presents more than one parallel to the Catholic crusade against the Albigenses, although it was fought with spiritual rather than military weapons. It was far more than dogmatic quibbling when the opponents from the outset arraigned Maimonides' emphasis upon immortality, rather than resurrection, in both the Code and the *Guide*. Although perfectly conversant with his *Commentary on the Mishnah,* where he had pronounced resurrection to be one of Judaism's foremost principles, they and even other, more impartial readers between the lines, clearly sensed the Fustat sage's underlying conviction that this doctrine is derived exclusively from revelation, and that it cannot be proved by logical demonstration. Indeed, many of his ardent admirers among the Spanish rationalists interpreted this, his reticence, as well as his outspoken contention that only the disembodied souls of the righteous will share in the world to come, as implied denials of bodily revival. Abraham Yarhi, a contemporary, relates: "when I arrived in Spain, I found people in many places who understood the words of Moses, may Peace rest upon him, to mean that their hope has turned into despair and their expectation has been frustrated, because they denied resurrection" (Higger, "Yarhi's Commentary on Kallah Rabbati," in *JQR,* XXIV, 342). Soon other elements of Maimonidean philosophy were dragged into the controversy, until the very legitimacy of Aristotelian interpretation of Judaism became the object of concentrated attacks. While the philosophically trained Spaniards, particularly Judah Alfakar, used Aristotelian weapons in combating the alleged subordination of Scripture to philosophy, the northern French rabbis more naïvely, but no less effectively, invoked the testimony of both the aggadic and the common-sense interpretation of the Bible to reject philosophic allegorization of any kind.

The battle in Provence became ever more bitter and reached its climax in the early years of the fourteenth century, when it was suddenly terminated by the expulsion of the Jews from France in 1306. Notwithstanding numerous reverses, the anti-rationalists, buttressed by the progressive deterioration in the Jews' social and legal status, won the upper hand, and the study of the *Guide* was now permitted only to men above twenty-five years of age. For a time they did not venture much further. Asheri, the German rabbi of Toledo, would have welcomed a more sweeping condemnation, since for him Torah and philosophy were "two opposites" (*Responsa* 55,9), but he had to accept the more moderate views of his Spanish colleagues. Even the latter, however, laid increased emphasis upon the Talmud as the prime source of truth. The Aggadah, whose authoritativeness had long been impugned by the geonim Sherira and Hai, now found in Adret an eloquent champion; he simply declared that each and every legend, deemed worthy of inclusion by the redactors of the Talmud, must have been based upon tradition. Even the philosopher, Hillel of Verona, could no longer reject the authenticity of the legendary records. When, for opportunist reasons, the Jewish delegates in Tortosa, as Nahmanides before them, tried to argue in favor of such rejection, they were not unjustifiedly threatened by Jerome of Santa Fé with prosecution as heretics. Undoubtedly the bulk of Jewish public opinion then and afterwards regarded such denial, if uttered without outside pressure, as a serious deviation from the highway of orthodoxy. This growing literalism brought forth the remarkable *Ketab Tamim (The Unblemished Work)* of Moses b. Hasdai Taku, a fervent anti-Maimonist, which postulated the belief in the corporeality of God as an irretrievable dogma of Judaism. Not even such German mystics as Eleazar of Worms, however, dared go to such an extreme.

More than the struggle itself and the somewhat lame fight put up by the advocates of philosophy, the speedy eclipse of Jewish rationalism in southwestern Europe was an incontrovertible sign of its inherent weakness under changed social conditions. It is truly illuminating to compare the rapid decline of Arabic and Jewish Averroism with the great strides made by this school of thought in the awakening Christian environment. Facing a disintegrating Moorish society in Spain, Averroës himself vainly offered to withdraw his doctrines, if proved to be contrary to religious dogma. He was denounced as a renegade and secret convert to Judaism, and banished from Cordova. His influence upon oriental Arabs was almost nil. Unlike their Moroccan confreres, the Muslim writers of the East, and with them Aaron of Nicomedia, the Karaite, still dealt with the dialectics of Kalam, as if Averroës and Maimonides had never lived. In Western Christendom, where Aristotelianism was more in harmony with social needs, it gained ever more adherents, despite the condemnations of the papacy and the universities of Paris and Oxford. In its older form, as Thomism, it soon became the dominant and all-embracing system of Catholic theology, and even the more radical Christian Averroism speedily developed into a major force in western thought. The contrast was so obvious that Ibn Kaspi, in 1332, dolefully complained:

Woe unto us that we have sinned! Jews despise or neglect the *Guide* nowadays, though the purpose of that treatise is to demonstrate the existence and unity of God. The Christians honor the work, study and translate it, while even greater attention is paid to it by the Mohammedans in Fez and other countries, where they have established Colleges for the study of the *Guide* under Jewish scholars. [I. Abrahams, *Wills,* p. 154.]

In the Jewish West, Gersonides is the last great representative of medieval Aristotelianism. Following in Averroës' footsteps, he even attacked his Jewish predecessors for their belief in God's knowledge of particulars. His own reconciliation of the dogma of God's knowledge of universals only with that of God's omniscience, was achieved through the desperate expedient of holding that particulars, being contingent, cannot be known by God. This was the most daring view expressed on the subject, among the leading medieval Jewish scholastics. If such radical philosophy were to stand on the basis of Judaism, it had to rationalize away most supernatural elements—as when Gersonides gave a decidedly naturalistic bent to the doctrines of providence, miracles and prophecy—or else to transfer more and more beliefs from the province of reason to the province of faith, a hazardous escape, indeed. No wonder that, notwithstanding Gersonides' great reputation as a Bible commentator and scientist, his standard work, *The Wars of the Lord,* was more and more widely classified as a book of wars *against* the Lord.

The more orthodox Crescas is the truer representative of Jewish philosophy in Christian lands. A distinguished man of affairs, he held his finger on the pulse of his time. If he became a philosopher at all, it was not, as had been the case with the leading thinkers from Saadia to Maimonides, to combat rationalistic skeptics and win them back to religion. It was because he feared that the inroads of Greek thought might lead to apostasy in the direction of the ruling faith. Just as he had courageously written (in the troubled years after 1391) a Spanish polemical treatise against Christianity, based on the accepted philosophical arguments of the day, so he attacked Jewish Aristotelianism with pungent Aristotelian weapons.

Since the reliance upon the words of the Greek [Aristotle] and his logical demonstrations is the mainspring of error and confusion, I have deemed it proper to point out the fallacy of his demonstrations and the delusion of his arguments also with respect to those which the master [Maimonides] derived from him. It will be shown on this day before the eyes of the nations that it is the Torah alone which removes confusion in matters of creed and which illumines the darkness. [*Or Adonai,* Intro.]

Although acting under this somewhat extraneous impulse, Crescas became the most penetrating philosophic critic of Aristotle in his day. That this critique, springing from a fertile mind, led him to new philosophical ideas, was an incidental gain of prime importance. Indeed in him may be found the first adumbration of a philosophic reformulation of spatial infinity, destined to become such an integral element in the modern outlook. His conception of time, although partly deriving from ancient sources (Plotinus), is likewise more modern than was the prevalent scholastic view. Abraham bar Hiyya had already shown dissatisfaction with the Aristotelian theory that, since time is merely the function of motion in space, one must believe that, like space itself, it was created by God, and thus reconcile scientific cognition with religion. Bar Hiyya's answer was that time possesses no objective entity, but "exists only in the consciousness of man" (*Megillat ha-Megaleh,* VI,23). Crescas, in direct opposition to Aristotle, evolved the theory of time as equivalent to indefinite duration, thus making it independent of space and not subject to creation. Perhaps the most remarkable among his numerous other teachings was his insistence upon the restriction of the immortality of the soul to those who fear and love God, the love of God being one of the keynotes of his entire work. His equally revolutionary doctrine of matter as the universal substance, possessing without form actuality, and not merely potentiality, and his remarkable paraphrase of the aggadic saying that God is "the place of the world," brought him perilously near to both pantheism and affirmation of God's corporeality. But he was too much of an ethical monotheist, emphasizing particularly the elements of love and will, to accept the former; and too much of a philosopher to share, in any fashion whatever, Moses Taku's palpably materialistic conception of the divine.

In his immediate disciple, Albo, he found a popularizing rather than original follower, for whom the defense against Christian polemists became an even more outspoken issue. His teachings were to reach their highest fruition only through a much more remote disciple. The genius of Spinoza, who, shifting in his early years from Maimonides to Crescas, soon combined the methods and findings of the medieval Jewish schoolman with the teachings of Leone Ebreo, Giordano Bruno, Descartes and others, succeeded in building a system of metaphysics and ethics which has had lasting influence upon western thought. In many ways Spinoza represents the culmination of medieval Jewish philosophy, while being among the pioneers of general modern philosophy. His attempt to identify God with nature, and to explain ethics through physics was, in one sense, a negation; in another, however, it was the necessary consequence of Jewish scholasticism. As it appeared, combined with a most radical criticism of the Bible and of Jewish religious institutions, it proved to be too much even for the Sephardic community of Amsterdam, which excommunicated him, while the Jewries of Germany, Poland and Turkey ignored him completely.

The political security and economic affluence of sixteenth-century Polish Jewry undoubtedly created temporary conditions which were favorable to an awakening of philosophical interests. Indeed an opponent, such as Solomon Luria, contended that he had found Aristotelian letters in the very prayer books of young students. He also reprimanded Isserles for his numerous citations from the works of the scholastics. But separated from the living stream of contemporary European thought, speaking the language of another age and society, the few philosophically minded Jews of Poland became typical epigoni. Moreover, the new stimuli, perhaps the stirrings of a new consciousness, as well as their social background, vanished rapidly in the rougher atmosphere of the Chmielnicki era.[15]

KABBALAH

European Jewry had more interest in, and made more notable contributions to, mystic philosophy. Jewish mysticism, the Kabbalah, was largely of ancient origin and was always close to Graeco-Oriental gnosticism, Neoplatonism and Islamic mysticism. It reached its highest degree of achievement, however, in medieval Europe and among the Spanish refugee communities in the East. There we find its two classical periods: the thirteenth century, beginning with the Provençal "father of the Kabbalah," Isaac the Blind, and culminating in the publication of the Zohar; and the sixteenth century, especially in the memorable Safed circle of Isaac Luria and Moses Cordovero. No wonder that the radiating light of these two great periods has largely obscured the previous history of Jewish mysticism, and that new contacts were soon established with the occult western trends.

The name Kabbalah means tradition. Zunz's well-known animadversion that "curiously the name was given to a science in which everything was young and new and in which every author transmitted only his own ideas" (*Die gottesdienstlichen Vorträge,* pp. 403 f.), largely reflects the antikabbalistic bias which dominated Jewish historiography in the nineteenth century. To be sure, the individual had a great deal of liberty. Nowhere in the Halakah could one find a statement like that of the author of the classical *Maareket ha-Elohut,* (*Order* [or *Battlefield*] *of the Deity,* usually ascribed to Todros Abulafia or Peres ha-Kohen) concerning his theory of *sephirot:* "I know very well that not all the kabbalistic sages acknowledge what I have written, but I have found no other way to explain these matters, in which all the experts have hitherto built upon castles in the air." Mystic experience is essentially ultrapersonal, and only the powerful impact of history upon the Jewish mind forced these extreme individualists to contend that their ideas were part and parcel of a continuous line of "tradition." For many centuries they had avoided publishing works under their own name, rightly fearing that they would soon be accused of heretical innovation. Little wonder that uncritical readers, impressed by these books, readily ascribed them to one or another eminent figure of the ancient world. Numerous apocryphal and pseudepigraphic writings found their way into the ever-growing circles of pious men (as, for example, during the Second Commonwealth) notwithstanding the protests of even sympathetic outsiders, such as Saadia. The *Book of Creation,* the classic-work of pre-Islamic Jewish mysticism, came to be generally ascribed to Abraham the Patriarch. Outdoing the ancient believers in the authenticity of the Book of Enoch, their medieval successors gloried in the possession of a series of works written by Adam, Seth and Noah. It is worth noting that the first kabbalist definitely known by name is Aaron of Bagdad, who, in the ninth century, transplanted the mystic lore of the East to Italy. Such anonymity and, even later, the great restraint practiced in making public personal mystic experiences, offer a striking contrast to the frequently over-communicative, if not tiringly loquacious, self-revelatory mystics of the other medieval nations, Christian as well as Muslim.

For over a millennium Kabbalah (the designation itself emerged in the thirteenth century) voluntarily restricted its appeal to a select group of the initiated. Occasionally we find them gathering in small conventicles. The talmudic injunctions against public instruction in matters of cosmogony and of Ezekiel's vision of the *Merkabah* (chariot) imposed a high degree of self-control. But from the thirteenth century on, the trend was reversed and there began a conscious process of propagating kabbalistic tenets among the mass of Hebrew readers. Even the theory of "left emanation," explaining the origin and power of evil, long kept in strict secrecy, was divulged to the Spanish-Provençal reading public in a special treatise under this title, by Isaac b. Jacob ha-Kohen (recently made accessible by G. Scholem in *Tarbiz,* II-V). Nevertheless, constant supervision by communal authorities maintained the unity of Judaism.

The bonds of unity were strengthened through the positive relation of the Kabbalah to the Halakah. True, whenever antinomian tendencies came to the fore, the Kabbalah furnished elaborate arguments for the superiority of spirit over action. In such extreme cases as Shabbetianism and Frankism, they resulted in apostasy from Judaism. The considerably milder opposition to strict legal observance, which was at times fairly widespread in southwestern Jewry, often took refuge behind the elasticity of kabbalistic allegory. The Zohar's attack upon the literal interpretation of Scripture was a ready rationale for the disregard of certain traditional commandments.

Said R. Simon: doomed is the man who says the Torah intends to reveal only simple stories and words of the man of the street. If that were the case we should be able, even today, to produce with ordinary words a Torah of higher quality. . . . But all words in the Torah are superior words and superior mysteries. [Behaalotka, 152 a.]

Abraham Abulafia haughtily dismissed the argument: "the words of the Torah in their ordinary sense are destined for people of crude intellect, but to those familiar with the secret lore (*yode hen*) it is given to detect, through the various combinations of the letters in the Torah, the mysteries of the sublime." The fourteenth-century author of *Peliah* and *Kanah* (cf. Horodezky, *Hatekufah,* X, 283-329), indeed, voiced overt antihalakic sentiments. The most authoritative writers, however, were anything but antinomian. Here and there the Zohar may indulge in witticism at the expense of the rabbis; the author of one fragment, *Raya Mehemna* (*The True Shepherd*), may try to modify some old and introduce a few new ceremonies. In essence, however, not only the ceremonial law, as such, but the actual Halakah as a whole retained full force. Its nonritualistic elements, and especially its civil and criminal law, were left unchanged. Only the strictly cultic sections of the law underwent minor adjustments.

The opposition of leading rabbis to the Kabbalah was reciprocally rather half-hearted from the outset. Saadia's rationalism, for example, was so little militant that subsequent mystics, invoking the testimony of his well-known commentary on the *Book of Creation,* regarded him as one of their spiritual fathers. During the great kabbalistic expansion in Spain and Provence, some halakic leaders were benevolently neutral, others positively friendly. To be sure, about 1240, Meir ben Simon of Narbonne, in a book entitled *War for Religion,* sharply attacked the then most prominent kabbalistic work, the *Book Bahir.* "We have found in it," he declared, "that they ascribe it to Nehoniah ben ha-Kanah, whereas the language of the book and its content prove that it was written by a man with no proper command of Hebrew and that it contains heretical and atheistic statements in many passages" (*MGWJ,* XXX, 299). Therefore, with the alleged support of Meshullam ben Moses, he exhorted his readers to search for such books and to extirpate them from the earth. But, like the most rabid anti-Maimonists of southern France, he seems to have been seized by the intolerant spirit of the Catholic crusaders against the Catharists, whose teachings, strongly permeated with Manichean elements, showed far-reaching affinities with the kabbalistic remnants of the ancient Jewish gnosis. As the Kabbalah, after a few decades, turned out to be the most successful competitor of rationalist philosophy, the rabbis became ever more approving in considering the mentality of those who did not find complete satisfaction in the broad but uniform road of the Halakah. On the other hand, in the process of transformation into a mass movement, the Kabbalah divested itself of many heretical ingredients, conceived in the uncontrolled obscurity of the conventicles, and compromised with the overwhelming force of halakic tradition. Apparently through a curious self-censorship, the kabbalists eliminated from their texts of the *Bahir* all passages found objectionable by their opponent of Narbonne.

Beginning in the days of Nahmanides and his disciple Adret, even the leading halakists became kabbalists of higher or lower order. The impact of the Kabbalah, especially upon the Spanish rabbis, is perhaps best illustrated by the case of Joseph Karo. By nature his was a legal mind, pure and simple, but under the prevalent fashion he too had to profess belief in the superior value of the Kabbalah. The contrast between his intrinsic indifference to the teachings of the great Isaac Luria, during whose memorable discourses he is said to have fallen asleep, and his enthusiastic acceptance of the leadership of Solomon Molko, the much younger and much more superficial though brilliant preacher, exemplifies the irresistible trend of the age. Under its influence, he even believed throughout his life that he heard an inner voice dictating his actions to him. Once, for example, he decided after prolonged reflection to go to Salonica, but when his inner *maggid* commanded him to proceed to Palestine, he unhesitatingly obeyed. His book, *Maggid mesharim* (*The Righteous Preacher*), reporting these inner voices in their chronological sequence, constitutes one of the most remarkable diaries in the history of letters. Nevertheless, in his halakic work he is a very sober jurist. In his entire Code he yielded to the authority of the Zohar on only a few insignificant modifications of talmudic law. Although few doubted the revealed character of the main documents of the Kabbalah, or even that they had been composed in the tannaitic period or earlier, the supremacy of the Talmud in the field of Halakah remained uncontested throughout the ages. Isserles, for example, firmly believed that "the words of the Zohar were given on Sinai"; but argued that, since the accepted author of the book in its present form is R. Simon b. Yohai, his legal opinions have no greater claim to acceptance than those ascribed to him in the tannaitic literature. There they are frequently overruled in favor of those advanced by R. Judah. In fact, even the halakic regulations of the medieval jurists were accepted by Isserles and others as more binding in practice than "the mysteries of the Zohar." Neither did the kabbalists ever impugn the Jewishness of those who devoted themselves to the study of the Halakah alone. At most, they comforted themselves with the hope that "he who had not busied himself with the orchard will come back to it in another life" (Isaac b. Solomon Luria's *Shulhan Aruk*, No. 18).

While the ever-rejuvenated force of the Halakah imposed compromises on the kabbalists, the decadence of scholastic philosophy encouraged the mystics in their attack on rationalist thinking. At first the influence of scholasticism was felt strongly. In fact, the contribution of the first classical period (thirteenth century) consisted primarily, as G. Scholem says, in "transplanting the Kabbalah from the world of the gnosis into that of Neoplatonism, and in the attempt to unite the old currents, flowing vividly in the channels of mythology, with the totally divergent ones of scholasticism" (*KA*, IX,18). Not only must we regard Gabirol as a fountainhead of classical Kabbalah (incidentally also of much medieval Christian mysticism, e.g., that of Eckhart), but even Maimonides deeply impressed the early mystic thinkers. "We are his disciples to the extent of our limited capacity," wrote Isaac ha-Kohen from the very center of the anti-Maimonists, Provence (Scholem, in *Tarbiz*, II,194). Similar affirmations were frequently heard in that Provençal circle, from the time of Todros Abulafia to that of Isaac b. Sheshet. To some, the great rationalist appeared little short of a mystic in disguise. Abraham Abulafia's "Guide to the Guide" (more correctly called *The Mysteries of the Torah;* cf. Steinschneider, *Die hebräischen Handschriften . . . München*, No. 341/7) is but a comment upon Maimonides' work in a kabbalistic vein. Shem Tob b. Abraham, an enthusiastic exegete of Maimonides' Code, could not refrain from saying that he had seen in Spain an ancient parchment which read: "I, Moses ben Maimon, when I descended into the secret chambers of the Merkabah, meditated on the problem of the last things" (*Migdal oz* on Mishneh Torah Yesode ha-Torah, I,10).

Soon, however, with the growth of antirationalist forces, most kabbalists rejected Maimonides and all scholasticism. With Nahmanides, the antiphilosophical reaction received the stamp of approval from a revered rabbinical authority. For example, the scapegoat prescribed in the Pentateuch had appeared to medieval thinkers as an obnoxious heathen custom. Ibn Ezra, who sojourned for long in the nonphilosophical northern communities, in explaining this passage, merely dared to hint at the abolition of this custom by the subsequent, more purified, monotheistic doctrine. This attempt at higher biblical criticism provoked a sharp reply from the Gerona rabbi.

I shall not be able to explain it [he finally admitted, however] because we would have first to shut the mouths of those naturalistic casuists who follow the Greek [Aristotle] in his denial of everything that is not perceived by the senses. He, and his wicked disciples following him, had the temerity to believe that whatever he cannot conceive through his reason is not true. [*Commentary* on Lev. 16:8.]

Notwithstanding the continued use of philosophical terminology, such as the *illat ha-illot* (the cause of causes), even by the Zohar, it became quite customary for a kabbalist to look down upon philosophy. One of the most violent arraignments of scholasticism can be found in the kabbalistic works of Shem Tob ibn Shem Tob (*ca.* 1400). Notwithstanding the considerably friendlier attitude of his son Joseph, who, in his *Kebod Elohim* (*The Glory of God*), spoke regretfully of his father's unreasoning hatred; and of his grandson, Shem Tob, who even wrote a new commentary on the *Guide,* scholasticism totally lost its hold upon the mystic minds of subsequent generations.

With the exception of a few semirationalists, such as Moses Cordovero, who contended that "in metaphysical matters the true masters of Kabbalah are frequently in agreement with the philosophers," but added the significant reservation: "nevertheless their way is not our way" (*Elimah Rabbati,* I,16), later kabbalists joined with the majority of halakists in rejecting scholasticism, on the ground of its alien character and origin. To be sure, it has become customary in modern times to detect in the Kabbalah itself ever more foreign ingredients. To each and every mystic current encountered by Judaism in its march through history—from the ancient Babylonian astral cults, Persian angelology and Indian transmigration of souls, to the Trinitarian principle of the Christian gnosis, the magic beliefs and practices of the ancient mystery religions, the numerical symbolism of Neopythagoreanism and the emanationist doctrines of Neoplatonism and Islamic Sufism—there has been attributed some influence upon its secret lore. Even in the Middle Ages some scholastic opponents of the Kabbalah, referring to the doctrine of *Sephirot,* contended that "the Christians believe in Trinity, the kabbalists believe in ten-in-oneness" (Isaac bar Sheshet's *Responsa*, No. 157). In the modern period, the partisan bias of most western Jewish scholars was greatly enhanced by the strong impression made by the Kabbalah upon the Christian mystics. Although Pico della Mirandola's pronunciamento that there is no science which can more firmly convince us of the divinity of Christ than magic and Kabbalah, provoked the anger of the Church, it necessarily increased the suspicions of Jewish critics ever since the time of Leon of Modena. Even those who, on apologetical grounds, were wont to point with pride to this distinguished Florentine Hebraist, the initiator of Latin translations of Recanati's Bible commentary and other kabbalistic works, contended that Jewish mysticism was directly dependent upon Christian prototypes.

It is, however, precisely in the field of occult and mystic sciences that similarity of ideas is in itself no evidence of common derivation. Outwardly, to say the least, the Kabbalah belongs to the most Jewish expressions of the Jewish spirit. Almost all its works are written either in Hebrew or in Judeo-Aramaic. The use of Aramaic by many European writers and liturgical poets was obviously a survival of preclassical Kabbalah. It had so widely prevailed in the pseudepigraphic writings of the semignostic conventicles in twelfth and thirteenth-century Provence that the authors of many Zohar fragments merely followed an already well-established trend, regardless of their own, often imperfect, command of that medium. This extraordinary conscious archaization was rationalized and artificially prolonged on the basis of the talmudic legend concerning the angels' unfamiliarity with Aramaic. A belated Arabic work of Ibn Wakar, a North African kabbalist of the fourteenth century, is truly an exception which proves the rule. Methodically, too, the Kabbalah, although wholly dependent upon the allegorical interpretation of Scripture, differed greatly from the Philonic and patristic exegesis, inasmuch as it allegorized exclusively the original Hebrew text. The *Book of Creation* had already erected many a speculative structure upon the twenty-two letters of the Hebrew alphabet, and their nexus with the five organs of speech. The Zohar and all subsequent writers utilized extensively the rules of Hebrew grammar and certain abnormalities in biblical language, for purposes of mystic allegorization. The chief means were the *gematria* and *notarikon,* which, although evidently taken over from the Greeks, were applied by the Jews with greater zest and mastery. Jacob ben Asher, for example, wrote a commentary on the entire Pentateuch, explaining the esoteric meaning of most passages through an extremely ingenious combination of the numerical value of the Hebrew letters contained in them.

The Jewish character of the Kabbalah is evident also in its teachings. Rarely did kabbalists pride themselves on being the recipients of direct revelation. They went no further than Joseph bar Judah Gaon's public reference to the appearance of the Prophet Elijah in the presence of his friends and disciples, and Jacob Halevi's publication of a collection called "Responsa from Heaven." The following introductory remark of an enthusiastic adherent, found in a manuscript of this work, describes the author's communion with God:

And such was his way all the time that whenever he was in doubt concerning a legal problem, he ordered the doors of his study shut, and then God appeared to him in a vision and all his doubts were resolved. This is a matter of common knowledge that he knows and sees nothing and does not wake up until they place a certain thing at the study door, whereupon he instantly awakes from his slumber. [A. Marx, "A New Collection of Manuscripts," *PAAJR,* IV, 153.]

The overwhelming power of tradition, which ascribed direct communication with God to Moses alone among men; and which agreed that later Israelitic prophecy, enabling a few chosen individuals to penetrate at least the secondary world of the "chariot," had also come to an end; prevented even the convinced kabbalist, after his mystic union with God, from claiming to have been in the divine presence itself. An intermediary had to be invoked. Even Abraham Abulafia, the most self-assertive of kabbalists, was satisfied with a hazy: "The Lord of all things revealed himself to me, divulged to me his secret, and let me know the end of the exile and the date of the beginning of the redemption" (in Jellinek's *Ginze hokmat ha-Kabbalah,* p. 18). Equally Jewish are the other kabbalistic doctrines. Undoubtedly, the fundamental principles of all esoteric philosophies are strikingly analogous. Having its own logic and mode of thinking, mysticism naturally operates similarly through the minds of all mystics. On the other hand, the highly personal nature of the mystic experience lends great variety to all its manifestations, so that it is very difficult to generalize the teachings of any school of esoteric thought. One can, nevertheless, perceive that the Kabbalah uniformly believes in the election of Israel, the eternal validity of the Torah and of all its commandments, and in the coming of the Messiah. It accentuates these fundamentals of Judaism by ascribing to them cosmic, rather than human or Jewish, significance. That these Jewish teachings are imbedded in a peculiar system of metaphysics, physics, anthropology and psychology, detracts from their Jewish character no more than Halevi's, Heller's or Elijah Gaon's metaphysical and psychological speculations compromise the Jewishness of their world outlook.

The force of Jewish tradition militated against extreme pantheism, so prevalent in other mystic currents. Expressions such as Hallaj's "I am God," or that of Angelus Silesius, "I am as great as God, He is like me so small," can hardly be duplicated in kabbalistic literature. Its prevailing, panentheistic opinion was to regard the universe as identical with God, but not God as identical with the universe. Like other mysticisms, however, the Kabbalah so stressed God's all-inclusiveness that there remained no positive differentia to distinguish his essence from other entities. God can be perceived by man only through a system of "negative theology." He is the *Eyn Sof* (the Infinite). Although, according to G. Scholem, this term occurs no more than fifteen times in the original sections of the Zohar, it belonged to the most popular of the later kabbalistic letters. The Neoplatonic doctrine of emanation, combined in the sixteenth century with the Lurianic concept of contraction (*simsum*), explained how there evolved from this Infinite, first the primordial nothing (*Ayin*), and finally the world of the *Sephirot*. To quote Hayyim b. Joseph Vital, chief representative of that post-Lurianic synthesis:

As long as the world was not created, He and his great name, the "Eyn Sof," filled the entire universe, and there was no empty space for the erection of the worlds, because the emanent light extended *ad infinitum*. That is why when God willed to emanate the emanations . . . He contracted himself in the middle of his light . . . and there remained a vacuum in between . . . until finally the world of emanation and all the other worlds found themselves placed in this vacuum, while the light of "Eyn Sof" surrounds them on all sides. [*Oserot Hayyim*, beginning.]

The light must not be regarded, however, as identical with God, as it appears in many mystic philosophies. Perhaps warned by Ibn Zaddik's determined stand against such identification, which he regarded as sheer anthropomorphism, the authors of the Zohar and the later kabbalists clearly distinguished between God and the primordial light created by him. Many minor thinkers relapsed into such pantheistic identification, however, and occasionally even the more important writers used loose expressions.

Enormous importance was attached by the kabbalists to emanation through a process of generation by the male and female principles. The system of the ten Sephirot, fundamental for the entire kabbalistic doctrine of emanation since the *Book of Creation,* was built upon such successive generations from the male and female elements into a synthesis of both, which again parts into the two sexes to generate a new combination. The Sephirot were regarded variously: by David b. Judah Messer Leon, as identical with God's substance; by Menahem Recanati, as mere instruments of the Divine; and finally by Moses Cordovero, as an amalgam of substance and instrumentality. In any case, they filled the being of the universe, and became the objects of prayerful adoration, as in the hymn of Moses ben Isaac Alashkar:

> They are ten, inseparably welded,
> The likeness of a sapphire ten-hued,
> They are one, all children of one father
> As fire blends with the coal it subdued.
> [Prayer, beginning *Adon hakol.*]

Toward the end of the Middle Ages, this system of Sephirot was increasingly expanded to include four "worlds," a concept which, owing to the space-time combination in the Hebrew word *olam,* long oscillated between the Neoplatonic ontological idea of impersonal *kosmoi* and the gnostic mythological doctrine of personified *aeona*. The two lines of thought were finally synthesized; and the fourteenth-century kabbalist, Isaac of Acco, dealt with the four worlds as with a well-known mystic entity, already using for them the abbreviation *Abia*. Those four worlds of emanation, creation, formation, and creative matter, constantly repeat the eternal bisexual generation of the Sephirot, on successively lower, more materialistic levels. The school of Luria explained the progressive materialization and deterioration by the increasing refraction of the light through the so-called "breaking of vessels." At the end of this process is the wretchedly imperfect sublunary world. While retaining the Ptolemaic cosmography, the kabbalists had many remarkable mystic intuitions of physical realities. For example, R. Hamnuna's statement: "the entire world rotates like a ball" (Zohar Vayikra, III, 10 a), if not the survival of a gnostic undercurrent from pre-Ptolemaic days, shows an extraordinary insight.

It was only natural that, with the acceptance of a cosmic bisexual generation, the mystic Triad should impose itself upon the kabbalistic mind, as it did upon so many other mystic currents in the world. Deterred by Christian Trinitarianism, however, the leading kabbalists tried to avoid this consequence by immediately enlarging the number to four. For example, the Sephirah *Binah* lends itself easily to an esoteric identification with Ben (son) and YH (YA). The Zohar, however, immediately adds to it its synonym *Tebunah,* which can be presented as standing for Ben, Bat (daughter) and WH, which supplements the previous YH to make a complete tetragrammaton. The obnoxious "Bar" in "Kiss the Son" (Psalms 2:12) is explained by the author of the *Tikkune ha-Zohar* as meaning the one who is "outside," and as referring to a righteous man who is exiled from his place.

In contrast to many other mystics, the kabbalists were led by the grandeur of the universal Eros to a most emphatic affirmation of human sex. Prompted by the principle of procreation, integral to an ethnic religion, the authors of the Zohar, and their successors, condemned celibacy and the celibate as harshly as the Halakah or Aggadah. To Moses alone they conceded the distinction that, because of his abstinence from women during the crucial days of Sinai, he achieved a mystic union with God unparalleled by any other mortal. Permanent abstention, however, would have been sinful. Friday evening having long been acknowledged as the time of divine and earthly love, its services were permeated with mystic eroticism by reading of the Song of Songs, excerpts from the Zohar (e.g., *Kegavna,* in section on Terumah, f. 135), prayers and table songs especially composed by kabbalistic poets. The Sabbath, the divine bride herself, was exalted in many poems, and Solomon ben Moses Alkabis' *Leka Dodi*

(*Come My Beloved*) soon became the climax of the orthodox service. Earthly love, sometimes even sinful love, was thus elevated by the Kabbalah into the realm of cosmic events. Nowhere do we find a kabbalist half cynically explaining, as did Ibn Arabi, "If I use the language of love to explain lofty thoughts concerning spiritual mysteries and the teachings of philosophy and ethics, it is because men are prone to dally with such amorous fancies and are the more readily attracted to the subject of my songs" (quoted by Bension, *The Zohar*, p. 45). For the Jewish mystics, the universe is out of order when a man and a woman, given each other by divine decree before their birth, are not united. Eventually they must meet, even at the price of sin—the secret of David and Bathsheba. One can only gauge the grandeur of this concept, when one considers the Kabbalah's basically ascetic outlook. But extreme sanctification, through helping maintain Israel and the world, this is the paradoxical watchword of a trend of thought where, alone in medieval Judaism, the magnificent combination of the prophetic ideas of holiness and sanctification with those of Israel's chosenness had been restored to their pristine purity.

The Kabbalah would, indeed, not have been truly Jewish, had it remained a speculative theology. Ibn Chikitilla, Ibn Latif and Cordovero, the philosophers among the kabbalists, were to a large extent activistic, rather than purely speculative, mystics. The writers of the Zohar fragments and Luria always kept in the forefront of their mystic contemplation the actions of man. Not only the active love of God, but even the passive fear of God, means for them good actions or the abstention from bad. Even to their purely metaphysical teachings they give an ethical turn, as when, for instance, Moses de Leon draws a parallel between the three "worlds" and the ethical values of thought, speech and deed. The Zohar tirelessly reiterates the constant interplay of the upper and lower worlds, and ascribes to each and every action of man and, especially, of the Jew, a direct influence upon the divine government of the universe. That is why kabbalist psychology, with its various degrees of souls (the highest, the *Neshamah,* dependent on the Sephirah *Binah,* being "an entity more subtle and spiritual than the angels" [Cordovero, *Pardes*, Chap. 31]), is so profoundly oriented toward the commandments of Judaism. The mystic concept of a "Treasury of Souls," from which hail both just and wicked souls; the idea that just souls sometimes "impregnate" a weak soul, and support it in its struggle against sin; the belief in transmigration of souls—all offer a new rationale for traditional Jewish law and ethics. The metempsychosis, long accepted by the early mystics, and the book *Bahir,* although unanimously rejected by scholasticism from the time of Saadia down and hotly debated throughout the Middle Ages, became ever more firmly rooted in the "system" of the Kabbalah, as it was integrated in the Jewish view of punishment and reward. Little wonder that the "practical" Kabbalah, with its magic rites, amulets, incantations, exorcisms and the like, appealed so strongly, even to the best minds of the school. Not only an outspoken kabbalist such as Nahmanides, but a mere sympathizer such as Hai Gaon, fully approved the vagaries of the practical Kabbalah, trying to forestall at most some of its patent abuses.

The fact that the most distinguished philosophers and kabbalists throughout the ages lived in Spain, southern France, Italy or the eastern Mediterranean countries, is no doubt a reflection of social conditions. Philosophy never obtained a real hold on the mind of northern Jews. Here not even the Kabbalah, which eventually penetrated the life of Ashkenazic Jewry, produced an Abulafia, a Moses de Leon, a Luria (of German descent, but living in Egypt and Palestine), a Cordovero or a Luzzatto. Isserles and Eibeschuetz left a permanent imprint on the history of the Halakah, but their contributions to kabbalistic thought were negligible, compared to those of the southerners. The only German mystic of considerable renown, Eleazar (Rokeah) of Worms, seems to have been a faithful transmitter of oriental gnosticism, rather than a creator in his own right. In the entire medieval German Kabbalah, says G. Scholem, "there is nothing of German origin, except a number of old Germanic superstitions." [16]

ETHICAL LITERATURE

Nevertheless, the religion of Ashkenazic Jewry was not merely halakic, and still less purely legalistic. In accordance with their petty-bourgeois, social outlook, and the tendencies prevailing in their immediate environment during the major part of the Middle Ages, they turned avidly to the popular ethical literature. An abundant output of sermons, commentaries on the Bible and special treatises devoted to edification rather than instruction, supplied moral philosophy for daily reading. Beginning with the twelfth-century *Book of the Pious,* the output increased steadily. Widely read, this literature, especially in the northern countries, influenced the religious outlook of ordinary Jews much more than did the more renowned scholastic or mystic works of the period. Although increasingly permeated with kabbalistic doctrines, on the whole this literature is merely a continuation of the talmudic Aggadah. Indeed, direct quotations from the sayings of the rabbis constitute an integral, sometimes a preponderant element. There were doubtless in every age Jews whose personal inclinations or mental capacities led them away from the study of the Halakah, notwithstanding its multicolored pattern. These usually turned to the aggadic portions of talmudic literature, whose study they, too, regarded as an imperative duty. Through the *piyyutim,* some of the homiletic sayings of the rabbis had even been incorporated in the liturgy. Again, the striking similarity of many phases of Persian culture to medieval folk life, and of the underlying social conditions of Babylonian Jewry to those in the medieval Ashkenazic communities, obscured the essential distinctions between those two worlds. For instance, Persian angelology and demonology, which colored some talmudic legends, found a striking counterpart in the medieval belief in spirits and witches. Even the Kabbalah, particularly in its practical and magic, and therefore more popular aspects, could thus be embodied in the dominant system of moral philosophy without causing much suspicion.

In many ways the great popularity of the ethical literature rested upon the close affinity of its appeal to that of the Halakah; both were more activist than speculative. With the exception of such a treatise as Bahya's *Duties of the Heart,* a border-line case between scholarly and popular philosophy, which contains a chapter on the unity of God, most writings of this sort are but little concerned with purely theological problems. They devote all their attention to practical behavior. Despite the reverence paid the genius of Maimonides, his thirteen principles of Judaism, which soon inspired many rhapsodists to compose liturgical poems and which were, under more than one guise, incorporated in every Jew's daily prayers, received but scant attention in moralistic literature. The homilies of both the southern and northern preachers, and even the semiphilosophical works of Jonah Gerondi, Bahya ben Asher, Al-Nakawa, Aboab, Arama and Isaiah Horowitz, rarely contained more than casual, self-evident assertions with respect to any of these fundamentals. When distinguished philosophers, such as Gabirol and Falakera, condescended to write a popular ethical treatise, they conspicuously avoided basic theologumena, and were satisfied with composing "an epistle teaching the right way" (Falakera, *Ha-Mebakesh,* Preface). Ibn Kaspi reiterates, in his *Guide to Knowledge,* his undoubtedly sincere and profound admiration for Maimonidean philosophy, but "admonishes" his son merely by stressing the ways of virtuous behavior. Still less metaphysical are, of course, Nahmanides and Asheri in their ethical wills. As to the truly popular northern homilists, such as Elijah de Vidas, Ephraim Lentshits and Zebi Hirsch Kaidanover, they could not indulge in speculations "beyond nature," even had they wished to do so. So averse was the mass of Jewry to every attempt at dogmatizing the Jewish religion!

On the other hand, the ethical literature, with its strong emphasis upon the intentions underlying human actions, counterbalanced the dangers of legalistic extremism inherent in the overwhelming power of the law. The saying of the rabbis that "sinful meditations are worse than sin itself," was a leitmotif of this literature. The following passage from a long lucubration of Israel ibn al-Nakawa, where kabbalistic anthropology is used to fortify the conviction that in every wicked thought grave dangers are inherent, may serve as a case in point:

When a man thinks of wicked and impure matters, his thought in its impurity attaches itself to the upper [worlds]. His soul thus becomes responsible to Heaven, since it makes [everything] impure by touch. But if he commits a sin below and its effect does not reach Heaven, it will rest less heavily upon him than a bad meditation which is attached to the upper [worlds] and is closely related to the "cutting down of plantations." From this point you will understand the mystery of one who entertains impure thoughts during the intercourse. [*Menorat ha-Maor,* edited by Enelow, IV, 107.]

The ethical and the legal writings were, however, not antagonistic, but complementary, forces. Together they represented a single whole of medieval rabbinic literature, a unity reminiscent of that of the Talmud itself, with its intermingling of the halakic and aggadic elements. Whenever a medieval Jew, whether Spaniard or German, Pole or Turk, was confronted by the question, which is the more important, he unhesitatingly answered, the Halakah. The Halakah was social, authoritative, disciplined; the Aggadah individual, free, uncontrolled. In view of the preponderance of the group over the individual throughout the Middle Ages, the supremacy of the Halakah was uncontested. It found its symbolic expression in communal life: the primacy of the rabbi over the preacher.[17]

On the fringe of this popular ethical literature was one which appealed to still wider masses: folk tales and folk songs in the vernacular, and especially in Yiddish. One-half of the Jewish people, the women, received practically no education beyond learning to read and write. Although a few exceptional women engaged in the pursuit of knowledge, although Glueckel of Hameln wrote an autobiography of real historical and esthetic significance, and occasionally wives of rabbis were able to discuss certain legal matters intelligently, the majority of Jewish women were nearly illiterate. Their knowledge of Hebrew being, as a rule, limited to the mumbling of prayers they did not understand, a special literature in the vernacular had to be created for them. Wherever male education was not universal, male readers swelled the ranks of the public to whom this literature appealed. More general social forces stimulated the demand for it. Even in the economically, fairly homogeneous German and Italian communities, there were groups of peddlers and journeymen in direct contact with the masses of Christian peasantry and urban workers. For them the language of the people among whom they lived was the chief medium of intellectual enjoyment, and they felt strongly the impact of local folklore and folk attitude to life.

Through the mist of the few extant records, one can sense today an eternal undercurrent of revolt against the supremacy of rabbinic theology and practice. The closer the relations of Jewish village peddlers with the peasants, the more exuberant became their desire to experience life in all its fullness.

Rabbinic law, with its emphasis on the golden mean, did not provoke any widespread resentment, but the popular ethical literature, aimed exactly at these circles, stressed too much a semi-ascetic mode of life. Eleazar of Worms' relentless insistence upon fasting (he spoke of 84 or 164 fast days as a prerequisite for the forgiveness of certain transgressions), may not have been fully shared by his successors. The observance of every Monday and Thursday as days of fasting was regarded by all as a prime virtue. Exaggerations, such as exposure of the body to ice and snow in winter and to flies, ants and bees in summer, naturally found very few followers. But one cannot lightly dismiss the fact that even the generally moderate author of the *Book of the Pious* advises the repentant adulterer in winter, "to break through the ice and remain immersed in the water up to his mouth or nose for the same period of time as that which elapsed from the inception of his flirtation to the consummation of the sin" (Section 19). The principle, moreover, that a sinner "should mortify his flesh, subdue and cleanse it . . . in order that he may live in the world to come, the true and the eternal," was generally accepted by the rabbinic teachers. Poets and preachers, kabbalistic and ethical writers, joined in singing the praises of repentance, the *teshubah*. This moderate asceticism appealed to the persecuted ghetto dwellers, but not to the Jewish farmer, where such survived, nor to working-class Jews, who retained a healthy appetite for worldly enjoyment. The endlessly reiterated moralistic exhortations made them impatient of their generally revered, but sometimes unsympathetic leaders.

In the earlier Middle Ages, western romances and legends (including the Arthurian cycle), adapted to their particular tastes, were extensively read by women and the uneducated masses in both the southern and northern countries. In thirteenth-century Germany, the more intellectual preachers of the school of Judah the Pious condemned the popularity of these books of chivalrous adventure. As a kind of compromise, a large body of Bible paraphrases, moralistic fiction and popular ethical treatises in "Yiddish," began to replace the more colorful imitations of European romance. The *Seenah u-Reenah* of Jacob ben Isaac Ashkenazi (a Yiddish paraphrase of the Pentateuch written before 1620); the anonymous *Maaseh Buch* (before 1602); and the *Bovo Buch* of the famous grammarian, Elijah Levita (a paraphrase of an Italian version of Bevis of Hampton, apparently first printed at Pesaro after 1507), are classics of that literature; they were to be found in almost every Jewish home throughout the Ashkenazic world.[18]

HASIDISM

At one point this rebellious undercurrent led to open revolt. In the Ukraine and Eastern Galicia, the number of Jews settled in villages became so large as to outnumber the urban Jewish population. It is estimated that of the Jewish population of Poland-Lithuania, one-third was concentrated in rural districts. These people lived, especially, upon the vast latifundia of the Polish aristocracy in the southeastern region, but even in sections of Lithuania and White Russia, rural Jewry rivaled in size that of the towns. For the first time in many centuries, an imposing section of the people lived, generation after generation, in direct contact with nature and with those close to nature. Although the livelihood of most of these Jews was derived from tax farming, the liquor trade and money lending, their attachment to the soil and their intimacy with the earth-bound peasantry far exceeded those of any other medieval Jewish group. The revolt of these masses, long slumbering under the surface, finally broke out in the form of a religious revival called Hasidism.

Hasidism is, most of all, the rebellion of the half-illiterate rural Jew against the supremacy of the learned urban Jew. Too long had the "village Jew" accepted a position of inferiority. Even in the synagogue he was subjected to ridicule and contempt whenever he came to town for the high holidays. To penetrate the walls of social prejudice he had to be extremely wealthy, to make large charitable and educational contributions, and to acquire as a son-in-law a promising poor scholar. In western Poland and Lithuania, the compact, organized, intellectually alert urban majority forced him to bow his head to the overwhelming power of rabbinism. In the extensive rural possessions of the Polish landlords in the southeast, however, he was more independent. Even the little towns were under the lash of a landlord, who ruled the whole area like an absolute sovereign. The subjection of the Jewish community to the whims of the lord and of his Jewish or Christian administrators; the relative scarcity of large urban settlements; the climatic, social and spiritual influences, emanating from generations of life on the soil, all these inspired in the rural Jew greater confidence to assert his own philosophy of life publicly. He was also for centuries exposed to the influences of the Greek Orthodox (or Graeco-Catholic) environment, with its outspoken contempt of learning as the mark of intellectual haughtiness, and its glorification of good deeds performed out of humble, blissful ignorance. The breakdown of centralized Jewish self-government in 1764, when the Council of the Four Lands was disbanded, and the partitions of Poland soon thereafter, still further weakened the influence of the rabbinical centers on the peripheral settlements, thus greatly facilitating the expansion of Hasidism. Folklore, reaching back to ancient Palestine, soon intensified by a popular adaptation of the Kabbalah and Jewish ethics, molded during the later centuries the ideology of this Jewish religiosocial movement, one of the profoundest in the recent religious history of mankind.

Hasidism had in Israel Baal Shem Tob (Besht) a great religious genius. As with all great religious founders, popular fancy has overlaid the few truly historical reminiscences, to form an indistinguishable whole of hasidic legend. Story telling, which until that time had been a surreptitious indulgence, was now sanctioned as a meritorious deed. A Hasid of Bratslav, even today, prays for the ability to tell stories of the righteous men and their wonders "in such a fashion that I may deserve to attract to me their great holiness and that I shall be enabled thereby to purify my thought from all confusion and chaotic knowledge and from all sorts of queer and strange ideas" (Nathan of Niemirow's *Likkute tefillot,* No. 105). Old legendary motifs, often of a positively Christological character, combined with local Ukrainian folklore to make the Besht a mythological figure of cosmic dimensions. The famous collection *Shibhe ha-Besht (Excellencies of the Besht),* first published in 1815, contains an amazing assemblage of legends which cropped up during the decades after the founder's death. Here are remarkable analogies to Gospel mythology. We learn, for example, that the Besht associated only with villagers and suspicious characters, and that a sinful woman, having been saved by him from the revenge of her brothers, repented and became righteous. More significant, we read that, although for fourteen years he abstained from intercourse with his wife, during this time his son Hershele was born by the word of God. Again, a girl "became pregnant as a result of his prayer" (No. 29). Finally, he rose from the dead, and again engaged in teaching his disciples. A work by his grandson tells us how he once crossed the Dniester, a river of considerable width, simply by casting his girdle over its troubled waters; a motif which, however reminiscent of the mantle of Elisha, first became frequent in the description of miracles performed by the various hasidic masters. Here are astounding parallels to early Christian, if not to the ancient Babylonian and Iranian, mythological motifs. No wonder messianic expectations were occasionally connected with the person of the Besht, and many Hasidim still hope that at the end of days he will reveal himself as the true Messiah. All this may be a survival of ancient Palestinian folklore, or an offshoot of Christian mythology, a certain familiarity with which on the part of the village Jews in the Ukraine may be taken for granted. But in any case—even in the hasidic acceptance of an immaculate conception—Jewish monotheism was unimpaired. God is never the father of a messiah; at most the Messiah, through his prayer, can alter the order of nature and bring about the birth of an ordinary child miraculously.

Apart from independent creations of folk phantasy, a large circle of disciples has transmitted its own, more disciplined tradition. Here, too, is found an analogy to the history of Jesus. The greatest of the Besht's disciples, Ber of Meseritsh, the St. Paul of Hasidism; and Jacob Joseph of Polonoye, who was, so to speak, its foremost evangelist, both repudiated the Besht at first. Jacob Joseph, later the celebrated author of the *Toledot Jacob Joseph* (first published in 1780), is said to have long persistently rejected the advances of the renowned healer and miracle worker. He was converted suddenly, on finding his synagogue empty and the entire congregation flocking to the market place to listen to the preachment of the Besht. The Besht, like Mohammed, seems to have made a special virtue of his lack of higher education. He always underrated his own knowledge, in order to raise the dignity of the common man. He did not, however, pretend to be wholly illiterate, in order to prove the superhuman character of his writings, although he seems to have written nothing but a few epistles. Like Jesus, he was close to the people, listening to the rumblings among the Jewish masses, and gathering new impressions and new ideas, even when they were out of line with the established tradition. As Ber of Meseritsh later said, "he had taught him the language of the birds and of the trees; revealed to him the secrets of the divine Names and the professions of the unity of God; led him into the book, *Maayan ha-hokmah* [*The Source of Wisdom*], explaining to him every letter, and showed him in the Book *Raziel* the letters and the script of angels" (*Maggid debarav le-Yaakob*, Intro.).

The Hasidism of the Besht and his disciples was hardly a new philosophy of religion, although in many ways it embodied a new sectarian trend. Its ideas of God and the creation, divine government and the physical composition of the world, its anthropology and psychology, are all taken from the popular Kabbalah and earlier ethical philosophy. Were the Zohar pure speculative philosophy, it never would have obtained its supreme position in hasidic thought. Being for the most part a pure aggadic Midrash, with strong kabbalistic ingredients, it easily lent itself to popular adaptation. The Lurianic Kabbalah, with its greater emphasis upon practical and magic aspects and especially upon the "intentions" in prayer, was incorporated in hasidic doctrines with equal ease. Many kabbalistic prayers, such as the *Brik shme demare alma* (Blessed is the Name of the World's Master) of the Saturday morning services, were altogether devoid of strictly speculative elements. Taking many kabbalistic theorems for granted and amplifying or embellishing them by folkloristic similes or folk songs, the hasidic teachers established a doctrinal basis upon which they built their activist philosophy of life.

Everything that Isaac Luria, blessed be his memory, discovered [pointedly says a hasidic biographer], is in Heaven above, in the upper worlds and the upper lights, and not every brain has the capactiy of grasping things so high above. But the Besht, blessed be his memory, discovered godhead here on earth, especially in man, the earthly creature. In man there is neither a member nor a force which is not invested with power divine, this power being hidden in him as well as in all things that exist in the world of reality where there is no place void of God's presence. [*Seder ha-dorot he-hadash*, p. 7.]

To the domain of action, Hasidism brought a novel orientation. Kabbalah and popular philosophy, creations of the intellectual upper or lower bourgeoisie, preached abstinence, self-mortification and ascetic repentance. Hasidism, the revolt of the rural simpleton long familiar with hunger and destitution, sounded the keynote of joy and exaltation in both prayer and life. *Simhah* and *alisut* (joy and exuberance), frowned upon by both rationalists and mystics since the fall of Jerusalem, came into their own. Said Menahem Mendel of Vitebsk:

Rejoice that you have the opportunity to sing unto God. Rejoice that you are a Jew. Rejoice that you are able to pray, to study and to perform God's will. Before the endlessness of God, the highest saint and the lowliest commoner are equal. Be contented with your achievements in the affairs of the spirit, as well as with your worldly status. Do not doubt yourself, but enjoy the Light of God. [Newman, *Hasidic Anthology*, p. 203.]

All authority, past and present, was defied to bring about joyous exaltation as a means of unison with God. Age-old memories of the Second Commonwealth, long subdued, were revived. The common meal, the holy communion of the initiated, which had disappeared from Jewish worship since the days of the Essenes, was restored to its former glory. Especially the third Sabbatical meal at the dim hour of sunset, when Princess Sabbath was leaving the congregation, was imbued with mystic meaning. Pagan songs and pagan dances were now revived as a means of mass ecstasy.[19] Even hard liquor, in so far as it helped to arouse mystic enthusiasm similar to that of an ancient mystery cult, was soon elevated to serve as the *tikkun* (improvement) of the human soul. White costumes during the divine services, reckless ecstatic gestures of forgetfulness and surrender, transformed the simple and somewhat colorless worship of the synagogue into a frenzied communion with God. Only sexual debauchery, which gained no hold, despite the erotic raptures of kabbalistic and hasidic theory, was lacking to recall fully the orgiastic cults so prevalent among ancient and medieval sectarians.

This is the more remarkable in as much as women became active participants in the hasidic movement. Sharing the illiteracy of the rural Jew, excluded from participation in public life, more deeply attracted to the popular folkways, the Ukrainian Jewish woman, often a business entrepreneur and organizer of great ability, found an unexpected medium of self-expression in Hasidism. The Besht's daughter Adel, in many ways a counterpart of Mohammed's Fatima, and the daughters and wives of other leaders, achieved great prominence in hasidic life. Occasionally a simple girl of the masses rose to a position of leadership by an inner urge. The tragic story of Hannah Rachel, "the Ludmirer Maid," the St. Joan of Hasidism, is illustrative of the equality of opportunity for the women within this sect. Little wonder that, as in the early days of Christianity, women were the first to be converted in large numbers. Today, the women devotees of the saddikim do not fall behind the male adherents in number or intensity of feeling.

Characteristically, this powerful mass movement could not get along without representatives in authority. The Besht and his disciples were soon elevated to the position of cosmic intermediaries between God and suffering humanity. Moreover, with the publication of the *Noam Elimelek* of Elimelech of Lezajsk, in 1788, *saddikism* became a fundamental factor in the hasidic outlook. Quoting from the ancient Aggadah and from medieval literature, the hasidic teachers saw the saddik (the righteous man) as "the very foundation of the world." Cordovero had already taught the superior duty of the chosen few. "When a pious man sins," he declared, "his punishment will be much more severe than that of a worthless person . . . because he instantly retards the flow of emanation and the rest of the world darkens on his account" (*Pardes,* Chap. 32). According to Moses Hayyim Ephraim of Sudilkow, the Besht's grandson, the very body of the true saddik is not really material. "The saddik's body is tied up with his soul and his soul with the Sephirot and the Sephirot with the Eyn Sof, blessed be He, who is the soul of the whole world." Or, in another connection,

it is evident that all the worlds were created through the Torah. That is why all the worlds are included in the mystery of the righteous man, because the Torah is identical with Man. [*Degel Mahneh Ephraim*, on Gen.]

By grace divine the saddik can transmit his power to his son and his disciple. This doctrine of a hereditary superman became the chief tenet of Hasidism for generations to come. No matter how degenerate some successors of the early enthusiasts were, no matter how much they turned the implicit faith of their adherents to their own advantage, every hasidic group has always found in its recognized leader the guidance, consolation and, above all, the focus of hopes and yearnings for which it looked. When David of Tolnoye acquired a silver chair, a foolish luxury, reminiscent of the excesses of the parvenu of every age; or when Israel of Rushin, the great-grandson of the great "Preacher" and the founder of the Sadagoran dynasty, built a magnificent castle and lived the life of a *grand seigneur* at the expense of thousands of poverty-stricken followers, the Hasidim saw therein only the partial restoration of the glory of the Israelitic kingdom. Nahman of Bratslav taught that "the saddikim resemble their Creator, and just as one asks questions with respect to the divine government, so also necessarily questions arise with respect to the saddik" (*Likkute Maharan*, II).

Hasidism, not satisfied with its great initial successes, became in the days of Ber of Meseritsh a truly propagandist creed. Two of his disciples, Azriel and Israel of Polotsk, wandered from place to place, preaching the gospel of their master, and often insinuating themselves into the hearts of congregations by their beautiful songs and prayers. They searched everywhere especially for a man with a "heart of flesh," whom they tried to induce to go to Meseritsh to the school of Rabbi Ber. Such disciples would often return to their village or town, and constitute, so to speak, a hasidic "cell." Solomon Maimon, the philosopher, reminiscing about his youth in Poland, tells us that numerous young men left their parents, wives and children, to gather at Meseritsh and to listen to the celebrated "Preacher."

This agitation could not long be ignored by official rabbinism, which took up the cudgels in its own defense. To be sure, the customary view, that rabbinic Judaism had become senile and needed replenishment from the vigorous young blood of Hasidism, has no historical foundation. Then and later, in the large urban ghettos of Poland and Lithuania, rabbinism was the broadest and most satisfactory channel for religious and intellectual self-expression. Since Judaism had always shown remarkable tolerance of doctrinal discrepancies, antihasidic resentment here was directed, not so much against the new religious ideology, nor even the outspoken denunciation of rabbinical leaders—Jacob Joseph, for example, called them "little destructive foxes . . . who have risen to power on account of money, while they are really petty, immature men" (*Toledot Jacob Joseph,* ed. Warsaw, p. 98)—but against the ritualistic innovations. The prayers outside the stated hours; the change from the Ashkenazic to the Sephardic ritual because the latter had been imbued with the spirit of the Lurianic "intentions"; and above all the heterodox use of a sharpened knife in the ritual slaughtering of animals, were stigmatized as truly heretical deviations. From 1781 on, many an excommunication was hurled at these sectarians by regional authorities. Shortly before his death, in 1796, Elijah Gaon of Vilna lent the authority of his great name to rally all rabbinical Jews in outlawing Hasidism. The texts of the bans reveal what were the major issues. The community of Cracow, for example, in 1786 ruled specifically "that no one of the members of our community should raise his hand to organize a congregation of his own in order to pray with all sorts of gestures, twisting lips, clapping hands and shaking heads as if they were drunk, or else to introduce whatever change into the ritual which the saints on earth have created for us" (Dubnow, *Toledot ha-Hasidut,* p. 451).

The more disorganized Eastern European Jewry became, in the period of the Polish partitions, the less effective were such bans. Some Hasidim haughtily dismissed the attacks of the rabbis.

The generation has not yet achieved the distinction [they comforted themselves], to understand the great depth of his [the Besht's] words, in every stroke of which are hidden mounds upon mounds of secrets and mysteries. The explanation of his work will come with the advent of the Messiah, and Elijah the Prophet will expound it in the future. [Ironically quoted by the rabbinical opponent (David of Makow?), in his *Zemir Arisim,* f. 6 a.]

More authoritatively Moses Hayyim Ephraim taught that "the leaders of every generation complete the Torah, because the Torah is interpreted anew in every generation in accordance with its needs and out of the depths of its soul" (*Degel Mahneh Ephraim,* on Genesis). Others could not suppress their public rejoicing over the death of the great Gaon Elijah, a reaction fully understandable in a period of strife when the community of Brody publicly burned Jacob Joseph's great work. A native of that city, Loeb Melamed, composed a treatise sharply attacking the *Turim* and the *Shulhan Aruk,* the two most revered codes of law. This treatise never appeared in print, however, and all such antirabbinical, though far from antinomian tendencies, quickly spent their forces.

In fact, the basic reason for the partial victory of Hasidism was its speedy compromise with rabbinism. In Ber of Meseritsh and his disciple, Shneur Zalman of Ljosna, Hasidism found leaders who successfully synthesized the teachings of the Besht with the established rabbinic tradition. Ber was a great Halakist in his own right, and Shneur Zalman, with his encouragement, actually composed the most significant halakic code of the last two centuries. Reverence for traditional rabbinism could hardly find better expression than in the latter's general acceptance of all rabbinical decisions. "They deserve," he writes, "to be relied upon and followed in every instance," and "one has no right to take a more lenient attitude wherever the latter authorities have adopted a stringent interpretation" (*Responsa,* Nos. 12,18). Elimelech of Lezajsk, sending to one of his followers an extensive set of rules of hasidic behavior, mentions in the first place: "Learn Talmud and the Code *Orah Hayyim* and pray that you may understand it correctly" (In Newman's *Anthology,* p. 280).

The battle raged, indeed, only on the periphery of Polish Jewish life, where Lithuania, White Russia and Eastern Galicia met Podolia, Volhynia and the Ukraine. In Poland proper (*i.e.,* in regions ethnically Polish) rabbinism easily retained its hold upon the mind of the Jews. From the outset, the progress of Hasidism in the districts of Cracow, Lublin and Warsaw, was determined by the degree of its harmonization with the rabbinical teachings and institutions. In Posen the impact of Hasidism was practically nil. In fact, outside of the Polish-Ukrainian center, the neighboring Moldavian and Slovakian provinces and, through immigration, Palestine,

Hasidism achieved at most temporary successes. Such were those in Frankfort and, more generally, in the growing Eastern European immigrant ghettos of the West. Even after peace had been restored, rabbinism remained so deeply rooted as to undergo no appreciable transformation in its general method or specific application. Those great halakists of the nineteenth and twentieth centuries who lived in the midst of the hasidic communities of Galicia and Ukraine, differed little, if at all, in method and outlook from such predecessors as Isserles or Solomon Luria. As in the seventeenth, so also in the nineteenth century, we find talmudic dialectics inspiring thousands of young and adult students, and giving them an intellectual satisfaction, hardly paralleled in intensity by any form of study in the contemporary West. It is absurd to speak of ossification or desiccation of a school of thought which had so many enthusiastic adherents. The progressive decline of rabbinism and, for that matter to an even higher degree, of Hasidism (after 1815), was due not so much to their lack of vitality, as to the sudden total transformation of the social scene, and the concomitant politico-intellectual developments of enlightenment and emancipation.[20]

SUBSTITUTES FOR STATE AND TERRITORY

The European ghetto thus became the embodiment of talmudic Judaism, in a form perhaps even purer than the community in Babylonia. Socially an almost uniform group of lower bourgeoisie; economically organized as a guild of money lenders and their associates; legalized as a corporation apart from all others with unique features of its own; territorially and culturally segregated from the rest of the population by thick walls at whose gates stood ever-suspicious watchmen; dominated by a communal organization combining the powers of a strong state and church—European Jewry lived its life as though it were still listening to the waves of the Euphrates or watching the falls of the Jordan. Centuries of uninterrupted life in a given country could not make the Jews feel that they were other than temporary sojourners, or make their neighbors regard them in any other light. Unceasingly they dreamed of a glorious return to their native land, never dismayed by recurring frustration. Ahasuerus, the Wandering

Jew, was always on the move, but not only because he had to—he wanted to move. Out of his dreams and nightmares, he created substitutes for a state and a territory, without which even he could not survive as a living organism; being artificial, these substitutes could never seriously threaten his historic progress toward emancipation from nature.

Such was the ideal, the pure ghetto, of which the physical ghetto, the segregated Jewish quarter, was merely an imperfect symbol. At the very moment when the former's evolution seemed to reach the highest point, at the turn from medieval to modern times, it had become so untrue to its own realities, that church and state had to buttress it by the force of legislation in support of the latter. Then and only then did the entirely artificial, technical ghetto spread through central Europe. The greatest centers of Jewry—Spain, Poland-Lithuania and the Ottoman Empire—had never known such a crystallization of economic endeavor and lack of social differentiation, the physical ghetto's necessary prerequisites. The intellectual and religious life of Spanish Jewry clearly reflected the variegated pattern of Jewish society. If, in Poland and Turkey, Jewish social and religious life seemed more drab and uniform, this was due not to peculiar Jewish developments but to the general decline of these two countries soon after the settlement of the Jewish masses. Having made a marvelous start during the sixteenth century, Jewish energies were quickly exhausted by an environment increasingly anarchical. Even then the contributions of Polish and Turkish Jewry to all the typically Jewish aspects of religion and culture, to Halakah and Kabbalah, popular philosophy and Hasidism, remain memorable. For all Jewry, however, the physical ghetto was a symbol, as the pure ghetto was an ideal, molding Jewish destinies, even when they could not confine the multifarious social and religious trends. It is in this sense that the ghetto typified medieval Jewish life, and that its gradual breaking up heralded the advent of a new era.

XI

EMANCIPATION

FROM the seventeenth century on, new forces began to operate in Jewish life, in large measure reflecting transformations going on in European society. "Emancipation," as the most important movement in modern Jewish history is called, usually carries only a political connotation. Along with political emancipation, however, which during the last century and a half admitted the Jews to full citizenship in most countries of the world, went economic and intellectual emancipation. In fact, political and legal rights came later and were but the formal acknowledgment of conditions already established in economic, social and intellectual life. Jewish history here, as often elsewhere, merely followed the lead of general European history. Whether the breakdown of medievalism took place first economically or intellectually; whether the prime determinant was early capitalism in Italy and the Netherlands, or the forces of art, religion and science released by the Italian Renaissance, the Protestant Reformation and the philosophical Enlightenment, is still debatable. But that the surge of the modern state toward democracy, the political revolution, was the climax of these earlier, more basic though less spectacular, revolutions, is indisputable. For the Jew, too, there was a preliminary economic emancipation, beginning early in Italy and continuing during the seventeenth century in Holland; as well as the intellectual emancipation in these two countries, later climaxed by the Berlin and Eastern European Haskalah. Both these took place long before the changes received recognition in public law, as "equality of rights." Jewish emancipation, moreover, merely followed upon the heels of the more fundamental European emancipation of the individual from the dominance of the corporate group. In the economic system of capitalism, as well as in the religious Reformation and the intellectual Enlightenment, the European had cast off the bonds of medieval society long before he won actual participation in government. The Jews, too, as individuals, were being emancipated in all these respects; while the Jewish group, as a communal entity, was losing its distinctive grip over its members.[1]

For the Jew, however, these general trends were particularly revolutionizing. Not only did Jewish emancipation, for the bulk of the people, begin much later, but the individual Jew had a double responsibility: a readjustment of relations to his own group, and to the European world outside. From a medieval ghetto Jew, he was to be transformed into a full-fledged modern Jewish European. In a period of less than three centuries, he was to accomplish a task twice as arduous and intricate as that performed by the other Europeans in more than half a millennium. This rapid readjustment produced a confusion from which the Jewish people as a whole have not yet recovered.

INCREASE IN POPULATION

The mid-seventeenth century was a notable turning point in both European and Jewish history. Such events as the Treaty of Westphalia and the English Revolution, and, in Jewish history, the revolt of Chmielnicki and the Shabbetianic movement, mark the end of one, and the beginning of another epoch. Not least among the startling changes were those of geographic distribution. Europe increased its population unprecedentedly, and founded a series of colonial empires. At the same time the Jewish population increased to an even greater extent. It is estimated that Europe about 1650 held approximately 100,000,000 inhabitants, or one-fifth of mankind. After the bloody Cossack revolts, the Jews seem to have numbered no more than 650,000 in Europe and 250,000 more in the rest of the world, apparently the smallest number since the days of the Judges. The ratio of Jews to the world population amounted to less than 0.2 percent, while their proportion to the European population was 0.65 percent. After 1848 the world population was more than 1,000,000,-000, the total Jewish world population 4,250,000, *i.e.*, approximately 0.4 percent. The European population was

250,000,000, and the Jews in Europe 3,700,000, or 1.5 percent. That is to say, while mankind doubled during this period and the peoples of Europe increased by only 150 percent, the Jews of the world multiplied nearly 5 times, and European Jewry almost 6 times. During the following sixty years the same tendencies continued with ever-increasing speed. Only the last decades indicate a slowing down of the pace. Population figures for 1936 are approximately as follows: 1,900,000,000 human beings exist in the whole world, and over 500,000,000 in Europe; world Jewry numbers more than 16,000,000, European Jewry almost 10,000,000. The proportion of Jews has thus further increased, to more than 0.8 percent of the world's population, and to almost 2 percent of the European population.[2]

Even more remarkable are the variations in growth among different groups of Jewry. In the middle of the seventeenth century, Ashkenazic Jewry, embracing at that time Poland, Germany and parts of the Dutch and Italian settlements, constituted roughly one-half of the total Jewish population. Sephardic, Italian and oriental Jewries made up the other half. In 1850 all non-Ashkenazic groups together still constituted about one-fifth of the whole. Today their number probably does not exceed 1,250,000, or 8 percent, leaving for the Ashkenazim more than 90 percent.

This astounding disproportion of 11:1 inevitably obliterated some ancient antagonisms. "If a Portuguese Jew in England or Holland married a German Jewess," writes a Sephardic apologist in 1763, "he would of course lose all his prerogatives, be no longer reckoned a member of their Synagogue, forfeit all civil and ecclesiastical preferments, be absolutely divorced from the body of the nation and not even buried with his Portuguese brethren" (*Letters of Certain Jews to Monsieur Voltaire,* English transl., pp. 37 f.). As late as 1812, the marriage of Moses Montefiore to Judith Cohen, of a prominent Ashkenazi family, was frowned upon by his Sephardic confreres, although the greatest Sephardic rabbi of the post-expulsion period, Joseph Karo, had no hesitation in marrying the daughter of Zechariah Seblish Ashkenazi. Today most "Sephardic" congregations in the New World have a predominantly Ashkenazic membership, and even in the former citadels of Sephardic "superiority," Holland, England and Palestine, the distinctions are rapidly melting away.

This remarkable development must be credited chiefly to Eastern European Jewry, to the Jewish masses of what was Poland in 1650. The remaining Ashkenazim, living mostly in Germany, increased at a much slower rate. The difficult economic situation down to the nineteenth century, governmental restrictions, and numerous conversions, contributed to retard the growth of German Jewry. Their proportion in the population of Germany today exceeds but slightly their proportion in 1650. At the same time the considerable German-Jewish emigration to the United States, England, etc., during the last century, was more than made up for by a steady influx of Jews from eastern Europe. Moreover, when Prussia swallowed a considerable portion of Poland, she at once incorporated an Eastern European Jewish mass many times larger than the number of her previous Jewish subjects. In 1816 Posen Jewry outnumbered their coreligionists, not only of Prussia but of the entire Germanic Confederation outside Austria. Since that time, this eastern province has poured its Jewish settlements into the rest of Germany. Today it is hard to determine which of the present so-called "German Jews" in the West are descendants of older German families or of immigrants (one might say re-immigrants) from Cracow, Kalisz or Vilna, from Posen or Bromberg. That the overwhelming majority of British, French, American and Palestinian Jewry hail from the Eastern European reservoir need hardly be emphasized. Taken as a whole, the descendants of the Polish-Lithuanian Ashkenazim of 1650, amounting at that time to less than 40 percent of world Jewry, may be said to constitute at least 80 percent of all Jews today.[3]

This tremendous growth was due entirely to natural increase. Unlike the period of the Second Commonwealth, modern times have witnessed few conversions to Judaism. As a matter of fact, in every generation a large number has left the fold. Considering its long history of intellectual achievement and physical suffering, Eastern European Jewry has revealed truly astounding regenerative powers. Rabbinic legislation encouraged early marriage and large families; both were common, down to the middle of the nineteenth century.

A Polish census of the eighteenth century, for example, mentioned a Jewish wife eight years of age. In 1712 the burgomaster of Amsterdam prohibited a marriage of a Jewish couple, both of whom were below the age of twelve.

Although similar cases also occurred in the population at large, there operated numerous checks, both positive and preventive, to use the Malthusian terms; while religion, ethnic segregation, and the peculiar economic and political lot of the Jews tended to counteract such checks much more effectively. Not only was birth control rejected, but the "moral restraint," of which Malthus spoke, was not regarded as moral. Family purity, general in the ghetto, also prevented corroding "vice." The Jewish people, for the most part, lived on a lower middle-class level; parents were not so prosperous as to use birth control for convenience, nor so destitute as to be unable to take care of children. A far lower mortality rate among the Jewish infants, as compared with that among the masses of poverty-stricken peasants, also had a decisive influence. Of course, no definite figures can be quoted for the period previous to the nineteenth century, but probably out of every 1,000 births 300 to 400 infants died during the first year, especially in the more backward countries of eastern Europe. In periods of distress, the proportion must have been still higher. The economic situation of the Jews; their communal charities; the superiority of medical care in towns; the better hygienic conditions, even within the crowded ghettos; and the sentimental devotion of Jewish parents to their children, fostered through centuries of concentrated family life—all contributed substantially to reduce Jewish infant mortality. Illegitimate births, with concomitant social ostracism and parental neglect, which everywhere else greatly increased the ratio of infants succumbing to disease and misery, were practically unknown in the ghetto. Today the number of illegitimate children in a city like Vilna is less than one out of a hundred among the Jews (0.5 percent, 1929; 0.9 percent, 1930), as against fourteen among the Catholics. No wonder that even in New York City, where these social distinctions have lost much of their force, Jewish infant mortality in 1915 was 78 for each 1,000 births, while that of the other "races" was 105. This and the equally favorable difference in child mortality for the ages of two to five, necessarily resulted in a higher excess of births over deaths in the Jewish population. In Lorraine in 1783, for example, the proportion of Jewish mortality to natality was 714.6 :1000, while among the rest of the population it was 871.9 : 1000. The result was that, although Lorraine Jewry registered only one birth for each 37 persons, as against 24 among the non-Jews, it multiplied one and a half times as fast as the others. How much more rapid must the Eastern European rate of increase have been, if, as is likely, Jewish natality equaled that of their neighbors.

The great destructive forces, contagious diseases and wars, seem to have claimed fewer victims among the Jews than among their Gentile neighbors. It is quite possible that Jewish religious life, through its prescriptions of continual washing, discrimination in food, a strict day of rest, and the like, helped build up greater resistance. The relatively longer experience of civilized and urban life may have endowed the Jewish race with a degree of immunity to certain bacilli, higher than that of their European neighbors. Until the end of the eighteenth century, the Jews were exempt from military service, and even during the early decades of the nineteenth century they sustained fewer casualties than Gentiles. Poland-Russia and Turkey, among the most important countries of Jewish settlement, did not begin drafting Jews into the army until 1845 (in Russia proper, 1827), and 1908 respectively. Except in 1812, the nineteenth-century wars involving Russia, Austria-Hungary and Turkey, were fought far from the dense Eastern European Jewish settlements, thus sparing their civilian population.

To be sure, throughout the ages special wars, namely pogroms, were directed against the Jews. But during the 220 years from 1660 to 1880, there was only one major pogrom movement by Gonta and Zelezhniak in the Ukrainian region of Humań, in 1768. The Jewish victims in this and other assaults were certainly fewer than the number of European soldiers killed or crippled during the incessant wars. Even the Ukrainian massacres of 1918-20 (the most extended and sanguinary pogrom movement since the days of Chmielnicki), which, according to a most conservative computation, affected at least 531 localities and destroyed directly "only" 34,719 Jewish lives (although we must add at least as many victims who died from wounds, assaults on trains, etc.), caused a proportionately smaller decrement in the man power of Russian Jewry than that resulting from the 12,000 war victims in 1914-18 in that of the German community. Coming on top of the losses in the World War and the enormous sufferings of the entire population in a territory ravaged by foreign invasion and civil war, the massacres, of course, devastated the Ukrainian sector. But numerical growth, so large in the preceding generations, was arrested for only a short time. Thus within less than three centuries, Jewry has risen numerically from the lowest to the highest point in the history of the dispersion.[4]

GEOGRAPHIC EXPANSION

These masses of Jews had to find space to expand. After the numerous expulsions from the thirteenth to the sixteenth centuries, the Jews had been restricted to a relatively small area in Europe, which included Poland, Turkey and parts of Italy and Germany. At the same time, their economic life had been increasingly confined to money lending and a few branches of industry and commerce. Correspondingly, the number of Jews diminished from generation to generation. Conversions, pogroms, and suffering during migrations counteracted whatever expansive powers still remained in the much-harassed people. In the friendlier period after 1650, a prodigious expansion, both geographic and economic, set in, materially broadening the economic basis and reciprocally influencing the steady growth of the population. Not only was the surplus economically absorbed, but the standard of life of the average Jew became much higher.

The partitions of Poland, especially, proved to be an effective lever for transplanting large masses of Jews. In 1772, Russia, which had consistently refused admission to Jewish travelers, was suddenly possessed of 27,000 Jewish subjects. The subsequent annexation of the other provinces of Poland brought in still larger masses of Jews. True, Catherine II and her successors soon erected the "Pale of Settlement" to exclude them from the interior, but the vast "Neo-Russian" steppes in the South, and to a certain extent the Baltic provinces, had to be opened to Jewish immigration. As a result, the Jewish population of three southern provinces (Kherson,

Taurida, Ekaterinoslav) is said to have increased by 333 percent in the years 1844-80, while its ratio in the general population rose from 2 to 5.6 percent. In the province of Kiev, there were 870 Jews in 1792, and 183,629 sixty years later. The inclusion of Galicia in the Hapsburg domains in 1772, opened the road not only to a steady influx of Jews into the neighboring provinces of northern Hungary and the Bukovina but, notwithstanding legal obstacles, to their gradual infiltration into the western provinces. In vain did the Austrian government maintain in Bohemia and Moravia the system of so-called *Familienstellen,* by virtue of which the number of Jewish families was limited, and only one son could marry and inherit the family's residential right. In vain did Vienna, the capital, after the expulsion of 1670, bar all Jews except those admitted through special individual grants of "tolerance." After 1848 and 1867, the pressure increased to such a degree that Vienna before the World War harbored the second largest Jewish community in Europe. Similar developments in Hungary raised that in Budapest to the rank of the third largest European community. Proof that neighboring countries could not long resist the pressure is best seen in Moldavia. This Rumanian province, until 1878 under the overlordship of Turkey, is estimated to have had only 12,000 Jews in 1803. Their number increased to 80,000 in 1838, to 119,000 in 1859, and to 196,000 in 1899. Today, in short, a century and a half after the first partition of Poland, the whole Ukraine and White Russia, Poland, Lithuania and Latvia, the northern sections of Greater Rumania, Slovakia and Carpathian Ruthenia, constitute one large block of Eastern European Jewry, with a proportion of Jewish to general population ranging from 6 to 12 percent. Odessa, Jassy or Munkacs are now as intensely Jewish settlements as Vilna or Lemberg, although two centuries ago these districts had very sparse Jewish communities or none at all.

Of equal significance was the expansion to the West. The year 1648 was a turning point also in the history of Jewish migrations. The influx of Ashkenazic Jewry into Poland and the drift of the Sephardic exiles toward the eastern shores of the Mediterranean was now reversed. The era of western migration, which was to reach its climax in the early years of this century, set in, to the sombre accompaniment of Cossack massacres and Shabbetian frenzy. At first the eastern Jews departed with great reluctance. Moses Rivkes, one of the prominent refugees of 1648, sounded an often-reiterated complaint. Safe in Amsterdam, he concluded his commentary on Karo's and Isserles' Code, entitled *Beer ha-Golah,* with the prayer that God return him to his former station in life and to the city of Vilna, a wish realized in the last years of his life. Gradually, Polish Jewry became more and more accustomed to wandering. Especially those who migrated to the United States became enthusiastic admirers of their adopted country, often urging relatives and friends to follow them.

In the West, the eastern immigrants encountered another wave of Jewish wanderers. The Spanish-Portuguese refugees, Jewish and Marrano, had throughout the sixteenth and seventeenth centuries settled in all western lands. Their superior wealth, trade connections, and familiarity with western manners and culture, more easily razed walls of prejudice. Numerically often insignificant, sometimes of dubious allegiance to Judaism and, as a rule, less steeped in Jewish tradition than their Ashkenazic brethren, these Sephardic merchants, physicians and writers constituted the vanguard of world Jewry in its amazing geographic expansion.

Holland was the first to open its gates to these newcomers. Not only individual Neo-Christians, but even a congregation of professing Jews was legalized in 1593, and more definitely in 1619. In the following decades, the Thirty Years' War and the Chmielnicki revolt caused the ingress of many German and Polish Ashkenazim. The Jewish population of Holland increased from some 3,000 in 1650 to more than 50,000 in 1790. The temporary decline during the revolutionary wars (according to Montalivet's report to Napoleon in 1811 to 39,575) was soon overcome by fresh waves of Eastern European immigrants.

Dutch Jewry, in turn, soon assumed leadership in settling Jews in new countries. Neighboring Belgium was the first goal. Strengthened by the provisions of the Peace of Westphalia, certain Amsterdam Jews applied for admission to this Spanish province. The few settled in Antwerp negotiated with the city council for the creation of a synagogue. Although, owing to the intervention of the pope, these efforts were frustrated, the Jewish population gradually grew to 1,044 by 1811. Later the eastern immigrants established a vigorous Jewish community in the diamond center, Antwerp.

The more spectacular negotiations of Menasseh ben Israel with Cromwell (1655) and Queen Christina of Sweden (1651) had little immediate success. In England the celebrated Amsterdam rabbi, whom Grotius had described as "a man of great usefulness to the state and to science," and whom Rembrandt's brush has immortalized, obtained the declaration of the Whitehall Conference that no law prohibited the return of the Jews. The life of the Marrano community, which under Elizabeth had already numbered some eighty or ninety members, thus became much less precarious; and in 1656, when war with Spain jeopardized the subsistence of these "Spaniards," they threw off their mask and declared themselves Jews. The Sephardic congregation in London, which long centered in the famous synagogue at Bevis Marks, now began to grow steadily. Although founded later and forced to overcome many adversities, the Ashkenazic community grew even more rapidly, making the capital of the British Empire, with its 200,000 Jews, today one of the foremost political and economic centers of world Jewry.

In Sweden, on the other hand, the economic and ethnic situation was far less favorable. The romantic leanings of Queen Christina, her friendship with Jewish bankers in Hamburg, and the liberalism of the librarian Vossius, were all of no avail. Not until the eighteenth century were the Jews slowly planted on Swedish soil. The career of one early settler, Aaron Isaac, has become known through a remarkable autobiography. Norway resisted still longer, and in its constitution of 1814 stated succinctly, "Jews are excluded from entering the country" (Art. 2). In 1833 an illegal Jewish entrant was kept in prison for twenty-eight days; in 1844 another was fined 800 thalers, of which 40 were turned over to the informer (cf. I. M. Jost's *Geschichte der Israeliten*, X, 2, 27). This prohibition was repealed in 1851. Altogether a few thousand German and Eastern European Jews have found refuge on the Scandinavian Peninsula.

France offers a striking illustration of the gradual advance of the Sephardim from the South and the Ashkenazim from the North. Almost immediately after the final expulsion of the Jews from Provence and the Dauphiné, Marranos began trickling into the southern regions. Soon entire communities arose in Bordeaux, Bayonne (or rather its suburb, Saint-Esprit) and Toulouse. To the French government, aware of their growing contributions to international trade, their clandestine adherence to Judaism was for long an open secret. Although as late as 1615 it reiterated its intolerance of professing Jews, the administration fostered the commercial activities of these Neo-Christians by all possible means. Sooner or later, however, the existence of Jewish communities had to be recognized. The development was accelerated when, in 1648, France annexed Alsace with several thousand Ashkenazic Jews, to which were added in 1766 those of Lorraine, and in 1790 the more Italianized ghetto Jews of Avignon and Carpentras. Together with the Marranos of Rouen, etc., these Jewries encircled Paris. In vain did the police of the capital search the inns at five o'clock each morning, in order to expel undesirable Jewish sojourners. On the eve of the Revolution, some 800 Jews had established their residence there. Natural increase and immigration rapidly swelled their number, especially in the two northern provinces. Alsatian Jewry multiplied from 3,665 in 1637, to 15,225 in 1760, and to 26,000 in 1810. In Lorraine their number grew from 1,000 in 1752, to 10,545 in 1810. The fact that all these Jews were concentrated in 18 percent of the Alsatian and 6 percent of the Lorraine municipalities, in a few of which they amounted to 40 percent of the population or more; that Strassburg, which had long effectively resisted their incursion, had 1,467 Jews in 1810; that the Metz community had grown from a handful in 1650, to more than 2,000 in 1789, made the increase even more conspicuous. In 1791 all restrictions were removed, and the Jews spread irresistibly all over the country. Today Paris, with a Jewish population exceeding 150,000, includes more than three-quarters of all Jewry in European France.

The Jewry of the New World was for a long time predominantly Sephardic. Starting with Luis Torres, Columbus' Marrano interpreter, who settled in Cuba, their number grew by voluntary and involuntary immigration, especially to Brazil, long a prisoners' colony for Portugal. With the temporary transfer of this province to Dutch rule, many Marranos declared themselves Jews and enemies of intolerant Portugal. After 1654, when Portugal with the financial assistance of a Marrano, Duarte da Silva, reoccupied this colony, many Jews emigrated into the Dutch possessions of Surinam, the West Indies and New Amsterdam. Soon afterwards, however, the British colonies, offering greater attractions, economically and politically, became the main centers of Jewish life. Ashkenazic Jews, also, such as Jacob Barsimson in New Amsterdam, the first Jew to settle in what is now the United States, began to realize the extent of the new opportunity. German and even Polish Jews arrived in ever-increasing numbers, and a Polish Talmud-Torah school was opened in New York in 1808. Nevertheless, in 1818 the total Jewish population in the United States seems not to have exceeded 3,000, in a total of about 9,500,000. But the great periods of the German and Russian immigration were soon to come. Today the compact Jewish masses of America may be considered another geographic extension of eastern Europe. The same holds true of Palestine, Argentine and the other more recent centers of Jewry.[5]

JEWS AND CAPITALISM

Hand in hand with the geographic expansion, went the intensification of Jewish economic life. Early capitalism, an acid which gradually dissolved the guild system, opened new fields of endeavor to Jews, as to all individuals. In a sense, the change in economic trends favored the Jew, for the first time in centuries. With the Commercial Revolution, land was no longer the principal element of economic and, consequently, of political life. Money, in the form of cash or credit, now ruled. The free entrepreneur, through private initiative assembling raw material, distributing it among hundreds and thousands of home workers and then marketing the finished product, was the pacemaker for the Industrial Revolution, with its concentration of wage earners in factories. In either case, the entrepreneur had to have at his disposal resources, cash or credit, to support a production process sometimes extending over many months. The man with initiative and capital, the upper bourgeois, now became the leading protagonist in the economic and political drama.

The Jew, in so far as he belonged to that upper-bourgeois class, could capitalize his former disabilities. Medieval regulations, centering in the guild system, were discarded or superseded by others more in line with the inherent forces of capitalism, favoring the individual without respect to race or creed. Forced in the medieval era to accumulate large sums in cash, the Jew's experience as the leading medieval banker stood him in good stead, in a world in which banking was the artery of economic life. Furthermore, in their own life and law the Jews had succeeded in perpetuating many elements of a similar capitalistic age in the early Roman Empire. So with Europe at large only beginning to reshape its own legal structure through the "reception" of Roman law, Jewish law was more easily adjustable to the new conditions.

In themselves, these factors would have been enough to secure for the Jews a more important rôle in modern capitalism than their number warranted. Their peculiar ethnic and religious experiences, however, gave them further advantages. Their whole history had molded mind and outlook, conscious and unconscious attitudes, in a manner suitable to modern capitalism. The psychological implications of their detachment from the soil, the bourgeois spirit of their urban life, the artificiality of all Jewish existence, the consequent prevalence of speculative thinking, as against peasant concreteness —all these were contributory factors. The pilpulistic speculations of the talmudic rabbis, reaching their height in sixteenth-century Poland, have often been denounced as aberrations of the Jewish mind. Basically, however, they were only the customary speculative method of all advanced juridical and logical thinking. Between the reasoning of Solomon Luria or Shabbetai Cohen and the rationalizing decisions of European and American courts of justice, there is little intrinsic difference—no more than there is between the latter and the arguments of modern philosophers and economic theorists. Unlike western scholarship, however, talmudic lucubrations were not limited to a small class of jurists, philosophers and economists, but became the discipline for a whole people. The statement of a Polish chronicler of the seventeenth century may be exaggerated: "There was practically no home in all the provinces of Poland where the Torah was not studied" (Nathan Nata Hannover, *Yeven mesulah*); but there is no denying that almost all educated Jews, particularly among the Ashkenazim, had an intensive training in such dialectics. Capitalism, in essence "artificial," based upon an exchange of abstract values, represented by the most abstract and irrational of values, viz., money, found the Jews ready to carry its implications to the logical extreme.

Sombart's exaggeration of the Jewish share in the development of modern capitalism has been criticized by many scholars in the last two decades, but it remains true that the Jewish contribution to the capitalistic transformation of western society far exceeded the numerical proportion of Jewry, particularly in western Europe. The often-quoted phrase of the German economist, "Israel passes over Europe like the sun: at its coming new life bursts forth; at its going all falls into decay" (*The Jews and Modern Capitalism,* English transl., p. 13), is special pleading rather than scientific statement. It contains this much truth, however, that those countries in which the Jews happened to settle were really hastened on their way toward capitalism. Nor is it merely a coincidence. Led by an intrinsic, one might say, metaphysical sympathy, Jews unconsciously found their way to countries in which new centers of economic and intellectual life were to evolve.[6]

This does not mean that the Jews were the fathers of modern capitalism, in Sombart's sense. His contention that most capitalistic, commercial as well as legal, instruments were derived from rabbinical practice, has been justly discredited. Rabbinic law may have influenced European legislation in such minor details as the bona-fide acquisition of stolen goods. But the vital innovations of paper currency, international bills of exchange, the stock exchanges, etc., reveal little, if any, Jewish influence in their early stages. If one dates the rise of early capitalism at 1300 rather than 1500 or 1600, such an assertion becomes a truism with respect to the Puritans. On entering the scene, Jews and Puritans found most of the new methods in business and public finance already firmly established. What is true is that, once actively engaged in their exploitation, the two religious groups contributed to their further growth in a more than proportionate degree.

Earlier Jewish participation in the development of capitalism had been checked by the geographic and political situation of the Jews. As is well known, the foundations of modern capitalism were laid in the thirteenth and fourteenth centuries in the North Italian republics, from which Jews were then totally excluded. When, for instance, Como, about 1250, introduced paper money as legal tender, there were no Jews in the city to handle it. In Genoa, the development of the famous banking houses and the establishment of what might properly be called the first modern stock exchange, went on without Jewish coöperation. When the influx of Jews, and especially of Jewish bankers, took place after 1400, northern Italy was already declining from its position of leadership. These Jewish bankers, moreover, were restricted by the stipulations of the *condottas* to petty money lending of a local character. This primitive type of banking doubtless became increasingly vital, and even the popes of the Counter Reformation recognized its indispensable character. After a brief period of exclusion, Sixtus V readmitted the Jewish money lenders to Rome in 1586, and allowed them to open fifty-five banking houses, probably thus averting a disaster such as befell Sicily after the expulsion of the Jews. His successor not only raised the number to sixty-four in 1590, but between 1587 and 1669 other popes granted them about one thousand special licenses, even in cities without ghettos, such as Bologna, Perugia and Città di Castello, and others outside the State of the Church. For example, in 1597, a concession was granted to two Jews "yet to be named," to trade in Nancy and Saint-Nicholas in Lorraine. In 1559 Yehiel Nissim da Pisa, a leading scholar and banker, stated that "in this country the custom of lending money to Gentiles has spread more than in all the other parts of the Diaspora" (A. Marx, "A Description of Bills of Exchange, 1559," *American Economic Review*, VI, 609-14).

Nevertheless, neither the Italian Jews nor the *montes pietatis*, their most important competitors, can claim credit for any significant contribution to capitalist evolution. The Jewish money lenders had so small a share in the international transfer of money and in the deposit business, both soon to become the basis of modern banking, that Da Pisa apologized for discussing at all the trade in bills of exchange, although "they are not current among the Jews of our time." When, in seventeenth-century Venice and Leghorn, Jewish merchants and shipowners began playing a really prominent rôle; when in 1619 Abraham del Banco helped establish the renowned Venetian *Banco di Giro;* and in 1686-1706 Aaron Uziel paid nearly half a million ducats into the Venetian treasury in customs dues alone, Italy on the whole was trailing far behind her western rivals in the general capitalistic procession. Vast regions on the Peninsula, moreover, remained closed to the Jews. The attempt of Charles Bourbon and his "enlightened" councilors, in 1740, to extend toleration to Jews in the kingdom of Naples and Sicily for a period of twenty-five years, was frustrated by a great popular outcry.

Much more important were Jewish contributions in the Iberian Peninsula which, during the fifteenth and sixteenth centuries, wrested from Italy the leadership in capitalistic enterprise. The Jews of Lisbon soon controlled the maritime trade of that distinguished port, while the Jewish bankers of Castile saved their country the usual embarrassment attending great foreign indebtedness. This development was cut short, however, by the successive expulsions, which left behind them smoldering ruins of the Jewish communities. Only Marranos remained to carry on their trade, which they did so effectively that many emerged as undisputed leaders of the Commercial Revolution in Spain, Portugal and their dependencies. Duarte da Silva, for instance, controlled, through his agencies in London, Antwerp, Rouen, Venice, Leghorn, Rome and the New World, a large part of Portugal's foreign commerce. Another Marrano, Manoel Pimentel (later known as Isaac ibn Yakar), was for a time a playmate of Henry IV, in France, and became one of the leading international merchants. In his will, written in 1616, he spoke of investments in Spain, Holland, Venice and Constantinople. In the early years after the discovery of America, Luis de Santangel obtained the first royal grant to export grain and horses from Spain to the new colonies. Torres, settled in Cuba, is believed to have been the discoverer of tobacco and its first exporter to the Old World. Jacob Rodrigues Rivera introduced the manufacture of sperm oil into America, where it soon became a leading industry. In Peru, Marranos became the masters of international trade. While the majority of Spanish, Portuguese and colonial Neo-Christians were eventually lost to Judaism, many were salvaged by emigration to other lands. It was precisely this Marrano Diaspora, which, like that of the Puritans and Huguenots, became the yeast in the capitalist fermentation.

For the most vital Jewish contributions to capitalism, it is customary to look to Holland and England, the main capitalist centers from the seventeenth century on. Even in the Netherlands, with their relatively larger Jewish population, the beginnings of capitalism go back to the period when Antwerp, already a commercial center of prime magnitude, had no more than a sprinkling of influential Marranos. After 1650, Amsterdam, at the height of her power, included hardly more than 3,000 Jews in a population of 115,000. Later, the Jews waxed tremendously in number and wealth, owning at one time, it is said, 25 percent of the shares of the East India Company. On one occasion the combined wealth of 40 Jewish guests assembled at a wedding ceremony was estimated in excess of 40,000,000 florins. De Pinto is said to have commanded a fortune of 8,000,000 guilders. Anthony Lopez (Isaac) Suasso allegedly financed William III's expedition to England in 1688 by extending him a loan of 2,000,000 guilders without interest, notwithstanding the tremendous risks. These few illustrations of individual Jewish wealth (however exaggerated the specific figures may be); as well as such ideological contributions as Joseph Penso de la Vega's first comprehensive theoretical treatise on the stock exchange, entitled *Confusion de Confusiones,* published in 1688; and the commercial journal issued for the Jews of Holland, the *Gazeta de Amsterdam,* which appeared in the years 1677-78, clearly indicate the extent of Jewish participation.

In England there is a direct connection between the Marrano banker Alvaro Mendes, personally recommended by Queen Elizabeth to the Sultan in 1592 as "a man of consequence most ready in the furthering of business and our affairs for many years" (L. Wolf, *Jews in Elizabethan England,* p. 27), and Carvajal, the financier and contractor of the Cromwellian armies, to Sir Solomon Medina and Samson Gideon. Gideon, the most active of the twelve Jewish brokers regularly admitted to the London Stock Exchange since 1697, is said to have handled one-quarter of all public loans negotiated by the British government in his day. He underwrote, for example, a loan of £1,500,000 in 1745. In both the British and the Dutch colonies, Jews played a prominent rôle. Moses

Lindo, arriving from London in 1756, is said to have invested £120,000 in raising indigo in South Carolina. Dr. Nuñes introduced indigo into the new colony of Georgia. In Newport, R. I., Lopez owned thirty ships and, together with the Gradis, Bordeaux Jewish sugar kings, extensively participated in the transatlantic sugar trade. Sugar, tobacco, indigo and coffee (which some rabbis called the "Jewish drink") became the staple articles of international Jewish commerce. These articles, destined for mass consumption, contrasted with the much narrower field of commerce in luxuries, conducted by the Jews in the early Middle Ages.

With the gradual spread of capitalism to central and eastern Europe, the active participation of the Jews rose in proportion to their numbers. The first Portuguese settlers in Hamburg, officially recognized in 1612, established far-flung commercial relations. By 1650 one-fifth of all freight leaving the harbor went to Spain and Portugal. A curious entry in the minute book of the Portuguese community mentions an Italian goldsmith, who, coming from Brazil, arrived in Hamburg, with the intention of proceeding to Poland. In 1725 Solomon Behrens' wealth amounted to 600,000 marks, and that of two other Jews to 400,000 marks each. But it was the older Jewish community of Frankfort which became the home of Jewish banking for all Germany. Between 1690 and 1790, it included among its members not less than 33 court Jews of various German princes. A counselor of the Winter King's son advised him to give his money to a Frankfort Jew for safe-keeping, because it was as secure there as if deposited with God Himself. In 1800 the city counted 111 Jews, possessing more than 10,000 guilders each, headed by Isaac Michael Speyer, the imperial court agent, who commanded 420,000 guilders. In near-by Württemberg, Suess Oppenheimer was very influential in government affairs. Few of these financiers, however, rivaled in significance the court Jews of the emperor. David Gans, the historian, spoke of Simon Ginsburg, who "made a great fortune of several hundred thousand guilders, a fortune the equal of which there existed none among our coreligionists in Germany in our generation" (*Semah David,* Prague, 1592, I, 63 b). The vicissitudes of the Oppenheimers and Wertheimers, whose financial management so greatly contributed to the Austrian military successes in the French and Turkish wars, and whose downfall in 1703 and 1733, respectively, for reasons beyond their control, markedly disturbed the financial equilibrium of the Empire, are typical both of these imperial bankers' highly influential position, and its inherent instability. Even a hardened Fugger was aroused over the cruel extortions perpetrated, at the emperor's command, on the family of the court Jew, Mordecai Meisel, in Prague, which yielded the handsome amount of 516,250 florins to the imperial treasury (V. Klarwill, *The Fugger News-Letters,* English transl., pp. 239 f.).

Less familiar are the careers of the many court Jews in the smaller German principalities. In 1723 the Bavarian state owed 20 percent of its public debt to Jews, and from 1801 to 1808 81 percent of all Bavarian loans were subscribed by Jewish bankers. The bankruptcy proceedings of the brothers Behrens in Hannover led to the exchange of notes between the kings of England, Prussia and Poland, in the years 1721-23. These few facts give a sense of the impact of Jewish finance upon German economy and politics of the period. The great Leipzig fairs attracted, in the years 1675-1764, 81,937 registered Jewish visitors from all the European ghettos. Their "corporal tax" (*Leibzoll*) alone yielded 719,661 thalers to the state and municipal governments. No wonder the fairs of Frankfort on the Oder and Breslau tried to obtain a slice of this profitable trade by extending considerable privileges to the Polish Jewish merchants. Nowhere, however, were the commercial and industrial contributions more vital for the development of the Jewish settlement than in Prussia. The burgomaster of Senssburg applied to the government, in the name of the city, that a wealthy Jew be allowed to settle there and supply the population with fine linen and other merchandise. In the privilege granted, in 1717, to the Jews of Neumark, they were specially enjoined to do their best "to market abroad all the wares produced in Our provinces" (S. Stern-Taeubler, *ZGJD,* V, 214). From the days of the Great Elector, cities like Berlin, Halberstadt, etc., included communities tolerated exclusively on account of such contributions. The 1807 Berlin directory of industry listed thirty Jewish against twenty-two Christian bankers. It was about that time that Jacobsohn of Memel was able to threaten, with success, to depart to Courland, should certain disabilities not be removed.

The most spectacular rise of the Jews under capitalism came in the first half of the nineteenth century. Under the leadership of the Rothschild family of Frankfort, London, Paris, Vienna, and, temporarily, Naples, the Jewish bankers and industrial entrepreneurs secured a position unrivaled in Jewish history. The Napoleonic wars, involving the constant transfer of large British subsidies to the Continental allies, and offering great opportunities to contractors supplying the belligerent armies, opened the road to the glamorous career of the house of Rothschild. Funds, handed over by the fugitive Landgraf of Hesse to Meyer Amschel Rothschild, yielded in his hands substantial returns to both banker and depositor. Nathan Meyer Rothschild, settling in 1797 in Manchester to engage in the textile trade, with a capital of only £20,000, could before long undertake the shipment of large amounts to the Continent, supplying Wellington's army in Spain with as much as £800,000 in gold. The Rothschild firm emerged as one of the main victors of the Napoleonic wars. In quick succession, they handled public loans of almost all the governments of Europe, totaling $650,000,000 between 1817 and 1848. Among the early borrowers appeared: Prussia, with a loan of £5,000,000 in 1818, and £3,500,000 in 1822; England, £12,000,000 in 1819; Austria, 106,000,000 guilders in 1820-21; Naples and Sicily, 40,000,000 ducats in 1821-22; Russia, £10,000,000 in 1822; France, 23,-000,000 francs in 1823; and Brazil £5,200,000 in 1824-25.

Although at first skeptical, they [the Rothschilds] early realized the importance of railways and took an active part in their promotion. They backed railways in England, the first railways in Austria, the largest railway in France, the great network of Belgian railways and were identified with railway financing in Brazil and the United States. [J. Strieder, in *Encyclopædia of Social Sciences*, s. v. Rothschild.]

An unsympathetic observer, such as the Bremen burgomaster Smidt, asserted in 1820 that the house of Rothschild "has to such an extent acquired control of the money market that it is in a position either to hinder or to promote, as it feels inclined, the movements and operations of potentates and even of the greatest European powers" (quoted by E. Corti, *The Rise of the House of Rothschild*, English transl., p. 263).

Lord Byron, then at the height of his European popularity, further dramatized the bankers' position:

> Who hold the balance of the world? Who reign
> O'er Congress whether royalist or liberal?...
> Jew Rothschild and his fellow Christian Baring
> Those and the truly liberal Lafitte
> Are the true Lords of Europe. Every loan
> Is not a merely speculative hit
> But seats a nation or upsets a throne.
> [*Don Juan*, XII, 5-6.]

The Polish poet, Krasinski, unmistakably made Rothschild the embodiment of the spirit of evil in his *Undivine Comedy*.

After the Rothschilds, came other distinguished financial and industrial leaders in Europe and in America. Émile Péreire built the first large French railroad in 1835, and earned the popular title of *pontifex maximus* of the French railway system. Together with the Paris Rothschilds, the Péreires later won control of a large part of the Caucasian oil fields. About 1910 the Jews owned some 15 percent of the production and 40 percent of industrial refining, of crude oil under the czars. In the United States the establishment of numerous Jewish banking houses by immigrants from Germany between 1840 and 1860, enabled them to participate in the huge profits furnished by the Civil War and the subsequent Reconstruction. In Germany, the establishment of the "Big Four" in the private banking system was largely due to Jewish capital and initiative.

Even in Russia and Poland, the first stirrings of capitalism brought Jewish merchants and industrialists to the fore. The "discovery of Volhynia," so dramatically depicted by Mendele Mocher Sefarim, duplicated that of America in opening new avenues of economic endeavor. In 1832 95 percent of the merchants of the "first guild" (those paying a high amount of taxes), and 93 percent of all factory owners in Volhynia were Jews. The Ukrainian and Polish sugar industry flourished under Jewish entrepreneurs of the type of Brodsky, Saitsev and Epstein. Leopold Kronenberg, of Warsaw, was the most prominent merchant in Poland about 1850. Later, the growth of Lodz, as a textile center, was brought about by the combined efforts of German and Jewish capitalists, the Jewish population of that town having increased twentyfold between 1860 and 1897. Even decaying Turkey had room for a great financier, Count Abraham Camondo.

To recapitulate, the Jews did not create capitalism or generate the capitalist spirit. But when their settlements, old and new, were reached by the progress of capitalist evolution, they, in turn, made contributions far beyond their numerical strength.[7]

ECONOMIC THEORIES

Economic theories, as usual, reflecting the conditions of life, eventually became a living force in the shaping of the destinies of the Jewish people, as well as of western civilization in general. The dominant theory of early capitalism, "mercantilism," was favorable to Jews under the conditions of the time. Reflecting the gold famine of the age, it stressed money as the chief element of economic and political power. Every state, leading economists taught, must strive to increase its reserves of precious metals. Wherever gold and silver were available in colonial mines, the direct importation of such treasures might solve the problem. Other countries could attain the same end only by increasing exports and decreasing imports. In such countries, national production, and especially industry and international commerce, must be fostered by all political, legislative and economic means. To mercantilist statesmen, therefore, even the Jews were welcome. They were capitalists, endowed with fortunes, skilled artisans and industrial entrepreneurs, who might help develop manufactures, or prosperous merchants with commercial contacts and family ties in foreign countries. The rivalry among European nations led to a high appreciation of population increase as such, as every immigrant could be regarded as both a potential soldier and a workingman. Frederick the Great's crude statement is representative of the age: "I regard them as a herd of deer in the park of a lord which has no other function but to populate and fill the preserve" (*Briefwechsel*, letter to Voltaire, Aug. 24, 1741). Although the Jewish question was too thorny for such a simple approach, as was proved, for example, by Frederick's own reluctance to admit more than a limited number of Jews to Prussia, such convictions could not fail, in the long run, to affect the attitude toward the Jews as individuals.

Throughout the West, Jews began to be regarded as an additional source of national power. When the merchants of Marseilles, in 1663, complained of Jewish competition, Colbert succinctly replied that the Jews were useful to the state as a whole. When Christian IV of Denmark founded a new commercial center in Glückstadt, he issued a specific invitation to the Portuguese Jews to settle there under very advantageous terms (1618-23). England and Holland had a prolonged dispute over the Jews of Surinam, whom the British wished to take with them to Jamaica, and whom the Dutch tried to retain. Menasseh ben Israel's negotiations with Cromwell aroused the Dutch government, which suspected that the Jews of Holland might remove their domicile to the British Isles. To allay these apprehensions, Menasseh announced that he had intervened only on behalf of his brethren who were persecuted by the Inquisition. Von Wolframsdorf, in his *Portrait de la cour de Pologne* (quoted by Priebatsch) argued that Jewish immigration into Saxony might swell the treasury income by five millions; and as late as 1819, Professor Lips explained the prosperity of Fürth, in contrast to declining Nuremberg, on the ground of the former's tolerant policy toward the Jews. Simone Luzzatto, in his *Discorso circa il stato degli Hebrei,* and Menasseh ben Israel, in his various political pamphlets, utilized these mercantilistic teachings as apologias of the Jewish people and their function in European society.

Perhaps it is no mere accident that Spain and Portugal, having command of vast colonies with rich mining resources, thought they could dispense with the Jews. But Holland, France, England and even Brandenburg-Prussia, being able to increase their national wealth only through production and exportation, were hospitable to Jewish newcomers. In time, the silver flotillas of Spain ceased to replenish the national treasury, while the northern countries made rapid progress in their more solid industrial expansion. By the time the Iberian countries began to issue decrees forbidding the Marranos to leave and carry their fortunes to foreign lands, irreparable harm had already been done. Moreover, laws were seldom successful in preventing a Marrano's flight, in the face of the danger of an auto-da-fé. Even the physiocratic reaction in the eighteenth century, with its emphasis upon agriculture as the only real source of all production, could not stem the tide. Capital remained the chief force, and the Jewish capitalists achieved a preëminent position.

The full release of Jewish energies came, however, only with the climax of capitalism, viz., economic liberalism. Mercantilism, although hostile to corporations, raised the flag of nationalism in the economic field, rendering the state supreme over the individual. Liberalism relegated the state itself to the background. The Jews, now firmly implanted upon capitalist soil, were among the earliest and most influential spokesmen of the movement. "Just as if Adam Smith in his system be said to stand at the end of the period in which the Stock Exchange was in its infancy, Pinto may be regarded as standing at the beginning of the modern era, with his theory of credit in which stock and share speculations have become the center of economic activity, and the Stock Exchange the heart of the body economic." Thus Sombart (*op. cit.*, p. 97), with his usual exaggeration, characterizes Isaac de Pinto's *Traité de la circulation et du crédit,* published in 1771. But whatever Pinto's merits, there is no doubt that in David Ricardo, the English Jew, liberalism has found an economic theoretician second to none in logical cogency and in influence upon subsequent economic doctrines.

The Jews could not help benefiting from such a theory and its practice. It may almost be stated as a historical law, that whenever society as a whole controls economic life through intricate regimentation of its activities, the Jews do not fare so well as under a liberalist régime, where state interference is restricted. Even in the mercantilist age, Jews derived relatively small advantage from the concentrated state power of enlightened absolutism. In Germany itself, where the court Jew materially helped the prince in building up the modern state against the combined opposition of the other privileged classes, he was merely an instrument of the monarch, who often abused him. In a democratic state, where the will of the majority of the population is supposed to decide, the Jews never constituted a majority. All forms of state socialism, however sympathetic their professed attitude, are necessarily subversive of Jewish prominence. One may see historical justice in this unconscious revenge of the state for the insistent Jewish denial of statehood.

The sentiments of the population, for the most part, remained hostile to the Jews. Capitalist evolution necessarily led to the overthrow of well-established modes of earning a living and to the ruin of many vested interests, the Jew becoming the scapegoat. As a rule, it was the old-type producer and distributor who felt threatened. Since the peasant masses of central Europe benefited greatly from the increasing competition and consequent decline in prices of industrial commodities, they now often favored the Jew against the Christian burgher. Unfortunately the power of the peasant had been broken, in the unsuccessful peasant revolts of early modern times. For a time the Jews won support from artisans, to whom they offered cheaper raw materials and a larger market for their wares. For example, in the city of Neustettin a number of guilds (bakers, butchers, brewers, shoemakers and smiths) appealed to the king in favor of the Polish Jews. But Christian artisans, too, were soon to bear the brunt of Jewish competition; they answered with a religious fanaticism which made increasing use of economic arguments. The Jewish usurer, rarely presented upon the medieval stage, became both on the Continent and in England a stock character in sixteenth-century drama. Stirred by the trial (or rather mistrial) of the Queen's physician, Roderigo Lopez, even Shakespeare created Shylock, who evidently could have had no prototype in the England of the pre-Resettlement days. Plays, satires and pictorial caricatures of Jews became extremely popular. Not even the royal protectors of the court Jews were exempt. In Prussia, in 1673, there was widely circulated an alleged testament of the court Jew, Israel Aron, the first paragraph of which read, "His Highness the Elector is requested to pay off the debts of the testator." So successful was anti-Jewish propaganda that in Lübeck, where Jews were unknown until that time, the artisan guild petitioned the government to refuse admission to a Jewish applicant on the ground of his intolerable odor, which would speedily exterminate both man and cattle.

The breakdown of prejudice followed very slowly upon the improvement of the economic and political status of the Jews. Wherever they lived in masses, only a small upper layer entered the top ranks of capitalistic endeavor. The large middle class and, where it existed, the urban and rural Jewish proletariat, continued in traditional occupations. Alsatian Jewry, in the first years of the Revolution, exemplified the prolonged resistance of the Jewish masses to modern forms. Even after the "emancipation," Jews did not immediately avail themselves of the legal opportunity to become farmers, French soldiers or public employees, but continued lending money on customary terms. So long as the inflation of paper currency boosted the prices of estates and crops, the peasants, who had borrowed heavily from the Jews to obtain abandoned estates of the nobility cheaply, were well satisfied. But when stabilization and deflation came, the high rates of interest weighed heavily upon the mortgagors. More and more peasant holdings were foreclosed for the benefit of Jewish creditors, who thus reluctantly came into the possession of extensive landholdings. The government estimated that, within fifteen years after the Jewish emancipation of 1791, Alsatian farmers were indebted to Jews to the extent of one-sixth of the total value of their estates. This relationship, so analogous to that of American and European farmers and bankers in 1933, brought the province to the brink of open revolt.

In eastern Europe, the Jewish position was further aggravated by the permanent agrarian crisis before and after the peasant liberation. Down to the twentieth century, capitalism touched there merely the surface of Jewish life. Long after the three partitions of Poland, the overwhelming majority pursued the medieval callings of *arrendators* (tax farmers and innkeepers) in the villages, and petty merchants and artisans in the towns. Jewish artisans remained the chief industrial producers in many regions. For example, in 1820, 101 out of 116 towns in Podolia had an exclusively Jewish artisan class; the craftsmen of the remaining 15 towns were predominantly Jewish. The rapidly increasing population soon outstripped the productivity of these traditional pursuits, however, and the nineteenth century witnessed an intense pauperization of the Jewish masses. In Odessa, one of the wealthiest Jewish communities in Russia, a disproportionately large number was supported by communal charities, and 63 percent of all burials had to be performed free of charge. In 1849 Miliutin wrote, on the condition of Russian Jewry, that "only three out of a hundred possess smaller or larger capital and . . . are not public charges upon their brethren, while the majority . . . is doomed to a life of destitution and beggary" (*Ustroistvo i sostoianie evreiskikh obschestv v Rossii,* p. 226). Nevertheless, the government policy, initiated by Catherine II, of keeping Jews (often also Christian merchants) out of the villages, supposedly to protect the peasants against exploitation, merely camouflaged the feudal ruling class's fear of the infiltration of more advanced ideas. This policy sharpened the perennial conflict between the Jews and the peasant masses, whom they could not help exploiting through money lending and the sale of liquor, since the bulk of the profits went to the landlords and the government. It was only after 1861 that the liberation of the peasants and the opening of the semicapitalistic age of Alexander II, made it possible for a few Jewish entrepreneurs and a minority of Jewish employees and workingmen to penetrate the thin capitalist superstructure. But capitalism in Russia was still a weak growth when the Communist Revolution broke out and—to speak in Marxian terms—the country skipped a historic stage, passing from feudalism, over capitalism, to socialism at a single bound.

JEWS AND SOCIALISM

The contributions of the Jews to modern socialism rank with their contributions to capitalism. Apart from the intrinsic affinities between the two trends, there were the perennial prophetic and rabbinic traditions of social justice, which prompted many Jews to join radical, equalitarian movements. They have supplied leaders to the socialist parties, too, far beyond their numerical proportion. In their overeagerness to accomplish the reign of justice, and in their logical extremism, they have often underestimated the power of traditional imponderables, and thus isolated themselves from the masses they led. But with their fervor, their organizing abilities, and especially their logical clarity in abstract thinking, they have often supplied theoretical bases as well as practical programs for the unconscious strivings of the masses.

There were, of course, also many Jewish antisocialists.

Disraeli could assert with some justice that the Jew, by virtue of his attachment to religion, family and property, is temperamentally a conservative rather than a radical. But others, with equal justice, could invoke the testimony of the Israelitic prophets and Jesus, to stamp the Jews as the hereditary revolutionaries. The strong sense of communal responsibility, permeating the ghetto, likewise stimulated opposition to anarchical liberalism. Whether their conservative or radical proclivities came to the fore, depended largely on the particular local situation. Disraeli himself, and his fellow archconservative, Frederick Julius Stahl (Schlesinger), the greatest theoretician of German junkerdom, were born Jews. Indeed, Jews are still almost entirely absent from the ranks of the British Communist and Independent Labour parties; few of them, in fact, have joined even the moderate wings of the Labour party. Owing to their class position, they belong, for the most part, either to the Conservatives or to the Liberals. In the France of 1789, the Jews, living far from Paris, had little share in the revolutionary movement. On the contrary, their religion soon bore the brunt of persecution on the part of the worshipers of Reason, and, being associated in the popular mind with wealth and usury, they were frequently denounced by provincial radicals. In 1794 the popular societies of Nancy and Toul demanded from the convention the expulsion of all Jewish stockjobbers. In October, 1793, the municipality of Nancy, controlled by the Jacobins, withheld the delivery of passports to Jews. That, in the course of the Revolution, these inimical trends were submerged in the great humanitarian wave of liberation, was mainly due to the impact of the general revolutionary principles, inculcating equality of man regardless of race and creed. This did not prevent the Portuguese priests, in 1808, from raising the effective battle cry against the invading French, "Death to the Jews and Jacobins," just as ten years before, Italy, temporarily "freed" from French domination by Suvarov, resounded with the hostile shouts, "French thieves," and "Death to the Jews." Even later, Fourier and his school were anything but friendly to the Jews, whom they regarded as the embodiment of the French bourgeoisie. On the other hand, among the more religious-minded Saint-Simonians, Jews, such as Émile Péreire, the editor of its main organ, *Le Globe,* and Benjamin Rodrigues, played prominent rôles.

Jewish leadership assumed importance only in the socialist movement of Germany and Russia, among whose foremost leaders have been Moses Hess, Karl Marx, Ferdinand Lassalle, Eduard Bernstein, Gustav Landauer, Leon Martov, Rosa Luxemburg and Leon Trotsky. The greatest of them, Karl Marx, with all his conscious negation of Judaism, was mentally, no less than physically, a true descendant of a long line of rabbis, reaching back probably to Meir Katzenellenbogen of fifteenth-century Padua. Ferdinand Lassalle, born of a line of Silesian ghetto Jews, remained a Jew throughout his checkered career, and his body is buried in the Jewish cemetery of Breslau.

But in all western countries, the Jewish socialist leaders were the spokesmen of the general, and not of the Jewish, proletariat. Sometimes they merely rationalized the grievances of the persecuted, ethnic minority, into the protest of all oppressed classes. In fact, until the 1890's there was practically no Jewish working class west of Poland. In Russia the growing Jewish proletarian masses, suffering doubly as workingmen and as Jews, were even more prone to join radical movements than their fellow workers among the Christians. But their Jewish consciousness usually led them to organize separate Jewish socialist parties, which sooner or later assumed a definitely nationalistic tinge. In short, the major contributions of the Jews to western socialism are, like those to capitalism, the work of individuals rather than of the masses, and this work was successfully carried on, except in the Russian Revolution of 1917, only in regions of sparse Jewish settlement.[8]

REFORMATION AND COUNTER REFORMATION

Intellectual and religious developments paralleling the rise of capitalism, accentuated the pace of the transformation of Jewish society. The Reformation, the Counter Reformation and the Enlightenment destroyed the general frame of medieval culture. New forces inside the ghetto, contact with Italian and Dutch cultures, the beginnings of neo-Hebrew and Yiddish literature, and the Jewish *Haskalah,* were successive stages in the emancipation of the Jewish individual from group predominance.

Reformation and Counter Reformation were by no means directly favorable to the Jews. In few periods was the anti-Jewish spirit more rampant than in the sixteenth century. In the recriminations between heretical and orthodox Christians, the accusation of Judaizing had long proved an effective tactical weapon in all hands. John Huss was burned in 1415, to the accompaniment of the bishops' voices making the preposterous accusation, "Oh, thou accursed Judas who, breaking away from the counsels of peace, hast taken counsel with Jews" (*Historia et monumenta Joannis Hus,* 2d ed., II, 518). It matters little that Huss appears to have had as few dealings with Jews as one could possibly have in his native Bohemia, a country humming with Jewish life. All the great reformers of the sixteenth century were decidedly anti-Jewish. Zwingli reiterated the Church's old assertion that, since the days of Jesus, the Christians have assumed the position of Israel, the chosen nation, whereas the Jews have degenerated into a Gentile people. Calvin burned Servetus because of his "judaizing" anti-Trinitarianism, while Servetus denounced Calvinistic legalism as Jewish.

None, however, used such violent terms in the denunciation of the Jews as Martin Luther, the fervent anti-Semite of German peasant stock. To be sure, he started his career as a friend of toleration, and declared that if he were a Jew he would rather suffer ten times the most terrible of deaths than join the papacy. Luther long cherished the hope that the Jews would become converted to his cause; if only a few rabbis would relinquish their faith, he sighed, the others would speedily follow. In *That Jesus Christ Is a Born Jew* and in a letter to a Jewish convert, both written in 1523, he denied the futility of missionary work among the Jews: "I think the cause of this ill-repute is not so much the Jews' obstinacy and wickedness, as rather their absurd and asinine ignorance and the wicked and shameless life of the popes, priests, monks and universities" (*Briefwechsel,* IV, 146; in the English transl., by Smith and Jacobs, II, 186). But like Mohammed, he was soon thoroughly disillusioned. In 1543 he published his *On the Jews and Their Lies* and *On the Shem Hamphoras,* a violent transcript of a fourteenth-century treatise. That this change of attitude was due to no temporary impulse, may well be seen from his book against the Sabbatarians, several of his harsh *Table Talks,* his "On the Last Words of David" written likewise in 1543, his epistle of 1545 to the Elector of Brandenburg, and his final "Exhortation against the Jews" of February 15, 1546. To quote only a few typical statements,

The Book of Esther is dear to the Jews, it is so well in line with their bloody and poisonous sentiment. There is no people under the sun so avid of revenge, so bloodthirsty, believing itself to be God's people merely in order to strangle and immolate the heathens.

. . .

Know, Christian, that next to the devil thou hast no enemy more cruel, more venomous and violent than a true Jew.

. . .

These are thieves, brigands who do not eat any food, do not wear on their bodies a single thread which they have not stolen from us and taken away by the most voracious of usuries.

. . .

Who prevents the Jews from returning to Judea? Nobody. . . . We shall provide them with all the supplies for the journey, only in order to get rid of that disgusting vermin. They are for us a heavy burden, the calamity of our being; they are a pest in the midst of our lands. [*Von den Juden und ihren Lügen,* in *Werke,* LIII, 433, 482.]

Luther, in fact, directly and indirectly instigated the German princes to banish the Jews from their lands. He concluded his last sermon with the injunction:

If the Jews wish to be converted and give up blaspheming and everything else they have been doing to us, we shall readily pardon them. If not, we shall not bear and tolerate them amongst us. [*Werke,* LI, 196.]

Although the unusually harsh language of the anti-Jewish pamphlets displeased even some of his followers (Heinrich Bullinger, for example, called them "impurissimae," while the Zurich reformers spoke of the "swinish, filthy Shemhamephorash"), and their sales remained far below his earlier pro-Jewish missionary treatise, they have exercised a great influence, even in Catholic countries such as Italy and France.[9]

The Catholic reaction was no less violent. Recognizing the great dangers threatening the unity of the Church, the papacy felt that even limited toleration of the Jews might considerably complicate its position. The granting of sufferance to out-and-out infidels embarrassed its campaign of fire and blood to extirpate the growing Christian heresies. Moreover, the very existence of the Jews, with their polemical and apologetical literature and their personal influence, seemed a threat to conformity. For example, in his remarkable *Colloquium heptaplomeres,* the semiheretical Jean Bodin introduced a Jew into the imaginary discussion, to reëcho the age-old arguments of Jewish apologists.

In the first half of the sixteenth century, the Renaissance popes still looked with composure upon the rising dissensions. They treated the Jews and even the Marranos with great friendliness, seeing in them merely a prodigious source of revenue.

How [writes a contemporary polemist] can one bear seeing a man persecute Lutherans in his country on account of religion and at the same time tolerate the Jews to such a degree? . . . Never have Christians been endowed with such favors, privileges and concessions, as have the Jews in these years under Paul III's pontificate. [Sadoleto, *Epistolæ,* XII, 780.]

Characteristically, the Council of Trent, convoked to restate the doctrine and the ritual of the Church, had nothing of importance to say on the Jewish question. Only toward the end of its twenty years' session did it adopt a resolution, reformulating ecclesiastical policy on Hebrew books. Nor did the greatest instrument of the Counter Reformation, the Jesuits and their founder Loyola, take much cognizance of the Jewish people. On the whole these interterritorial counter-reformatory agencies would have produced no change in the Church's attitude to the Jews, had it not been for the popes. In almost direct reversal of the medieval situation, when general councils often transplanted provincial anti-Jewish sentiment to a relatively tolerant center, the popes, starting with Paul IV, now began to denounce Jewish influence wildly. More persistently than ever, they demanded the segregation of the Jews in ghettos, the burning of allegedly dangerous Jewish books, and even the imposition of economic restrictions. Paul IV, under whose pontificate Rome became "a veritable monastery of St. Francis," issued, in 1555, the notorious bull *Cum nimis absurdum,* which marks a turning point in papal-Jewish relations. Officially introducing the technical ghetto into the ancient city and heaping new upon old disabilities, it poignantly enumerated the crimes of that nation "upon whom God has imposed serfdom as long as it does not recognize its errors." Even to address a Jew as "Sir" was prohibited. Pius V, in 1569, and Clement VIII, in 1593, went still further and tried the experiment, previously unknown in pontifical history, of expelling the Jews from the Papal States. They exempted, however, the Jewries of Rome, Ancona and Avignon.

Under the impact of the Counter Reformation, the position of the Jews in Catholic lands declined markedly. Their readmission by Clement VIII to the pontifical state meant only partial restoration. Their money-lending activities, while recognized as vital to papal economy, were more rigidly supervised. The special banking concessions were, as a rule, now issued only for a limited period of years. The rate of interest was restricted to a maximum of 18 percent per annum, and in Ferrara to 15 instead of 20 percent, as previously. The admission to medical practice of individual Jews, such as Raphaele di Modigliano (1602), a graduate of the medical and philosophical faculties in Siena; or of Moise Cordovero, of Leghorn (1677), was altogether exceptional. Jewish physicians were permitted to attend Christian patients only in the presence of Christian colleagues. In 1645 the Roman Inquisition decreed that no Jew could be authorized to practice medicine within the papal boundaries. The hand of the tax collector lay very heavily upon Jews. In addition to many other assessments, they were subjected to a 5-percent property tax in Rome and a 3-percent tax in Ferrara. Missionary activities were now pursued with greater zeal. An eyewitness graphically describes a baptismal ceremony in 1599:

Early last Sunday the Pope celebrated Mass in the Chapel of San Giorgio. There were there seven Jewish persons, three men and four women dressed all in red. These the Pope baptized himself in the presence of nineteen Cardinals, seven of whom he appointed as godfathers. [Klarwill, *op. cit.*, p. 220.]

In 1704 Clement XI renewed the custom of performing in person baptismal ceremonies of Jewish neophytes. Clement's successors imitated him; Benedict XIII during his pontificate personally baptized no less than twenty-six Jews. (In the Middle Ages such performances had been very infrequent. When in 1377 Charles V of France served as godfather for a convert of Castile and named him Charles, this was regarded as an exceptional favor.) More insistent than the medieval popes, Gregory XIII and his successors realized what Ramon Lull and the Council of Vienne had once mildly suggested, and introduced weekly missionary sermons before forcibly gathered Jewish audiences. The activities of the Inquisition in Spain and Portugal were no longer hampered by papal authority. In fact, on one occasion the Hapsburg imperial government tried to make use of canon law to lay hands upon the large fortune of the Hamburg Texeiras. The culmination of all papal anti-Jewish legislation was the bull of Pius VIII of 1775, which reads like a codification of all intolerant enactments in canon law. What a contrast to the medieval privileges, which, beginning with Calixtus II, had emphasized only that law's pro-Jewish side!

In short, before the Reformation, the papacy, forced to defend the Jews against intolerance, stressed toleration above restriction. Now, with Europe tending increasingly toward tolerance, emphasis shifted to disabilities and accusations. No wonder ghettos spread from one Italian city to another in the seventeenth century. Charles V, though willing in divided Germany to renew (in 1546) the old imperial protection, was most inflexible with respect to Jews and Marranos in Spain and the Netherlands. The influence of Joseph of Rossheim, that most indefatigable of *shtadlanim,* addressed by Luther himself as "Mein lieber Josel," waned outside the boundaries of the Holy Roman Empire. Even in the France of Voltaire and Rousseau, prosecutions for witchchaft and sacrilege were as numerous as before. The purchase of an estate, with its patronage over a Catholic parish, by the Jewish baron, Liefman Calmer, stirred anti-Jewish opinion during the pre-revolutionary years, and even found an echo in the Polish press.

Popular passions likewise often rose to a high pitch. As always, the passion plays incited the populace against the "Christ-killers." One performed in Frankfort, in 1506, by 270 actors, is said to have ended with the baptism of several Jews. While charges of violation of the Host lost much of their point in the face of the raging controversy over transubstantiation, the blood accusation remained quite common in central Europe and, if anything, became more frequent in Poland. It recurred even in France about 1670, in connection with the mysterious disappearance of twenty-six young men. As before, the popes refrained from encouraging this libel, but they made fewer vigorous protests. The intervention of Clement XIII in 1763, based upon the legal opinion of Cardinal Ganganelli, was obtained by Jacob Zelig, special envoy of the Council of the Four Lands, after protracted negotiations. After the Napoleonic wars, Catholic reaction was so strong that most Italian states hastened to restore their previous anti-Jewish legislation.

Only among the semisectarian, often persecuted, minority trends in modern Catholicism, such as the Franco-Italian Jansenism, mystic exaltation of the chosen people, combined with millennial yearnings, lent a friendlier tinge to the lucubrations on the position of Jewry. They were all predicated, however, on the expectation of speedy conversion. The greatest and most sober of these mystics, Pascal, merely extolled the Jews as the "depositaries of the true religion." "I find this faith," he wrote, "wholly divine in its authority, its duration, its perpetuity, its morals, its conduct, its doctrine, its effects" (*Pensées*, III,196 f.). Others, such as Abbot Claude M. Duguet, the Dominican Bernard Lambert, Degola and the famous poet, Manzoni, meditated on the restoration of converted Israel to Palestine, which would reëstablish the unity of the Church and usher in the messianic era. Among these "planners of a system of converting the Jews," there were some who strikingly resembled the Jewish "computers of the end." One, writing in 1730, calculated that the arrival of Prophet Elijah and, hence the restoration of Israel, was to take place in 1748.[10]

The future of the West, however, was determined in Protestant countries. Protestantism, allied with the rising capitalist spirit, unintentionally tore down many walls of prejudice against the Jews. The Lutheran insistence upon faith as against works, was a repudiation of the entire system of canon law. No matter how vigorously Luther reiterated the canonical principle of just price ("for the selling should not be a work that is within thy own power or will, without all law and limit, as though thou wert God, bounden to no one"), his teaching that worldly pursuits are outside the scope of faith, fostered in the long run an independent development of secular economy and politics. Much against Luther's intention, such independence from ecclesiastical interference turned out to be favorable to Jewish enterprise. The more Calvinism, especially its Puritan branch, stressed the merits of this-worldly behavior; the more it saw in the worldly "calling" the fulfillment of a higher call, and in business success a sign of divine grace; in short, the more it rationalized secular life, emotional as well as utilitarian; the nearer it came to toleration of Jews. Max Weber's identification of capitalism with Protestantism and especially Puritanism, may be almost as exaggerated as Sombart's effort to establish a connection between Judaism and capitalism. There is enough truth in both theories, however, to indicate a certain affinity between the two religious trends and economic forms. These affinities encouraged mutual understanding and toleration.

Better understanding was also promoted by the revival of Hebrew studies in early modern times. In Italy and Germany, even before the rise of the great Protestant sects, Hebrew studies pursued by Cardinal Egidio di Viterbo, Pico della Mirandola, Johann Reuchlin, Sebastian Muenster, and others, attained considerable vogue. In the prolonged and sensational controversy, stirred up between Reuchlin and the Dominicans by the Jewish apostate Pfefferkorn, enlightened opinion rallied behind the humanist. The revival of the classical tongues, the rise of critical standards of scholarship, the achievements of Renaissance historiography, contributed to increase doubts as to the canonical authority of the Vulgate. Protestant emphasis upon the Bible necessarily stimulated interest in the original language of the Old Testament. Luther was a poor Hebraist (he is said not to have recognized a Hebrew prayer book) and in his old age opposed consultation of Jews on the meaning of biblical passages. He could not help referring to the Hebrew original in his epochal translation of Scripture, however. Other Hebraists, Catholic as well as Protestant, frequently sought the advice of Jewish grammarians. Elijah Levita (Bahur) was not only allowed to teach Hebrew in Italian Renaissance universities, but was offered a chair at the University of Paris, citadel of Catholic theology. Through Protestantism and especially Cranmer's translation of the Bible, Hebrew studies penetrated into England, to reach a climax in English seventeenth-century Christian-Hebrew scholarship. In John Weemes's *The Christian Synagogue* (1623), it found a curious expression, in John Milton's works (beginning in 1642) a significant one; while in the King James version of the Bible, Walton's Polyglot Bible (incidentally subsidized by Cromwell), and Kennicott's collation of hundreds of biblical manuscripts, it left enduring monuments of penetrating and tireless research.[11]

Little wonder that English and American Puritanism was deeply imbued with the Old Testament spirit. "It was," says Froude, "because in the Old Testament they found, or thought they found, a divine example of national government, a distinct indication of the laws which men were ordered to follow, with visible and immediate punishments attached to disobedience" (*Short Studies,* II,49). Unfamiliar with the Jewish tradition and with postbiblical Jewish life, they followed even Old Testament admonitions long discarded by the Jews. Witchcraft, for example, was not merely believed in on biblical authority by Bodin, Shakespeare, Milton and Cromwell, but the legal prosecution of witches, unknown to medieval Jewry, was also introduced into Protestant countries.

Protestant social revolutionaries invoked the Old Testament in support of republican ideas. For example, Rev. Samuel Langdon, president of Harvard College, bluntly stated in an election sermon in 1775 that "the Jewish government, according to the original Constitution which was divinely established, if considered merely in a civil view, was a perfect republic" (In J. W. Thornton's *Pulpit of the American Revolution,* p. 239). Cromwell, the greatest of the Puritan rebels, recited biblical passages in the midst of every battle. It is no mere chance that almost all of the recorded citations are from the Old Testament. Not even the excesses of bibliolatry on the part of the Levelers and the Fifth Monarchy men discredited the trend. In America, where a belief in the identity of the native Indians with the lost Ten Tribes of Israel was gaining ground, Jewish Scripture played a unique rôle in the fervid partisan struggles of the Pilgrim Fathers and their descendants. In his widely read *Moses, His Judicials,* John Cotton in 1641 advocated the adoption of a New England constitution modeled on Mosaic patterns.

This new attitude naturally had a favorable effect on the position of the Jews. In 1649, even before Menasseh ben Israel, Johanna Cartwright and her son, Ebenezer, British Puritans, living in Amsterdam, addressed the English government asking the recall of the Jews to England. In his *Oceana* (1656), James Harrington preached the return of the Jews to the soil as in Bible times, and suggested their wholesale transplantation from the Continent to Ireland. Roger Williams, the founder of Rhode Island, who incidentally exchanged with John Milton lessons in Dutch for instruction in Hebrew, became the famous apostle of liberty of conscience, and advocated the admission of the Jews "for whose hard measure, I fear, the nations and England hath yet a score to pay" (*Hireling Ministry None of Christ's,* 1652; cf. O. S. Strauss, *Roger Williams,* p. 178). To be sure, some Protestant churches emulated Catholicism and introduced missionary sermons before Jewish audiences, which were often, as for instance in Giessen in 1643, complete failures. In 1703 the Protestant government of Jamaica decreed that the Jews must not have Christian servants, under the severe penalty of a fine of £500. Nevertheless, true to its own demands of individual freedom and in the face of the enormous differences within itself, Protestantism finally arrived at religious tolerance. Often Protestants sought relief from Catholic oppression by arguing that they should not be treated worse than the Jews. The wars of religion in the Old World and the vicious sectarian struggles in the New, eventually brought mutual toleration, pronounced a basic principle of international law in the Peace of Westphalia in 1648. Full liberty of conscience and even separation of church and state soon appeared as the only logical consequence.

EUROPEAN ENLIGHTENMENT

From the Reformation it was only one step to secular Enlightenment. Under the leadership of great scientists, philosophers and jurists, the entire system of human relations was reinterpreted, until it reached its classical absolutist formula in Hobbes and its democratic counter formula in Rousseau. Enlightenment, becoming more and more cosmopolitan, individualistic and secularized, was on the whole friendly to the Jews. The increasing emphasis upon the law of nature, whose eternal validity was contrasted with the relative force of positive law, had direct bearing upon the fate of the Jews. The law of nature was frequently identified with Old Testament law. Undoubtedly, argued these Christian jurists, Mosaic legislation was abrogated by the preachment of Jesus. But since it had once been divine law, it could not possibly be regarded as in contradiction to the essentials of immutable natural law. Consequently, any plea for the "natural" validity of a legal postulate was reinforced by evidence of scriptural support. Thomas Aquinas had already stated, "The old law showed forth the precepts of the natural law and added certain precepts of its own" (*Summa theol.*, II, 1,98,5). Jean Bodin, disregarding the Thomistic qualification, simply declared that the Mosaic legislation, being identical with the law of nature, suffices for human happiness; or, even more pointedly, "the authority of Moses alone is so high in my eyes that I prefer it by far to the writings and opinions of all the philosophers" (*Methodus*, Chap. VIII). Hugo Grotius, the most systematic jurist of the seventeenth century, well conversant not only with Hebrew Scripture, but, unlike most other Christian Hebraists, able to read the Talmud, inevitably became a political friend of the Jews. Appointed in 1619, together with Van Pauw, to report upon toleration, he advocated the admission of Jews to Amsterdam and freedom of public worship for them on a par with Catholics. His special code of forty-nine articles retained only a few disabilities, such as exclusion from public office, the prohibition of intermarriage, and the limitation of the number of Jewish families in the city to a maximum of three hundred. John Locke went a step further half a century later, and drew up a constitution for the Carolinas which included full liberty of conscience "to Jews, heathens and other dissenters" ("Constitution for Carolina," 1669, Art. 97).

As opposition to the Church from the French encyclopedists and Voltaire increased, however, Judaism, too, became the target of iconoclastic attacks. It was now blamed for being the parent religion of Christianity, and a source of obscurantism among the Jewish masses. Voltaire especially, having had in addition disagreeable pecuniary experiences with individual Jews, lashed with his sharp tongue the most revered Jewish institutions. Enlightenment could hardly attack the orthodox conviction of the divine origin of the Bible, as such. To every question concerning a contradiction or historical incongruity, there was the ready answer that God Almighty could have changed the course of nature and that it is our shortcoming in grasping his unfathomable ways which is to be blamed. The most effective method of the agnostics was, therefore, to heap ridicule upon traditional concepts, rather than to make a frontal attack. In this Voltaire found no rival. Such biblical criticism was effective, but shallow and incomparably inferior to the work of the Dutch critics or Jean Astruc. In addition Voltaire also attacked pitilessly the contemporary Jew. The closing sentence of the first section of his article "Juif" in the widely read *Dictionnaire philosophique* typifies his hasty generalizations:

In short, we find in them only an ignorant and barbarous people, who have long united the most sordid avarice with the most detestable superstition and the most invincible hatred for every people by whom they are tolerated and enriched. Still, we ought not to burn them. [English transl., IV, 214.]

Although in his answer to the challenge of Isaac de Pinto, the distinguished social philosopher, he mitigated it slightly, this violent arraignment best epitomizes his innumerable references to Jews and Judaism throughout his literary career. Diderot, too, has a number of sarcastic observations in his *Voyages en Hollande;* he presents two amusing Jewish types in his *Neveu de Rameau,* and attacks the Old Testament, Jews and Judaism in his encyclopedia articles, especially that on "Juifs."

The Jews found, on the other hand, French friends in such leaders of the Enlightenment as Montesquieu and Mirabeau. Although without any real understanding of the situation and character of the Jewish people (as illustrated in his essay in *Mélanges inédits,* pp. 139 f.), Montesquieu, always moderate in his opposition to the Church, often refers with sympathy to the Jews. He lays particular stress upon their commercial contributions and is apparently the first to attribute to the exiles from Spain the invention of the bill of exchange. In Germany Gotthold Ephraim Lessing, combining the cosmopolitanism of the Enlightenment with a new and deeper historical conception of religion, produced in his *Nathan the*

Wise a most eloquent apology for the Jewish people and the principle of mutual toleration. These enlightened concepts gradually filtered into wider circles. An audience in Copenhagen, for example, once vociferously rejected an anti-Jewish play. Thus it was the Enlightenment much more than the Reformation, that paved the way to the political emancipation of the Jews.[12]

JEWS AND THE REFORMATION

The reverberations of these powerful influences in Jewry were many and varied. To find the beginnings of Jewish enlightenment in Mendelssohn, is a curious misjudgment, due mainly to the provincialism of German Jewish historiography. In most fundamentals the process can be traced back to Italy and Holland of the sixteenth and seventeenth centuries, where intellectual changes had kept pace with economic transformation. That these achieved their culmination in the Berlin enlightenment and the Eastern European Haskalah was primarily the result of the rise of the Ashkenazic sector and of the incipient process of political emancipation.

The Reformation, as such, had indirect rather than direct effect upon the Jews. Not until nineteenth-century Reform did Protestantism exercise an influence upon Jewish theology. On the other hand, Jewish messianic hope surged higher and higher under the impact of Christian schismatic movements. According to Franz Delitzsch, a legend was current among the Eastern European Jews that Isaac Luria in Safed had foretold the birth of Martin Luther as an event of great significance to the salvation of the world. More realistically, another kabbalist, Joseph of Arli, prophesied that "our salvation will descend upon us when the belief in Jesus shall fall to the ground through the various new denominations" (quoted in *Hebräische Bibliographie,* V,45). The western Marranos particularly, having long combated the Church secretly, relished the new schismatic trends. Not only Calvinism with its religious affinities to Judaism, but even Lutheranism appealed to them. Most London Marranos attended Lutheran churches. According to the papal nuncio, the Jews spread Spanish versions of Luther's works all over Flanders and Spain as early as 1521. Some even seem to have been brought to Jerusalem. In the troubled year 1566, a Marrano, Marcus Perez, was chief of the Calvinist consistory in Antwerp. Neo-Christians were quite prominent among the later Huguenots, coming in part from the Marrano center of Bordeaux. Michel de Montaigne, the famous essayist, was an offspring of the Protestant Lopez family. Jean Bodin's alleged partly Jewish ancestry may have been the source of his impulse to preach universal religious toleration. The Huguenot, Isaac de la Peyrère, apparently born a Marrano, reiterated for the last thirty years of his life his ideal of the restoration of Palestine to the Jews, although calling for their previous conversion to Christianity.

The professing Jews, however, kept aloof, preserving strict neutrality in the incessant wars of religion. As individuals, some were friendly with Ziška, the Hussite leader; while others maintained amicable relations with Emperor Sigismund and Pope Martin V. Even this moderate fraternization evoked the protests of the rabbinate, which enjoined the Jews "not to take part in quarrels which are not of their concern and in which the expression of their opinion is wholly uncalled for" (quoted by Bondy and Dworsky, *Juden in Böhmen,* II, 910 f.). During the Thirty Years' War they assisted the Winter King, Gustavus Adolphus and the French armies as much as the armies of the emperor and of Spain. Conversely, Catholic as well as Protestant generals often spared the Jewish population of a besieged town, so as to prevent a total breakdown in the economic life of the district. Even in times of peace, the Jews came to terms with their respective masters. In Göttingen, for example, there were two synagogues, one "Lutheran" and one "Catholic," so called from the religion of the two lords of the district.

ITALIAN AND DUTCH HASKALAH

Much more significant was the influence of the Enlightenment upon the Jews. Beginning with the first stirrings in the sixteenth century, Italian Jewish life aligned itself with humanism. Not only did personal relations with Christians reach an intimacy hitherto unparalleled even in Spain, but the new forces assumed definite shape in the general as well as in the inner life of Jewry, in its thought as well as in its literature. Jewish musicians, artists and physicians vied with Gentiles in popularity among noble patrons. Azariah de' Rossi's and Leon of Modena's great intimacy with Christian theologians gave no offense, even to conservative contemporaries. The hold of the community and of rabbinical authority was assaulted not only from below, as later in Polish Hasidism, but also from above, by the wealthy and educated classes, as in Russia during the nineteenth century. Leon of Modena complained about "those common people who call themselves *parnasim* and chiefs, while their intention is always to degrade the power of the Torah, to prevent the wise from safeguarding the administration of the law and even to voice opinions about things ritually permitted or prohibited" (L. Blau, *Modenas Briefe,* p. 171). Apparently the heads of the community resented the cloistered scholarship of their rabbis, whose worldly knowledge did not keep pace with the growing complexity of mercantile civilization. Demands were even heard that rabbis shorten their garments to suit the changed fashions of the age.

Leone Ebreo's *Dialoghi di amore,* although apparently written first in Hebrew, is so remarkable an example of nonsectarian philosophy that, were it not for the name of the author, one might mistake it for the work of a non-Jew. Indeed on the title-page of the second, the Aldine edition of 1540, the unwarranted assertion is made that Leone was a Christian convert. Even such a fervidly anti-Jewish thinker as Giordano Bruno came under the spell of his teachings. This eldest son of Don Isaac Abravanel speedily became very popular with the European reading public (the "Dialogues" appeared in Italian five times within twenty years, and were soon translated into Spanish, French, Latin and Hebrew), and, through Bruno and Spinoza, markedly influenced modern European thought. The work of Judah (Leone) Muscato, written in Hebrew, is more in the line of medieval Jewish scholasticism. But he, too, betrays in many ways the changed outlook of the Renaissance. The revival of historical interest among the Jews, due both to the emotional reaction against the upheavals of the sixteenth century and to the influence of Renaissance historiography, was not satisfied with a mere recital of the sufferings in Usque's *Consolaçam,* the Portuguese classic, nor in the Hebrew works of Joseph Hacohen,

Ibn Verga and Ibn Yahia. In Abraham Zacuto's "Book of Genealogies" an attempt was made to review the literary history of the people more critically. Azariah de' Rossi, exhibiting the critical spirit of Bruni and Blondus, transplanted into the Jewish field, searchingly examined the records of the past in order to reconcile them with a modern point of view. De' Rossi did not refrain, for example, from questioning the historical validity of Jewish chronology. This startling attempt aroused a storm of protest among the scholars of Safed and Prague. The Italian rabbinate, however, influenced by Moses Provençale and Muscato of Mantua, merely limited the reading of de' Rossi's work to men of mature age. The awakened spirit did not fully subside, even under the blows of the Counter-Reformatory reaction and the spread throughout Italy of the factual ghetto. Through Leon of Modena, Simone Luzzatto and Joseph Solomon Delmedigo, seventeenth-century Italian Jewry revealed all the fundamentals of Haskalah. In Delmedigo, indeed, we find the most remarkable, although half-hearted, attempt in Hebrew letters to reconcile Judaism with modern natural science. Emasculated, however, by the combined pressure of economic decline and ecclesiastic reaction, this movement largely spent its force before it could communicate itself to the masses of central and eastern Europe. None the less, the leaders of the nineteenth-century Italian Haskalah, Samuel David Luzzatto, I. S. Reggio and Lellio della Torre, may be regarded as lineal descendants of de' Rossi and Modena. It may be asserted that the influence of Mendelssohn was not indispensable to the appearance of Italian thinkers of this school.

The new spirit reached its highest point in capitalist and Protestant Holland. The tremendous power still wielded by the Jewish community was a partial check, but it was now wielded by secular rather than rabbinical leaders. A contract signed in 1763 between the newly elected Chief Rabbi of Dutch Surinam and the Portuguese *parnasim,* all of them from Amsterdam, in which the rabbi pledged himself never to interfere with the will of the *parnasim* and always to take their part against the majority of the congregation, reflects prevalent usage in the mother country. The shadow of their Marrano antecedents, to be sure, stimulated among intellectual leaders mystic rather than rationalist and historical thinking. Some of the most distinguished of modern kabbalists (e.g., Abraham Herrera) were Dutch Marranos. But changed environment and social status were reflected by renewed Jewish participation in general science. Some of the leading medical men of the age were Amsterdam Sephardim. The importance of a social thinker of the rank of de Pinto has already been mentioned. Secular studies were not discouraged by the communal leaders; true to their old Spanish traditions, they assigned to them a considerable place in the curriculum of the famous Yeshiba *Ets Haim* of Amsterdam. The Dutch Jewish school system, at least, anticipated many postulates of the later Haskalah. Even a conservative visitor, such as Sheftel Horowitz, could not fail to be impressed by the Amsterdam schools, so orderly and scientific compared to the undisciplined and too-much *pilpul*-ridden Polish and German schools.

The critique of the Jewish religion by Uriel da Costa and Spinoza clearly revealed the individualistic trends within Amsterdam Jewry. Da Costa, chiefly a theologian, discussed the respective truths of Christianity and Judaism in the vein of contemporary Christian reformers. His public avowal of allegiance to Judaism was seriously influenced by the oft-repeated medieval argument that, while both Jews and Christians acknowledged the divine origin of the Old Testament, the Jews denied that of the New. Later in life, however, he turned this *consensus omnium* argument against Judaism, pointing out that many nations reject both Christianity and Judaism—an obvious reflection of the enlargement of the ethnological horizon through the great voyages of discovery. It was only natural that such a romantic Marrano should, in his Jewish superpatriotism, show an intrinsic affinity with the ancient Sadducees. He objected, for example, to the Pharisaic modification of the biblical "eye for an eye," and attacked the doctrine of immortality, which brought upon him the wrath of Samuel da Silva, Menasseh and even Spinoza. De la Peyrère, another nationalistically minded Marrano, preached the return to Palestine, as we have seen, even at the cost of religious apostasy. Here was clearly the revival of the supreme political principle of the pre-Sadducean Hellenizers.

Spinoza, although towering high above all his confreres, was not unaffected by the heated religious controversies; and yet he sounded the keynote of enlightenment and the rational revolt against religious authority. Forced carefully to scrutinize every word with respect to the Christian Gospels, his criticism of the Hebrew Scriptures was much sharper than that of the New Testament. In fact, an impression of leaning backwards when speaking of Jesus and the Gospels, while giving free reign to his emotional rather than intellectual opposition in discussing Mosaic legislation and Hebrew prophecy, is unavoidable. His reticence is thrown into bold relief when contrasted with the free New Testament criticism in the *Colloquium heptaplomeres* of Bodin. In his *Theologico-Political Treatise,* a classic of early Bible criticism, Spinoza combined negative theological strictures with a positive political theory. This he did, not merely because he had to defend himself against the "vulgar" opinion that he was an atheist, and to teach in every possible way "the freedom of philosophic speculation and of expression of what we feel" (*Ep.* 30, in *Opera,* IV,166). Nor, as insinuated by Hermann Cohen, was he trying to mix polemics against Judaism with an apology for the Dutch system of government. The source of the combination is rather the Protestant background of the period, which sought in the Old Testament the vestiges of a purified law of nature and of perfect government. That his expressions are often harsher than is warranted by the argument itself is due both to personal bitterness and to pioneering iconoclastic zeal. "Am Judengott frass Judenhass," to quote Nietzsche's famous poem.

That is why Spinoza also indulged in unbridled accusations against Maimonides, to whom, next to Crescas and Descartes, he owed more than to any other philosopher. Spinoza's most important theoretical criticism was of Maimonides' distinction between God's knowledge (God always knows) and God's will (he sometimes wills and sometimes does not will, which is no reflection on his power). He also stressed the importance of right living as against right thinking—strongly emphasized by Maimonides in his evident desire to secure a place for philosophy within activist Judaism—and refused to accept the medieval skepticism, which had argued that the unreliability of human reason leads to the interest in revelation and hence to the belief in revelation. Nevertheless, he took over so many Maimonidean teachings that, under other circumstances, he might have become a direct successor of the great medieval schoolman. Under the pressure of a novel situation, personal as well as general, however, he preferred to attack Judaism, and, rather than defend himself for deserting it, to transfer the burden of proof to his inherited religion. It is especially interesting to see this son of Jewish martyrs ridicule Calvin's exaltation of Mosaic legislation. No wonder he glorified the state as no Jew, with the exception of Stahl, had done before or after him. Meeting Hobbes, the great protagonist of absolute state power, on common ground; declaring that "every state ought to retain its form of government and, indeed, cannot change it, without danger of the utter ruin of the whole state" (*Theologico-Political Treatise,* Chap. XVIII end, *Opera,* III,228); throughout his philosophical system turning to a static rather than dynamic conception of the universe—he became the profoundest theorist of the political principle in human morals.

Spinoza and da Costa were singular phenomena, but everyone familiar with the religious and intellectual fermentation going on in Amsterdam Jewry will easily perceive that firm foundations were laid there for the secularization of Judaism and the incorporation of the Jews into the general cultural and political life of the western nations. Even the best-known Dutch rabbi, Menasseh ben Israel, owes his fame chiefly to his influence among the non-Jews. Not only in his political pamphlets and petitions, but in most of his scholarly writings, he addressed himself, long before Mendelssohn, to a Christian audience. He wrote fluently in Latin, Spanish and Portuguese, and his *Hope of Israel* appeared in no less than six languages and twenty-six editions. In all these fundamentals, the Dutch Jewish enlightenment adumbrated the vital transformations of the emancipation era.

Formally, too, the Italian and Dutch developments laid the foundations for the Central and Eastern European Haskalah. Not only were Jews productive in the vernacular to a much higher degree than even their medieval Spanish ancestors, but they evolved new Hebrew literary forms. Business needs and fresh interests in the surrounding cultures united with growing government pressure to induce the Jews to make use of the European languages. Thus the minutes of the Roman community, of which twenty volumes covering the years 1536-1620 are extant, were written until 1577 in Hebrew, afterwards in Italian. That this change was due to papal interference, appears plausible, especially since the popes after Sixtus V demanded the use of Italian, or at least Italian script, for Hebrew entries by all licensed Jewish bankers in their private ledgers. Even the religious literature of Italian Jewry showed the impact of the native language in a measure unparalleled since Islamic days. The prayer book was translated into both Spanish and Italian for the use of Marranos, women and uneducated men. At first printed in Hebrew script, partly on account of the Church's suspicion of its possible missionary effect, the Italian version made its appearance in the Latin alphabet in 1786. Most significantly, Italian rabbis used Italian, even in their responsa deciding ritual questions.

Dutch Jewry was forced from the outset to use the vernacular because of the numerous secret coreligionists who had no knowledge of Hebrew. Even the Hebrew text of the prayer book had to be transliterated into Latin script—a practice totally unknown in medieval Judaism. The publication of the *Gazeta de Amsterdam* and the economic treatises of De la Vega and Pinto in Spanish or French, was undoubtedly a question of commercial advantage. The official minutes of the Sephardi *Maamadim* of Holland (and England) were written exclusively in Spanish and Portuguese. The clash between the Iberian Ladino and the Dutch of the native majority, however, decreased the speed of linguistic assimilation, which otherwise might have exceeded that in Italy.

The beginnings of the Hebrew drama also marked a most significant innovation in Hebrew letters. Dialogue, chorus, and dramatic action may have been known in ancient Israel (Job, Ezekiel, Song of Songs); and the "Exodus" of the Alexandrine Jew, Ezekielos, reflected the influence of the Greek drama. Medieval Jewry made no attempt whatever to evolve its own dramatic literature, however. Religious antagonism to the theater, with its intrinsically pagan or Christian associations, was strong. There were, moreover, the perennial mourning for Jerusalem, and the impossibility of arranging expensive public spectacles in the small western communities. Not even the Persian-Arabic *medda* seems to have had a Jewish counterpart. It was only under the impact of the modern Spanish and Italian theaters that a few Hebrew poets, later stimulated by the genius of Calderon and the success of Lope de Vega, turned to the drama. The earliest Hebrew comedy thus far known is Joseph ben Samuel Sarfati's translation, in the early 1500's, of the famous Spanish *Comedia de Calisto e Melibea* (better known as *Celestina*) of the Marrano, Fernando de Rojas. It was followed by an original comedy, apparently composed about 1550, by Leone da Sommi of Mantua, the distinguished theoretician of Italian theatrical arts. About the same time appeared the first Spanish-Jewish drama *Esther,* by Solomon Usque and Lazaro Graziano, later translated into Italian by Leon of Modena. Two seventeenth-century Amsterdam Jews, Moses Zacut and Joseph Penso de la Vega, the economist (who for a long time was erroneously regarded as the father of the Hebrew drama: *pensavit carmina primus*), wrote three dramatic pieces in Hebrew. They were soon overshadowed by Moses Hayyim Luzzatto (of Venice and Amsterdam!) in the eighteenth century, a distinguished kabbalist and philologist, messianic dreamer and poet, who incidentally produced three plays, which, according to a popular fallacy, inaugurated modern Hebrew literature.

All these, of course, were closet dramas, not intended for public or private performance. The various "Purim-Spiele," which might be classified as folk drama, were written in the vernacular. These Yiddish plays, as well as the folk songs, prepared the ground for the nineteenth-century renaissance of Yiddish letters. However clumsy and artless, they performed a pioneer service among the Jewish masses, affecting especially the women. A recently discovered Yiddish library of an Italian Jewish woman strikingly reveals how broad were the intellectual interests of the Italian (and Dutch) women.[13]

GERMAN HASKALAH

The scene was thus set for a profound transformation, which emanated from the German and eastern Haskalah. Even before the time of Mendelssohn, signs of change were to be seen throughout Germany. In seventeenth-century Worms, Jewish children frequented the German schools without provoking articulate opposition on the part of either Jews or Christians. The University of Duisburg in Brandenburg, founded in 1665, began to admit Jewish students, who had previously been able to attend universities only in Italy and Holland. Among the seventy-five doctors of medicine graduated between 1726 and 1750, were seven Jews. At the express order of the Great Elector, two Jews from Poland were given scholarships and duly matriculated as medical students at the University of Frankfort on the Oder (1678). While the dissolution of traditional patterns was most noticeable in Berlin, no less than forty cases of Jewish illegitimate births and sexual transgressions with Gentiles were brought to the attention of the municipal authorities in the gay city of Mannheim during the eighteenth century.

Jewish enlightenment took on a definite and increasingly militant program, with Mendelssohn and his disciples. In addition to releasing the individual from the bonds of his social group, as has the European Enlightenment, it had to integrate the Jew in western society and culture. The leaders of the movement were only partly aware of its extent. Had the emancipation of the individual Jew from the Jewish group been complete, it would have meant the abolition of both Jewish religion and nationality. The European or American had in his language, literature, state, etc., manifold expressions, conscious or unconscious, of his national life. The Jew had no such immediate substitutes for tradition. Of course, many wished to see the Jewish culture of the past vanish, and such had a simple way out. In the first rush, a great wave of baptism swept Western European Jewry, particularly in Germany. The total of 204,542 baptized Jews in the years 1800-99, in addition to 19,460 baptized children of mixed marriages, given by the missionary, de le Roi, seems decidedly exaggerated (*Nathanael, Zeitschrift,* XV,65-118). Nevertheless, many Jews, encouraged by the "Christian" governments of Prussia and Russia in the nineteenth century, abandoned their inherited creed.[14]

All who remained Jews felt more or less explicitly that some part of traditional Judaism must be preserved if the Jew were to survive. Hence Jewish enlightenment was, on the whole, much less radical than the European movement, especially in its French manifestation. Mendelssohn himself devoted much of his effort, especially in his most important work, *Jerusalem,* published in 1763, to a defense of the Jewish religion and, in particular, of Jewish law. His general outlook may best be defined in his own words, "Comply with the customs and the civil constitutions of the countries in which ye are transplanted, but, at the same time, be constant to the faith of your forefathers" (*Jerusalem,* English transl. by M. Samuels, I,162). In his opinion, rather than give up the religious law, one should forego civil union with the Gentiles. Characteristically, this disciple of supposedly "unhistorical" enlightenment, who was personally devoid, in fact, of all historical interest and even opposed to Lessing's idea of a progressive "education of mankind," frequently reiterated the historical proof of Judaism. While Voltaire, himself a distinguished historian, was ready to condemn the past whenever it differed from rational standards, Mendelssohn, true to Jewish tradition and keenly aware of the unsatisfactory condition of his people, treated the processes of historical evolution with greater reverence. Neither was he a militant reformer. All his struggles against Lavater, Michaelis, and Jacobi, were forced upon him, much against his will, by untoward circumstances. Even his German translation of the Bible, which turned out to be the most revolutionary act of his life, was done primarily, as he himself asserts, for the benefit of his children. There certainly was nothing heterodox in his fundamental theory that Judaism is less a dogmatic creed than a law and mode of life, and that all the descendants of Abraham are in duty bound to observe each and every minute prescription.

There were, however, in all his writings, numerous utterances—the author himself being often evidently unaware of their far-reaching implications—which revealed that, after all, he was the spokesman of a new generation. So when he tried to distinguish between the rationally comprehensible moral law, valid with respect to all mankind, and the irrational, but revealed, ceremonial law, which binds the Jews alone, he stated that God constantly reveals the creedal tenets to the Jews, "as to the rest of mankind, by nature and by events, but never in words or written characters," and that the laws alone needed support by revelation (*Jerusalem,* English transl. by M. Samuels, I,89). Perhaps half unwittingly he thus established a novel contrast between faith and knowledge, in opposition to all previous philosophy of Judaism. In a private letter to Homberg, he also admitted that ritual law had lost much of its significance as a symbol and remained mainly a tie uniting all true "theists" (*G.S., Jubiläumsausgabe,* V,669). Through his own widely heralded works in general philosophy and his profound indebtedness to Plato, Leibnitz and Wolff, however, he contributed much more than through these doctrinal deviations, toward the secularization of Jewish intellectual life. True, even his greatest philosophical treatise, the *Phaedon,* is not devoid of hidden apologetics. His emphatic attempt to explain the immortality of the soul rationally, as a necessary culmination of ethics, was doubtless provoked by such "enlightened" thinkers as Locke, Leibnitz and Lessing, who had stressed the superiority of Christianity over Judaism, because it had added faith to the this-worldly law of the mother religion and, with it, the reward of immortality. Mendelssohn might have answered by historical reference to the Pharisaic doctrine of resurrection, which antedated the rise of Christianity. But he preferred to argue, in the philosophic jargon of the day, that immortality was a general human belief, based upon reason and not upon the preachment of Jesus; and that, consequently, it is as germane to Judaism as it is to Christianity or any other advanced religion. Nevertheless, Mendelssohn's philosophy was outwardly primarily German and secular, and its great popularity among contemporary German intellectuals brought the author great influence among Jews, whose growing sense of inferiority throughout the emancipation era made them extremely sensitive to all signs of approval from outside.

Mendelssohn's followers were forced largely to abandon or pass over in silence the theoretical teachings of the master. For a while they remained faithful to Hebrew, which their master had tried to resuscitate and had glorified as the language "supreme in quality and oldest in time" (*Kohelet Musar,* reprinted *Festschrift . . . Budapest,* Hebrew section, p. 65). But, with the swift pace of social transformation, they had to lay increasing stress upon secular education. Focusing on the *Ha-Meassef,* founded in Königsberg in 1783 (it was the first Hebrew periodical, if one disregards Mendelssohn's sporadic attempt of 1750), they preached with increasing zest *rapprochement* with the German environment. Hartwig Wessely, particularly, a protagonist of educational reform, saw in the new school an instrument for the improvement of the social and intellectual status of his people. Educational changes had often been preached among the Jews; for instance, Loew b. Bezalel, the conservative rabbi of sixteenth-century Prague, led the struggle in his day. But now, under the pressure of adjustment to the new environment, and under the influence of Rousseau's *Émile,* the reform of Jewish education was regarded as the paramount problem of the day. Wessely withstood the concentrated attack of several revered orthodox rabbis. The foundation of a modern school in Berlin by Friedlaender in 1776, followed by similar institutions in Trieste, Frankfort, Seesen and Wolfenbüttel, can be traced to his preachment. One of his less worthy allies, Herz Homberg, was asked by Joseph II to serve as inspector of the Jewish school system in Galicia. Soon every Jewish man and woman of the province had to pass an examination on Homberg's German catechism of the Jewish religion in order to get a marriage license.

In literature Wessely and his friends applied the medium of poetry to revitalize the Hebrew language. Although most of them despised the Yiddish idiom, some used it for propaganda. It was propagandist fervor, rather than poetic inspiration, which guided the pen of Wessely in his Hebrew *Songs of Glory* and especially his *Words of Peace and Truth.* Propaganda was also the chief aim of Isaac Euchel in his *Rab Henoch,* the first Yiddish comedy of a literary nature; and Aaron Wolfson's publicist articles in the *Ha-Meassef,* as well as in his Yiddish work *Leichtsinn und Frömmelei.* Characteristically, Euchel himself in commending the use of Yiddish complained that, in contrast with 1783 when their periodical was founded and when "every young Jewish littérateur regarded it as a distinction to learn Hebrew," in 1797 its study was greatly neglected ("Ist nach dem jüdischen Gesetze das Übernachten der Todten wirklich verboten?," *Ha-Meassef,* VII, 364).

All these writers were clearly aware of their indebtedness to the Italian and Dutch Haskalah. Mendelssohn had already encouraged the translation of Menasseh's *Vindiciae* by Marcus Herz, the distinguished physician and philosopher. Apart from counting among their coworkers Dutch and Italian poets such as Franco Mendes and Samuel Romanelli, the *Meassefim* republished de' Rossi's historical work, and wrote the biographies of Abravanel, Joseph Solomon Delmedigo, etc. But they focused their attention primarily on the popularization of the ethical and literary standards prevalent in contemporary German letters, such as Wessely's *Songs,* depending greatly on Klopstock's *Messiah.* Symptomatically, Goethe and Schiller found no appreciation among these self-appointed literary guides of their people. More important, although far less influential, were the innovations in the philosophic field. Almost simultaneously with Solomon Pappenheim's largely prehaskalic meditations came Lazarus Bendavid's posthaskalic, assimilatory rationalism. Above them towered Solomon Maimon, the profoundest Jewish thinker of the eighteenth century, who tried to reconcile Kantian philosophy with that of Maimonides. His *Gibeat Hamoreh,* a commentary on the *Guide,* was the first attempt to synthesize Judaism and idealistic German philosophy.[15]

The belated German-Jewish enlightenment, however, came upon a world which no longer wanted enlightenment, a world no longer satisfied by rationalism. The post-Mendelssohnian generation coincided with the rise of German romanticism and the "historical" schools. Kant had already challenged the supremacy of human reason. With Fichte and Hegel, a distinct reaction began in philosophy, literature, art, law and history. Society, in all its aspects, came to be regarded more and more as the result of implacable historical forces, the outgrowth of a slow evolution not to be overturned by even the strongest will of any one generation. As to the Jews, Herder's glorification of ancient Hebrew poetry was merely in line with his sincere conviction that diversity of culture, rather than cosmopolitan leveling of differences, is the aim of historical evolution. His eloquent proclamations that the older a people, the more distinctive its individuality, that Israel's chosenness is the essence of Jewish history, and that the burden of the law is an integral part of Judaism, made a tremendous appeal to the young Jews. They were prone to disregard his dire prediction that the Jewish people will always remain an alien, Asiatic element in western culture. Hegel's gigantic conception of the progression of the "subjective spirit" through history, acknowledging ancient Israel as a vital stage of that development, flattered the vanity of intellectual Jews. His assertion, on the other hand, that the slavish bondage of the Israelitic individual before God had been overcome by the freedom of Christianity, stimulated opposition and dialectical defense. History itself now came to be recognized by both progressive and conservative Jews as the principal means of reconciling Judaism with western culture.

WISSENSCHAFT DES JUDENTUMS

Out of this conviction was generated the most enduring and, in its permanent effects, the richest Jewish movement of the nineteenth century: the *Wissenschaft des Judentums*. Represented by pioneers of the rank of Zunz, Jost, Frankel, Geiger and Graetz in Germany; S. D. Luzzatto, and Reggio in Austrian Italy; and Krochmal, Chajes, Rappaport, and Schorr in Austrian Galicia, it opened a new chapter in the history of Judaism, a chapter whose most important pages are perhaps still unwritten. Historicism, awakened in sixteenth-century Italy, had long been withering in the unfavorable atmosphere of "unhistorical" Jewish enlightenment. Mendelssohn himself admitted,

What do I know of history? All that bears the name history . . . has never got into my head; and I yawn all the time when I am bound to read anything historical. [*G. S.,* 1844, V, 342.]

In the seventeenth and eighteenth centuries the major work in Jewish history was performed by non-Jews, such as the Dutch Orientalists, Selden, Surenhusius, Vitringa; the positively anti-Semitic Schudt; the Bible scholars, Tychsen and Michaelis; and, most of all, by the Frenchman Basnage. Now the Jews assumed uncontested leadership in the field of postbiblical Jewish history and, for a while—in the persons of Geiger, Frankel and Luzzatto—made imposing contributions to biblical learning as well. A wide search of the libraries of Europe brought to light unknown treasures of the past. Through philological and historical criticism, these savants sifted the available material and reconstructed it in ever-new syntheses. All this scholarship has sometimes been called lifeless. But the great builders of this new science were perfectly aware of the immediate relevance of their work to the task of transforming Jewish life. The interrelation of Jewish studies and the struggle for political as well as intellectual emancipation, came clearly to the fore. Leopold Zunz, for example, in the introduction to his classical work, *Die gottesdienstlichen Vorträge der Juden*, wrote,

> Through wider intellectual culture and a deeper understanding of their own affairs the Jews would achieve a higher degree of recognition and consequently of right. Many a legislative blunder, many a prejudice against Jewish antiquity, and many a condemnation of the new aspirations, has been simply the result of the desolate condition into which Jewish literature and science have fallen during the last seventy years, especially in Germany.

To Rappaport and Luzzatto, on the other hand, the studies in Jewish history, Hebrew philology and literature appeared as the chief means of rejuvenating Jewish national and religious feeling.[16]

GALICIAN AND RUSSIAN HASKALAH

Practically every great leader had his own conception of Judaism and Jewish needs. Each not only reflected the wide variations in the conditions of Prussian, Lombardo-Venetian and Galician Jewry, but also the different stages at which assimilation to the surrounding culture took place. Berlin Jewry had entered modern capitalism as a kind of advance guard; but Italian and Galician Jewry, although living in a relatively progressive empire, lagged far behind. Italian Jewry, furthermore, was inextricably linked with Italian culture, which had not yet responded to the impulses of the nineteenth century. In Galicia the problem was much more complicated, many contradictory tendencies tugging at one another; while Germanization was fostered by the imperial government of Vienna, Polonization was demanded by the local ethnic majority; while the capitalistic advance of western Austria went on, Galicia's backwardness was deliberately preserved; while the Jews of the western provinces were being urbanized, the majority of Galician Jewry lived in rural districts or small towns. Moreover, German philosophy and poetry, now in their flower, were widely read by all the Eastern European Jewish intelligentsia.

The greatest difference, however, consisted in the aggregation of Jewry. In Germany, where the Jews constituted an insignificant minority of less than one percent, the overwhelming influence of German culture could hardly be resisted. In eastern Europe the Jewish mass population, outnumbering the Christians in many a township, long continued to live an essentially Jewish life. The contradictory influences of Russo-Polish and German cultures weakened both these forces further. The knowledge of the German language was limited to a cultivated few and all German culture was merely "book" culture in the East. Here Jewish national life was easily able to weather the threat of disintegration, while in central and western Europe the very existence of the Jewish nationality was seriously threatened.

During the first half of the nineteenth century the leadership of Galician Jewry in the eastern Haskalah was uncontested. Following an early group in Tyśmienica about 1730, Mendel Lefin Satanover, who came from Podolia to Brody, soon became the spokesman of the Mendelssohnian ideal. Under the influence of the liberal Polish statesman, Prince Adam Casimir Czartoryski, Lefin published in 1791 a pamphlet whose title clearly indicated his objectives, *Essai d'un plan de réforme, ayant pour objet d'éclairer la nation juive en Pologne et la rédresser par ses moeurs.* In order to reach the Jewish masses, Lefin wrote extensively both in Hebrew and Yiddish, and published a Yiddish translation of parts of the Bible. He even wrote a German paper, thus far unpublished, "concerning the importance of popular writings in Yiddish for the culture and enlightenment of the Jewish inhabitants in Poland" (quoted by I. Weinlös, in *JB,* II, 345). He also published a Hebrew translation of a popular medical work (of Tissot), which Mendelssohn recommended for consultation in all places where there was no expert physician. His translation of Benjamin Franklin's *Poor Richard's Almanac* was not only republished by Israel Salanter and others, but initiated a kind of youth movement in Galicia and Podolia, where special groups were organized for the purpose of living in accordance with the ethical standards expounded in that work.

The great era of the Galician Haskalah did not set in, however, until Krochmal (originally Krochmalnik) began his quiet but effective teaching activity, which culminated in the posthumous publication of his *Guide of the Perplexed of Our*

Time. Accepting the general theory (advanced by thinkers from Vico to Hegel) of the three stages of all civilizations—birth, growth and decay—he claimed exceptional eternity for the Jewish people, in whose history each such cycle ends only to give rise to another. Since "God accompanies Israel in all his migrations," Jewish history, although otherwise determined by the ordinary natural processes, is not merely a stage in the objectivization of the Absolute, but its eternally recurrent self-realization. Simultaneously, Zebi Chajes undertook a scientific reformulation of the Talmud, and Joseph Perl launched both his memorable attack on Hasidism and his educational reform in Tarnopol. Hasidism was regarded as the main enemy. In 1816, even before Perl's anonymous *Megalleh temirin* (The Revealer of the Hidden), similar in character and effect to *Epistolae obscurorum virorum,* one of his disciples (apparently Bezalel Stern) circulated a German polemical description of the sect. This pamphlet was to exercise lasting influence upon the view taken of that movement by German Jewish historians, such as Jost and Graetz. The number of Galician Haskalah poets and writers, headed by Isaac Erter, and especially scholars and publicists, is too large to be enumerated. Curiously, however, their force spent itself quickly, as the emancipation movement, after 1848, went far beyond the Haskalah. With the assumption of power by the Poles, there began large-scale Polonization of the Jewish intelligentsia. Galician Jewry, after 1867, had the choice of being assimilated to Polish culture, of emigrating to the West, or of following traditional Jewish patterns with as little change as possible. Between the extremes of rigid orthodoxy and Hasidism on the one hand, and far-reaching assimilation on the other, the Haskalah had little chance to survive. One of the Haskalah leaders, Joseph Samuel Byk, increasingly disgusted with the barrenness of "enlightened" ideology, went over to the enemy camp and became a sympathizer of Hasidism.

It was in Russia that the Galician Haskalah found its direct continuation. Such important writers and educators as Simhah Pinsker, Eichenbaum, and B. Stern, emigrated from Galicia, especially to the newly established center in Odessa. The writings of the Galician leaders, including such minor lights as Mieses, Letteris and Goldenberg, found their most enthusiastic readers across the border. Conversely, I. B. Levinsohn, the most influential personality in the Russian Haskalah, frequently visited the commercial city of Brody, where he received much stimulus for his work. Indeed, Brody furnished more subscribers for his *Admonition unto Israel* than any other city. Unlike Galicia, however, Russia did not emancipate her Jewry until the Revolution of 1917, by which time the Haskalah had long been diverted into the channels of the national renaissance.

Although it had antecedents in the circle around Elijah Gaon of Vilna, the Russian Haskalah boasts no such towering personality as that of Nahman Krochmal. Neither did it have scholars of the rank of Rappaport, Chajes, Luzzatto, Reggio or Schorr. On the other hand, it had more distinguished men of letters, such as Abraham Mapu, often called the father of the Hebrew novel; Abraham Ber Lebensohn, a skilled versifier; his more gifted son, Micah Joseph Lebensohn; and, finally, Yehudah Loeb Gordon, the most prominent poet of the Haskalah period. That most of these poets' writings bear the stamp of this period so clearly is chiefly due to their programmatic militancy. The Russian Haskalah was also more negative in its immediate aims than was the Galician enlightenment. With the exception of I. B. Levinsohn, most Russian writers combated not only Hasidism but all forms of traditional Judaism. Schorr had attempted a scientific, though not unbiased, critique of the Talmud, and suggested numerous emendations to the Old Testament text. But his Russian disciples, Gordon and Lilienblum, at times voiced decidedly heterodox opinions with respect to the Bible itself and, writing as poets and publicists rather than scholars, carried their antireligious crusade to the masses. One member of this circle, Abraham Uri Kovner, not only rejected the "useless minutiae" of Hebrew scholarship, but, despairing of the survival of Hebrew letters and of Judaism, proceeded to the baptismal font.

The Yiddish Haskalah was, on the whole, still more antagonistic to tradition. The Kahal had become an instrument of government oppression, especially after 1827, when it became responsible for the delivery of a fixed number of Jewish boys to the army. In this situation, the social antagonisms within the ghetto grew sharper and sharper. The proletarian masses resented and finally rejected the leadership of the arbitrary *parnasim*. The rabbinical leaders, although often of the highest personal integrity and imbued with the finest traditions of Jewish learning and morals, were much too often cloistered scholars, unable to counterbalance the excesses of the lay leaders. Thus they made themselves guilty of tacit coöperation. In reaction, one of the most gifted dramatists of the Yiddish stage, Jacob Gordin, founded a kind of agnostic, ethical-culture movement in Russia. The effect of Yiddish letters upon the masses can easily be measured by the great popularity of certain authors. Eliezer Pavir's otherwise altogether insignificant drama, *The Greatness of Joseph* (1801), a paraphrase of an equally insipid Hebrew play, *War in Peace,* of Hayyim Abraham, the Maggid, went through forty-odd editions.

Still more extreme were the protagonists of Russification among the Jews. At first Vilna and Odessa tended toward German culture, knowledge of Russian being slight even among the Jewish intellectuals. After 1860 both these cities became centers of Russian culture, while Warsaw focalized the forces of Polonization. Originally only a few rich Jews and those in public employ agitated for full linguistic assimilation, but in the liberal era of Alexander II many Jewish intellectuals preached the adoption of one or another of the Slavonic cultures. Even in the synagogue such men as Zebi Hirsh Dainov, called the "Slutsker Maggid," preached the ideal of Russification. Indeed some began to address synagogue assemblies in the Russian language. An increasing number of converts became sworn enemies of Judaism. For example, Jacob Brafman, through his *Book of the Kahal,* purportedly a collection of minutes of the Minsk community, became one of the most dangerous informers of the nineteenth century.

The Russian government supported all these tendencies, morally as well as financially. Nicholas I saw in the widespread educational activity of the imported German rabbi, Dr. Lilienthal, nothing but a step toward full Christianization. His decrees outlawing the peculiarly Jewish dress, the traditional earlocks, etc., breathed the same missionary spirit. Under the more liberal government of Alexander II, secular assimilation replaced the ideal of religious conversion; the

"Society for the Promotion of Enlightenment among the Jews in Russia," founded in 1863, became one of the main vehicles of assimilatory propaganda. Little wonder that the Haskalah was greatly distrusted by the orthodox masses as a preliminary to the final absorption of the Jews by the surrounding nationalities.[17]

EMANCIPATION AND ASSIMILATION

The problem of denationalization and assimilation became dominant also in the political arena, where the emancipation of the individual meant the destruction of the corporation. Since the modern state was from the outset radically opposed to corporate entities within its borders, Jewish corporate life had to disappear sooner or later. Even absolute monarchy had gradually dissolved the different "estates" by concentrating all the state power in the hands of a single person, the king. The state, absolute or democratic, was now the supreme institution of public and, in a sense, even of private life.

The Jewish "corporation," *i.e.*, the Jewish community, lasted longer than the other corporations, owing not to its corporate, but to its peculiar Jewish, features. Because in the West the Jews were few in number, their "corporations" could be overlooked or ignored temporarily. To take an extreme example, the legal fiction that Jews were not admitted to England was maintained at a time when a synagogue was located in the heart of the capital, and when Jewish bankers had become very influential. Eventually, however, the state simply had to take some cognizance of this anomalous body; it had to try to absorb it like others. With free competition established under the new capitalistic order; with its standing armies of mercenaries or the *levée en masse;* and with the progressive secularization of education, arts and sciences; the modern state sooner or later had to dispense with the economic guild, the noble army and the ecclesiastical estate. The Jews, too, gradually lost their specific function within the political organism. Although for its military and administrative ventures the state needed money and credit more than ever, no single group of rich Jews could provide the necessary loans and taxes. The whole people had to be drafted for both supplying the normal revenue and subscribing to public debentures. The Jewish banker remained instrumental in the distribution of securities, but his function was no longer specifically Jewish, and the Jewish community as a whole had nothing to do with it. Under these circumstances, the existence of a Jewish corporation became more and more gratuitous. Even had the economic and intellectual advances of the Jews not prepared the way for their political emancipation, the modern state, for reasons of its own, would have sooner or later destroyed that Jewish corporation and distributed its members through the whole body politic.

For this reason, wherever emancipation came, the expectation of assimilation moved not far behind. To be sure, that was not the case in Russia, Turkey or even Austria-Hungary. By the time these three empires liberated the Jews by general constitutional legislation, it had become perfectly clear that assimilation of the Jewish group could not be accomplished overnight. But the earlier emancipations, starting with the American and French Revolutions, took for granted that the consequence would be speedy assimilation to the dominant nationality. In some countries protagonists, in others opponents, of emancipation demanded prior assimilation. Assimilation and emancipation thus became associated as a single solution for the Jewish problem.[18]

Assimilation had many aspects. Full assimilation could only mean the abandonment of all distinctive elements. Logically, it would lead to conversion to Christianity and gradually to the extinction of the Jewish race through intermarriage. Europe had behind it, however, two fixed traditions: the wars of religion, culminating in freedom of conscience; and the historic futility of all attempts at converting the Jews. If the state did not wish to compromise the principle of noninterference with the belief and worship of its citizens, the Jewish religion had to be tolerated. At most the state arrogated to itself supervision of the external forms of religious life. Even to such control there was objection by extreme advocates of the separation of church and state. The Jewish faith thus had to be maintained as one of the permitted religious denominations.

As to the Jewish "race," there was the hope and expectation that intermarriage might solve this problem without legal prescription. Napoleon alone tried to have the state and Jewish leaders support intermarriage. But even the Paris Sanhedrin, a mere instrument of imperial policy, opposed the emperor on this point. Napoleon had suggested a resolution encouraging one mixed marriage to every two Jewish marriages. The Jewish elders refused to sanction even the performance of such a ceremony by a rabbi. At most, they acknowledged the validity of mixed nuptials performed by the civil authorities, quoting for their support the old talmudic principle, "The law of the kingdom is law." In the other Catholic countries, moreover, the old canonical prohibition counteracted such tendencies. Even today, for example, the civil law of the Austrian Republic retains the canonical *impedimentum cultus disparitatis*, and no Christian is allowed to marry a non-Christian. Even where intermarriage became admissible under the law, modern constitutions have, as a rule, granted citizens enough personal liberties so that the authorities have been barred from interfering with this most intimate sphere of private life.

On its march toward consolidation, the modern state encountered no slight obstacle in Jewish communal organization. The material as well as spiritual power possessed by communal leaders, represented vested interests of considerable magnitude. The obvious foreignness of the Jews, their indifference to a particular territory, their transient sojourning and frequent expulsion, their special privileges, favorable and unfavorable—all put the Jewish group beyond the normal range of "Christian" society. This fact was recognized by both Jew and non-Jew, each finding adequate comfort in his own rationalization. The modern state, however, had to batter down this refractory group, this nation within the nation. Emancipated Jewish individuals were, for their part, perfectly ready to give up a special status, which was, in so many ways, a handicap. But the great Jewish masses living in eastern Europe or under Muslim domination, barely touched by modern capitalism and the intellectual enlightenment, ardently clung to their familiar way of life. Thus a great battle ensued. In each state progressive forces combined with a small vanguard of Jews against reactionary forces allied to the masses of Jewry. Radical anti-Semites often echoed demands for Jewish autonomy, as expressed by the most unyielding traditionalists among the Jews. The trend toward complete emancipation, however, was accelerated by many economic factors. All Jews, even the most orthodox, wished civil emancipation (*privatbürgerliche Emanzipation*), which would give them ampler opportunities of earning a living. The tremendous pressure of the rapidly increasing Jewish population made a diversification of economic activities more and more inevitable, and this meant the removal of the manifold legal disabilities which had shut out the Jews from various pursuits. But precisely these economic implications provoked relentless opposition among certain classes of the non-Jewish population, who saw their vested interests seriously threatened. Political emancipation, on the other hand, the granting of the rights of citizens, implied forfeiture of Jewish autonomy. It was on this score that the modern statesmen were most insistent, whereas the Jewish masses often considered the price too high.

As early as the days of Joseph II, Jewish hostility to his radical measures caused much concern to the benign emperor. Orthodox Jewry in France, even in the predominantly Sephardic community of Bayonne, received the emancipatory decrees with mixed feelings. In 1792 the powerful community of Fürth successfully resisted Hardenberg's early attempts at partial emancipation. The Jews instinctively sensed that behind the new, friendly spirit lurked much of the conviction, voiced already by Christian Wagenseil, that while the Jews could not be led to abandon their faith through force, appointment to public office and other friendly gestures would accomplish this end. When, finally, in the wake of the French emancipation, there arose the cult of Reason, with the concomitant outlawry of Judaism; when Sabbath observance was forbidden; when a rabbi like Sinzheim had to hide his library and become a wanderer; when all the Jews, like the Marranos of old, had to perform their rites in strictest secrecy; and when a conscientious objector, Jean Mendès, probably a descendant of Marranos, was condemned to death —the suspicions of orthodox Jewry seemed fully confirmed. The further east, the more numerous were the adherents of Saul Ascher's vigorous objections to the artificial suppression of Jewish nationality. In Padua, Luzzatto time and again reiterated his belief that the fortunes of our people do not depend upon emancipation, but upon our love of one another and upon our being united with ties of brotherhood like children of one family. That is our fortune which is diminishing and being lost in the shadow of emancipation. [Letter to Jost, 1840; *Iggerot Shadal*, V, 660.]

He found influential allies in the orthodox rabbis Akiba Eiger, in Posen, and Moses Schreiber, in Pressburg. Even in the West, for example in Amsterdam in 1796 and in Baden in 1846, much articulate opposition had to be overcome. Sir Moses Montefiore, a most popular champion of Jewish rights throughout the world, advocated, in the midst of the most heated controversy in England, many minor reforms in Jewish legal status, including admission to Parliament, but was opposed to full emancipation.

The European governments could not fully ignore this attitude. In Holland, especially, the Jewish opposition influenced the democratic constitution of 1796 which read, "No Jew may be deprived of the rights connected with Batavian citizenship as long as *he wishes* to make use of them, on condition that he satisfy all demands and fulfill all duties fixed by the Constitution." The Germanic Act of Confederation of 1815, and many minor edicts, reiterated this *condition*. The governments were clearly aware then, though it appears to be forgotten now, that emancipation was an exchange rather than a one-sided gift, and that the Jews might reject their part of the bargain.

The Jews did not reject it. Age-old habits of obedience to state authority, the pressure of economic needs, the social and intellectual interests of progressive leaders, eventually subdued all opposition. The advocates of equality, in almost messianic expectation of a new epoch of universal happiness, were deaf to the rumblings among the masses. They spoke in the name of the entire people. The community of Frankfort, dispatching delegates to the Paris Assembly of Notables, enthusiastically announced that "never yet had such a happy era dawned upon the Jewish people as today" (Quoted by Klibansky, in *REJ*, LXXXIV, 99). The president of that assembly, Abraham Furtado, incidentally a son of Marrano parents, untiringly voiced similar exalted sentiments. In Breslau a Jewish publicist called himself Lewin Benjamin Dohm, out of gratitude to the Christian spokesman of Jewish equality, and in 1807 the community expressed public thanks to the Christian burgesses for permission to take part in the defense of the city. The trend was quite irresistible.

JEWISH DIPLOMATS

The progress of Emancipation was, none the less, slow and full of sudden reversals. On the whole, it may be asserted that Western European Jewry was emancipated in the eighteenth, Central European Jewry in the nineteenth, and the Eastern European Jewish masses in the twentieth century. Forebodings of political change could be felt even earlier in the growing influence of Marrano and Jewish diplomats, bankers and contractors, upon the public life of Holland, England and France. Not only did Jewish representatives of Muslim powers receive diplomatic standing in the West, but even Christian countries frequently availed themselves of the services of these able negotiators. In 1573 Solomon Ashkenazi was sent by Turkey to Venice, where he was received with high honors as the main negotiator of the much-desired peace treaty. Solomon Cormano journeyed to London in 1592, where, as the representative of Alvaro Mendes and indirectly of the Sultan, he organized the first public Jewish services in centuries. Samuel Palache was permanent envoy to Holland of the Sultan of Morocco. These were but a few of the numerous Jews in Muslim diplomatic service. Even more significant was the appointment, in 1655, of Abraham Senior Texeira as diplomatic representative of Sweden in Hamburg by Queen Christina, a Christian sovereign with no Jewish subjects of her own. In 1684 the queen appointed Miguel Osorio as her representative in Holland. Jacob Cohen served there as agent for Prince Maurice of Nassau, and David Bueno de Mesquita as resident of the Margrave of Brandenburg. Daniel and Jacob Abensur served in the same capacity in Hamburg for the king of Poland while Gabriel Gomez represented the king of Denmark in that city. Israel Conegliano, as a member of the Venetian delegation, proved to be a very resourceful negotiator, and became instrumental in the successful conclusion of the Carlovitz peace treaty of 1698.

Paradoxically, Spain and Portugal made by far the most extensive use of the services of Jewish diplomats. This contrast between foreign and domestic policy, often discernible in anti-Semitic governments today, did not escape the notice of contemporaries such as Sir William Temple and Schudt. The diplomatic relations between Portugal and Hamburg in the years 1640-1795 were maintained through the Portuguese family Nuñez da Costa, while another branch of that family filled a similar position in Holland until the middle of the eighteenth century. In 1746 David de Oliveira served as Portuguese agent in Leghorn; a century earlier Manuel Fernandez de Villareal held a similar position in Paris. When, in 1652, he unsuspectingly visited Lisbon, he was burned at the stake. Anthony Lopez Suasso was made Baron of Avernas Le Gras by Charles II, in reward for the diplomatic services rendered by him to Spain. For several decades Baron Manuel de Belmonte represented the king of Spain in the Netherlands, and in 1693, in recognition of his great services, he was created Count Palatine by the emperor. The emperor also conferred the title Marquis de Montfort upon Franciso de Sylva, whose son Fernando, the second marquis, publicly returned to Judaism under the simple name Isaac de Silva Solis.

Apart from these half-Jewish, half-Christian diplomats, numerous German court Jews rendered spectacular services to their respective princes. For example, Samson Wertheimer was instrumental in bringing about Hapsburg military victories in Italy and Turkey. It was not without reason that one of the greatest generals of the age, Prince Eugene of Savoy, favored Jewish resettlement in Milan. Lefmann Behrens, in Hannover, considerably helped his sovereign obtain the title of elector. Behrend Lehman of Halberstadt was partly responsible for the election of the Saxon king to the throne of Poland. De Pinto's services to Holland in 1748 received the public recognition of the secretary of state, "You have saved the country!"

EMANCIPATION IN WESTERN EUROPE AND AMERICA

The prominence achieved by these individuals naturally threw a sharp light on the disabilities of the people at large, and served as a constant stimulus to reform. The first voice in favor of unrestricted Jewish emancipation came characteristically from the British Isles, which had readmitted Jews only a short time before. John Toland, in a pamphlet entitled *Reasons for Naturalizing the Jews in Great Britain and Ireland,* published in London in 1714, may be regarded as the initiator of the literary struggle for emancipation. Before that time Hugo Grotius had advocated equality in principle, while insisting upon the maintenance of specific disabilities. In 1614, Leonard Busher, an Englishman living in Holland, demanded readmission of the Jews to England. He was followed three decades later by the Americans, Roger Williams and Hugh Peters. But all these were much more concerned with the problem of religious liberty in general than with the details of legal equality. It was left to Toland, the deist, who had long contended that "Christianity is not mysterious," to open the frontal attack on Jewish disabilities.

The legal status of British Jewry at that time was quite unsettled. Although the prominent jurists of the 1655 Whitehall conference (especially Glynne and Steele) had advised Cromwell that the expulsion of 1290 could not be regarded as a legal impediment, and that "there was no law which forbids the Jews' return to England"—a conception apparently already entertained by the crown jurists of Queen Elizabeth —the British government had preferred to maintain silence on the subject. Thus arose the legal anomaly, under which Jews were neither admitted nor excluded by law; and it was left to the courts to settle each individual case as it came up. In 1608 (before the definite "Resettlement"), Lord Coke could declare that "infidels including Jews are subjects of the Devil and perpetual enemies, with whom and Christians there is perpetual hostility and no peace." In 1667 the King's Bench, on the other hand, declared that Jews might serve as witnesses and swear in accordance with their own ritual. In 1677 the court calendars were so arranged as not to force a Jewish party or witness to appear on a Sabbath or on Jewish holidays. When, in 1697, the London Stock Exchange permanently admitted 12 Jewish brokers (out of a total of 124), the new rules specifically provided that they might be nonfreemen and take a modified oath omitting the Christian formula. In the following year the House of Commons rejected by a decisive majority of 140 against 78 a clause in the Blasphemy Act which would have driven Jews out of the kingdom, because, the hypocritical argument ran, in remaining "they have the means and opportunities to be informed of and rightly instructed in the principles of the true Christian religion" (Henriques, *The Jews and the English Law*, pp. 16 ff., 167). How uncertain, nevertheless, the legal status of the Jewish religion was, in 1744, may be seen in the famous case of Elias de Paz's testament in which £1,200 were bequeathed for the maintenance of a Yeshibah. Declaring such a legacy for the propagation of the Jewish religion illegal, the court decided to apply the bequest to related charitable uses, and so transferred £1,000 to the Foundling Hospital to help support a preacher and instruct children in the *Christian* religion. These contradictory opinions were not harmonized until 1833, when Lord Chancellor Brougham decided "that His Majesty's subjects professing the Jewish religion were born to all the rights, immunities and privileges of His Majesty's other subjects, excepting so far as positive enactments of law deprive them of those rights, immunities and privileges."

In this fashion the reticence of the British government in dealing with the Jewish question, like that of the early Roman Empire, brought about a comparatively favorable legal status. It certainly contrasted with the extensive anti-Catholic legislation, which in 1759 was well epitomized by the Lord Chancellor, "The Law does not suppose any such person to exist as an Irish Roman Catholic except for repression and punishment." The Jews, as a matter of fact, enjoyed almost full equality in civil law, and exercised some political rights. Their disabilities mainly arose from certain general requirements, such as the taking of an oath which, since it must be couched in Christian terms, automatically barred them from many offices and guilds. But there was, for instance, no special Jewish taxation such as had existed in all countries of the dispersion since Roman times, and, except for one futile attempt, none was proposed.

Two legislative acts of the eighteenth century, however, had far-reaching significance. In 1740 the British Parliament passed a Naturalization Act for the American colonies which dispensed with the Christian ceremony for "such who profess the Jewish religion"; and in 1753 Prime Minister Pelham put through Parliament his "Jews' Bill," which was to remove most of the Jewish disabilities. The Naturalization Act, which established a sharp contrast between the status of the Jews in the colonies and that in the motherland, merely reflected the desire of the British government to colonize the vast unexploited territories with white men, regardless of race and religion.[19] None the less, it greatly advanced the general cause of equality for Jews in America. In 1658 Dr. Jacob Lumbroso was prosecuted in Baltimore for "blasphemy," on account of his Jewish persuasion. The same man was, in 1663, one of the first Jews to be granted letters of denization (J. N. Hollander, in PAJHS, I, 25, 29). The Quebec Act for Catholics also had a favorable effect upon the status of Jews in the British colonies. Eventually the Virginia Declaration of Rights of 1776, the Constitution of the United States and the First Amendment (1791), established general equality without specifically mentioning the Jews. In several letters to Jewish congregations, George Washington expressed the hope that the growing spirit of liberality and philanthropy among enlightened nations would accrue to the benefit of the Jews all over the world. Nevertheless, it was several decades before all minor disabilities, especially through state laws, were removed. North Carolina, which had long treated the Jews somewhat better than it did "papists," did not drop its last discriminatory regulations until 1868. Today, certain minor questions, such as Sunday rest legislation, may still be debated. But the occupancy in 1936 of three governorships, two Supreme Court justiceships and other positions of confidence and trust by Jews is a visible sign of full-fledged political emancipation.

Equality of rights in Canada was granted in 1832, likewise many years before it was obtained in the mother country. The other British colonies, such as South Africa, Australia and New Zealand, from the outset pursued a liberal policy toward Jews. The development is best symbolized by the fact that one Jew was commander in chief of the Australian expeditionary army during the World War, and another served as her governor general, the first native to be appointed to that supreme office.

For the first time since the days of the Roman Empire, Pelham's Jews' Bill established almost full equality of rights for Jews on European soil. Under the pressure of public opinion, aroused by widespread anti-Jewish agitation, Pelham himself had to revoke it after a few months. Nevertheless, Continental advocates of emancipation often cited this constitutional experiment in a country whose system of government was generally admired. The struggle for the removal of disabilities was reopened in England only after the Catholic Emancipation of 1829. The contrast with the British colonies, later remarked Sir John Simon, a native of Jamaica, "was so galling that I vowed never to rest... until I saw my people enjoying the same rights in the mother country that they possessed in the colonies" (*Jewish Chronicle,* Nov. 13, 1891, p. 6). The London *Times,* in its issue of April 19, 1833, advocated full emancipation, characteristically arguing that the Jews were not only good citizens, but so few in number that there was no fear of their exerting too great an influence. In advance of contemporary opinion, young Macaulay, the historian, in his maiden speech in Parliament as well as in an article in the *Edinburgh Review,* pleaded that equality was not incompatible even with the survival of a Jewish national entity. Lord John Russell, Robert Grant, and others consistently favored the admission of the Jews to Parliament. But the conservative forces, at first led by Wellington, succeeded in delaying admission for almost three decades. A distinguished Tory, Henry Drummond, so completely misjudged the situation as to see in the repeated elections of Lionel Rothschild as the parliamentary representative of the "City" nothing but that "the rabble of London, partly out of love of mischief, partly from contempt of the House of Commons, and partly from a desire to give a slap in the face to Christianity, elected a Jew." As late as 1869, Queen Victoria objected "to a Jew being made a Peer." Nevertheless, successive bills of 1858, 1866, 1871 and 1878 opened the highest government and university offices to Jews; and in 1885 the queen herself, at Gladstone's insistence, created the first Jewish peerage. Finally, in 1890, it was declared that any public office, with the sole exception of that of the British monarch, was open to Jews. In the few decades since then, beginning with Sir George Jessel's appointment in 1871 to the post of solicitor general, Jews have held high offices, including those of viceroy of India, lord chief justice, lord chancellor and cabinet minister. Only the office of prime minister has not yet been occupied by a professing Jew, although the baptized Jew, Disraeli, was one of the most distinguished in the brilliant galaxy of British premiers.[20]

Today the Anglo-Saxon countries are of the highest significance to the life of Jewry. But in the eighteenth century their Jewish policies were far overshadowed by those of the French Revolution. When France emancipated not only her own Jews but those of Holland, Belgium, Italy and the German Rhinelands, and, to a certain extent, those in the Duchy of Warsaw, she broke down the walls of legal discrimination against a large portion of the people. Even before the Revolution, the necessity of change commended itself to all far-sighted observers from the Seine to the Vistula. As early as 1748, Montesquieu wrote in favor of the Portuguese Jews in France. The most influential publicist utterance, however, was Christian Wilhelm Dohm's *Ueber die bürgerliche Verbesserung der Juden,* which appeared in two volumes, in Berlin, 1781-83. This was written on the occasion of the request of Alsatian Jewry to Mendelssohn to prepare for them a memorial to be submitted to the French government. Dohm's work soon exerted considerable influence on European opinion, especially after 1782, through a French translation of the first volume made by Bernouilli. Dohm's arguments were reëchoed by Mirabeau in his work *Sur Moses Mendelssohn et sur la réforme politique des Juifs,* in 1787; by an anonymous writer, in 1782; later by Butrymowicz, Czacki, and others in Poland. It was the most effective weapon in the struggle for equality. The Edict of Toleration of Joseph II in 1782 and, in its wake, several minor legislative measures of Louis XVI, marked the beginnings of reform on the part of the two most powerful European governments. At the same time, the Emperor tried, through harsh legislative and educational measures, to break the back of Jewish "separatism." The French *lettres patentes* of 1784 were predicated on the assumption that even Alsatian Jewry was no longer a corporate body, so that the Keeper of the Seal refused acceptance of a memorandum simply because it spoke in the name of all the Jews of that province.

The battle was decided suddenly in the first year of the French Revolution. In the numerous cahiers which instructed members of the National Assembly in an anti-Jewish sense, in the frequent debates of the Assembly itself, in the agitation in various municipal councils, the political clubs and the press, almost all the arguments heard throughout the nineteenth century for and against emancipation came to the fore. The friends of equality included humanitarian clergymen like Abbé Gregoire, liberal statesmen such as Count Mirabeau, convinced democrats such as Clérmont-Tonnère and Duport, and radicals such as Robespierre. Humanitarian considerations of a cosmopolitan nature, coupled with the recognition of the necessity of an equalitarian democratic state, induced all these men, despite their temperamental differences, to attempt to incorporate the Jews in the French national body. The opposition, too, united disparate forces. A popular agitator, such as Marat, voiced the inarticulate atavistic sentiments of the masses; the crude and unscrupulous Rewbell pleaded the cause of the Alsatian peasants against Jewish exploitation; most significant of all, Abbé Maury voiced the apprehension of the Church with respect to the equality of infidels, as well as that of the French nationalists that the Jews would always remain a nation within the nation. With the exception of a few intellectuals, such as Cerfberr and Zalkind Horowitz, the Jews were objects rather than subjects of the discussion. The pressing needs of the modern state, however, decided the issue; in 1790 the Portuguese and Avignonese Jews, and in 1791 the German Jews of France, were declared equal citizens. As soon as the new French constitution was adopted, a deputy, Regnauld, remarked: "I demand that a vote be taken without listening to those who wish to speak against this proposal, since it is the Constitution itself that they will combat" (September 27, 1791; in *Revue des grandes journées parlementaires*, I, 61). This simple comment put an end to the heated debate.

The French armies speedily established equality of rights in all countries under their control. In the Batavian Republic of 1796, they encountered stiff opposition on the part of both conservative Christians and orthodox Jews. The resistance of the Jews was strengthened by their bonds of fidelity to the house of Orange and their manifold economic ties with England. This resistance, however, and even the sad interlude of the Napoleonic legislation of 1808, retarded the pace of emancipation only slightly. The spectacular convocation of the Great Sanhedrin left a deep impression, even outside of France. Metternich, then Austrian ambassador in Paris, informed his government on October 23, 1806, that "if the Emperor has not conceived the idea of the Great Sanhedrin with the intention of making it coincide with his military operations, there is nevertheless no doubt that he will not fail to present himself to the Christian people of Poland as a liberator, and as a messiah to its immense Jewish population" (Gelber, "La Police autrichienne," in *REJ,* LXXXIII, 137). Indeed, the Russian government, frightened by the French appeal, withdrew its decree of expulsion from the villages, issued in 1804, and pretended friendliness to the Jews. These tactics, reënforced by the strained Polish-Jewish relations, succeeded in dividing Eastern European Jewish public opinion sharply when it had to choose between France and Russia in 1812.

To be sure, the disillusionment of the Frenchmen over the slow process of Jewish assimilation, the social revolt of Alsatian peasantry against Jewish money lending, the "scandalous struggle" between the Christian debtors and Jewish creditors in the Rhenish provinces, publicist agitation cleverly conducted by Bonald and Poujol, and Napoleon's anger over Jewish "lack of patriotism" (he accused them of shirking war service and of espionage for the allies)—generated the "infamous decree" of March 17, 1808, which imposed severe disabilities. But, from the outset, it was a reformatory measure limited to ten years, and exemptions were granted in one province after another, even sooner. Of some 80,000 Jews under the sovereignty of Napoleon in 1811, one-sixth had already been exempted, while the others were about evenly divided between those who wished to be exempted and those who made no such demand. Some of the most discriminatory provisions of the decree (e. g., obligatory military service, without the right of substitution), were soon greatly modified by Napoleon himself; while the vassal states of Holland, Westphalia and the grand duchy of Frankfort never adopted them at all. Even the reactionary government of Louis XVIII did not venture to prolong their validity beyond 1818. Notwithstanding several petitions to this effect, the French Parliament let the period of renewal lapse without action. With the establishment of the "bourgeois monarchy" under Louis Philippe, the last vestiges of discrimination were removed. The French government, from 1831 until the separation of the church and state in 1906, financially supported Jewish religious officers on a par with Catholic and Protestant clergy. The removal of the oath *more judaico* in 1846 fully established legal equality between Jew and Gentile.

The progress of assimilation, on the other hand, was equally rapid. With subdued irony, Louis Philippe once praised

the capability of the Jews to become civilized. Regardless of the religious tie which unites them in the various lands, they have succeeded in becoming Frenchmen in France, Englishmen in England and so on. ... They were almost wedded to the good qualities, sometimes even to the faults of the nations in whose midst they lived. [Feb. 12, 1846; Jost, *Geschichte der Israeliten*, X, 2, 218.]

The Netherlands, reëstablished as an independent state in 1815, included a Protestant majority in Holland and a Catholic majority in Belgium. Equality of all inhabitants, without regard to religious conviction, was consequently indispensable for the inner peace of the country. It received international sanction by the treaty of July 2, 1814, between the Netherlands and the allies. By implication, the rights of the Jews were thus internationally guaranteed—for the first time in modern history. Owing to the consistently tolerant policy of the government, these international safeguards never had to be tested. In fact, going beyond its international obligations, Holland voluntarily extended financial support to the Jewish religious bodies. This interpretation of equality was maintained, after 1831, in independent Belgium, the government granting the small Brussels community a subsidy of 80,-000 francs, a sum in excess of the total revenue from Jewish taxpayers.[21]

EMANCIPATION IN CENTRAL AND EASTERN EUROPE

The example set by western Europe had an immediate effect upon the condition of the Jews in Germany and Italy. In the prerevolutionary period, in 1699, Samson Wertheimer had to persuade the fathers of his native city, Worms, not to press the point of Jewish "serfdom." In the 1740's, Maria Theresa, against the advice of her counselors, and Charles

Bourbon, against his own will, banished the Jews from Prague and from the Kingdom of Naples respectively. The renewal of this notorious medieval means of adjusting Judeo-Christian relations, demonstrated the untenability of the Jewish status in "modern" society and state, even more clearly than did their numerous specific disabilities. Maria Theresa's two sons, indeed, took an active part in initiating far-reaching reforms. Leopold of Tuscany, apart from removing many civil disabilities, admitted his Jewish subjects to the exercise of the most important political rights, viz., to vote in the municipal elections. Joseph II, after issuing his Toleration Edict, amplified it in the following years through many detailed legislative measures. Most significantly, in 1788, he was the first European monarch to draft the Jews into the Austrian army, thereby not only preparing the ground for their full incorporation into Austrian society, but also removing the main political justification for legal discrimination. At this juncture came French emancipation, which gave direct impetus to all liberal forces; but, on the other hand, it aroused grave suspicions among the conservatives, and strengthened their resistance to any reform whatsoever.

It would far exceed the limits of the present work to narrate all the vicissitudes in the protracted struggle for emancipation in Germany (including Austria), that classical laboratory for the Jewish question in the nineteenth century. Each of the numerous states pursued an independent policy, and a wide variety of attempted solutions were produced. Even within the boundaries of a single state, the status of the Jews was by no means always uniform. After 1816 Prussia possessed twenty-one different legal systems in various provinces, ranging from full emancipation in parts of the West to the fully medieval conditions in Posen and Saxony. The liberal forces of the Franco-German Enlightenment and of the French Revolution encountered the stubborn opposition of the conservatives, as exemplified in Emperor Francis I and King Frederick William III, who distrusted every liberal move as a sign of revolution. While in Austria the traditions of "Josephinism" survived into the nineteenth century, in Prussia and in most other principalities, the tendency of enlightened absolutism to educate the Jews toward full citizenship was now replaced by the general romantic aims of the historical schools to maintain feudalistic medieval patterns so far as possible. In Prussia the highly efficient bureaucracy, at least, pursued a certain steady line, but in the smaller states reaction often knew no bounds. Fiscal considerations greatly complicated the problem. On the one hand, they led to toleration. For example, even in the prerevolutionary age, the peasantry of the Buseck Valley in Hesse had admitted more Jews into the eight villages under its sovereignty than there were in all the twelve Hessian cities combined. In 1776 a writer complained that the Buseck Valley "is a little Palestine, although of the dirtiest kind" (quoted by Bodenheimer, in *ZGJD,* IV 19). On the other hand, the Austrian Minister of the Interior, Count Saurau, declared in 1820 that there was no possibility of emancipating the Jews without renouncing considerable revenue from their special taxes and thus causing further disequilibrium in the empire's budget.

At any rate, little remained of the full emancipation achieved in Westphalia and Frankfort during the Napoleonic era. The Prussian edict of March, 1812, however, which had granted the Jews full equality with the exception of appointment to public office, remained in force in these territories. In many regions along the Rhine, French emancipation remained unaltered, except for the Napoleonic decree of 1808, the validity of which was indefinitely prolonged beyond 1818. All this was in accordance with the confederate constitution of 1816, which, while holding out a promise of future full equality throughout the Confederation, insisted upon the maintenance of all rights already granted to the Jews by the various states.

The subsequent struggle for emancipation in all the confederate states was forcefully directed by such Jewish leaders as the Frankfort Rothschilds, Baruch, Friedlaender and Jacobsohn, and later especially Gabriel Riesser. It was actively supported by the most influential Austro-Prussian statesmen, such as Metternich, Hardenberg and Humboldt, and backed in its initial stages by England and Russia, the guarantors of the Germanic constitution. Nevertheless, its progress against the alliance of vested interests, political reaction and romantic dreams was very slow. Even the achievements of the Revolution of 1848, when the national parliament of Frankfort and the diets of Kremsier and Berlin proclaimed democratic constitutions for Germany, Austria and Prussia, and when national insurgents tried to rebuild Hungary on an independent democratic basis, were soon frustrated by the Austrian and Prussian reaction. Not before 1867 in the Austro-Hungarian empire, and 1869 and 1871 in the North German union and the German empire, was full equality of rights constitutionally granted to the Jews. Down to the time of the World War, both imperial governments continued to discriminate against Jews in making appointments to high positions in administration, army and university. These were, however, only minor shortcomings of an otherwise complete emancipation, which lasted until the recent reversals under the Hitler régime.

In Italy, too, the pattern was variegated during the reactionary period after 1816. Fully medieval conditions were reëstablished in the two largest states, those of the Church and Piedmont-Sardinia, to give way, after 1848, to the democratic constitution of an increasingly unified Italy. The Jews long remained inactive. When an unknown Italian urged the Jewish communities on the peninsula to appeal to the congress of Aix-la-Chapelle in 1818, his suggestion went totally unheeded. It was chiefly the publicist agitation of the non-Jew, Massimo d'Azeglio, which paved the way to equality. The patriotic activity of some Jews, such as Isacco Artom, Cavour's intimate associate, helped break down barriers. Since 1871 Italian Jews, although slight in number, have held positions of confidence and trust in the highest public service. Even the Fascist régime of the last decade has not seriously affected the political equality of the Jews. Switzerland, forced by foreign pressure to emancipate the Jews in 1874, has, on the whole, lived up to the letter and spirit of her constitution. The same holds true of the Scandinavian countries, where Jewish emancipation, including admission to public office, was accomplished through progressive legislation: in Denmark, 1814-49 (Schleswig 1854, Holstein 1863); in Sweden, especially 1860-70; and in Norway, 1851-91.[22]

The Russian Jewish emancipation movement progressed most irregularly. Catherine II granted her first Jewish subjects a large share in municipal government, which meant almost political equality under the circumstances. At the same time she laid the foundations for the future Pale of Settlement (1791). The contradictory policies of Alexander I, who forcibly expelled Jewish farmers from the villages, while encouraging their first large-scale colonization and issuing high-sounding humanitarian declarations on an international scale; the strongly anti-Semitic and missionary tactics of Nicholas I; the short liberal interlude of Alexander II; the sharp reaction of the "May Laws" of 1882, extended to Poland in 1892; even the reluctant granting of the political franchise to Jews during the Revolution of 1905—reveal the perplexities of the political problem of that largest sector of world Jewry. The Pale of Settlement and the progressive exclusion from rural districts, which made it impossible for a Jewish landowner to spend a night on his own estate, were aggravated in 1844 by the expulsion of Jews, indiscriminately denounced as smugglers, from an area some thirty miles wide, along the entire western frontier. Most inhuman of all was the compulsory military service (the "rekrutchina," established in Russia in 1827 and extended to Poland in 1845), which annually pressed thousands of Jewish boys, often only eight or ten years of age, into a protracted demoralizing occupation, and served as a constant impetus to conflicts within the Jewish community. This impossible system was abolished by Alexander II in 1856. The toleration and, in some cases, encouragement of mass pogroms by the government in 1881-82, 1903 and 1905, in order to divert the rising tide of social revolution into anti-Jewish channels, showed how precarious was the political situation of Russian Jewry at the beginning of this century. It sharply contrasted even with that of medieval Jewry, when secular and ecclesiastic authorities had attempted, however ineffectively, to protect the life and limb of Jewish subjects. With the progressive disintegration of the "Kahal" and its legal abolition in 1844, the great compensating factor in medieval life, unhampered Jewish self-government, likewise vanished.

Most tragic, however, was the fact that discriminatory laws forced the Jews to concentrate on a few trades, some of which, like the liquor trade, allied them with feudalistic forces as class enemies of the peasant masses. Moreover, when the struggle for emancipation entered a decisive stage, toward the end of the century, the experiences of emancipated Jewry in the West had already caused a great deal of disillusionment.

The new demand of Russian Jewry was for emancipation, combined with the protection of minority rights. The realization of this double purpose was not to come, however, until the revolutionary upheavals of 1917.

In Poland the first stirrings of reform were clearly discernible even before the French Revolution. Especially when the Quadrennial Diet (1788-92), at the eleventh hour, undertook a thorough overhauling of the foundering ship of state, hopes surged higher and higher that the Jewish question would also be solved in a more satisfactory manner. Jewish opinion was divided. Progressive leaders, including the Chelm rabbi, Herschel Józefowicz, joined the chorus of such Polish publicists as Butrymowicz, who demanded thoroughgoing reform; Mendel Lefin preached cultural-political regeneration, and Simon Wolfowicz of Vilna, the abolition of the *Kahal;* the court factor, Abraham Hirszowicz, submitted to King Stanislaus August a detailed memorandum on Jewish reform; and Solomon Maimon dedicated one of his philosophic works to the king, in a letter stressing the political import of the Jewish question. At the same time, the leaders of the then-illegal Lithuanian Council collected money to send representatives to Warsaw to "forestall the danger so that, God forbid, no new reforms be introduced" (A. [E.] N. Frenk, *Ha-Ironim ve-ha-Yehudim be-Polin,* pp. 107-8). Since the opposition of the Polish arch-conservatives was equally steadfast, the famous constitution of May 3, 1791, had no provisions concerning the Jews. Although the diet's committee on Jewish affairs finally adopted an extensive project of Jewish reform in May, 1792, the plenary session merely saved its face by promising action in the future.

The nineteenth-century Polish-Jewish relations were often full of insoluble perplexities. The policy of Austria, Prussia and, especially, Russia was to sow discord between the two minorities, while the growing Polish middle class resented the overwhelming share of the Jews in industry and commerce and soon also in the professions. On the other hand, the recapture of Polish independence was contingent upon the realization of the liberal, democratic and humanitarian tendencies in Europe. Some Polish nationalists extended a brotherly hand to their Jewish fellow sufferers; hailed Jewish patriots, such as Colonel Berek Joselowicz; and, in Towianism, dreamed of a forthcoming messianic era to be realized through the combined efforts of the two messianic nations. But others bitterly resented the support lent by certain Jews to the oppressive governments, as well as the general apathy and neutrality of the masses. They also hated the people as a whole for their stubborn refusal to surrender their identity and become assimilated with the Polish majority. The result was that in the short-lived Duchy of Warsaw, the equalitarian provisions of the constitution of 1808 were speedily suspended (October 17, 1808); that the republic of Cracow (1815-46) kept her Jews in their prerevolutionary status; and that the leaders of the revolutions of 1831 and 1846 sought to discourage Jewish participation. After a friendlier interlude in the Wielopolski era, during the upheaval of 1863, the relations became increasingly envenomed under the impact of czarist oppression and the Prussian anti-Polish legislation. Hostility reached a climax in the Polish boycott of Jews in Congress Poland in 1912, and was carried over into the tragic War and the early postwar years. It decidedly diminished the mutual benefits and the better understanding which otherwise might have emanated from the liberal Polish constitution of 1920, granting the Jews full equality of rights.

Nor was the emancipation of the remaining Jews of eastern Europe achieved before the beginning of the twentieth century. Although Turkey, in the laws of 1838 and 1856, promised equal treatment to all subjects, the peculiar structure of society permitted the state to continue to discriminate against the large *raya* (Christian and Jewish) sections. Only with the "Young Turk" revolution of 1908 did the country receive a constitution modeled on western patterns and including real equality for Jews.

The vicissitudes of Rumanian Jewry, to whom the Congress of Berlin promised equality of rights under international safeguards in 1878, are well known. By surreptitiously declaring all Jews aliens, the Rumanian government, notwithstanding the protests of the United States, Great Britain and other powers, successfully evaded the application of Article 44 of the Treaty of Berlin. In the years 1879-1911, it naturalized by special acts of parliament but some 2,000 Jews of the more than 200,000 then living in the country. Only the Peace treaties of Bucharest in 1918, and especially those of Saint-

Germain and Trianon in 1919, brought real constitutional equality for all Jews of Greater Rumania.[23]

In short, the overwhelming majority of world Jewry still lived under nonemancipated conditions at the beginning of this century. To this day the emancipation has by no means been fully realized, even in legal theory. Quite apart from the most recent developments in Nazi Germany, there are still Muslim countries, such as Iran (Persia) and Yemen, where emancipation is not yet legally established. There the Jews are frequently persecuted, kept out of public office and, in Iran, forbidden to emigrate. In Morocco and Tunis, under French domination, the Jews still live in medieval ghettos. Only the Jewry of Algiers acquired French citizenship (1871), largely through the instrumentality of Adolphe Crémieux, then a member of the revolutionary government. Christian Ethiopia is another instance of a country which, until its recent conquest by the Italians, consistently refused to grant her Falasha Jews equal treatment. All in all, however, only some 2 or 3 percent of the Jewish world population is included in these regions.

THE REFORM MOVEMENT

The Jewish religion now had to take over the burden of adapting Judaism to the new Jewish status of citizenship. Just as the Haskalah had been in essence a preëmancipatory adaptation, so was the more radical adjustment of the Jewish faith a necessary complement to emancipation. The Jewish community no longer determined the ethnic and religious allegiance of every Jewish individual. No longer could the London Maamad, for example, prevent its members from publishing books on religious or political subjects without obtaining its previous consent. No longer did the tiny community of Sugenheim, in Franconia, impose those severe penalties for chatting during synagogue hours, which had been enacted in its *Pinkas* of 1756. Now Jewish institutions could be changed to suit new needs, with comparative ease.

Characteristically, even these tendencies conformed to the traditional line of Judaism, reforming the *actions* of the Jews, rather than their beliefs. Jacobsohn's, Friedlaender's and Hess's early attempts, and the entire Hamburg movement, centered on certain innovations in synagogue service, such as the German sermon, German prayers, decorum and orderliness, with little, if any, discussion of theological fundamentals. Friedlaender's offer to Pastor Teller to embrace Protestantism with the exception of certain Christian *dogmas* undoubtedly stressed dogmatic differences. Friedlaender was even ready to accept Protestant ceremonies, "as a mere form, prerequisite to admission into a social group." But even here the emphasis on the actions of believers revealed itself in the most naïve fashion. Jews may become Christians, Friedlaender thought, if they follow Christian observances, while rejecting the basic creed. This tender had to be dismissed by Teller courteously, but firmly. Even later, many struggles between the conservatives and reformers converged on details of synagogue ritual. Thus the first move of Holdheim, in Mecklenburg, was to introduce the reading of the Torah in the ordinary intonation of a German reader of the nineteenth century, instead of in the traditional cantillation. But this minor innovation sufficed to stir the orthodox section of his congregation to violent opposition. Such a conservative as Frankel was stoned in Töplitz on account of his omission of a few *piyyutim*, often discarded or curtailed even by orthodox Eastern Europeans.

J. King, in London, in 1812, confined himself to suggestions as to how to avoid the indecorum of the traditional service. The final break in 1840 and the establishment of the *West London Synagogue of British Jews* resulted chiefly from the desire of a few prominent business men and intellectuals to have a synagogue in the western part of the metropolis, "where a revised service may be performed at hours more suited to our habits and in a manner more calculated to inspire feelings of devotion" (D. Philipson, *The Reform Movement in Judaism*, p. 96). This was also the professed aim of the Association for Effecting a Modification in the Liturgy of the German Jews, organized in London in 1874. The initiators of the Charleston movement, in 1824, likewise laid exclusive stress upon "the more rational means of worshipping the true God," and suggested for "the Hasan, or reader, to repeat in English such part of the Hebrew prayers as may be deemed necessary" (B. A. Elzas, *The Reformed Society of Israelites of Charleston, S. C.*, p. 17). Throughout the nineteenth century, periodical crops of revised prayer books in the United States resulted in total anarchy in the reform ritual, which was checked only by the publication of the official Union Prayer Book in 1892-95 (revised in 1918-22). In Germany such unification was not achieved until 1929. In other words, as in most other religious upheavals, reform of ritual rather than of theologumena was the starting point. It goes without saying that sooner or later a rationale was sought and that, once found, it exerted, in turn, powerful influence upon ritualistic adaptations.[24]

Outside the synagogue, too, practical attitudes were more pressing than theoretics and theologies. As under Hellenism and Islam, assimilation involved considerable disregard of Jewish ceremonial law. With or without theological justification, many Jews were forced by their occupations not only to neglect some such religious duties as daily attendance at the synagogue, but also some legal fundamentals such as Sabbath observance. Without much speculation or many scruples, they began to flout many obligations of their religion. As far back as 1770, an anonymous Dutch writer advocated the abolition of the Sabbath and holiday rest because it entailed many special expenses and caused the loss of working days. In those years many Berlin Jews largely discarded the ancient rites. Mendelssohn himself is said to have transgressed important ritual laws in later years, although in his youth he refrained from seeing his fiancée rather than comb his hair on the Sabbath, and in theory always held them inviolable. Ever-continuing pressure soon brushed aside all half-hearted attempts.

In addition to denationalization and economic pressure, the changes in the social structure and the intellectual environment also made necessary a reorientation. No longer were the Jewries of Berlin and Frankfort predominantly of the lower middle class, which had generated the typical ghetto life. Many now entered the upper bourgeoisie of bankers and intellectuals; there was intercourse with the German aristocracy and littérateurs in the famous salons of Berlin and Vienna. Life was increasingly molded in accord with the general standards of "society." Of course, many "patrician" Jews consciously cultivated the inherited mode of life. Not only the Oppenheimers or Wertheimers of the previous centuries, but also the Rothschilds long remained observant Jews.

As late as 1869, Lionel Rothschild contended, "We are emancipated, but if our emancipation should damage our faith, it would be a curse instead of a blessing." The most revered leader of British Jewry, Sir Moses Montefiore, wrote in a similar vein in his *Diaries* (July 9, 1837), "I am most firmly resolved not to give up the smallest part of our religious forms and principles to obtain civil rights"; he remained unflinchingly orthodox throughout his life. Several other bankers in London, at the top of the social ladder, were likewise observant Jews. The mass of the upper class, however, not high enough in rank to disregard snobbish social isolation, sought as close an adjustment as possible to the life of their Gentile acquaintances. Rationalist philosophy, as usual, became popular among them.

The social and intellectual emancipation of the Jewish woman also demanded religious recognition. Although the position of woman in Judaism had always been rather high, she had not taken active part in public life. *Mulier taceat in ecclesia* was also true of the synagogue, as far as its public functions were concerned. To be sure, encompassing all domains of private life the Jewish religion recognized the broad functions of the woman in the family, in education, in charity, and similar spheres. Even the talmudic opposition to the higher education of women was modified by great rabbinical authorities from Moses of Coucy to Isserles, who taught that a woman is obliged to learn the laws she is bound to observe. In the nineteenth century, however, the Berlin society lady, often superior in culture and brilliancy of mind to her wealthy but uneducated husband, wanted a more active share in public life, including the synagogue. Many Jewesses of that age altogether deserted Judaism and married Christian husbands. For those who remained within the fold, the outward expression of equality became the family pew. The institution of the family pew may be said to have torn down the walls of a sort of special ghetto within the ghetto.[25]

The influence of Protestantism was also deeply felt. In the first half of the nineteenth century, there arose in Germany and in England religious movements which tried to rejuvenate the Protestant churches. This religious spirit permeated literature and philosophy. In the philosophy of Hegel, particularly, Protestantism was regarded as the climax of all religious history. Hegelian theories, viewing the history of mankind as a unit in progressive development, tremendously appealed to the best minds of Jewry, imbued with Judaism's traditional emphasis on history. The Berlin Society for Jewish Culture and Science, under the leadership of the jurist, Eduard Gans, was a center of Jewish Hegelianism. Even far away in Galicia, Krochmal tried to strengthen Judaism with Hegelian buttressing. The reigning philosophy thus united with Protestant currents, such as those led by Schleiermacher, Bunsen and the British pietists, to determine the religious outlook of young Jews. It is no mere accident that the Jewish Reform movement reached its highest flower in Protestant countries—Prussia, and later America. In the sparse and scattered congregations of Sweden, the most important innovations found early and uncontested acceptance. On the other hand, in almost all Catholic countries, including France and Italy, where assimilation was so facile, Judaism largely clung to the traditional. Even in Hungary, where Reform was quite vigorous for a time, there was at least a strong Protestant minority. At the same time, English Protestantism was not quite as conducive to Jewish Reform as German Protestantism, owing both to High-Church affinities with Catholicism and to the generally conservative mood of the English upper classes.[26]

Out of all these circumstances sprang the Jewish Reform movement, next to Hasidism the most important religious trend in modern Jewish history. Hasidism was the creation of the Polish Jewish mass settlement in the ghetto era. Jewish Reform was a direct offshoot of the struggle and winning of emancipation. Later reformers, it is true, often protested against this identification. Friedlaender, in his letter to Teller, was still ready to admit that both "duty and conscience demand from us, that we should improve our civic position through the purification of our religious constitution." But Geiger, Holdheim and others refused to admit any such political aims. Riesser, the staunch champion of equal rights, was especially vehement in deprecating state interference in matters of religious conviction or observance. But all these protestations, however sincere, could not obscure the real connection. The logical sequence remained: emancipation, assimilation, reformation.

One emphasis common to German, Hungarian and American Reform and insisted upon by the leaders from the outset, was that Judaism be reduced (or exalted) to a creed alone, and that all national elements be eliminated. There could no longer be a belief in a personal messiah to redeem the Jewish people and lead it back to Palestine. The true messianic hope is in a messianic age when ethical monotheism, bringing justice and peace to all, will be fully realized. The mission of Israel is to work collectively for this prophesied end; this is the real messiah. Therefore, all references to a personal redeemer, Palestine, Zion or bodily resurrection must be discarded. The longing for Palestine, particularly, was long denounced as unpatriotic. Like the modern Christian, it was asserted, the modern Jew owes undivided loyalty to the country of his birth and citizenship. It could not escape the keen-minded leaders, however, that this narrow conception of religion, possible perhaps within Protestantism with its great stress on state supremacy, but impossible even within all-embracing Catholicism, was diametrically opposed to their claim of the universality of Judaism. Even Holdheim could not avoid proclaiming the inalienability of Judaism to all born within its fold—obviously a concession to the ethnic principle. Very few reformers, facing the disintegrating force of intermarriage, were ready to renounce the ethnic element of preservation. The Paris Sanhedrin and the Brunswick Conference of 1844 were at most ready to concede that intermarriage was not forbidden. But few German or even American rabbis have performed the wedding ceremony when the couple persevered in its religious disparity. The Augsburg synod of 1870 and the Central Conference of American Rabbis on various occasions evaded the issue. None the less, Abraham Geiger felt entitled to contrast, in 1870, the Philadelphia conference with the more moderate Leipzig synod and to declare:

The cultural evolution now tends to emphasize its general humanitarianism. Judaism, too, must get out of its national enclosure and, secure in its eternal validity, penetrate without hesitation the wide halls of humanity. [*Jüdische Zeitschrift für Wissenschaft und Leben,* VIII, 2.]

Reform was not a reformation in the sense of a complete return to Mosaism. On the whole, talmudic and rabbinical teachings were conscientiously ignored, and there was an outspoken reversion to revelation through the prophets as the chief source of Judaism. But that the leading reformers, even among such radicals as the founder of the Frankfort *Reformverein* in 1843, confined their attacks to the Talmud and avoided discussion of Mosaic Law, was due primarily to political considerations. "The Bible is treated gently," wrote Gabriel Riesser, himself sympathetic to Reform, to Dr. Stern, "because of its noble kinship with Christianity and on account of the august police" (*G.S.*, I, 358). In fact, however, the laws of the Pentateuch had also been discarded. Moreover, the force of tradition as well as the training of the leaders often brought them to the citation of talmudic support for their innovations. Aaron Chorin, Michael Creizenach and Samuel Holdheim, especially in their younger years all keen Talmudists but poor historians, found many a *heksher* (dispensation) through an adroit pilpulistic adaptation of talmudic passages. Creizenach wrote a large work in four parts, significantly entitled *Schulchan Aruch,* for the purpose of "helping regulate Israel's religious life through a distinction between talmudic interpretations and talmudic aggravations" (subtitle of the second part). Walter Josephs issued, in 1874, a circular letter urging "the desirability, nay the necessity of a modification in the Liturgy and Ritual of the Synagogue . . . on Talmudical principles" (quoted in L. Wolf, *Essays,* p. 348). It was, on the other hand, Holdheim himself who pronounced the only logical and consistent principle, "The Talmud speaks out of the consciousness of its own age and thus far the Talmud was right; but speaking out of the higher consciousness of my age, I am right" (*Das Ceremonialgesetz im Messiasreich,* 1845, p. 50).

He spoke, indeed, in the name of a large body of his coreligionists, who felt that, in order to achieve full emancipation, the Jew had to become a German, Hungarian or American in every respect but one, his creed. In the short space of a generation, all those "secular" elements, which since the Middle Ages the state had progressively arrogated to itself, had to be eliminated from the Jewish religion. Very few leaders were aware that what was possible in centuries of development, with the state approving Christian churches, did more than violence to the essentially nonpolitical Jewish religion.

The most radical among the reformers refashioned Judaism into a dogmatic creed, after the model of Christianity, in which certain theological principles became the essence of religion. Disregarding Geiger's and Holdheim's tireless reiteration (with minor reservations) of the Mendelssohnian principle that Judaism knows no dogma, the American reformers made haste to formulate a system of creeds and beliefs. At the two most significant gatherings, in Philadelphia in 1869 and Pittsburgh in 1885, they proclaimed creeds obligatory for every true Reform Jew.

Once creed was substituted for law, the disparagement of all ceremonial observances appeared quite consistent. The Sabbath, to be sure, not only sanctified by ritualistic tradition but also praised as one of the greatest Jewish contributions to civilization, presented a stumbling block which the various conferences in Germany and America tried vainly to overcome. Rabbi Hofmann of Hildenburghausen, who, interpreting with great latitude the talmudic injunction that "the law of the kingdom is law," permitted the Jewish pupils of the local schools to write on Sabbath, was decidedly an exception. Against this motivation, which was also used by Holdheim to justify his extremist views on the invalidation of Jewish marriage laws, protested not only conservatives, such as Frankel, but also Leopold Loew, the leading Hungarian reformer (1862; cf. *G.S.*, III, 347-58). With respect to the Sabbath, Rabbi Voorsanger undoubtedly rendered the opinion of the overwhelming majority when, in his report to the Central Conference in 1902, he declared emphatically, "The non-observance of the Sabbath by millions of Jews does not invalidate the fact that, as an historical institution, it represents principles that are a part of the lifeblood of our religion" (*Yearbook CCAR*, XII, 119). But pressing economic necessities swept away the half-hearted compromises of the leaders. Circumcision, on the contrary, although rejected in principle by the Frankfort reformers,[27] Holdheim and (privately) Geiger, as well as by many of their American disciples, proved to be less discordant to the new realities of Jewish life. It has survived within all wings of Jewry as the major form of initiation into Judaism.

These and other exceptions, however significant in themselves, do not alter the fundamental trend in Reform: No longer shall the force of tradition and common participation in a system of ceremonial regulations be the uniting link, but those "eternal" truths, unto the validity of which the Jew shall bear witness until their final adoption by all mankind. Although the essence of Judaism was thus found to be in adherence to these creedal principles, public worship of an altered sort was maintained. Organs were introduced into the synagogue, sexes seated together, prayers and sermons offered in the vernacular. In the most radical congregations, the Sabbath was transferred from Saturday to the rest day of the majority of citizens.

To an impartial observer, such a deviation from previous history must have appeared as a break with the historical principle per se, an invitation to individual whim and arbitrary decision. Who could decide and on what grounds, what Judaism in very truth should be? The attempt to find a unity in dogmas was an effort to crystallize religious life and to counteract the main trend of Reform itself, viz., steady readjustment to the ever-changing needs of life. These dangers were not overlooked by the great Reform leaders. In order to counteract both anarchy and a new ultraconformity, the idea of a synod was conceived. A synod of representative rabbis and laymen, invested with the authority of the ancient Sanhedrin, would, it was thought, formulate a new uniform code of belief and behavior. As a permanent institution, it would issue new ordinances to conform with ever-changing reality, and give definite expression to "the convictions and aspirations that animate modern Judaism" (Enelow, in "Report of the Committee on the Synod," *Yearbook CCAR*, XIV, 117; cf. also his *Selected Works*, IV, 41-79). The two synods of Leipzig and Augsburg in 1869-70, however, revealed such disparity of views and tendencies that they had to be satisfied with a few lame compromise resolutions. Thereafter no synod met in Germany. In America, where most other postulates were pursued to their radical conclusion, ever-recurring agitation for the convocation of a synod did not have even such futile results. Solomon Schechter's keen analysis: "If the Synod should become a blessing, it must first recognize a standard of authority, and this can be no other than the Bible, the Talmud and the lessons of Jewish history as to the vital and the essential in Judaism" (in Central Conference of American Rabbis, *Views on the Synod,* p. 140), revealed the fundamental weakness of the agitation which, by disregarding historical continuity, necessarily failed to consolidate the opinion of world Jewry. The Synod's main substitutes, the rabbinical conferences, became the medium of expression of but one group, with all its local and social limitations.

The more moderate wings in Reform, led by Abraham Geiger, the greatest of all Reform thinkers, tried to reconcile history with the newly framed creed. This meant moderation and a slowing up of the revolutionary transformation. But it meant also a greater degree of continuity and a safeguard for the future. Geiger's type of Reform has triumphed over the radical wings since the middle of the nineteenth century. In America, radicalism was for a long time predominant, but recent tendencies likewise reveal a recovery of historical perspective. That Reform wing especially which, led by Bernhard Felsenthal, Gustav Gottheil and Stephen S. Wise, has tried to synthesize Reform with Zionism, looks for a return to the mainsprings of historic Judaism. Wise's significant warning at the twenty-fifth anniversary of his entry into the rabbinate, has been heeded by many younger Reform rabbis and laymen:[28]

Reform, if it become as it is fast becoming a Jewish sect, may for a time survive as a sect. But it will cease to be Jewish, as every Jewish sect has passed, save for the Pharisaic, which was not a sect, but a vital movement of a people in the interests of national as well as religious self-preservation. [*Opinion,* I, Pt. 21, 6.]

Reform Judaism has, on the whole, enriched neither creedal nor ceremonial Judaism. It has, in the main, eliminated a few of the older tenets and rites, substituted for venerable old Hebrew, shorter made-to-order vernacular prayers, and shifted the center of gravity in worship from the congregation to its minister. If compared with the orthodox theology formulated by Joseph Albo, Reform has maintained the belief in the eleven principles, fundamental and derived ("principles and stems"), "Existence of God, unity, incorporeality, independence of time, freedom from defect, prophecy, authenticity of the messenger, revelation, God's knowledge, providence, reward and punishment" (*Book of Principles,* I, 26, 7;

English transl. I, 202). It has rejected only a part of what Albo classified as branches. While hesitant in passing judgment as to creation *ex nihilo* and the position of Moses, it has repudiated the belief in the eternity of the Torah, in the attainment of human perfection through the fulfillment of the Law, in bodily resurrection, and in the coming of a personal messiah. Even more conspicuous is Reform's lightening of the burden of the law. In view of this incontrovertible curtailment of creed and ritual without a corresponding amplification through new beliefs and observances, one can hardly agree with Emil G. Hirsch's exclamation,

My Radicalism and it is that which I imbibed at the feet of my own father and teacher and found in the instruction of my master Geiger, both of blessed memory, the Radicalism of Einhorn and Samuel Adler intends to be more Jewish than ever was official orthodoxy. We hunger for more Judaism, not for less of it. [*My Religion*, p. 294.]

With all the emphasis placed by Samuel Hirsch and Guedemann upon the translation of Torah by *Lehre* rather than *Gesetz,* one of the major weaknesses of Reform has been its failure to develop further either the dogmatic or the ceremonial side of Judaism. A faith which demands little sacrifice from its adherents must not pin too great hopes on their loyalty and devotion.

The reaction of the Jewish masses to Reform varied. The millions settled in Russia, Poland, Galicia and the Ottoman Empire pursued the age-old policy of ignoring all liberalism. Jewry in those countries was still in the preëmancipation state —in need of enlightenment, but not ready for reformation. The national sentiment of the masses was too staunch to be impressed by a denationalized Judaism. Not even the new *Mussar* (ethical) movement of Israel Salanter (Lipkin) in Lithuania and Königsberg revealed distinct traces of Reform influence. It was altogether a native growth of the Eastern European ghetto, a non-hasidic synthesis of Hasidism and Rabbinism. Just as Ber of Meseritsh and Shneur Zalman of Ljosna had perpetuated Hasidism by reconciling it with talmudic Judaism, so the Mussar movement, often called the Hasidism of the "opponents," reinvigorated rabbinism by focusing attention on the ethical, rather than the strictly legalistic and speculative, aspects of Jewish tradition. It also served to reconcile the various classes in Lithuanian Jewry. The talmudic leaders, after a brief hesitancy, accepted the innovation, and classes in ethics soon became a regular part of the curriculum in most northern academies.

In Posen, Austria and Hungary, the borderlands, the old type of orthodoxy, led by the great halakists, Eiger, Banet and Schreiber, reacted with denunciations and even excommunication. As in former ages, they registered their opposition to the practical rather than the theoretical innovations. Following the lead of, say, Haham Zebi Ashkenazi of Amsterdam, who had refused to take action against a pantheistic sermon of Rabbi David Nieto in London (*Responsa*, No. 18), his successors in orthodox leadership combated mainly the arbitrary changes in ritual. "If we should permit ourselves," declared Eiger, "to invalidate one letter in the words of the Sages, serious danger would threaten the entire Torah." In the Hamburg controversy and in the Geiger-Tiktin affair, their implacable insistence upon all traditional observances found an often disagreeable expression. A widespread, well-substantiated rumor had it that the sudden death of Abraham Kohn, the reform preacher in Lemberg, in 1848, was due to poisoning by orthodox fanatics. The more the traditionalists' vested interests clashed with the social and political aims of the reformers, of whom Banet pointedly said that "their only purpose was to curry favor with the Christians," the more fiercely did the controversy rage.

NEO-ORTHODOXY

Frankfort and Hamburg orthodoxy, however, with a social status similar to that of the Reform group and facing the same problems, felt that some sort of reinterpretation was indispensable. It was Samson Raphael Hirsch who reworked the theology of orthodox Judaism. Stating that the belief in one God converts a heathen into a man, and that the fulfillment of the Law converts a man into a Jew, he hastened to draw therefrom the conclusion that the difference between a liberal and an orthodox Jew is greater than that between a Protestant and a Catholic. Indeed, his constant agitation led to frequent secessions of his adherents from the united communities, and he won his greatest victory when, in 1876, the German diet adopted a new statute which enabled a Jew to secede from the community and yet remain a professing Jew. Not unjustly, therefore, his faction was nicknamed *Trennungsorthodoxie*. Extreme intolerance on account of theological disparity was thus introduced into the fabric of Jewish life.

It must be remembered, however, that a concern with theology, as such, is not native to Judaism. In opposing Reform with his own type of orthodox Judaism, which came to be known as neo-orthodoxy, S. R. Hirsch largely accepted the premise of Reform that Judaism can be viewed as a dogmatic religion. Neo-orthodoxy, without being quite aware of it, constituted in itself an equally fundamental deviation from historical Judaism. In his ultimate acceptance of emancipation Hirsch is likewise ready to give up the Jewish nationality, or, at most, to limit it to a *Religionsnation*. Unwittingly, he is driven thereby to surpass his Reform opponents (except Holdheim) in their denial of Jewish nationalism, and to declare that, even in the period of Israel's independence, state and territory were merely a means of the people's "spiritual calling." He also believed in the Jewish religious mission as fervently as any humanitarian Reform dreamer. Neither his admission that Judaism had never been a "religion," either in the Roman sense of *religio*, or in its more modern theological connotations, and that the Hebrew language did not even possess an expression for religion (*dat* originally being the equivalent for "law"), nor his decided preference for "Torah" as the all-embracing term (*G.S.*, I, 80), could save neo-orthodoxy from tending to crystallize the Jewish religion around a definite set of beliefs and observances. No less than Reform, it thus abandoned Judaism's self-rejuvenating historical dynamism.

CONSERVATIVE JUDAISM

For this reason we may say that another indirect offshoot of Reform, the "positive historical" Judaism of Zacharias Frankel and Michael Sachs, and the "conservative" Judaism of America, have been much truer to the spirit of traditional Judaism. By maintaining the general validity of traditional Jewish law and combining with it freedom of personal interpretation of the Jewish past and creed, Frankel and his successors hoped to preserve historical continuity, in the face of the unprecedented perplexities of the new era. On the other hand, this conservative wing, representing a middle course, reveals all the strengths and weaknesses of compromise. At any rate, notwithstanding Frankel and Guedemann, Morris Joseph, Schechter and Kaplan, it has not yet succeeded in developing an all-embracing philosophy, common to all who, though estranged from orthodoxy, are reluctant to join the Reform camp.

True, on one point all conservatives do lay great stress: the obligation of the Jew to adhere to the whole body of the Law. In practice, however, they, too, make certain concessions to new conditions. But they are so little in agreement on the extent of these concessions, as well as on theological fundamentals, that M. M. Kaplan himself, in many ways one of conservative Judaism's foremost exponents, speaks of two distinct groups as belonging to the Right Wing of Reformism and to the Left Wing of Neo-Orthodoxy.

That conservative and neo-orthodox Judaism were both a reaction to Reform and emancipation is self-evident. Both, however, disclaimed any connection with emancipation no less vigorously than did the Reform leaders. S. R. Hirsch's pronunciamento expresses beautifully the conscious attitude of the orthodox and conservative leaders, "I bless emancipation if Israel does not regard it as the goal of its task, but only as a new condition of its mission, and as a new trial, much severer than the trial of oppression; but I should grieve if Israel understood itself so little, and had so little comprehension of its own spirit that it would welcome emancipation as the end of the Galut and the highest goal of its historic mission" (*The Nineteen Letters of Ben Uziel,* English transl., p. 167).[29]

Stealing the thunder from enlightenment, governmental and Jewish, which had tried to educate "enlightened" rabbis in the semisecular rabbinical colleges of Warsaw, Padua and Metz (1826-30), both reformers and conservatives speedily founded theological seminaries to supply the much-needed leadership for their congregations. Ludwig Philippson and Geiger had long postulated the establishment of a liberal theological faculty, but the conservative theological Seminary of

Breslau was founded first. Under the guidance of Frankel and Graetz it tried to instill in its students the spirit of "positive historical" Judaism. The founding of the liberal *Hochschule* and the neo-orthodox *Rabbinerseminar*, both in Berlin, followed in the years 1872-73. In America, on the contrary, the Hebrew Union College in Cincinnati (1875) preceded the conservative Jewish Theological Seminary of America (1886). They were followed in 1896 by the Rabbi Isaac Elhanan Yeshiva, and in 1922 by the liberal Jewish Institute of Religion. The alumni of these institutions, as well as those of London, Vienna, Budapest, etc., have ever since exerted a marked influence on Jewish movements far beyond the confines of the countries in which they happened to be placed.[30]

REFORM'S HISTORIC POSITION

Curiously, the political sentiments of the reformers were not entirely reciprocated by either Christian society or the state. To be sure, Napoleon saw in the reformation of Judaism a means of more effectively controlling the Jewish group and pressing it into the service of the state. But the governments of the most important centers of Reform—Prussia, Hungary and the United States—had an indifferent and sometimes antagonistic attitude. In Prussia, particularly, all innovations were looked upon with serious misgivings before 1848. The Prussian ministry of cults suspected that social and political radicals were being harbored in the Jewish Reform group, as among the young Protestant theologians. Disturbances in the Jewish community, caused by religious dissensions, for a time appeared to the rigid Prussian police as a source of disorder to be suppressed. Instigated, moreover, by the new Berlin Missionary Society, which hoped thus to make more converts, the Prussian government in 1823 forbade Reform services of any kind. Nevertheless, the social forces behind Reform carried it to victory in Prussia in the first decades of the century, and in America in the second half of the century. When these social forces had spent themselves, or were replaced, the evolution of the Reform movement was retarded, and finally even reversed.

From the outset, Reform's greatest handicap was its confinement to a limited circle of business men and intellectuals, in a few countries of the dispersion. At the very height of its American achievement in the Union Prayer Book, it seemed to appeal to "a people composed of retired philanthropists and amateur social workers" (S. S. Cohon, *Yearbook CCAR,* XXXVIII, p. 250 n. 5).[31] It merely shared therein the fate of religious liberalism in the Christian churches, which "has never been and gives no promise of becoming a majority movement" (A. C. McGiffert, in *JR,* XV,174). Unlike Christian liberalism, however, Reform Judaism suffered from its original intimate connection with the struggle for emancipation. Its greatest undeniable historical achievement had consisted in having partially checked religious indifference, and retarded the pace of baptism and intermarriage. The warning sounded by a French reformer of 1859, "Wait another half century and Reform will find no persons to deal with" (G. Levy, *Orgue et Pioutim,* p. XXIX), was more than a phrase. Indeed, religious indifference is more widespread in the Jewries of France and Italy, the two Catholic countries where assimilation found no counterpoise in Reform, than in America, England or Germany. In radically disrupting the flow of historical continuity and in denying the great historic reality of the Jewish ethnos, however, Reform had put itself into opposition to the yearnings and aspirations of the masses of the people.

Owing to the experiences of the World War, the Palestine mandate and the minority rights treaties, as well as to the enlarged scope of the World Union for Progressive Judaism, organized in 1926, a new period began in the history of the movement. There is also a growing recognition of the fact that too much stress has been laid upon ethics and the systematization of theology, and too little upon actual religious experience and the warm appeal of ceremony. All these facts point to a religious reorientation of untold possibilities in the near future.

CONFLICTING FORCES IN EMANCIPATION

The emancipation of the European man and the Jew, to sum up, opened a new chapter in the history of both. As in all other historical developments, the changes were not sudden nor the reactions immediate. Even the great revolutions in the western countries and the grant of full citizenship to the Jews were merely climactic expressions of long developments. There was, however, not a simultaneous evolution in all domains of life. The inner development of the Jews did not always coincide with transformations in the outside world. The sudden emancipation of Alsatian Jewry by the French Revolution, for example, necessarily followed the profound changes in French society at large, but the condition of the Jew in these northeastern provinces remained essentially medieval. On the other hand, Prussian Jewry had been ripe for equality long before the official emancipation of 1847. These not infrequent contrasts between potentiality and actuality were a permanent source of new conflicts.

The dispersion of the Jews and their continual migrations, produced further complications. General emancipation of the individual in economics, culture and politics, progressed with increasing speed from West to East. The same holds true of Jewish emancipation. But while the richest, most popular and, in a sense, most important European nations were in the West, the Jewish masses lived in the East. The early participation of the Jews in capitalism, enlightenment and political equality was therefore limited to an insignificant number. On the other hand, the tremendous increase of the Jewish population throughout the period, caused a steady translocation of large groups from the East to the West, *i.e.*, from one stage in emancipation to another stage. This presented still graver problems of adjustment to such Jews, forcing them to skip many generations of evolution. From members of a solid Jewish community, they had to become free individuals, and at the same time be integrated into a society even stranger than the previous near-by Gentile milieu. For the earlier settled groups of western Jewries, the influx of these newcomers spelled retardation, in some respects a direct reversal of the main trends in their own development, which was often equivalent to salvation from imminent extinction as Jews. The most important religious movement of the age, Jewish Reform, was consequently not only split up into many opposing camps, but exercised a direct appeal merely upon a small minority of world Jewry. Soon a new force appeared, which tried to overcome these confused and centrifugal tendencies—Jewish nationalism.

XII

NATIONALISM

DURING the last half century Jewish nationalism has again become a dominant force in Jewish life. Ethnic affirmation has become as important to Jewry as emancipation once was. Every Jew at all conscious of his Jewishness has been obliged to assert or deny openly his allegiance to the Jewish ethnic body. Those lacking in social consciousness or absorbed in an economic routine, might remain indifferent to this as to other social problems, but all vital groups in Jewry have had to take a stand.

Jewish nationalism is the belated offspring of European nationalism. The peculiar position of the Jewish people in dispersion delayed the rise of Jewish national consciousness until internationalism had begun to replace, or at least effectively supplement, nationalism in general. This internationalism is to be distinguished from the eighteenth-century cosmopolitan spirit which contended for the universality of mankind as *against* its ethnic differentiation. Modern internationalism acknowledges the discreteness of each cultural and ethnic entity, striving to build upon them a superstructure of brotherhood. Internationalism thus conceived really presupposes nationalism, of which it is the ideal fulfillment. Cosmopolitan Enlightenment, on the other hand, with its negation of the *ethnos,* was as inimical to Jewish nationality as was the jingo-patriotism of the early eighteen hundreds. To be sure, in the eighteenth century everybody spoke of a Jewish nation. Even such friends of Jewish emancipation as Mendelssohn, Dohm and Mirabeau, indiscriminately used the expressions, *jüdische Nation* and *jüdisches Volk, la nation juive* and *le peuple juif.* As emancipation came increasingly to be associated with assimilation, however, these terms began to disappear in favor of terms emphasizing equality of rights.

Early nationalism had for its ultimate goal the erection of a national state for each nationality. The Jewish nationality, which could not hope to erect its own national state embracing the bulk of Jewry, represented a serious obstacle. Every national state, it was further felt, should become as purely national as possible, which presupposed also the absorption of the Jews by the various ethnic majorities. Thus integrated into the national state, they would not interfere with its ethnic homogeneity. In western Europe, therefore, as well as in Germany and Italy, which were at that time driving toward national unification, the comparatively small Jewish population was increasingly regarded as a religious rather than an ethnic group.

Even in the Polish ethnographic region, at that time under the domination of Russia, Austria and Prussia, a similar theory was advanced by the leading proponents of Polish nationalism, and accepted by the "enlightened" leaders of Jewish public opinion. The Polish nation, torn asunder by three mighty empires, never gave up its dream of ultimate unification into a national state. Successive waves of Polish revolutionary *émigrés* were among the staunchest supporters of extreme nationalism, even in the countries of western and central Europe to which they fled. There was no room for a Jewish nationality in their program for a future Polish national state. The Jews were expected to sacrifice their national identity and to be completely absorbed. Even the mystic dreamers among the Paris *émigrés,* under Towianski and Mickiewicz, who saw in Poland and in Israel two suffering messiah peoples, visualized the Polish state as nationally pure. The Jews of Poland would have to be denationalized.

No reaction set in until toward the end of the century, when dissension among the nationalities reached its peak, and wars of nationalism threatened to frustrate forever the hope of human unity. The increasing difficulty in ethnically mixed territories, so common in central Europe and the Balkans, revealed the impossibility of a full realization of the idea of an exclusive national state. Each of these rising national states would in that case be forced logically to decree the extinction of its conationals outside its own boundaries. The cohesive forces behind certain states of multiple nationalities, especially Austria-Hungary and Russia, also counteracted this extreme nationalism, which was gradually undermining their imperial framework. Out of these circumstances grew the conviction that a state may include national minorities without damage to its political existence. Hence came the demand for recognition and even protection of a Jewish national minority along with other minorities.[1]

MIGRATION AND URBANIZATION

These political forces were strengthened by many social and economic factors. The enormous growth of the Jewish population during the last centuries reached its peak after 1880. During the last fifty years the Jewish population of the world increased by more than 100 percent, and the dislocation of the Jewish masses increased accordingly. Even without the Russian pogrom wave of 1881, emigration to America would have been inevitable. In fact, Russian Jewish emigration from 1881 to 1890, although much larger than in the preceding decades, was very small in comparison with the myriads which left the country after 1890. The Jews of the other eastern European countries also participated in this exodus, which had been made compulsory by economic necessity. Then, too, the Jewish emigration from eastern Europe constituted only a part, though a very significant part, of the transplanting of large sections of the general eastern European population to the countries of the West. Down to the 1880's, immigration into the United States was primarily western European, including Englishmen, Germans, Scandinavians, etc. In the two following decades the proportion of eastern Europeans grew immensely. The so-called "old immigration" reached its peak in 1882, with 87.1 percent of all newcomers. In 1907 the so-called "new immigration" from Austria-Hungary, Italy and Russia rose to 81 percent, while the old dropped to 12.9 percent. Similarly Russian Jewish immigration, which is said to have totaled 7,550 during the whole preceding half century, jumped to 41,000 in the ten years 1871-80. This sudden increase was primarily due to the Polish famine of 1869, as a result of which no less than 800 Jews were brought over to America by the Alliance israélite universelle alone. The Odessa journal *Den* and the Berlin *Allgemeine Zeitung des Judentums* of 1869-71, commented extensively on this exodus. The United States delegates to the Jewish World Conference in Paris in 1878 felt the necessity of uttering a warning against indiscriminate promotion of Jewish emigration to America. Nevertheless, the number of immigrants rose to 133,000 in the following decade, to 280,000 in 1891-1900, and to 704,000 in 1901-10. However, the proportion of Jews within the total immigration from Russia dropped from 73 percent in 1871-80 to 63 percent in 1881-90, to 55 percent in 1891-1900, and to 44 percent in 1901-10. The immigration from Austria-Hungary (including Galicia), although no spectacular pogroms occurred there, rose to 45,000 in 1881-90, 84,000 in 1891-1900, and 159,000 in 1901-10. At the same time, the proportion of Jews in the Austro-Hungarian emigration to America sank from 12.6 percent and 14.1 percent in the first two decades to 7.4 percent in 1901-10. Of course, the pogroms of 1881-82 and 1903-5 added impetus to such movements. Figures rose materially in years when such bloodshed took place, but soon afterwards they returned to a normal rate of acceleration. Notwithstanding the great contraction beginning with the World War (except the year 1921 which brought 119,000 Jews to America), and notwithstanding the practical stoppage of immigration during the last few years, the United States, with approximately 4,500,000 Jews, has become by far the largest Jewish center in the world.

As a whole, in the generation between 1880 and 1910 not less than 30 percent of all living Jews were on the road from one continent to another. Many more, willingly or not, changed their abode from one European country to another, or moved within a given country. The expulsion of Jews from the rural districts in Russia, in particular, and the immigration of the so-called "Litvaks" into Russian Poland, and of Galician and Hungarian Jews into western Austria, swelled the number of migrants for which, for obvious reasons, no statistics are available. It was a truly astonishing movement of a whole people, of which about one-fifth was transported from eastern Europe into the United States within a generation.

But this stupendous movement was not unique. Ireland's population, which had amounted in 1840 to 8,200,000, gradually diminished during the following sixty years to 4,400,000, or to almost half its former total. In contrast to this actual decline, eastern European Jewry, while losing large masses of emigrants, simultaneously increased in Russia, Poland, Austria-Hungary, Rumania, etc. One can speak of a recession of the eastern European Jewish sector merely in relation to the rest of the population, whose rate of increase during those years was likewise enormous. The only eastern European community which has really become depopulated in recent generations, is Posen and its surrounding districts. The majority of its Jews had moved to other German territories, to England, or oversea. The return of that province to Poland in 1919, caused the final expatriation of a large part of the remnant. In the early postwar years one could frequently see in Warsaw or Cracow delegations of one or another decaying community, pathetically offering centuries-old scrolls of law for preservation and use in these large congregations. During the last few years, however, the trend has been reversed and, under the economic pressure, numerous Jews have moved from central and eastern Poland, westward to Posen and Silesia. Thus, at least next to the Irish, the Jews have been the most migratory nation of modern times, continuing in a "voluntary" fashion their medieval wanderings.

Along with this process of displacement another vital transformation, the urbanization of the Jewish people, was going on. At present almost half of world Jewry lives in towns with a population exceeding 100,000, while more than one-fourth dwell in huge cities of a million inhabitants and more. Furthermore, the conglomeration of Jewry has gone so far that a majority of the whole people are massed in communities of more than 10,000 Jews each. The nearest example in the world at large can be found in England, where two-fifths of the population live in cities of over 100,000, and one-fifth in cities of over 1,000,000 inhabitants. For the United States of America in 1930 the respective figures were 30 and 12 percent; for Germany in 1933, 30 and 8 percent. More than one-ninth of world Jewry is concentrated in one city, New York. One may thus speak of the metropolitanization rather than urbanization of the Jewish people. This truly astounding accumulation, combined with the rise in economic and political power of the United States in general, as well as with the simultaneous disruption of Russian Jewry as a result of the

World War, lent further emphasis to the shift of the center of gravity of world Jewry from the East to the West.

This movement has not been arrested even by the contraction in Jewish migration in postwar years. New York, contrary to often-voiced expectations, did not distribute its Jewish masses all over the American continent. At the same time, the Soviet Union, with the breakdown of the Pale of Settlement, opened new metropolitan areas to Jewish settlers. While immigration into Russia has been restricted to a small number of skilled craftsmen, the government has effectively discouraged the emigration of Jews. Few Jews have been able to avail themselves of the opportunity offered by law during the last few years to acquire an exit visa at an average price of some $500. (This fee was considerably reduced in June, 1936.) Internally, Russia, since the Revolution, has witnessed a tremendous shift of Jews and others. Before the War there were in Moscow and Leningrad only 2,000 or 3,000 Jewish merchants "of the first guild," and intellectuals; today they have Jewish communities of some 400,000 and 250,000 respectively. The two Ukrainian centers, Kiev and Kharkov, harbor between them another 300,000 Jews. The mushroom growth of new industrial cities, such as Stalingrad and Magnitogorsk, has attracted many thousands of Jewish inhabitants. East European Jewry has thus been seized by the whirl of metropolitanization in one of its vital centers. The postwar rise of Warsaw and Budapest to the rank of cities with over 1,000,000 inhabitants has also added some 600,000 Jews to the "metropolitan" group.[2]

THE CLIMAX OF CAPITALISM

This transplanting of large groups of Jewry naturally had considerable economic significance. Not only had capitalism by that time begun to penetrate the eastern European countries, wrenching Jews as well as others out of traditional ways of life, but a large section of the Jewish people were now directly grafted on highly capitalistic organisms in America and western Europe. For the first time masses of Jews entered the capitalistic system at its height. Slowly they adjusted themselves to the new demands, as far as commerce, banking, liberal professions and a few industries were concerned. Commerce, including the money trade, remained their principal occupation. Undoubtedly the figures given for Prussia in 1925, according to which 59 out of every 100 Jews earning a living were engaged in commerce, transportation or the hotel business, as compared with 17 percent for the whole population, are not equally valid for other countries. But the preponderance of commercial activities everywhere cannot be doubted. In most countries 35-55 percent of the Jewish population derive their income from one or another form of merchandizing, banking, agency, etc. In contrast to this even the most mercantile countries, such as England, the United States and Germany, do not possess a commercial population of more than 12-15 percent, if one excludes from the census figures railroad and marine transportation which may be said to belong to industry rather than commerce.

At the same time, Jewish big business suffered a relative decline. Jewish bankers no longer exercised that overwhelming control over the international money market which had been theirs in the first half of the nineteenth century. The Rothschilds, to be sure, remained for a while the leading private bankers of Europe. It has been estimated that in the years 1817-1902, they negotiated public loans to the staggering amount of $6,500,000,000. Among their most spectacular transactions was the £4,000,000 credit for the acquisition of 177,000 shares of the Suez Canal, extended in 1875 by Lionel Rothschild on the spur of the moment to his personal friend, Prime Minister Disraeli. Through this loan, negotiated without the authorization of Parliament, "the French government has been out-generaled" (Disraeli to Queen Victoria, November 24, 1875, in W. F. Monypenny and G. E. Buckle's *Life of Benjamin Disraeli,* II,788), and Great Britain obtained control over that vital artery of Indian trade. But when the World War, entailing the destruction of enormous quantities of goods, forced the governments to borrow billions of dollars, no single banking concern could underwrite the tremendous bond issues. The belligerent powers appealed directly to the people by campaigns which largely eliminated the intercession of the private banker. At the same time, the rapid development of joint stock companies, through successive mergers, established financial powers far surpassing those of any private banking firm.

London, for more than a century the financial center of the world, offers the most striking illustration. The postwar "Big Five" among British banks, whose balance sheets for 1930 showed deposits of £1,700,000,000 against £280,000,000 deposited in the remaining twenty banks, have had few Jewish associates. Lloyd's and Barclay's had no Jews; the Midland Bank, only one among its directors. Only the National and Provincial Bank and the Westminster Bank have some Jewish connections (Reading, Montagus). Among the twenty smaller banks, six have been under partial Jewish control. Only one of the four leading investment trusts can be classified as predominantly Jewish. As against these huge corporations, the Jewish private bankers, the Rothschilds, Lazard Brothers, Montagues, and Sassoons, are only of secondary importance. Even in the acceptance business with the Continent, from which until the World War the big companies had held aloof, the monopoly of the private bankers is now gone.

In the various sections of the London financial market [writes P. Einzig, a local banker], it is only the bullion market in which Jews predominate. Their relative influence in the foreign exchange market has declined to a fraction of what it used to be, as a result of the extension of foreign business by the joint stock banks. Although there are many prominent Jewish Stock Exchange firms, in the aggregate, they form a small minority. As for the money market, it is essentially non-Jewish. [*The Banker,* XXVIII.]

In America Jewish bankers had a hard struggle from the beginning, against the older and well established non-Jewish firms. Haym Salomon, the Jewish financier of the American Revolution, was at that time an exceptional figure. By 1860, however, a number of banking houses had been established by German Jewish immigrants, which soon exercised considerable influence on domestic and international trade. Lazard brothers, hailing from Alsace; the Speyer family, descendants of the old distinguished Frankfort court Jews of that name; the Seligmanns from Bavaria, where early in the century Aaron Elias Seligmann (Baron von Eichstädt) had been the leading banker; the Lehmanns from Württemberg; the Belmonts from Frankfort, for a time representatives of the Rothschild interests; have all won a high position in American banking. Kuhn, Loeb and Company, the leading Jewish firm, was founded by Abraham Kuhn and Solomon Loeb from

Alsace, but achieved its greatest renown after 1875, under the guidance of Jacob Schiff of Frankfort. It has had a particularly far-reaching influence upon the development of American railways and the marketing of foreign loans in New York. For example, in conjunction with several other banking houses, it negotiated loans in excess of $1,000,000,-000 in the years 1881-1920, for the Pennsylvania Railroad Company, and in 1908 floated a loan of 460,000,000 Mexican dollars for the consolidation of Mexico's two main railroads. In 1900 it launched the first German loan on the American market, to the amount of 80,000,000 marks; and, in 1904 and 1905, spectacularly participated in lending Japan an aggregate of £55,000,000, largely on account of Schiff's enmity to Czardom, thus indirectly contributing to Japan's victory over Russia. These undoubtedly remarkable achievements of Kuhn, Loeb and Company, however, do not compare with those of J. P. Morgan and Company. The few joint stock companies controlled by Jews, largely of eastern European origin, such as the Manufacturers Trust Company, the Bank of United States, the Public National Bank and the Amalgamated Bank (controlled by Jewish needleworkers' unions), never held a position comparable to that of the Chase National Bank or the National City Bank. The crisis of 1929-33 hit Jewish banks harder than the older and more firmly established houses of Morgan, the Whitneys, the Bakers, etc. The Manufacturers Trust Company and the Public National Bank have been reorganized after an elimination of all Jewish directors; the Bank of United States was forced into bankruptcy. Kuhn, Loeb and Company's balance sheets, submitted to the Senate Investigating Committee, showed that in the years 1929-32 its assets were reduced by 70 percent.

On the European Continent the influence of Jewish banking has been most conspicuous in Germany and Austria. Many Jewish banking firms established during the Napoleonic wars, exercised great influence over central European economy. Such private bankers as the Mendelssohns and Bleichroeders in Berlin, the Warburgs in Hamburg, Lazard-Speyer-Elissen in Frankfort, and Arnstein and Eskeles in Vienna, had their counterpart in the numerous Jewish founders and directors of the German "Big Four" (Deutsche, Dresdner, Danat, Commerzbank), the Austrian Creditanstalt and Bankverein, the

Hungarian Kreditbank, etc. Eskeles was one of the founders of the Austrian National Bank in 1816, and Ludwig Bamberger contributed much to the establishment of the German Reichsbank in 1870. That many of these Jewish bankers cast off their Judaism and joined the dominant religion had little effect upon public opinion, which consistently saw in them the representatives of Jewish *Finanzkapital*. The small Jewries of France and Italy likewise produced such bankers as the brothers Péreire, the founders of the long-successful Crédit Mobilier, which in vain tried to undermine the financial predominance of the Rothschilds; Maurice de Hirsch, chief of the Paris banking firm, Bischoffsheim; Giuseppe Toeplitz, the Polish immigrant, under whose leadership the Banca Commerciale Italiana grew to its present position; and Luigi Luzzatti, the promoter of numerous banking coöperatives throughout Italy. Ironically, it was this Jewish financier and statesman who in Italy championed Schulze-Delitzsch's idea, which in Germany had provoked the most bitter attacks of another Jew, Lassalle. Although there were in Russia and Poland many large banks without Jewish connections, the Ginzburgs, Poliakovs and Epsteins undoubtedly were in the very first rank of Russo-Polish high finance.

The power of the Jewish banks on the Continent has waned during the last few decades. On the whole, this decline was merely part of the general retrogression of "financial capital." In the Anglo-Saxon countries, and especially in England, banking had never won as complete control of industry as in Germany or France. Correspondingly, Jews, entering from the financial side, scarcely penetrated manufacture and mining. Beginning with this century, and especially since the World War, Continental industry also began to emancipate itself from bank domination, thus largely shaking off Jewish influence.

OLD AND NEW INDUSTRIES

Jewish participation in light industries has always been more extensive than in heavy industries. American Jews were important producers of cloaks and suits as far back as 1885, long before the large influx of Eastern Europeans made itself felt. "A time was to come," say Charles and Mary Beard, "when the greatest industry in the land of John Alden and Cotton Mather was to be directed by a Portuguese Jew with an Anglo-Saxon name" (*The Rise of American Civilization*, I,640). In Brünn, a textile center of central Europe, the Jews are said to have controlled 80 percent of the total output in 1910. Leather production in all its forms has likewise long been identified with Jewish enterprise. American Jews have made notable contributions to the building industry. For example, Louis J. Horowitz, a poor immigrant, rose to head the Thompson-Starrett Company, which erected such imposing skyscrapers as the Woolworth, Equitable and Municipal Buildings in New York City. A Russian Jewish engineer, Moiseieff, was prominent in the construction of the Brooklyn, Williamsburg, Kings and other bridges. In recent years few architects have won such fame as Professor Erich Mendelssohn of Germany. The rôle of sugar refining of colonial and Russo-Polish Jews has already been mentioned. Nelson Morris, an immigrant from Bavaria, became one of the foremost meat-packers in Chicago, helping to develop that great middle-western industry in the crucial 1860's and 1870's. In the younger industries, of course, such as motion pictures, the manufacture of radio, gramophones, and artificial silk, the Jews have won great power.

The Jewish share in more basic industries, however, has been largely confined to railroad construction and management. The Rothschilds of Paris and Vienna, the Bischoffsheims of Brussels and Paris, the Poliakovs of St. Petersburg, and Kuhn, Loeb and Company of New York, were instrumental in spreading railways over a large part of the globe. The enthusiastic railway engineer, Theodore D. Judah, converted the American railroad magnates to the idea of a transcontinental line. Jews were relatively absent, however, from railroad construction in the British Empire, especially England. The same holds true with respect to the British, American and French merchant marine. In Dutch and Russian navigation, however, and especially in the Italian and German, Jews have been significantly active. Albert Ballin, to whom the Hamburg American Line owed its prewar greatness, was second to none among modern masters of shipping. The Lloyd Triestino was long controlled and run by Jews. On the other hand, Jews have never played a significant rôle in the coal or steel industries. The Friedlaender-Fould interests in the German coal regions, those of the Guttmanns in Dambrowa, and of the Vienna Rothschilds in the Witkowitz steel plants, are exceptional. The Jewish share in oil production has been much larger. Not only did Jews exercise an overwhelming influence on the oil areas of Poland and Rumania, but French as well as Russian Jews were prominently identified with the exploitation of the Caucasian oil fields which, before the War, held second place in the world's production. Jewish influence has been altogether negligible, however, in the two predominant systems of Standard Oil and Royal Dutch Shell. Hence, they have had little, if any, connection with the exploitation of new oil regions in Venezuela, Iraq and Persia. In considering mining, one must mention the Hendricks family in the United States, which as early as 1813, was prominent in the production of copper; and the Guggenheims, the copper kings of recent decades. Through American Smelting and Refining, the largest firm of its kind in the world, they have had effective control over many phases of production and marketing of semi-precious metals. Jews also took a prominent part in the output of Russian platinum. In 1912, of five directors of the "Platina" Corporation, which had a virtual monopoly of the Russian market, two were Jews. The South African Jewish pioneers, who contributed materially to British colonization, also became leaders in diamond mining. In 1905 J. Alfred Beit of Capetown, a partner of Cecil Rhodes, was regarded as the richest man on earth. "Gold mining," says an expert reviewer, "exploited and financed chiefly by Jews, is one of the very few industries in which English Jews still maintain a leading position, but this industry, on anything like its present scale, is of so recent a birth, that it is but natural that it should remain at present largely in the hands of its originators" (E. L. Franklin, in the *Contemporary Review,* CXLIV, 60).

During the last half century, the rôle of the Jews as employees and workers has also undergone significant changes. Immigration of Eastern European Jews into America, England and France resulted in a considerable increase of the Jewish industrial proletariat. Originally the western countries had few Jewish craftsmen. Frankfort in 1835, although not representative of all western communities, may serve as an illustration. Among the 434 Jews then engaged in gainful occupations, 251 were bankers and insurance brokers, 168 merchants in wool and clothing, 49 engaged in other branches of commerce, and 30 in the liberal professions. Only 10 were craftsmen. In the territories of Posen and Bromberg, on the contrary, the official statistics of 1825 show that among 13,060 Jewish heads of families, 46 were farmers and 3,663 artisans. The largest category was that of tailors who numbered 2,364. The proportion of artisans in other East European regions often exceeded 20 percent. It is revealing that fully 18.8 percent of Jewish immigrants into the United States in the years 1888-1911 declared themselves to be skilled tailors. Later, the Jewish clothing workers performed pioneering service in the unionization and development of collective bargaining of American labor.

These Jewish tailors [commented two enthusiastic investigators in 1930], have immeasurably enriched America. For while their fellow workers—diggers of coal, forgers of steel, weavers of cloth—are still widely denied a collective voice, the masses in the needle trades have been revealing what free, responsible citizens can contribute toward the development of life and industry. [S. Kopald and B. M. Selekman, in *MJ*, XVIII, 314.]

Eastern European Jews likewise swelled the ranks of labor in England and France. In the diamond centers of Amsterdam and Antwerp, most Jews joined the working classes. In recent years about three-quarters of all the diamond cutters in Amsterdam and more than one-quarter of those in Antwerp have been Jewish. Until the recent removal of the Greeks from Asia Minor, work on the docks of Salonica was regularly abandoned on Saturday, in deference to the numerous Jewish longshoremen. Even in central Europe the effects of legally opening the crafts to Jews were often startling. In Denmark the disability was removed in 1788; within twenty-six years there were 34 factory owners and 140 artisans, among the 2,400 Jews of the capital. In Bavaria Jews were admitted to crafts in 1813. In 1821 there were 169 Jewish artisans; in 1854, without any great increase in population, there were 4,813. The Jews of Prague so effectively availed themselves of the opportunity given them in 1797, that by 1840 they had four guilds in the typically Jewish crafts of tailoring, shoemaking, baking and goldsmithery. In 1824 Hamburg resorted to a *numerus clausus,* to keep Jewish artisans down to their proportion of the population. All these advances were made in the face of steady opposition from many quarters, especially the vested interest of established non-Jewish craftsmen. For example, in the early years of the French Revolution, Alsatian Jewry complained that its youth could not find positions as apprentices, the necessary prerequisite for future master craftsmen. Prussia's discrimination against foreign Jewish apprentices in the 1830's was the cause of extended controversy with several of her neighbors.

Today about 30 percent of world Jewry derive a living from some sort of industrial work. At first glance, this does not appear to be a small proportion, in considering fully industrialized countries as well as those largely agricultural. In England alone slightly more than one-half the population is engaged in industry; in Germany 42 percent, in the United States approximately 35 percent. On closer examination, however, the position of the Jews can hardly be regarded as enviable. While the overwhelming majority of the industrial population in these western countries consists of workers in factories and mines, the largest section among the Jews works at handicrafts. An illuminating example may be found in the statistical survey of Poland in 1921-22. Among the Gentile workers, 14.8 percent were engaged in minor crafts and 85.2 percent worked in factories, whereas the Jews showed the almost-inverted ratio of 78.6:21.4 percent. That the Jews prefer to be masters of the machine rather than its servants, may serve as a psychological explanation and as a solace. But such social stratification becomes increasingly dangerous, in view of the progressive mechanization of world production. True, the predictions of Marx and his contemporaries that, within a few decades, the artisan class will have been forced out of existence by mass production, have not materialized; nor are they likely to do so in the near future, since, with every new industry producing standardized goods on a large scale, there arises a class of people devoted to repair and other minor artisan tasks. Nevertheless, prospects for small craftsmen seem bad in every respect. In Soviet Russia, for example, while the government has greatly mitigated its early opposition to the artisan class as such, it has, by emphasizing the large-scale manufacture of clothing and leather goods, seriously endangered the two basic Jewish crafts.

The process of transforming the Jewish working classes into an industrial proletariat has thus far been slow. In America the proportion of Jews in such "Jewish" industries as the needle trades, has receded in recent years. On the other hand, since the War larger or smaller groups of industrial workers have arisen among the Jews in Poland, Rumania and Palestine. This is especially true of Soviet Russia. The shortage of labor caused by intensive industrialization under the two Five Year plans, has helped to attract a considerable number of Jews to new factories. Elsewhere the unemployment, which has become a more or less permanent feature of such industrial countries as England, Germany and the United States, is a serious deterrent.

These negative forces, however, are partly counteracted by other tendencies. As machines progressively replace manual labor, the proportion of brain workers is on the increase, even in factories. A significant example is revealed by recent German industrial statistics, which show a reduction of more than 4 percent in the number of workers, and an increase of about 50 percent in employees, between 1907 and 1925. The Jews, gradually driven out of independent commercial and industrial enterprises, may take up clerical work for mercantile and industrial corporations, provided, of course, that no extensive discrimination is directed against them.[3]

RETURN TO THE SOIL

The greatest transformation in the economic life of Jewry, however, has been the entrance of the Jews into agriculture, which had been closed to them for centuries. From the beginning of the emancipation era, it became constantly clearer to both friends and enemies of the Jews that a "productivization" of the Jewish masses is not only an economic, but also a political and cultural necessity. Productivization meant, in the first place, their return to that basic occupation which supports the vast majority of humanity. Theoretical demands for such return were voiced clearly by responsible leaders, both Jewish and Gentile, as far back as the eighteenth century.

These demands were greatly stimulated by the physiocratic school of economic thought, which stressed agriculture as the only productive occupation. While Frederick the Great, a true mercantilist, angrily refused the toleration of a Jewish cattle breeder, because he wished to see the Jews exclusively engaged in developing Prussian industry and commerce, a German political writer, Justi, suggested, in 1760, a plan to settle them on land in some unexploited territories. Christian Dohm, the famous protagonist of Jewish emancipation, advocated compulsion, if necessary, to force Jewish fathers to educate at least one son in a "useful" pursuit. Similar sentiments were expressed by the publicists Czacki and Herschel Józefowicz, and several deputies at the diet of 1793-95, in independent Poland. In 1825, one Moses Laski wrote a booklet emphasizing "the glory and the virtues of agriculture and all crafts" (cf. D. B. Weinryb, in *Tarbiz,* VII, 57-73). For other reasons, the socialist, Fourier, advocated stringent legislation, to "force the Jews to engage in productive work and not admit more than one-hundredth of their number to the pursuit of vice [Fourier's synonym for commerce], one merchant family only being allowed for every hundred agricultural and industrial families" (*Le Nouveau Monde,* p. 421).

These patent discrepancies in aims and in methods did not discourage the Jewish leaders from taking an active part in the process of occupational restratification. Special societies for the promotion of crafts and agriculture were organized by Jewish communities throughout the world, often enjoying the moral and financial support of the government. When Michaelis of Göttingen realistically objected: why should one try to make poor artisans out of good merchants, he was generally denounced as an anti-Semite. Great Jewish philanthropists, such as Baron Edmond de Rothschild, Baron Maurice de Hirsch and Sir Moses Montefiore, spent huge sums to facilitate the process of transformation on an international scale. Such interterritorial Jewish organizations as the Alliance israélite universelle, fostered the trend by extensive educational work, in which craft training was emphasized.

The earliest concrete official measures were adopted by Joseph II, the benevolent despot who endeavored to transplant 1,410 Galician families from commerce to agriculture. Jewish merchants were forbidden to settle in Bukovina when it was occupied by the Austrian army. As a result, half of the immigrating Jews had to declare themselves farmers. Indeed after 32 years, 150 Bukovinian villages had Jewish settlements and in the 1880's (20 years after their ownership of rural estates was legalized) Jews owned 37 large estates. In neighboring Galicia the Jews in 1902 possessed 7.4 percent of the entire cultivable area, a share nearly equal to their proportion in the population. The immigrants into Carpathian Ruthenia, moreover, largely Galician Jews, penetrated into agriculture so extensively that more than 28 percent of Carpatho-Ruthenian Jewry is still engaged in farming.

Most important, however, were similar developments in Russia. Soon after the third partition of Poland, mass settlement of Jews on land was advocated by the Jewish spokesman, Nathan Nata Notkin, in 1797; and the official Russian investigator of the Jewish question, Derzhavin, in 1799. Practical attempts to colonize the Jews in separate villages where they could combine farming with their accustomed national and religious life, began in 1806. The government set aside more than 80,000 acres in the neo-Russian province of Kherson, for young men who could prove their physical ability and who possessed 400 rubles per family. Soon seven colonies, carrying such picturesque names as *Sedeh Menuhah* (Field of Rest), *Har Shepher* (Beautiful Mountain), etc., were founded. In 1810 their population consisted of 1,690 Jewish families. After the famine years of 1821-22, the Russian government made another attempt, likewise with partial success. The call issued in 1835, that Jews settle in far-off Siberia, found such a responsive echo among the pauperized masses that Nicholas I became frightened. Several hundred Jews had already started on the road to Asia, when he suddenly revoked the order. The colonization movement, sporadically encouraged by the government and public opinion, gained momentum until 1865, when approximately 33,000 Jews were living on the land. Although in 1866, on the opening of the industrial era, Alexander II prohibited further colonization and in 1874 withdrew the land reserves previously set aside for this purpose, and although the May Laws of 1882 altogether shut out the Jews from the acquisition of rural property, the Jewish farming population grew as rapidly as ever. At the end of the century, it consisted of approximately 100,000 souls. In Russian Poland some 70 Jewish colonies were founded in the years 1817-70. While in 1861 only 374 families inhabited 57 colonies, the total Jewish agricultural population had been estimated at 28,391 in 1858.

From Europe the movement spread to the New World and Palestine. The *Am-Olam* organization of the 1880's made a concerted attempt to transplant Russian Jews to America and to settle them in socialistically planned agricultural colonies. Although supported by the United Hebrew Charities of New York and other American organizations, and guided by such able leaders as Herman Rosenthal and Michael Halprin, this attempt had little success. Colonies founded in the 1880's and the 1890's in Louisiana, North and South Dakota, Colorado, Oregon, Kansas, Michigan, Virginia and Ohio, coming at a time when the most fertile regions had already been occupied, could not long hold out against unfavorable natural factors. About the same time, Baron Maurice de Hirsch (stimulated by Wilhelm Loewenthal's description of his visit in the Argentinian province of Santa Fé, where 135 Eastern European Jewish families had taken up farming on their own initiative) set out to colonize 3,000,000 Russian Jews in the agricultural regions of South America within 25 years. Although supported by an endowment of some $40,000,000, his plan turned out to be little short of utopian. In 1891, in the very first year of the Jewish Colonization Association (ICA), 6,000 Jews were brought over to Argentina. Of these, 3,000 remained in Buenos Aires. In the next two years, the number of colonists dropped from some 2,850 in December, 1891, to 2,683 in October, 1893.

The tremendous pressure of the growing population, however, combined with the progressive mechanization and commercialization of agriculture after 1900, helped to overcome these initial difficulties. The shift to agriculture was stimulated by Zionist, Diaspora-nationalist, and socialist currents, and by the World War, which sent up prices of foodstuffs and raw materials. Apart from Palestine, Jewish colonization made considerable progress, especially in the two Americas and in Russia. In Argentina 80 percent of the initial 600,000 hectars (1,500,000 acres) acquired by the ICA in 1891 has been settled; over 60 percent (384,496 hectars on

January 1, 1931) is today under cultivation. Many farmers in the fourteen Argentinian colonies have paid off all mortgages to the ICA, and acquired full title to their property. In 1916 the large colony of Moiseville (named after Maurice de Hirsch) counted 60 members, with holdings valued at between $30,000 and $60,000. The progress can easily be estimated by noting that land sold to colonists by the ICA for years at $8.40 per acre had attained a market value of from $125 to $160 in 1927. All in all, as a result of ICA's total investment of approximately $4,000,000, about 45,000 Jews now live in these colonies, of whom 33,000 are farmers. In Brazil the ICA acquired 250,000 acres, and over 1,000 Jews are now farming in two colonies founded in 1904. Progress in the United States, stimulated by the organization of the Jewish Agricultural Aid Society in 1900, has been more rapid. Settling near large eastern cities, the Jewish colonists have engaged mainly in intensive dairy farming, for which those of Woodbine, N. J., have won more than one prize at agricultural exhibits. Jewish farmers rose to almost 100,000 in number, with aggregate holdings of more than 1,000,000 acres.

There is no branch of farming in which Jews have not achieved signal success.... They are among the largest producers [of tobacco in the Connecticut River Valley] and they raise a product of the highest quality.... In the Geneva [Ohio] grape district Jewish farmers, although in the minority, raise more than half of the crop. A Jew is known as the "Grape King."... Jewish farmers are in the front rank of the truck growers in the vegetable sections of South Jersey and Long Island.... [A Jew] has developed the "Spiegel" type of Gladiola, regarded by judges as one of the finest varieties.... The largest New Jersey potato farm is worked by a Jew. .... A 30,000 acre wheat farm in Kansas, a truly gigantic enterprise, is in the hands of a Jew.... This man's service to the agriculture of the region was fittingly recognized in a celebration in his honor.... The day of celebration was declared a legal holiday. [*Report of the Jewish Agricultural Society for 1900-1924*, pp. 46-48.]

Even in far-off Australia, an Australian Jewish Land Settlement Trust was organized in Melbourne, in 1927. In overcommercialized Germany a *Reichsbund für jüdische Siedlung in Deutschland* tried, in 1928-32, to utilize the pro-agrarian policies of recent German governments to facilitate the settlement of Jews on the land. It was only the Nazi legislation which, stressing particularly the racial "purity" of the farming population in consonance with its general "blood and soil" philosophy, put an end to these promising attempts.

By far the largest colonizing activity has taken place in Russia under the Soviets. During the early, anarchical period of the Revolution, the peasants, feeling that a Jewish share in responsibility would enhance the security of their own acquisitions, frequently invited the Jews to participate in the distribution of the large landholdings of the aristocracy and the Church. Somewhat later the Soviet law, excluding the urban population from government land grants, made a significant exception in favor of the Jews. The Jews, the legislators stated, had become exclusively urban only by virtue of discriminatory laws, especially the May Laws of 1882, and it would be unjust to perpetuate this untoward condition. In 1924, the Soviet government embarked upon an ambitious policy of mass colonization of Jews in the Crimea, the Ukraine, the Northern Caucasus (on both sides of the Sea of Azov), and later in Birobidjan. It was decided, with the help of world Jewry and especially the Agro-Joint, a subsidiary of the American Jewish Joint Distribution Committee, to build up contiguous Jewish settlements which might eventually qualify as independent Jewish republics. By 1927 the Jewish farming population of Soviet Russia included 33,357 families, or 165,000 persons, in these colonies, and 32,800 families in other regions. Since that time the rapid industrialization of Russia, the world-wide depression which diminished the financial resources of the Agro-Joint, the numerous disappointments of the first settlers in 1928-32, the red tape of the Russian administration, the war alarms in the Far East, etc., have all slowed down the process. Nevertheless, recent official estimates are that there are now approximately 300,000 Jewish farmers in the Soviet Union. From 2 percent at the beginning of the century, they had become one-tenth of the Jewish population, thus rivaling in size the steadily declining merchant group. It is a speedy advance, indeed, toward the goal announced by Tshemerisky at the All-Soviet Culture Congress of 1928, that "a lock be hung on the last Jewish shop."

Taking world Jewry as a whole, it may be asserted that at the beginning of this century the total agricultural settlement did not exceed 2 percent of the population, whereas it is now as high as 4 percent. The importance of the change can be seen when one realizes that in England the total agricultural population does not exceed 7.5 percent. Of course, England is an exception. Other industrial countries, such as Belgium, Germany and the United States still have 20 percent or more farming population. The Jewish farmers, moreover, do not live in England, Belgium or Germany, but for the most part in Russia, Palestine, Poland and Carpathian Ruthenia, where an overwhelming majority of the population is engaged in agriculture. Nevertheless, compared to the previous situation of the Jewish people, this return to the soil may be classified as one of the most revolutionary events in modern Jewish history. If continued, the increase in Jewish farming, combined with its simultaneous decrease within the world's most advanced nations, may eventually overcome the disparity between the general and the Jewish ratios.[4]

LIBERAL PROFESSIONS

An equally startling transformation has taken place in the field of the liberal professions. Even before the emancipation, Jewish physicians were more readily admitted to medical practice. In the rigidly organized legal profession, the main difficulty hinged on the admission to the various bar associations. In England the first Jewish solicitor appeared in 1770, the first Jewish barrister only in 1833. In France we encounter the first practicing lawyer, Michel Berr, soon after the Revolution. Dr. Rafael Joel, however, the first Jewish lawyer in Austria to arise from the "liberal" legislation of Joseph II, eventually landed at the baptismal font. With the progress of Enlightenment and emancipation, which opened the way to the study of western letters and sciences, Jews became prominent as physicians, lawyers, littérateurs, artists, musicians and theatrical producers. Postwar Germany, with more than 4 percent of Jews in these professions as against less than 2 percent in the total population, is a striking example of recent developments in the West. Elsewhere the relative figures are smaller, but almost everywhere larger than the Jewish share in the population. The old propensity of Jewish youth to study, and the desire of parents to see their sons become rabbis, has been changed to a general effort to enter the liberal professions. There is a typical dictum, reflecting Jewish self-irony, to the effect that every Jewish family has a lawyer among its sons, with the exception of those families that have two or three lawyers. Since the growth of clientèle cannot possibly keep pace with this increase of professional intellectuals, the eventual outcome is a general proletarization of the Jewish intelligentsia, and occasional recourse to dubious practices. And with the prevalent tendency to generalize regarding Jews, proletarization and unfair competition among individuals reflect upon the standing of the entire Jewish group in a given profession. The simultaneous growth of the professional classes in the non-Jewish population, instead of allaying the fears and suspicions against the Jewish intellectuals, frequently serves only to sharpen the competition and to increase the number, power and articulateness of their opponents. The preponderance of lawyers is the more disquieting if one realizes, with Abraham ibn Daud and modern communists, that, if the world were just, there would be no need of lawyers. Overproduction of Jewish intellectuals is true of all fields of art and science. Even in the plastic arts, from which the Jewish people, on the whole, kept aloof throughout two millennia, the Jews now proportionately outnumber the non-Jews. One need merely note the thousands of Jewish painters, outstanding and mediocre, assembled in Paris, to realize the profundity of the transformation.[5]

The economic life of the Jewish people during the last fifty years has been very far from normal. Only in the last two or three decades did increased participation in agricultural and industrial labor indicate that sustained attempts to normalize its economic structure are not utterly hopeless. The economic position of many Jewish individuals and even groups has undoubtedly improved considerably, especially of those transferred from countries with a lower to those with a higher economic status.[6] But even in advanced countries, they show an economic stratification distinctly at variance with that of the rest of the population, and their situation as a group remains exceptional in many ways. In a word, the much-heralded economic amalgamation of the Jews to the surrounding nations is still far from having been achieved.

CULTURAL TRANSFORMATIONS

Social, political and intellectual absorption of Jewry by the various national majorities appeared, on the surface, to have been much more complete. The entrance of the Jews into western European society early in the nineteenth century seemed to have destroyed thoroughly both the intellectual and the territorial ghetto. From Heine and Boerne to Schnitzler, Wassermann and Feuchtwanger, the creations of German Jews have been among the epoch's most notable works of literature. Russian letters were increasingly enriched by Jewish poets and writers, from Frug and Levanda to Ehrenburg and Babel. The press was soon largely dominated by Jews. Not only were such prominent organs as those of the house of Ullstein, the *Frankfurter Zeitung, Berliner Tageblatt, Neue Freie Presse,* and the *New York Times* owned by Jews, but the most renowned European news agencies, those of Reuter and Wolff, were founded by Jewish journalists. In scientific fields, too, the Jews became protagonists of western culture. Among the 141 Nobel prize winners in the years 1901-31, there were no less than 18 Jews, almost 13 percent. The prominence of Jews as composers, from Meyer Beer (Meyerbeer), Mendelssohn-Bartholdy and Halévy to Mahler and Schoenberg; as musical interpreters (the famous violinists of our day are almost all Jews); as theatrical and motion-picture producers and actors (Reinhardt, Granowsky, Eisenstein, Rachel, Sarah Bernhardt, Sonnenthal); and as painters and sculptors (Antokolsky, Liebermann, Israels, Chagall), is a matter of common knowledge. All this seemed to indicate that Jews had been completely transformed into Germans, Frenchmen, Englishmen, Americans, etc.

In western social life alone certain irrational impulses or inveterate habits delayed the desired amalgamation. In America, especially, the lack of a landed gentry and titles of nobility, and the prevalent political democracy, led to rigid social exclusiveness among the plutocratic families; more rigid, indeed, than anywhere in Europe. Judge Hilton's refusal, in 1877, to admit to his Grand Union Hotel in Saratoga Springs, Joseph Seligman, to whom President Grant had a few years before offered the post of Secretary of the Treasury, was an early instance of such social fastidiousness. Up to 1933, the exclusion of Jews from hotels, summer resorts and residential sections was not quite as obvious or frequent, even in anti-Semitic Germany. But this social aloofness could be explained away as the snobbery of a vanishing class. Moreover, in Europe many a wealthy Jewess succeeded in purchasing a poor, but titled, husband, thus forcing "society" to accept her, along with him. In the happy days of liberalism, the Jewish question seemed to be solving itself through these assimilatory processes. Many Jews, readily losing sight of certain disquieting phenomena, looked forward to the realization of Moses Mendelssohn's prediction:

The few points which still separate us [Jews and Christians], may remain open for centuries without interfering with the happiness of human society.... In our years these denominations would carry a connotation no more hostile than the names Cartesians and Leibnitzians. [*G. S.,* ed. 1843, III, 114.] [7]

MODERN ANTI-SEMITISM

Then came the sudden awakening. After 1873, the year of the great crash on the stock exchange and the collapse of the so-called *Gründer-Aera* in Germany and Austria, condemnation of the Jews and Judaism became general. It was engaged in, even by responsible publicists and scholars. An unceasing stream of pamphlets and articles reiterated the arguments of the first "classic" of modern anti-Semitism, D. H. Naudh's *Die Juden und der deutsche Staat* (1st ed., 1861). As in previous critical moments, mass dissatisfaction was largely diverted into anti-Jewish channels. This time the governments failed to take such repressive measures as those of the imperial and Prussian administrations against Eisenmenger's *Entdecktes Judenthum* in 1700, or of the general directorate of the occupied German territories in the Napoleonic period against all anti-Jewish and pro-Jewish works. The animosities of the early post-Napoleonic era, reflected in the philosophical and historical arguments of Professors Fries and Ruehs, were now revived with greater intensity. In Stoecker, Duehring, R. Wagner, Treitschke, Hartmann, Lagarde and Chamberlain, this new movement found leaders with great influence upon the educated classes; while popular agitators such as Marr, Glogau, Ahlwardt, Henrici, Schoenerer, Lueger and Istoczy, translated their teachings into a cruder and more practical form for the masses. French Jewry, too, after having been, through a century of emancipation and assimilation, lulled into a feeling of undisturbed security, awoke with a start when Drumont began his ferocious anti-Jewish campaign. His *La France juive* (1886), ignored by the Paris press for a while, soon became a best seller. Within a year there appeared one hundred editions, to which were later added seventy-eight more French editions and others in English, German, Spanish and Polish. Despite obvious shortcomings, this work, as well as Drumont's other writings and his paper *La Libre Parole,* established his reputation as a scholar and writer. Even Joseph Lemaitre praised him as the greatest historian of the nineteenth century, next to Fustel de Coulanges. Soon afterwards the Dreyfus affair, which kept Europe aghast for years, opened the eyes of many thoroughly assimilated western Jews. The heated discussions of the two opposing camps, which dominated French politics in the late 1890's, the outbreak of popular fury in Marseilles, Lyons and Bordeaux, as well as the genuine Algerian pogrom, revealed the deep dissatisfaction of the masses and the distrust felt by many high government and social leaders.

Simultaneously Russian Jewry suffered a severe shock. More than a century of Russian domination had passed, and popular animosity toward the Jews had never resulted in widespread violence. Like everyone else, Russian Jewry thought the day of medieval pogroms had passed. Even the serious outbreak of 1871 in Odessa was minimized. The sudden pogrom wave in 1881, which, beginning in April at Elizavetgrad, swept in a few months through 167 Russian towns and villages, filled the whole Jewish people with anguish and despair. The ever-recurrent acts of mass violence, increasing in intensity and geographic extension in the following four decades, as well as the endless flood of anti-Semitic outpourings, were all, to say the least, countenanced by the government. Plainly Czarism meant "business," when one of its spokesmen, Plehve, allegedly announced the program of making Jewish life in Russia as unbearable as Hell. It has been estimated that in the years 1905-16, there appeared in the country 2,837 anti-Jewish writings, of which 14,327,000 copies were distributed among the people. Nicholas II, it is asserted, spent 12,239,000 rubles from his private chest to subsidize this propaganda. What could this mean but an attempt to carry out the notorious dictum ascribed to Pobedonostsev, procurator general of the Holy Synod, that a third of Russian Jewry should be converted, a third forced to emigrate, and a third allowed to perish? The simultaneous, harsh persecution of the other racial and religious minorities was so adroitly managed that, rather than converting them into friends of Jewry, it intensified their own judeophobia. No less bloodthirsty were the numerous anti-Semitic writers in contemporary Poland, Rumania, Hungary and other countries.

Anti-Semitism—the word had just been coined, possibly by Marr or Renan—thus again became an openly active force in world affairs. The psychological, biological, religious, economic and political forces, which had operated throughout Jewish history in the dispersion, were now further complicated by the new turn in Judeo-Gentile relations. Physical differences between the majority and the minority had been but slightly mitigated by the Jews' adoption of western dress and manners. Whether or not Freud is correct in saying that circumcision has produced a kind of "castration complex" among Gentiles, there is no doubt that, from the Roman period down, this physical differentiation has been subjected to legislative restriction, mythological denunciation and popular suspicion. Whether the Jews, like, supposedly, the Mongol and Negro races, possess a corporal odor, different from that of their Aryan neighbors, a theory underlying the familiar literary and artistic presentation of Jewish types in the Middle Ages and recently reiterated by many anti-Semites, is yet to be proved. Their distinctiveness of physiognomy can hardly be denied, however. The so-called "Jewish nose," due to Hittite rather than Semitic antecedents, has become the most regular feature of anti-Semitic caricature. That 46 percent of the Bavarian population were found to possess hooked noses and that the majority of Eastern European Jews failed to reveal this "racial characteristic," has not mattered. Popular prejudice was easily nurtured by this or other, alleged or real, physical distinctions. It is a curious biological irony that the nonassimilated Jews of Eastern Europe possess so-called Jewish physical peculiarities in a much smaller degree than the assimilated Sephardic and German Jews of the West.

Another psychological factor of undeniable importance has always been the defenselessness of the Jewish minority, which provoked hatred and maltreatment. All the sadistic impulses which go to make child and wife-beaters arise at the sight of this defenseless object of hate. Organized Jewish self-defense has frequently staved off pogroms, not only by inspiring fear in the prospective assailants, but by removing this psychological provocation. In this sense, the post-emancipation regeneration of the Jewish physique and the Jewish participation in sports has certainly counteracted anti-Semitic feeling more than a flood of publicist apologias. The possibility of selling protection to Jews has been another incentive. For example, as far back as 1700-4, the Frankfort community offered 12,000 guilders to Eisenmenger for the suppression of his book (G. Wolf, in *MGWJ*, XVIII). Although anti-Semitic publicists soon grew beyond the capacity of the Jews to silence them by bribery, there always remained "yellow" journalists and unscrupulous politicians who hoped to obtain such hush money. A Jewish delegate to the Peace Conference in Paris (apparently Lucien Wolf, who afterwards reported the incident) was approached by an unknown Lithuanian, who promised for £10,000 to prevent the publication of the notorious *Protocols of the Learned Elders of Zion*. Jewish solidarity was another stumbling-block. Even after the disintegration of the ghetto, the undeniable group life of medieval Jewry, the ancient traditions of mutual responsibility, and the precarious position as a minority, maintained the fiction of Jewish solidarity. Jews and Christians alike almost unconsciously ascribed the deeds of an individual Jew to the Jewish group as a whole, the only difference being that Jews claimed credit for the entire people for the distinction won by any Jewish individual, while anti-Semites generalized individual Jewish crimes or misbehavior. Proud Jews asserted in vain,

We shall not renounce the right to have our Shylocks. The Lord has not created us as a living illustration to the song of the honest man. [Krojanker.]

The tendency to blame the entire people for the individual Shylock has persisted. Even the very long and distinguished history of the Jews could serve as an excuse for this "dislike of the unlike." The "immortality" of the Jewish people fascinated many, but provoked the wrath and anger of others. Even a liberal writer, such as Wilhelm Michel, has recently expressed this resentment of the Jewish refusal to die. Very eloquently he has written of the Pharisaic *hybris,*

which after the horrible experiences of the Exile embarked upon the most audacious and successful enterprise against death. A people, self-chained to life as to a galley bench, immured itself into Existence with wonderful enthusiastic fury. [*Der Jude,* Sonderheft I, p. 54.]

These psychological aversions were strengthened by manifold sociological realities. In many a western country the gradual infiltration of eastern Jews was blamed for the hostile outbreaks. Treitschke's poignant denunciation, "year after year there pours into Germany from the inexhaustible Polish reservoir a host of ambitious pants-selling youngsters whose children and children's children will some day control Germany's stock exchanges and newspapers" (*Ein Wort über unser Judentum,* p. 2), was often reëchoed in anti-Semitic circles. In France, the German Jews served as a target. Drumont argued that, instead of sacrificing thousands of Frenchmen to march to Berlin, the French should reconquer Paris from the German Jews. S. Neumann's reliable statistical surveys, revealing a very moderate eastern Jewish immigration into Prussia before 1880, were accepted by such conservative economists and historians as A. Wagner and Mommsen. But Treitschke and his associates continued to blame the eastern Jews for all the crimes and shortcomings, real and imaginary, of German Jewry. During the years 1914-20, the forcible evacuation of Polish and Russian Jews by the invading German armies, the Russian and Hungarian revolutions, and the Russo-Polish war, brought numerous eastern refugees to Germany. In addition a number of Jewish prisoners of war remained in the country. The general insecurity of the first postwar years was likewise conducive to migratory movements. Nevertheless, in 1925 there were, among the 560,000 Jews in Germany, less than 100,000 aliens (76,387 in Prussia). In this number were included Western European and American Jews, German women married to eastern immigrants, and a large number temporarily residing in Germany for business or educational purposes. Nevertheless, the hatred of the *Ostjude* has been artificially nurtured by anti-Semitic writers, not without the coöperation of some German Jews. These eastern aliens furnished also an excuse for the anti-Jewish measures of the Nazi government, although through a curious irony of fate they have been persecuted to a somewhat lesser degree than Jewish Reich citizens, because they enjoyed the protection of the Polish or other foreign governments.

Anti-Semitic religious traditions also persisted. The accusation of Christ-killing and the denunciation of the patristic and medieval writers lingered in pious Christian minds. To be sure, Catholicism was, on the whole, still opposed to rabid anti-Semitism, rejecting its nationalist haughtiness and lack of Christian humility. The universal Church necessarily saw in the doctrine of racial inequality a direct challenge to its own mission. Moderate anti-Semitism of the older religious and social character, however, found many a champion in the Catholic camp. In 1872-73, Pope Pius IX, unbalanced by the loss of Rome, launched an unexpected assault on Jewish liberalism and journalism. The traditions of the Counter Reformation had long sustained anti-Jewish sentiment among the peasant and lower bourgeois masses. Now the Christian Socialist movement often assumed a militant anti-Semitic character. Primarily disturbed by the growth of the Socialist parties, Stoecker and Lueger organized what Wilhelm Liebknecht characterized as "a bastard edition of socialism for the use of stupid people," using the "Christian" slogans to attract a large petty bourgeois following. Only in Protestant countries, where Catholics were a struggling minority, were the notable pro-Jewish utterances of medieval churchmen frequently cited. The struggle for equality of rights for all denominations, carried on by the German Center Party (after a few years of hesitation, during which its organ, the *Germania,* indulged in extensive Jew baiting) and by British and American Catholics, contrasted sharply with the Austrian Christian Socialism and the French Royalist clerical agitation. In Protestant Prussia, on the other hand, Luther was often invoked against the Jews. Prussian Protestantism, statebound and nationalistic, seemed less irreconcilable to racial superpatriotism, just as the more individualistic currents in American, British and Dutch Protestantism have been among the strongest bulwarks of individual and religious liberties. Ancient traditions of Byzantine intolerance survived in the semi-feudal Russia of the nineteenth century, without the mitigations provided by medieval Catholicism or modern Protestantism.

Popular suspicion was nourished at the troubled spring of folk culture. The blood accusation, in particular, continued to find widespread credence among the central and eastern European masses. The events at Tisza Eszlar, in Hungary, in 1880; at German Xanten, in 1891, and Konitz, in 1900; the Hilsner affair in Bohemia, in 1897; and the Beilis trial in the Ukraine, in 1911-13, fill some of the saddest and most discreditable pages in the history of Jewish-Christian relations. Christian theologians, such as Professor A. Rohling of Prague, in his *Talmudjude* (1st ed., 1871), and Professor Kossorotov and the priest, Father Pranaitis, prosecution experts in the Beilis case, furnished "scholarly proofs" of the truth of the blood-ritual charge against Jews. In September, 1928, the temporary disappearance of a Christian child induced the mayor of Massena, N. Y., to send a state trooper to ask the local rabbi whether Jews use Christian blood for ritual purposes. Recurrent protests of the most prominent Christian experts on the Jewish religion (Franz Delitzsch, Noeldeke, Wuensche, Strack, Kokovtzov, etc.), including several learned converts from Judaism, were of no avail. The Russian government failed to induce a packed jury to condemn Beilis, but did punish severely twenty-five renowned Christian and Jewish jurists, who had taken a stand against the prosecutor's unfair methods. As a last resort, many argued that, if not all the Jews, at least some obscure sect among them might still practice the sanguinary ritual. Drumont entertained no doubt that "the God whom they adore in the ghetto is not the God of Moses but the horrible Phoenician Moloch who requires human sacrifices of children and virgins" (*La France juive*, II, 405). Even in liberal countries the Jewish method of slaughtering animals was often viewed with disfavor. In 1891 Switzerland prohibited the *shehitah,* setting an example which Nazi Germany readily emulated.

The spirit of religious tolerance had become so strong, however, that anti-Semites preferred to advance economic, social and political arguments. Drumont altogether denied the religious nature of the Jewish question. "Always and everywhere it has been exclusively an economic question," he declared (*La Dernière Bataille,* p. ix). The economic distinctiveness of the Jews, their concentration in commerce and liberal professions, gave a fine opening for attacks. On the one hand, the Jews were identified with capitalism and the exploitation of the masses. Even Mommsen spoke of the story of the house of Rothschild, "more important than that of Saxony," as typical of Jewish history. Marx, identifying Judaism with the spirit of capitalism, found himself in strange company. On the other hand, Jews were attacked as socialists and communists, spreading Marxist doctrines among the workers. In fact, Lenin, discussing anti-Semitism in an address phonographically recorded in 1919, optimistically explained that antagonism to Jews can endure only in those countries where the landowners and capitalists keep the peasants and workingmen in complete illiteracy. Most recently it has become fashionable to assail the Jews as both capitalists and Marxists, as a people sordidly realistic, who, in theory and practice, champion the cause of the two contending materialistic philosophies against the reign of the spirit.

Jewish radicalism has often been a political stalking-horse. Disraeli's emphasis upon the Jewish propensity to preserve property, family and religion, which makes the Jews born conservatives, found little acceptance on the Continent, where the radicalism of numerous Jewish individuals was taken to represent the inherent trend of the entire people. As a matter of fact, ghetto traditions of social justice and democratic equality influenced many Jews to join "left" organizations, despite other, equally old, conservative impulses and interests. Continental conservatism was to a large extent feudalistic, monarchical and nationalistic. Consequently, each conservative party assumed a local coloring which differed in many ways from Jewish conservatism. Jewish conservatism, it was held, means in essence the preservation of a Jewish separate entity and distinct mode of life. The "Tivoli program" of 1892 of the Prussian conservatives, deeply indebted ideologically to the Jew, Stahl, included the statement,

We combat the intrusive and destructive Jewish influence upon our national life. We demand a Christian authority for the Christian schools.

Even more outspoken was the postwar German nationalist party of Junkers and great industrialists. "We emphatically reject," it proclaimed, "the preponderance of Judaism in government and public life which, since the Revolution, has become more and more disastrous." Equally anti-Semitic were the royalist parties of France and postwar Austria, the notorious Russian "Black Hundred," Koltchak, Denikin and the reactionary *émigrés* since 1917.

Jewish "internationalism," often identified with lack of patriotism, was also attacked from all sides. In Russia, Austria and Germany, in peace and war, despite all contrary evidence, one could often hear that Jews were poor soldiers, slackers and deserters. General Yanushkevitch, chief of staff of the Russian army, reporting the destruction of bridges along the front, to the minister of war, on April 27, 1915, concluded, "This is all done for money; probably the Jews are doing it. *There is no one else to do it*" (D. Lloyd George, *War Memoirs*, I, 448). When the great German offensive began a few days later, several hundred thousand Russian Jews were forcibly evacuated within forty-eight hours from their dwellings, many miles behind the lines of defense. The German war ministry, on the other hand, did not disdain to lend its moral support to similar contentions, when, in the midst of the *Burgfrieden* of 1916, it ordered a special census of Jewish combatants, the results of which it never published. It was only recently that the German-Jewish war veterans published a list of 10,623 known Jewish soldiers who gave up their lives during the War. Undoubtedly at least 1,000 more must have been from territories ceded by Germany to the Allied and Associated Powers, or among the unidentifiable victims. In any case, the number is well in excess of the Jewish proportion of the population. But against a deeply ingrained popular prejudice, such statistical surveys were ineffective. When, moreover, a Krupp or Skoda sold arms to potential enemies of the Central Powers, he was attacked as an individual. But when an Isidor Loewe of Berlin sold arms to France, the result was Ahlwardt's *Judenflinten* and an extensive anti-Semitic press campaign.

The Jewish "golden international" (so styled in a popular pamphlet by C. Wilmanns, a typical petty bourgeois anti-capitalistic reformer of the 1870's) was denounced from another angle, too. A most absurd notion was steadily gaining ground that the Jewish people were on the way to assuming world domination, through a conscious effort of their leaders. The prominence of certain Jewish politicians, such as Lasker and Bamberger in Bismarckian Germany, and Joseph Reinach in France, seemed to substantiate such claims. Although Lasker had done more than anyone else to unmask the Jewish and non-Jewish perpetrators of the great frauds of the *Gründer*-boom (Strousberg, etc.), the Jews were blamed for the prevalent political corruption. The opponents of Bismarck found an easy target in Bleichroeder, who had helped finance the great military victories of Prussia. One Rudolf H. Meyer wrote in 1877, "As long as Prince Bismarck remains the omnipotent idol, so long will the German nation be sacrificed for the sake of the Empire and the Empire for the sake of the chancellor; the chancellor in turn belongs to the Jews and the Gründer" (*Politische Gründer und die Korruption in Deutschland*, p. 204). About the same time Carlyle denounced the "Hebrew conjurer" Disraeli, and T. P. O'Connor portrayed the prime minister, then at the height of his diplomatic, basically pro-Turkish and anti-Russian, achievements, as "moulding the whole policy of Christendom to Jewish aims" (*Lord Beaconsfield*, pp. 612 ff.).

By a curious juxtaposition, Judaism was associated with Freemasonry in mysterious machinations to undermine Christian society. Conceived in the early period of the Rothschilds' financial preëminence, the idea of a Jewish world menace found eloquent champions in Marr, Drumont and others, until it culminated in the publication of *The Protocols of the Learned Elders of Zion*. This spurious document was compounded in 1902 by E. A. Nilus, from M. Joly's anti-Bonapartist pamphlet of 1865, H. Goedsche's fantastic novel of 1868, and other similarly dubious sources. It served the purposes of the Russian police, which, as early as 1895, had prepared a memorandum for the Czar on the "Secret of Judaism." After the Revolution of 1905, Count Lamsdorf explained to the Czar that the revolutionary movement was "actively supported and partly directed by the forces of universal Jewry," centered in the "Alliance" in Paris, "which possesses gigantic pecuniary means, disposes of an enormous membership, and is supported by Masonic lodges of every description." He suggested a confidential exchange of views with Berlin and the Vatican, first to organize a vigilant supervision, and later for active joint struggle against the common foe of the Christian and monarchical order (L. Wolf, *Diplomatic History*, pp. 57-62). After the War, German and English translations of the Protocols (in England under the title, *The Jewish Peril*) carried the propaganda over the entire world. Striking a responsive chord in the excited war generation, with its revolutionary and counterrevolutionary psychosis, the work was soon translated into many languages, including Chinese and Arabic, and produced a torrent of anti-Jewish writings in 1920-21. Among these the most influential were A. Rosenberg's *Die Protokolle der Weisen von Zion und die jüdische Weltpolitik; The International Jew,* a collection of articles which had previously appeared under the direction of Henry Ford in the *Dearborn Independent;* and a similar series of seventeen articles in the London *Morning Post,* republished in book form in England and America as *The Cause of World Unrest.* Although soon discredited by scholars and journalists such as L. Wolf, H. Bernstein, B. Segel and the London *Times'* Constantinople correspondent, the myth continued to excite the imagination of the uncritical populace and to furnish dangerous weapons to unscrupulous politicians. The impression it made upon two German youngsters led to the assassination of Walter Rathenau, one of the alleged "Elders of Zion."

Paradoxically, attempts were made to give anti-Semitism international form. An early congress was convened by Stoecker and Istoczy in Dresden in 1882, German and Austro-Hungarian anti-Semites attending its wholly secret deliberations. When Stoecker, disgusted with the intransigence of his associates, refused to participate in the second congress (at Chemnitz, half a year later), the movement died down. Stoecker's own attempt to win over British public opinion by his visit to London in 1883 ended in as dismal a failure as did Rosenberg's similar undertaking four decades later. Renewed international agitation resulted in a secret conference at Budapest in 1925. The participation of several Rumanian delegates, hospitably treated by the archenemies of their country, the "Awakening Magyars," created little short of a sensation. A secret meeting near Copenhagen in 1926 was comparatively large. The delegations included, in addition to Russian *émigré* whites, representatives from Germany, France,

England, Poland, Czechoslovakia, Hungary, Austria, Switzerland, Denmark and Holland. The result of the deliberations, however, was of no consequence, and the international agitation had largely died down when, under Hitler's chancellorship, numerous German emissaries began propagating Nazi ideologies on an international scale. In 1933 and 1934 secret anti-Semitic congresses, with the participation of delegates from many European countries, took place in Copenhagen and Brussels.

The very term "anti-Semitism" became a source of strength to those who gathered under it. Without positive connotation, it could easily conceal the divergence among the different trends. There was, in fact, not one anti-Semitic movement, but many. It included those who wanted the elimination of Jewish competition in the economic field; those who wished to destroy the Jews as capitalists; those seeking revenge on Jewish leaders of socialism; those who believed in racial purity, and the superiority of their own race over all others; those demagogues who detected in the excitation of popular anger against the Jews a means of personal political aggrandizement; and those who sought to deflect popular resentment of their own misgovernment into other channels. Such an omnibus term could easily cover a multitude of motives and impulses. As time went on, however, the inconsistencies of anti-Semitic ideology and the diversities of interest frequently came to the fore, and interminable dissensions followed. Personal improbity and mental aberrations of a number of prominent anti-Semites, likewise cast a shadow on the movement. In Germany, in particular, scandals followed in quick succession, when von Hammerstein, the editor of the conservative *Kreuz-Zeitung,* was convicted of forgery and larceny; Deputy Leuss sent to prison for perjury, and Ahlwart for extortion; Count Pückler confined to an insane asylum, and Deputy Schack forced to resign on the score of immorality. Unrest after the Great War, the revolutions and the peace treaties, revived by the horrible sufferings in the world-wide depression since 1929, resulted in an unprecedented renewal of anti-Semitic propaganda.[8]

Behind all these movements, whether childish and ignorant or mature and sophisticated, naïve and guileless or willful and misleading, sincere and innocent or scheming and consciously criminal, there stood one great reality: the failure of the Jewish group to succumb to ethnic or economic absorption. The increasing nationalism of the last decades whetted the resentment of the majorities. The unification of Germany had resuscitated the antagonism of the national state toward the Jew. On the other hand, in the struggle of nationalities in mixed empires, such as Austria-Hungary and Russia, the Jew was often a buffer and scapegoat. Feverish nationalist leaders were prone to overlook valuable services of Jews, and to have eyes only for those Jews in an opposing nationalist camp. In Bohemia, for instance, the opening of every public school, with either German or Czech as the language of instruction, became a serious matter for the whole Austrian Empire. Each Jewish child frequenting such a school brought denunciations down upon the head of all Jewry by the irreconcilables of the other nationality. The Flemish struggle for cultural independence generated similar dilemmas for Belgian Jewry. In prewar Great Britain and America, where national antagonisms remained in the background, anti-Semitism had been weak. For a few years after the War, the anti-Semitic propaganda of littérateurs and demagogues in England, of anti-radicals and Ku Klux Klan members in the United States, appeared as serious warnings. The whole movement soon spent its energy and, were it not for the Jews, the anti-Semitic outbursts of Henry Ford and Belloc would have been completely forgotten. When his anti-Semitism was threatened with reprisals by the motion-picture magnate, William Fox, and later, in 1927, squarely placed before a court by Aaron Sapiro, Ford withdrew from the fight, paid the high costs (some $106,000 to Sapiro alone), and apologized to the Jewish people. Belloc and his confrere, G. K. Chesterton, champions of Catholic medievalism, came to realize the danger to England and the Catholic Church of racial anti-Semitism, and their anti-Jewish fervor cooled decidedly after the Hitlerite excesses in Germany. The closing of immigration to Jews and others in England in 1905, and in America through the laws of 1924 and 1928, and President Hoover's executive order of 1930, was directed against all alien competitors in the labor market. The comparative quiet prevailing before 1933 in these two countries was not fully reassuring, however. The recent spread of Nazi propaganda, the agitation of Mosley, Pelley and others has demonstrated the vulnerability of even the relatively most secure bodies in Jewry.

NEW ACCUSATIONS

An examination of the anti-Semitism of the post-emancipation era reveals many relatively new features. Although much of the medieval temper lingered on among the masses, their leaders concocted new accusations and arguments. No longer was the primary concern the segregation of the Jews—their life as a nation within a nation. Precisely the opposite denunciation was hurled. They are corrupting the nation by insidiously boring from within! Not lack of western education, but domination over national arts, sciences and letters, became the avowed reason for opposition. Jews were said to insinuate everywhere their own alien temper. In 1845, using the old term in a novel sense, A. Toussenel, the monarchist and anticapitalist, readily acknowledged "the superior character of the Jewish nation" and its "enormous influence on the history of mankind," but deeply resented that "the Jew should reign and govern in France" (*Les Juifs, rois de l'époque*, pp. 4 f.). In 1879 Wilhelm Marr, with disingenuous pessimism, proclaimed to the world "the great historical triumph of Judaism, the record of a lost battle, without any extenuation for the beaten army" (*Der Sieg des Judentums über das Germanentum*, p. 4).

The foreignness of the Jews was thus still the trump card of anti-Semitism. A new pretext was discovered: *race*. Human biological distinctions, such as those detected in the eighteenth century by Linné and Blumenbach, were soon confused with philological differentiations. Following Schloetzer's suggestion in accordance with the biblical genealogy in Genesis 10, the ancient western Asiatic tongues were called "Semitic." Somewhat later Frederick Schlegel, romantic opponent of the cosmopolitanism of Herder and von Humboldt, began to glorify the "Aryan" tongues. Only a step remained to the sociological appreciation of race by August Comte. But, by an accident not wholly unworthy of a metaphysico-ethical reflection, it was a born Jew who first emphasized the historic importance of race. Disraeli's racial theory (developed in his novel, *Coningsby*, published in 1844, and reiterated three years later in *Tancred*) culminated in the exclamation, "All is race, there is no other truth" (*Tancred,* 1894, p. 149). Gobineau's classical treatise, *Essai sur l'inégalité des races humaines,* was written in 1851-54. Since then racial ideologies have found influential spokesmen in Renan, Taine, Chamberlain, Fischer, Guenther and others. The sheer juxtaposition of these names shows how much sincere and brilliant scholarship was mingled with platitudinous publicist agitation in this obscure field of knowledge. It mattered little that the world's foremost scientists were unable to agree upon any fundamental point concerning racial purity, racial characteristics, and their acquisition through heredity or social environment. The great philologist, Max Mueller, and the distinguished anthropologist, Luschan, in vain protested that to speak of an Indo-European skull was like using the term dolichocephalic dictionary or brachycephalic grammar. The terms Semitic and Aryan have been more and more generally accepted as expressing some kind of racial difference between Jews and western Gentiles. Of course, Germans, who today appear as champions of racial purity, show few so-called Nordic characteristics. There is no doubt that the Samaritans, the most authentic remnant of ancient Jewry, with their 30 percent of dolichocephalic, and only 22 per cent of brachycephalic, skulls far exceed the proportion of Nordic long-heads, even in northern Germany. Central and southern Germany, according to Eugen Fischer himself, have as many as 80-90 percent short-headed men. As mentioned above, the so-called Jewish nose is more frequently found in southern Germany than among Polish Jewry. Even blondness is a characteristic of but a minority, 20-30 percent, of southern Germans, a rate exceeded among Eastern European Jews. Blue eyes seem to prevail north of the Main, but even this feature is that of a minority in the south. In short, the majority of southern Germans have so-called Alpine or Dinaric characteristics, thus falling largely in the same semi-Asiatic category as the majority of Jews. The most distinguished Germans in history, Leibnitz, Kant, Schopenhauer, Goethe, Schiller, Bismarck, were all brachycephalic. Kant's head was almost a sphere. Among prominent German poets, Heine alone, like many Asiatic Jews and Arabs, had a long head. Practically, however, it remained generally possible to distinguish an individual Jew by his features, and it is easy to argue that physical differences reflect mental disparity, or even mental inferiority.

Characteristically, Disraeli, the father of racial theorists, was fully convinced of Semitic superiority. "Which do you think should be the superior race," a young Jewess asked his aristocratic hero, Tancred, "the worshiped or the worshipers?" (p. 196). In the elaborate chapter on the Jewish question in his biography of George Bentinck, Disraeli discussed how the world has discovered that it is impossible to destroy the Jews, and concluded triumphantly, "All which proves that it is in vain for man to attempt to baffle the inexorable law of nature, which has decreed that a superior race shall never be destroyed or absorbed by an inferior" (8th ed., p. 355). Even Gobineau was ready to admit the physical beauty of the Semites, but he denied the connection between race and religion. It was Renan who, in 1855, claimed for himself the credit of being the first "to recognize that the Semitic, if compared with the Indo-European race, represents an inferior combination of human nature" (*Histoire général des langues sémitiques,* p. 4). On the other hand, he refused to be classified as a Jew hater, and reiterated on all occasions that the Jews, having absorbed so many different strains in their extraordinary historic evolution, can no longer be regarded as Semites. He concluded, moreover, his famous lecture on "Judaism as a Race and Religion," by significantly emphasizing that

when the National Assembly, in 1791, decreed the emancipation of Jews, it paid very little attention to their race. . . . The achievement of the nineteenth century has been to batter down all the ghettos, and I do not compliment those who elsewhere wish to reërect them.

All reservations of the founders, however, were soon cast aside by disciples, who, discarding everything else, took over only what fitted into their picture of Jewish inferiority. Any admixture of Jewish blood, they proclaimed, is racial pollution and involves the impairment of the original racial spirit. While Mommsen's statement that even in the Roman Empire the Jews were an element of "national decomposition" was often invoked, his emphasis on the necessity and progressive function of such a leavening element was ignored. Largely disregarding the historical fact that the successive conversions of the Jews, enforced and voluntary, had injected much Jewish blood into the veins of all European nations, many a racial theorist insisted that his particular race was pure, brooking no such admixture, or, at least, could be made pure in the course of one or two generations. On the other hand, those anti-Semites who wished to cast aspersion upon the dominant classes gloried in the various "Semi-Gothas," "Semi-Kürschners," and "The Jews' Who's Whos," which showed how deeply the European aristocracy and intelligentsia are permeated with Jewish blood. They drew therefrom the conclusion that the Jews must be prevented from further contamination of the leading classes of European society.

Racial anti-Semitism thus became invested with a degree of finality which older religious Jew-hating never possessed. "A wide gulf separates the different races," declared von Hellwald as far back as 1872, "which, throughout recorded human history, has been unbridgeable and, in all probability, will remain unbridgeable" (*Das Ausland,* XLV, 901).

The aversion of the Teuton nations to the Semites [wrote the more moderate Viktor Scheffel] is not based upon the difference of creed and dogma, but upon the difference of blood, race, descent. . . . I have often talked about these matters with my friend Berthold Auerbach. [*Die Grenzboten,* XLIII/2, p. 513.]

Previously baptism had made a Jew a more or less welcome member of the Christian nation. Only in Spain and Portugal, as a result of Marranism, did racial *limpieza* long play a prominent rôle (as late as 1904, Prime Minister Miguel Maura was taunted in Parliament as a *chueta*). Elsewhere, at least the children or grandchildren of a Jewish convert to Christianity were accepted as full-fledged Christians. In recent generations, moreover, intermarriage with accompanying conversion to Christianity has often been encouraged by Christian ecclesiastical and political leaders. Even Bismarck advocated the mating of a German stallion with a Jewish mare, as recorded by his factotum, Moritz Busch, himself the spokesman of rabid racial anti-Semitism. "I do not know," the Chancellor significantly concluded, "what I shall one day advise my sons to do" (*Tagebuchblätter,* II, 33; in the English transl., I, 340). The anti-Semite of today, however, takes vengeance unto the third and fourth generation and even beyond that. The recent development of a large organization of "non-Aryan Christians" in Germany, among whom are some six hundred Protestant pastors and many persons who only recently discovered that they had had a Jewish grandparent, is a pathetic illustration of the tragi-comic extremes of racialism. Many professing Jews stay within the fold against their will and convictions. In this irreligious age there is little opportunity for mass conversion from one faith to another, while sheer agnosticism is no longer an escape. A Jew converted to Christianity may still be regarded by most Jews, and in many countries by the majority of Christians, as a non-Jew. But a Jewish atheist is classified by almost all Christians and most Jews as a Jew. This inescapability and immutability of Jewish allegiance has created a large group of involuntary Jews, numbering hundreds of thousands. These "inverted Marranos," as one might properly style them, constitute a problem no less grave than that of the true Marranos of the sixteenth and seventeenth centuries.[9]

What is to become of the Jews? For the extremists among the racial anti-Semites, there is no alternative but expulsion from the western countries, or extinction. Incitement to pogroms, economic boycott and political suppression have become increasingly vehement. In 1881 Duehring suggested international action to "huddle up and segregate" the Jews in a manner which, he emphasized, must not resemble a Jewish state. In 1926 Theodor Fritsch, the veteran fighter (whose name incidentally has now replaced that of Walter Rathenau on one of Berlin's thoroughfares), advocated the wholesale emasculation of Jewish youth. Ever since, Nazi medical societies have espoused "humane" and "innocent" methods of sterilization by X-ray treatment, to prevent Jewish procreation without harm to the Jewish individual. Treitschke himself still believed that

> no man with common sense would now think of the withdrawal or even restriction of emancipation. Such proceedings would constitute an overt injustice, an abandonment of the fine traditions of our country and would sharpen rather than mitigate the national conflicts which disturb us. [*Ein Wort über unser Judentum*, p. 4.]

But modern anti-Semites have frequently preached, and, under the Nazi government indeed realized, through the

Nuremberg decrees, the annulment of the constitutional equality of rights. That Germany had long refrained from public disavowal of emancipation was largely due to the fear that the Jews would automatically qualify as a national minority, and thus offer to the League of Nations full opportunity to interfere in their favor. Similar international considerations led the Hungarian Supreme Court in 1924 to deny that the Jews were a separate race. On the other hand, an anti-Semitic Austrian cabinet, wishing to prevent the naturalization of Jews who sought to exercise an "option" in accordance with the peace treaties, insisted that they do not by "race" belong to the Austrian population. Austria successfully defended this principle before the League of Nations. An attempt to force residents to declare racial allegiance, in the census of 1923, failed completely, however, and merely illustrated the enormous practical difficulties of applying such an equivocal term. In Anglo-Saxon countries, even racial anti-Semites have voiced much more moderate proposals. Their attitude may, perhaps, be best rendered in the words of H. Belloc, ". . . the Jews on their side shall openly recognize their wholly separate nationality and we on ours shall equally recognize that separate nationality, treat it without reserve as an alien thing and respect it as a province of society outside our own" (*The Jews*, p. 5).

Neither the old religious prediction of the survival of Jewry until the end of days, nor the recognition of Jewish contributions to civilization through their prophetic religion, have made any impression upon the racial anti-Semites. In the postulated Aryan revolt against every aspect of Semitism, they have demanded the rejection of all Semitic values, including the Bible and early Christianity. Indeed, for many of them emancipation from Judaism meant also emancipation from the Christian religion.

There were evidently many shades of opinion. Some wished to separate the Old from the New Testament. Schopenhauer had already suggested that the Gospels, because of their ascetic morality and pessimism, must have been of Indian rather than Jewish origin. In 1879 Professor J. N. Sepp argued that, since Jesus was of no human race, Christianity ought to repudiate the Old Testament and revert to the older cuneiform sources. With the full authority of his Assyriological scholarship, Frederick Delitzsch, ostentatiously honored by William II, insisted that the Hebrew Scriptures were merely inferior reproductions of great Babylonian ideas. He also stated that Jesus, according to cuneiform evidence, was "undoubtedly" a Galilean of non-Jewish descent, a hypothesis which, first voiced by Richard Wagner in 1869, contradicts both the Christian tradition of Jesus' Davidic descent and the results of modern research. He finally suggested that German children should be brought up on Germanic sagas rather than upon those of the Old Testament, with the exception of the Joseph legend. Others, however, rejected the New along with the Old Testament. Some adduced religious arguments. Maurras, for example, decidedly preferred the illustrious array of councils, popes and the modern élite of great ecclesiastics to the Gospels of "four obscure Jews." But the most significant opposition came from racial and imperialist doctrinaires. Even before the World War, voices were heard to say, "Woe to the nation which behaves in a Christian fashion at a time when a battle is raging over the possession of the globe" (E. Wachler, in 1909). H. Pudor incited his fellow Germans to annihilate the Jews because "the Christian religion has taught fear to Siegfried the Teuton . . . all Christianity is Judeo-Christianity and as such the most daring fraud perpetrated upon races and nations in world history" (quoted by I. Freund in his *Der Judenhass,* pp. 34 ff.). The theologian, Arthur Bonus, finally coined the slogan, "Germanisierung des Christentums," and gathered around it an ever-growing number of followers.

Little wonder that one of the intellectual leaders of Hitlerite Germany has declared that

The period of the Israelitic man and thought on earth is drawing to a close. The world of the Jewish dispersion and of Christianity is tired and exhausted. The Messiah, who had come to fulfill and not to destroy, has not fulfilled but destroyed! [Franz Hielscher in *Die Klärung,* p. 42.]

Nietzsche's voice, reverberating so powerfully in nationalist circles, was heeded, in so far as he denounced Christianity as a religion of weaklings. His profound admiration for the Old Testament was readily discarded, however, as was his conviction that an ingredient of Jews, whom he once called "the purest, strongest and most persistent race" in Europe, would be a welcome addition to the new western amalgam of races. These religious sentiments were soon embodied in an organization of "German Christians," founded by the Silesian pastor, Frederick Andersen. Since the publication of his programmatic *Der richtige Jesus* in 1926, the organization has grown by leaps and bounds until, under Hitler and Alfred Rosenberg, it has made deep inroads into the Protestant churches of Germany. Professor Ernst Bergmann's *Die deutsche Nationalkirche* and his "catechism" of the "Deutschreligion" are perhaps the best theoretical formulations of this trend. They culminate in his exclamation:

The period of world religions draws to its close. A people which returns to race and soil, which has recognized the world peril of international Judaism, can no longer tolerate in its churches a religion which calls the sacred writings of the Jews its "Gospel." Germania's reconstruction would be wrecked by this inner untruth. . . . That is why the watchword of the Germanic religion is: Away from Rome and Jerusalem! [*Die 25 Thesen der Deutschreligion,* p. 74.]

PRO-SEMITIC REACTION

The ever-swelling anti-Semitic wave necessarily provoked a reaction within Christian society. Liberals of all wings sensed the danger to their own view of life. The struggle was taken up not only by general leagues for human rights and the like, but by special societies to combat anti-Semitism. Richard Wagner's essay, *Das Judenthum in der Musik,* passed unnoticed in 1869, but within a short time after its republication in the troubled year 1879, it elicited 170 replies. In France, public opinion, rallied behind Zola's *J'accuse,* carried the liberals from victory to victory; since the turn of the century, French political anti-Semitism has been reduced to impotency. The achievements of the German *Verein zur Abwehr des Antisemitismus,* organized in 1890 by Gneist and later headed by Rickert, were much less enduring, notwithstanding its numerous publications, such as the *Antisemiten-Spiegel,* issued in several editions. In 1933, when a courageous stand on its part was most needed, it decided to disband. The work of the "Society for the Dissemination of Truthful Information concerning the Jews," organized in Russia in 1906, was no more effective. Sporadic protests were heard also in the Anglo-

Saxon countries, not only against the Russian and Rumanian pogroms, but against local anti-Semitic propaganda. Among dramatic public disavowals of anti-Jewish agitation was a proclamation prepared bv John Spargo and signed by Wilson, Taft, Cardinal O'Connell, and 115 other prominent Americans on January 16, 1921. "The anti-Semitic publications," they declared, "are introducing into our national and political life a new dangerous spirit, one that is wholly at variance with our traditions and ideals and subversive of our system of government." The United States, Great Britain and the French socialists sent special delegations to investigate on the spot difficulties in Polish-Jewish relations. In 1933 world opinion was stirred to its depths by the outrages of the Hitler régime. In Germany it was the churches which voiced the only articulate opposition to the Aryan principle, recognized by them as a threat to the very foundations of universal Christendom. Petitions signed by two thousand Protestant clergymen, leading New Testament scholars and the Marburg theological faculty, have been addressed to the government. The tenor of these petitions is well rendered in a Breslau protest: "The Church of Jesus Christ is no community of blood but a community of the Holy Ghost, and whoever strives to exclude evangelical Christians of alien stock denies the divine ordination of the church and the sacrament of baptism" (*New York Times*, November 26, 1933). Twelve hundred representatives of the American Protestant clergy, the Archbishop of Canterbury, and the leading clergy of other lands have likewise raised their voices in protest. But the lack of a persevering struggle against the incipient anti-Jewish virus has rendered ineffective the pathetic denunciations during periods of great stress.

Only the German and Russian socialists have maintained a consistent attitude of combating anti-Semitism, which often raised its head even in their own midst. Under the leadership of August Bebel, who characterized anti-Semitism as "the religion of fools," the German Social Democratic party repeatedly condemned as reactionary all anti-Semitic tendencies. The resolution of the Cologne Congress (1893) succinctly reads, "Social-democracy combats anti-Semitism as a movement directed against the natural evolution of society which, however, despite its reactionary character, promotes revolution against its own will" (quoted by O. Heller in *Der Untergang*,

p. 131). A similar stand was taken by the communists in Russia. A few months after they seized power, they decreed,

> The Council of the People's Commissars declares that the anti-Semitic movement and pogroms against the Jews are fatal to the interests of the workers' and peasants' revolution and calls upon the toiling people of socialist Russia to fight this evil with all the means at their disposal. . . . The Council of the People's Commissars instructs all Soviet deputies to take uncompromising measures to tear the anti-Semitic movement out by the roots. Pogromists and pogrom agitators are to be placed outside the law. [August 9, 1918.]

Indeed, the Soviet government has succeeded in suppressing all anti-Semitic outbreaks. Sporadic occurrences, reflecting an anti-Jewish undercurrent within the proletariat itself, have been dealt with summarily and, thus far, very effectively.[10]

NEW THEORIES OF NATIONALISM

What was the Jewish answer to the new challenge? Does Jewish nationalism merely represent—as is often asserted—a reaction of the Jewish people against anti-Semitism? Certainly not. The Jewish national consciousness might have been retarded in its development, but it could not have failed to rearise sooner or later. The sudden reorientation of Pinsker after the pogroms of 1881, and Herzl's "repentance" in a Paris resounding with the harangues of Anti-Dreyfusards, were important milestones, but neither was indispensable for the evolution of the national idea. Much earlier and without any such spectacular events, Moses Hess reached similar conclusions. The indisputable conservative function of anti-Semitism, already emphasized by Spinoza, was correctly defined by Max Nordau, himself one of its classical illustrations. "In the case of most Zionists," he declared, "anti-Semitism was only a stimulus causing them to reflect upon their relation to the nations, and that reflection has led them to results that must remain for them a permanent intellectual and spiritual possession, even if anti-Semitism were to vanish completely from the world" (*Zionism, Its History and Its Aims,* English transl. 1905, pp. 7 f.). Of still more affirmative nature was the Zionism of the eastern Europeans. Smolenskin's *Am Olam* (*The Eternal People*), published in the relatively quiet period of 1872, clearly was constructive rather than defensive. But it was Ahad Ha-Am, who, more than all his predecessors, stressed the positive character of Jewish nationalism, developing his biological theory of the innate will to live of every vital national organism—a theory which has greatly influenced all Zionist ideology. The realities of ethnic and economic non-assimilation, that lay behind the rise of anti-Semitism, had to be faced by the Jews themselves. Once stirred out of their apathy, the Jewish masses of eastern Europe brought with them the full consciousness of these realities. The policy of ignoring their true position, or barring it by fictitious constructions, had to yield. With or without anti-Semitism, a new, more realistic policy had to be adopted, new rationalizations sought to replace outworn assimilatory concepts.

Some of these realities were: a compact mass of several million Jews living between the Oder and the Black Sea, the Theiss and the Baltic, in its overwhelming majority dwelling in urban settlements, economically engaged in all branches of commerce and crafts, but not in agriculture, largely Yiddish in speech, living an intensely religious Jewish life, and segregated from all other peoples by barriers much stronger than law could erect of itself. On the surface, enlightenment and the culture of the surrounding nations have appeared as a dynamic force of transformation. But they were still limited to a small class of the intelligentsia, which had partly lost contact with the living organism of the people.

The changes in nationalist theory in Europe helped lend a theoretical formulation to these realities. Formerly nationalism in central and eastern Europe had the same connotation which, to a certain extent, prevails even nowadays in western Europe and America, namely, that nationality may be equated with state. Even today, to be of English or French nationality means to be a citizen of Great Britain or France. Such nationality could obviously not be claimed by Jews, who, in eastern Europe, were citizens or subjects of Russia, Austria, etc. The moment, however, the ethnic differentiation of Austria-Hungary, Russia and Turkey began to be a source of inner dissension (destined finally to disrupt these empires politically), there arose a new nonpolitical conception of nationality. Austria-Hungary, in particular, a vast experimental laboratory for all nationality problems, offered a striking contrast between political unity and linguistic, racial and cultural differences. It was the Austrian socialists, whose internationalist program forced them to recognize the rights of each nationality to independent ethnic and cultural existence, who formulated the new theory. Building upon the theoretical foundations of Adolf Fischhof, Renan, and Neumann, Karl Renner, and later Otto Bauer, established a nationality principle based exclusively upon the subjective elements of unity of destiny and culture (*Kultur- und Schicksalsgemeinschaft*), applying it first to Austria and then to the world at large. No longer is the state, territory or even language, race, and religion, each apart, the exclusive reason for ethnic allegiance. All of them constitute vital elements, but none is indispensable. The decisive factor is a common culture and the individual's own sentiment, which accounts for his membership in a group unified by a common past. The latter is what the German expression *Schicksal* means primarily. Reintroducing the medieval legal personality principle, Renner demanded the recognition of the various nationalities according to such subjective criteria. A census, in his opinion, should leave it to each individual to register freely his allegiance to one of the existing nationalities, regardless of his place of residence, his rights of citizenship, the language he usually speaks, the religion he professes, and the supposed racial blood flowing in his veins.

This conception of nationality became a tremendous force in central and eastern Europe, because it appeared to offer the only solution to the profound contradictions existing in all the objective elements of national life. In western Europe and in Germany, even the socialist advocates of internationalism long resisted subjective formulae. They demanded at least the recognition of language as the primary criterion. But detached sociological theory had, even before Renan, paved the way for the recognition of the subjective valuations. Nationally conscious Jews soon took an active part in the ensuing battle, effectively contributing to the final adoption of the new principle in international public law.

This subjectivization—if one may so term it—of the national allegiance, had a still deeper significance in its application to the Jews. Objective values were largely lacking. Certainly no state or territory could be regarded as predominantly Jewish. Undoubtedly millions of Jews spoke Yiddish, but other millions either had adopted a Gentile language or, as in the case of Sephardic and oriental Jewry, had never known Yiddish. To exclude such Jews from the Jewish national body was hardly justified in itself, and conflicted with the inherited feeling of solidarity of all Jewry. The main cohesive force apparently consisted in the common race and religion. Race, however, could easily be disputed from the point of view of anthropological theory, and many Jews no longer professed any religion. Notwithstanding all these contradictions, the unity of the Jewish people was for most Jews a reality. The actuality of a common past and heritage, even of a certain community of culture, were undeniable; in them each Jew could easily find a justification for his fealty to a Jewish nation. For more than two thousand years Jewish history had been the realization of such concepts of nationality, based upon a common history and culture, persisting even when deprived of state and territory. Were the Jewish people to abandon this idea, just as the world at large began to adopt it?

Jewish theoreticians soon found a formula for the Jewish people. At the end of the nineteenth century there began a prolonged struggle to obtain legal recognition of Jewish nationality in the countries of Jewish mass settlement. In partial analogy to the national demands of the other ethnic minorities, but in many phases markedly diverging, spokesmen of Jewish nationalism demanded national autonomy for their people. The interterritorial community, although in many ways different from its medieval predecessor, should, it was claimed, again become widely self-governing in matters of national life and culture. Characteristically, there was no demand for revival of the ghetto. In many eastern European towns the Jews, constituting a majority of the population, needed no such segregation. Elsewhere legal and cultural separation was deemed sufficient. Thus the principal demand of Jewish nationalism became an autonomy which was not to preclude, but to supplement, the full equality of rights. Of necessity, this post-emancipation autonomy was to differ from medieval autonomy. Moreover, it could be achieved only in connection with analogous rights granted other national minorities in eastern Europe, widely dissimilar in structure from medieval Jewry.

NATIONAL MINORITY RIGHTS

The term "national-cultural autonomy" was doubtless unhappy, since, to connote cultural and essentially nonpolitical self-determination, they used the Greek word for political sovereignty or semisovereignty. It also covered a multitude of aspects and was open to a variety of interpretations. In its extreme form, as demanded, for example, by the Polish populists (Folkspartei), it included separate national parliaments for each ethnic group, possessing exclusive jurisdiction over most of the group's cultural, religious and social affairs. The 1906 Helsingfors Conference of Russian Zionists adopted a more moderate program, "the organs of national self-government possess the right to found, conduct and support all kinds of institutions which serve the ends of 1) national education, 2) national health, 3) mutual and labor aid, 4) emigration and 5) matters of faith . . . as also to issue in accordance with the laws of the state and province . . . ordinances and regulations for their institutions" (quoted by Janowsky, *Jews and Minority Rights,* p. 110). Even this far-reaching delegation of sovereignty to the constituent national groups was not to infringe on the democratic equality of rights of all citizens. Only Nordau, confronted with violent Rumanian opposition to Jewish emancipation, was ready in 1900 to compromise on mere civil equality in return for extensive self-government. The shadow of the *privatbürgerliche* emancipation thus reappeared in the wake of the "autonomist" agitation.

The formulation of these demands was a slow growth. First appearing, in an inarticulate form, in the constitutional clauses inserted by the Austrian revolutionary diet in 1848 and the Frankfort National Assembly in 1849, minority self-government long remained an unclarified objective. Not until the 1880's and the 1890's did a few perspicacious scholars and statesmen begin to visualize, through the haze of endless nationalist dissensions, a new order. As far as Jewish autonomy was concerned, the proletarian publicist Chaim Zhitlovsky and the middle-class historian Simon M. Dubnow reached similar conclusions almost simultaneously. Zhitlovsky's *A Jew to Jews* issued in Switzerland in 1892, and secretly distributed in Russia, and Dubnow's widely read *Letters on Old and*

Modern Judaism (1897-1907) sounded the first distinct calls to action. In the following two decades the issue was gradually clarified. It won ever-wider recognition among the Jewish masses of Russia, Poland, Galicia, Bukovina and the eastern European emigrés in the West.

For a long time its main champions were the Jewish socialists. Although somewhat hesitant at first, the Bund, the largest Russian Jewish proletarian organization, adopted a definitely favorable stand in 1903. The younger socialist organizations which became active during the Revolution of 1905-6, the *Poale Zion,* the Socialists-Zionists *(SS)* and the *Seymists* (so called because of the emphasis they laid upon a Jewish diet), soon followed the Bund's example. In 1917, the Jewish socialists were the first to reap the harvest of prolonged agitation; in the February and October revolutions they played a leading part in bringing about partial realization of their own aims.

The Bund's initial hesitancy is easily understood when one considers the apparent difficulty in reconciling such a program with Marxian internationalism. Marxism glorified mankind above all groups, and proclaimed the solidarity of the world's proletariat in the class struggle against oppressors of all lands and nationalities. Even Aaron Liberman, the first Marxist to write in Hebrew, defined the aims of his socialist periodical *Ha-Emet* in its first issue of 1877, "Not love of our people has prompted us to publish this periodical, but the love of men generally and the love of our co-nationals, because they are men—this alone induced us to address them in a language which they understand and to tell them the value of truth." For a long time this was also the point of view of Lieberman's associates, E. Zuckerman, Vintshevsky, Y. L. Kantor, Y. L. Lewin —all protagonists of radical enlightenment, which had sought to disparage rather than promote Jewish cultural distinctiveness. The Bund itself had started as a purely Russian socialist organization, condescending to use Yiddish only to heighten the effectiveness of its propaganda among Jewish workers.

External obstacles were equally great. The general socialist organizations looked with suspicion upon this Jewish "separatism." Even in Austria, where socialists led the struggle for national-cultural autonomy, Otto Bauer, himself a Jew, expressly rejected the Jewish claim to national autonomy, in his

Die Nationalitätenfrage und die Sozialdemokratie (first published in 1907), the best expression of the Austro-Marxist conception of nationality. Not without justification did Lenin censure Bauer's attitude as inconsistent and insincere, since it excluded the only truly "exterritorial" nation from his scheme of exterritorial autonomy. Lenin himself, however, was even more outspoken in his opposition to Jewish autonomism. At the time of the breach between the Bund and the Russian Socialist party in 1903, he wrote that the idea of a Jewish nationality

has an evidently reactionary character not only in the form advocated by its consistent champions, the Zionists, but also in that of the Bundists who try to combine it with social democracy. This idea runs counter to the interests of the Jewish proletariat inasmuch as it creates, directly and indirectly, an attitude hostile to assimilation, a ghetto philosophy. [*Sämmtliche Werke*, VI,106.]

The Jewish socialists, however, argued that anti-Semitism and governmental oppression did harm to the Jewish proletariat and that the class struggle could proceed unhampered in the Jewish camp only after their elimination. As an orthodox Marxist, Ber Borochov, the ablest theoretician of "Jewish" socialism, characterized all national conflicts, even when masquerading as spiritual struggles, as strife for material possessions. He nevertheless insisted that "the national question of an oppressed people is divorced from its basis in the materialistic conditions of production; the cultural necessities acquire an independent significance and all members of the nation become interested in the freedom of national self-determination" (*Di klassen-interessen un di natsionale frage*, in *Poale Zion Shriften*, I,81).[11]

Paradoxically it was Lenin who, more than any other statesman, helped realize the national autonomy of the Jews. To be sure, he never abandoned his messianic hope that some day nationalities would disappear and give way to a united humanity. His disciple, Stalin, clearly restated his position when he addressed the Sixteenth All Russian Congress of the Communist Party in 1930.

We must let the national cultures develop and expand, revealing all their potential qualities, in order to create the necessary conditions for fusing them into one common culture with one common tongue. The flourishing of cultures, national in form and Socialist in content, in the conditions of a proletarian dictatorship in one country, for the *purpose* of their fusion into one common Socialist culture, common both in form and in content, with one common tongue, when the proletariat is victorious throughout the world and Socialism becomes an every-day matter—in this lies the dialectical quality of the Leninist way of treating the question of national cultures. [*Political Report,* p. 191.]

As a matter of fact, Lenin and Stalin have given full self-government to national minorities, including the Jewish. Just as Marxian theory distinguished the ultimate atrophying (*Absterben*) of the state and its exalted position in a transitional period, as the main vehicle of the revolution, so also nationality, although doomed to final extinction in the future, was to enjoy full self-determination during its brief span of life. In the very first days of the Communist Revolution, Lenin issued the famous decree of November 15, 1917, which granted to all ethnic groups full freedom of action to the extent of secession from the Soviet Union. Paradoxically again, it was the Jewish communists of the *Yevsektsia* (the Jewish section of the Commissariat for Nationalities) who had to apply this principle to Jewish life. Their spokesman, S. Dimenstein, frequently reiterated opposition to the enthusiastic affirmation of Yiddish as "holy Yiddish," and expressed readiness to see it abandoned in favor of the stronger national languages of the environment. He and his associates were, none the less, instrumental in organizing Jewish soviets in localities with a Jewish majority. In many regions, especially the autonomous republics of Ukraine and White Russia, judicial and administrative business are often transacted in Yiddish, official proclamations appear in Yiddish, and schools in which Yiddish is the language of instruction are supported by the government. In 1930 there were 130 Yiddish-speaking soviets in the Ukraine, 23 in White Russia and 14 in the Crimea. No less than 100,000 Jewish children went to Yiddish public and secondary schools. The departments of Jewish studies at the universities and academies of Moscow, Kiev, Minsk, Odessa, etc., have employed a larger personnel and offered greater facilities for Jewish research than perhaps all European and American universities combined.

The demand for Jewish literature is growing; about forty Jewish newspapers and magazines are now printed in the U.S.S.R. The number of books in Yiddish has increased from 399 in 1915 to 600 in 1933, with a circulation of over two and a half million copies. ["Position of the Jews in the U.S.S.R.," *Soviet Union Review*, XI,104].[12]

Jewish social stratification, however, pushed to the fore, not proletarian, but middle-class nationalism. In Russia, Galicia and America, as well as in western Europe, only a tiny minority of Jews were members of the industrial proletariat. Jewish socialist parties had to derive their main strength from petty artisans and shopkeepers, who in general were staunchly anti-Marxian, and, above all, from an intelligentsia dissatisfied through the double pressure of anti-Jewish discrimination and their own excessive numbers. Even in America the Jewish socialist leaders were for a long time brilliant writers and debaters, rather than real labor leaders, despite their influence over powerful labor unions of largely Jewish membership. In eastern Europe trade-unionism was in its infancy before the Great War, and the Jewish unions included only a fraction of their potential "proletarian" membership. For many years the more influential protagonists of Jewish nationalism were the professedly middle-class parties: Dubnow's autonomists, Prilucki's populists, and, far overshadowing them in significance, the Zionists of all lands. Like the Bund, the Zionists, after a short period of hesitation, adopted the program of national cultural autonomy. At first they feared lest concentration on the Diaspora problems divert the best energies from the work for Palestine. Some even denounced the futility of fighting for national rights against the overwhelming forces of assimilation, to which, they contended, all the Jews outside of Palestine must eventually succumb. But Herzl's motto, "Conquer the Jewish communities," although primarily aiming at the unification of Jewry for the sake of Palestine, laid the foundation for Zionist *Landespolitik*. In 1906, the Russian Zionists, gathered in Helsingfors under the stress of the Russian Revolution; and, in October, 1918, under the impact of the Great War, the Copenhagen executive of the Zionist World Organization, incorporated the demand for national minority rights in their official program. The "Copenhagen Manifesto," sanctioned in 1921 by a Zionist Congress at Karlsbad, is one of the most remarkable of modern pronunciamentos on the question of Jewish self-government.[13]

INTERNATIONAL SOLUTIONS

All these parties early recognized that the Jewish question could never be solved by action within a single state. The failure of emancipation taught them a lesson as to the futility of such isolated attempts. The Jewish question has always been international. During the Middle Ages Islam and the Church determined the position of the Jews, much more than any individual country. The state could withdraw its tolerance and forcibly baptize or expel the Jews, but, once admitted, the Jews had to live in accordance with the fundamental policies of the dominant religion. Little room was left for variations necessary to a locality. Caliphs and popes, Muslim and Canonical schools of jurisprudence, were much more decisive in molding the Jews' legal status than were the respective monarchs or states. It was the late-developing, medieval national state which gradually undermined the prevailing uniformity. Even in the modern period, however, when the unity of Christendom had been rent, the Jewish question retained many international features. Soon realizing that they could not crush Marranism within the confines of Spain without dealing with its more universal aspects, Ferdinand and Isabella exercised pressure upon neighboring Portugal to expel the Jews, and tried to influence even far-off England to refuse toleration to her few Neo-Christian settlers (1496-98). Approached by the Spanish ambassador, King Henry VII, "laying both hands on his breast swore that he would persecute without mercy any Jew or heretic that the King or Queen of Spain might point out in his dominions" (in L. Wolf's *Diplomatic History*, p. 126). The protracted negotiations between Portugal and the pope over the establishment of an Inquisition in the early sixteenth century, illustrated this internationalism as clearly as did the conflict between the sultan and the pope over the Marranos of Ancona a few decades later. Soon Dutch Jewry assumed leadership in diplomatic negotiations with many lands. Menasseh ben Israel's correspondence with Cromwell was only one link in a chain of recurrent interventions of the scholars and merchants of Amsterdam on behalf of their coreligionists in Germany, Belgium and other lands. The Treaty of Westphalia, proclaiming the principle of toleration for religious minorities, offered sufficient subterfuges for diplomatic negotiations.

European powers could recognize the international import of the Jewish question without prejudice to sovereignty. On the score of juridical right, as much as on that of humanity, they felt entitled to intervene in favor of individuals who, as their own nationals, were under their specific protection, and of whole groups, even though alien, for whom persecution made life unbearable. In the cosmopolitan and humanitarian seventeenth and eighteenth centuries, the great international jurists, Bacon, Grotius and Pufendorf, expounded the right of armed intervention in a neighboring country to eliminate misgovernment or oppression. True, the more nationalistically oriented European "Concert of Powers" gradually abandoned this principle in the nineteenth century. Yet it could never wholly refrain from diplomatic intercessions in cases of flagrant violations of human rights.

Napoleon's convocation of the Great Sanhedrin, purportedly an agency of world Jewry entitled to legislate for all Jews, was a striking modern recognition of that community of interests linking together emancipated and nonemancipated Jewries of all lands. The protracted negotiations on the German Jewish question at Rasstadt in 1803, at the Congress of Vienna in 1814-15, at Aix-la-Chapelle in 1818, at the Vienna conference of Ministers in 1820, and throughout the early sessions of the Germanic diet in 1816-24, showed the great powers to be aware that protective measures must forestall arbitrary decisions of smaller neighbors. The combined interventions of England, Austria and Prussia in favor of Frankfort Jewry in 1816, although expressly qualified as not purporting "to limit the city of Frankfort in her inner organization with respect to the participation of the Israelitic citizens in political rights," doubtless influenced the eventual compromise of 1824. The intercessions of these powers and Russia, as signatories of the treaty of Vienna, in Lübeck had at least great moral effects. At the Congress of Aix-la-Chapelle, Czar Alexander I, prompted by a British missionary, Louis Way, suggested an international reform of the Jewish status. The newly founded states of the Netherlands in 1815, and Greece in 1830, had to assume an international obligation to grant equality of rights to all subjects, Jews being tacitly included.

In subsequent decades the question of reciprocity attracted more widespread attention. As far back as 1718, the treaty of Passarowitz between Austria and Turkey established the reciprocal rights of domiciles for the subjects of the two empires. Confirmed by the treaty of Belgrade of 1739, this agreement had the ironical effect that for more than a century thereafter Turkish Jews could settle in Vienna more freely and under more auspicious conditions than the native Jews of the Austrian provinces. In the nineteenth century the numerous conflicts between Switzerland, which insisted upon its right to discriminate against foreign Jews as well as against its own Jewish subjects, and the countries which had emancipated the Jews and now demanded equal treatment of their Jewish and non-Jewish citizens, were more than merely controversial interpretations of a paramount principle in international relations. In 1833 France broke off diplomatic and commercial relations with the canton of Basel-Land. The French were soon supported by Great Britain, the United States and Holland, which had similar interests. Negotiations ultimately resulted in the Franco-Swiss treaty of June 30, 1864, which contained the juridical monstrosity, "All Frenchmen without distinction of creed shall in future be admitted to each of the Swiss cantons and treated on the same footing with the *Christian* citizens of the other cantons" (Brisac, *Ce que les Israélites de la Suisse doivent à la France,* p. 53). To put an end to this anomaly, the government hastened to grant equality of rights to the Swiss Jews. A similar controversy raged for thirty years between Russia and the United States with respect to the interpretation of a commercial treaty concluded in 1832. In 1912, under the pressure of public opinion, President Taft notified the Russian government that the United States had decided to terminate that treaty.

Apart from juridical controversies, there were numerous intercessions of the Powers in favor of Jews on purely humanitarian grounds. The outcry in all western countries against the anti-Jewish atrocities at Damascus in 1840; the official moves of Great Britain, Austria, the United States and Holland to protect the Damascus Jews; the forced "leave of absence" of the British Consul, Werry, because he had failed immediately to discountenance the blood-ritual libel; and Lord Palmerston's unprecedented proposal in 1841 that "the Jews in Palestine should be allowed to transmit to the Porte, through British authorities, any complaints which they might have to prefer against the Turkish authorities," were all notable expressions of international solidarity with persecuted Jews. The western governments pursued even more consistently the policy of protecting the *Rumanian* Jews, since all phases of Rumanian independence were of special concern to them. After several decades of negotiations, Granville proposed in 1872 an international conference to discuss the Rumanian persecutions. Although supported by France and Italy, this idea was frustrated by the opposition of the Czar's government which, as we know from the Silberman affair of the same year, was fomenting Rumanian instability. At length, in 1878, the Congress of Berlin adopted the famous Article 44, guaranteeing full equality of rights to the Jews of the new kingdom. Rumania's opposition, although again stiffened by the Russian Gortshakov, was overcome by the combined efforts of Bismarck, Disraeli and Waddington, the French representative, with the direct or indirect support of Italy, the United States and other countries. These renowned statesmen could not cope with Rumanian craftiness, however, and the Rumanian government succeeded for fully four decades in evading its clear treaty obligations. The protests of the various governments proved of no avail. Not even America's purported self-interest in keeping away from its shores immigrants "who came as outcasts, made doubly paupers by physical and moral oppression in their native land" (John Hay's note of July 17, 1902, in C. Adler's *Jews in the Diplomatic Correspondence,* p. 59), carried weight with the Rumanian government. After such experiences, the statesmen who gathered in Bucharest, Saint Germain and Trianon in 1918-19 took pains to specify all obligations in minutest detail. The diplomatic history of the last century and a half thus offered a convincing illustration of the adage that "the peculiar position of the Jews places them under the protection of the civilized world" (Dispatch of the British Consul General in Bucharest of August 2, 1867; *British and Foreign State Papers,* LXII, 1877, p. 705).[14]

During this period the attitude of the Jews to international action underwent a remarkable change. At first western leaders were so involved in their struggle for emancipation or so contented with its achievement that they shunned action on behalf of coreligionists in other lands. They feared that united action to bring about international intervention might be misinterpreted as a profession of international Jewish solidarity and a lack of patriotic allegiance to their respective native countries. This narrow local patriotism was well exhibited in the attitude of the first Jewish delegates to appear before a modern international assembly. The Frankfort spokesmen before the Congress of Vienna (Baruch and Gumprecht, later Uffenheimer) tried to defend only the rights of their own community, which really happened to be placed in a better juridical position than the rest of German Jewry. This particularism was thrown into sharper relief by the attitude of Buchholz, the Christian delegate of the Hanseatic communities, who consistently championed Jewish emancipation throughout the Germanic Confederacy. In later years, too, particularistic interests often militated against united action. At best, such individuals as the Rothschilds and Montefiore used personal influence on the chancelleries of London, Paris and Vienna, to help persecuted eastern coreligionists. The Rothschild family, cognizant of its exposed position, preferred secret diplomacy, while Montefiore indulged in spectacular journeys to the Orient, Russia, etc. Soon after the Damascus affair, a Russian law of 1844 provoked the interference of the Rothschilds in Vienna and Berlin, and resulted, after several years of urging, in Montefiore's visit to Czar Nicholas I in 1846.

This spasmodic, unorganized, back-door diplomacy increasingly gave way to concerted action. The more the Jews themselves ceased to believe that the "persecutions" directed against them were part of an immutable social order, the more inadequate appeared such individual actions. French Jewry, feeling securely emancipated, first ventured to move toward an international combination of Jewish forces. Prompted by the Mortara affair in Rome, the Moroccan and Damascus persecutions and the outbreaks in Rumania, the French leaders, Crémieux, Albert Cohn, Charles Netter, and others, founded in 1860 the Alliance israélite universelle, with the definite purpose of ameliorating the political, economic and cultural conditions of the Jews throughout the world. The Jews of central Europe, although tremendously impressed, were hesitant in following that lead. In Vienna, for example, the majority of responsible leaders sidetracked the proposal to establish a vigorous branch of the Alliance, lest the Austrian government suspect them of supporting the imperialistic policy of Napoleon III. They decided to found, instead, an independent organization, the *Israelitische Allianz*. In 1871 English Jewry organized the Anglo-Jewish Association, and in 1878 the British Joint Foreign Committee, representing both the Association and the Jewish Board of Deputies. During the years 1859-78, the Board of Delegates of American Israelites, and later the Jewish Alliance and the American Committee for Ameliorating the Condition of the Russian Refugees, had a more limited scope. But from these antecedents arose the American Jewish Committee in 1906. Consisting of a number of self-appointed notables, it was from its inception vigorously denounced as undemocratic. Even the Central Conference of American Rabbis, through its president, Rabbi Stolz, voiced an objection, "because the people who are clamoring for a democratic organization will never be satisfied with a self-constituted, self-perpetuating, mutually admiring aristocratic committee" ("Message of Rabbi Joseph Stolz," *Yearbook CCAR*, XVI, 230). The Committee, undeterred by criticism, pursued its constructive course under the able leadership of Sulzberger and Marshall, and achieved its greatest prewar success in the abrogation of the Russian treaty. In Germany all previous undertakings have been overshadowed by the *Central-Verein deutscher Staatsbürger jüdischen Glaubens*, which, founded in 1893, speedily became the central political body of German Jewry. In 1929 it counted 555 local units and over 60,000 individual members. Together with its numerous corporate members, it may be said to have then represented more than half of German Jewry. Prewar attempts to unify all these national organizations consistently failed. There were, to be sure, three important conferences in Brussels and Paris in 1872, 1876 and 1878, dealing chiefly with the problems of Balkan Jewry. But, like the international synods of the Reform rabbis and laymen of that period, they did not result in permanent world-wide organization nor even in regularizing the practice of joint conferences.

The World War brought a sudden change. The upheaval in Jewish life, the forthcoming territorial changes in eastern

Europe and the Turkish dominions, the larger problem of self-determination of the small nationalities and the hopes, rising higher and higher, that out of the catastrophe would emerge a new world order of peace and justice, placed the Jewish question, among others, in the forefront of international deliberation. American Jewry now assumed the leadership. Under the pressure of public opinion, a more "democratic" American Jewish Congress was organized in 1916. After much unsavory bickering, it obtained the coöperation of the American Jewish Committee, the Bnai Brith Lodges, and other national organizations. On June 10, 1917, 335,000 votes were cast for delegates to the Congress; in addition, there were delegates of affiliated organizations with a purported aggregate of some 450,000 members. Although the Central Conference of American Rabbis, the Union of American Hebrew Congregations and the Council of Jewish Women refused to participate, the right of the congress to speak in the name of American Jewry could hardly be contested. At the Paris Peace Conference of 1919, the Congress threw in its lot with the Jewries of eastern Europe, establishing the so-called *Comité des délégations juives,* which, as the main representative of world Jewry, entered into protracted negotiations with the Allied and Associated Powers. This committee, headed by Mack, Marshall and Wise on the American side, and by Sokolow and Motzkin on the European, enjoyed the coöperation of the British and, to a smaller extent, of the French Jewish representatives. It set out to secure for the Jews of the newly organized states both legal equality and national minority rights.[15]

Mainly under Jewish initiative, minority-rights clauses were inserted in the treaties with Poland, Czechoslovakia, Hungary, Austria, Rumania and Turkey. Finland, Estonia, Latvia and Lithuania had to pledge observance of these clauses when they were admitted to membership in the League of Nations. This innovation appeared to be "a necessary consequence and an essential part of the new system of international relations brought into being by the establishment of the League of Nations" (Clemenceau's Letter to Paderewski, June 24, 1919). The treaty with Poland, which served as a basis for all the subsequent pacts, provided in Article VIII that

Polish nationals who belong to racial, religious or linguistic minorities shall enjoy the same treatment and security in law and in fact as the other Polish nationals. In particular, they shall have an equal right to establish, manage and control at their own expense charitable, religious and social institutions, schools and other educational establishments, with the right to use their own language and to exercise their religion freely therein.

Articles X and XI of the Polish treaty contained in addition specific clauses, not repeated in the other treaties, safeguarding Jewish education and the Jewish Sabbath. The reason given for this discrimination was that "in view of the historical development of the Jewish question and the great animosity aroused by it, special protection is necessary for the Jews in Poland" (Clemenceau, *l.c.*). On the other hand, Rumania had to promise that the Jewish residents of old Rumania, as well as the nationals of the newly acquired provinces, would *ipso facto* acquire Rumanian citizenship and be protected as a national minority. The Turkish Treaty of Sèvres and again that of Lausanne, likewise contained a special provision in favor of the Jews. These minority clauses were made part of permanent international law, the signatories agreeing that they

constitute obligations of international concern, and shall be placed under the guarantee of the League of Nations. They shall not be modified without the assent of a majority of the Council of the League of Nations. [Article XII of the Polish treaty.]

This signal achievement of the minority nationalities was due largely to Jewish influence at the Peace Conference, which could make itself felt primarily for two reasons. In the drafting of the new world order, a permanent settlement of all the national disputes was attempted through the granting of political independence to the nationalities inhabiting contiguous territories. The Jews, as the only nationality which had no territory of its own, were the national minority *par exemple*. Secondly, under the peculiar circumstances of the time, the Jews alone among the prospective new national minorities had influential spokesmen at the councils of the potentates. There were other equally large minorities to be considered: the millions of Germans, Hungarians, etc. But they were members of the vanquished nations, whose voice carried little weight with the Big Four of the Paris Conference. The eastern Jews, on the other hand, had coreligionists in America, England, France and Italy, and were thus placed in a strategic position. In this fashion two decades of persistent propaganda were crowned with complete success, and another utopian dream was converted at least into a recognized rule of international law.

For the most part, however, this regulation has remained a dead letter. The only country which without reservation carried into effect the minority clauses was the Soviet Union, which was not a signatory to the treaties. While those officially bound by them proceeded to incorporate the clauses into their own constitutions, thus attaching to them national as well as international sanction, they found one excuse after another for postponing or evading their application. Czechoslovakia alone may be said, on the whole, to have treated the Jewish minority in accordance with her obligations. Estonia, Latvia (until the recent Fascist upheaval) and Bulgaria likewise conformed relatively. Lithuania started out with a special ministry for Jewish affairs, a Jewish national council, etc., but in 1924 suppressed all these self-governing agencies and began to deny all rights of the Jewish minority in rapid succession. Dictatorial Turkey has induced her minorities, the Jewish coming first, through appointed notables, to renounce their rights. However inadequate such a renunciation may be legally, without the approval of the Council of the League, it certainly has curtailed the freedom of the Jewish leaders to appeal to Geneva against infractions. The worst offenders, however, have been Poland and Rumania. Even under the relatively favorable governments of Pilsudski and Duca, no minority rights have been applied to Jews. In September, 1934, Colonel Beck, the Polish Foreign Minister, startled his colleagues of the League of Nations Assembly, by declaring that "pending the bringing into force of a general and uniform system for the protection of minorities, my government finds itself compelled to refuse as from today all coöperation with international organizations in the matter of supervision of the application by Poland of a system of minority protection" (*New York Times,* September 14, 1934). This declaration was effectively repudiated by the British and other members of the Council, but Poland, relying upon her greatly enhanced international position, persists in her defiant mood.

Still more serious is the position of the Jewish minority in countries where no minority clauses operate, as illustrated by recent events in Germany. The German delegates to the Versailles Conference made a splendid gesture, and promised to abide by the minority stipulations, and on June 16, 1919, the Allies "took note" of this statement. At that time, however, Germany was not considered to have any significant minority, and no one probed the legal import of the generous promise. When the Nazi government began to persecute Jews, it became apparent that, with the exception of Upper Silesia, where minority rights had been established by special treaty with Poland, the Jews could invoke the minority clauses morally, but not legally. This German Jewish problem has brought into bold relief the oft-debated universal extension of minority rights over the entire League membership, or, indeed, the entire world. The resolutions adopted by the League Assembly in September, 1922, and, 1933, have thus far been merely expressions of a pious "hope," while the Polish suspension of international coöperation has further accentuated the desirability of universal agreement. Although there is little promise of achievement in the near future, this ideal still constitutes the ultimate goal of Jewish nationalism.[16]

POLITICAL ZIONISM

Jewish minority rights were at the outset limited to countries of Jewish mass settlement, containing other national minorities in addition to the Jews. National autonomy for Jews seemed out of the question in western Europe or America. Here the Jews were less numerous. Here, too, the states were either fully national states, or ethnically so mixed that a new nation had begun to take form. The Jews themselves would have seen in such autonomy a limitation rather than an extension of rights, the reëstablishment of the much-deplored ghetto, with its concomitant restrictions in public and private life. At the same time, a Jewish nationalism, true to itself, could not abandon these considerable and influential sections of Jewry. Even in the western countries, moreover, a national reaction set in against the assimilationist tendencies of the previous two or three generations. The steady flux of migrations from East to West brought nationally conscious Jews from territories where autonomy was possible and desirable, into those where the reverse was the case. The realities of western life sufficiently fortified that consciousness. Not only did anti-Semitism everywhere denounce the Jews as a separate ethnic group; but orthodoxy, with its adherence to the time-honored traditions and laws, maintained essentially the old compound of religion and nationality, even in the West. To I. Breuer, the most fervent anti-Zionist, the Jewish people were still a *Religionsnation,* if nothing else. Reform Judaism, too, had at least continued to acknowledge the existence of a Jewish "people." This people, although stripped of all elements of political nationality, retained a great many of its cultural and historical ingredients. Now, under the new conception of nationality, the peculiar characteristics of this "people" could easily be extended and translated into terms of a "nationality." The distinctive economic stratification of the Jews throughout the world sufficiently accounted for the realism of such national convictions.

The anomaly of such a nation was nevertheless quite obvious. No wonder tendencies were in motion to "normalize" its situation. In economic life, we have seen, the whole drift of the age was directed toward an increased diversification of Jewish economic activities and, more especially, toward a return of the Jews to agriculture. Similarly, political normalcy meant the acquisition of a territory and, possibly, of a state. The Jews are a nationality apart, Jewish spokesmen argued, but precisely for this reason they should become a nationality like all the others, which means a nationality based upon state (or something approximating its sovereignty) and territory. From this root sprang political Zionism.

Zionism was an age-old heritage. The vitality of the messianic hope in Jewish culture was always in direct relation to the extent of extraterritorial features in the medieval ghetto, and the extent to which Jews were generally regarded as temporary sojourners. The debacle of the Shabbetianic agitation could not dampen the hope, and even the Marranos continued to pray for restoration to the "land of promise." Disregarding all protests and warnings, Jews the world over continued to settle in Palestine, in order to be buried in the sacred soil. Commenting on the Russian Jews in the middle of the nineteenth century, an eyewitness somewhat sarcastically remarked, "The numbers repairing to Jerusalem for the inestimable privilege of being buried there became alarming" (J. Finn, *Stirring Times*, I,113). Diaspora Jewry also regarded it as its solemn duty to maintain its poverty-stricken coreligionists in the Holy Land. Collections for Palestine, a more or less permanent feature in the history of the dispersion, received definitive organizational form in the nineteenth century. To administer *Halukkah*, as the "distribution" of these funds was called, was deemed a great honor by the most prominent Jewish leaders. The Amsterdam *Pekidim and Amarkalim* (e.g., Akiba Lehren) and the Russian and Polish *Nesiim*—no less honorific titles were chosen—vied for the distinction of supporting one or another Palestinian group, while Palestinian branches maintained a regular messenger service to Europe. Not all the administrative abuses, graft and discriminatory methods of almsgiving could diminish the profound interest of the Jewish people in the preservation of its Palestinian sector.

Hasidism, of both the pre-Beshtian and the post-Beshtian type, intensified this love of Palestine. The Holy Land had always occupied a focal position in Jewish mysticism. Isaiah Horowitz, in the eighteenth century, left his enviable position in one of the largest of Ashkenazic communities to go to Palestine. In 1699-1701 several renowned mystic rabbis left for the Holy Land with fifteen hundred Polish, Bohemian and Hungarian Hasidim. Although five hundred of their followers are said to have perished on the road, their example invited imitation in subsequent years. With what personal sacrifice did Nahman of Bratslav start on his pilgrimage, at the age of twenty-six! "You will proceed to your future father-in-law," he wrote in 1799 to his eldest daughter, "your older sister will become a servant, your little sister will probably be taken into some home out of pity, your mother will become a cook, and I shall dispose of all my household for traveling expenses." (*Shibhe ha-Ran,* chap. on Journey, section 6). But such sacrifices were as nothing to this hasidic rabbi, in whom the great Maggid of Meseritsh had instilled the belief that "Zion is the very essence of the world, it is the lifeblood of the universe; that is why it contains a portion of all countries, and every country draws her lifeblood and nourishment from that portion which is hers in Zion" (*Or Torah,* section Va-Era).

Among the western Jews, these messianic dreams were often hidden behind the mask of stern realism, but on occasions they ran to extremes. Mordecai Manuel Noah's appeal to the Jews of the world to settle in a country of their own, Ararat, a deserted region near Buffalo, although couched in apparently statesmanlike phrases, was no less visionary an undertaking than that of any medieval "false messiah." From the outset, Noah's plan was intended merely as a preparation for the final return to Palestine. In 1845 Noah himself admitted that "every attempt to colonize the Jews in other countries has failed; their eye has steadily rested on their beloved Jerusalem" (*Discourse on the Restoration of the Jews,* p. 4).

During the emancipation era, it appeared as if the Jewish people were ready, because of assimilation or Reform, to give up this messianic hope. At least its political aspects were to be translated into a religious vision without national restrictions. But when the emancipation proved to be an inadequate solution of the Jewish problem, the eyes of the people again turned toward Zion. With the need for further economic differentiation and the return to agriculture, and under the pressure of the Eastern European Jewish masses, which needed an outlet and found more and more countries closed to them, the erection of a Jewish homeland in Palestine became also an economic necessity. The conviction that Jewish separation from other nations will never be overcome, and the belief that the greatest achievements of Judaism, the prophecy and poetry of the Bible, could only be repeated by a people restored to Palestine, lent additional strength to both political and cultural Zionism.

The outside world was fully prepared, through centuries of international discussion, for the idea of a Jewish restoration. On the one hand, the more humane anti-Semites, wishing to see the Jews leave their own countries, proposed that they be settled anywhere in the world in a state of their own. For example, as far back as 1816, vom Stein, the great German statesman, wished "to populate the northern coast of Africa with them." Two years later an anonymous Polish writer suggested to Alexander I to rid Poland of her Jews by transplanting them to southern Russia, an idea which was seriously debated and resolved upon by the Polish diet in 1822. On the other hand, the famous proclamation of Napoleon to the Jewish people during his Egyptian campaign in 1799, although of little immediate consequence, symbolized Europe's acknowledgment of Jewish rights to Palestine. Napoleon was no idealist, seeking to solve the Jewish question on an altruistic basis; his shrewd recognition of the intense interest of the Jews, whom he attempted to enlist in his expeditionary army, and of the support the Jewish hope had received from French and English writers, is a barometer of the extent to which the European atmosphere was charged with these messianic expectations. French public opinion had, in fact, been prepared by more than a century of publicist agitation by Peyrère, the Marquis de Langallerie, Pierre Jurieux, and others. The municipality of Nancy on December 10, 1790, suggested, in a spirit not unfriendly to the Jews, that all French Jewry be assembled in a Jewish colony in the Champagne. Just before Napoleon's expedition, a public discussion on the topic of Jewish restoration to Palestine, begun by a Jewish pamphleteer, received favorable comment in the Paris press. Across the Channel, too, the British mystic, Henry Finch, had published as early as 1621 a pamphlet entitled *The World's Great Restoration or the Calling of the Jewes and with Them of All the Nations and Kingdomes of the Earth to the Faith of Christ,* in which he advocated the reconstruction of a Jewish kingdom in Palestine as a step toward the impending Jewish world dominion. Of course, he expected the Jews to have been converted to Christianity by that time. This combination of political restoration and conversion, preliminary to the second coming of Christ, has been frequently reëchoed in the western proposals for a Jewish Palestine. The Catholic Jansenists and Manzoni shared this enthusiastic expectation with the Puritans and English, American and German Pietists. At the Congress of Aix-la-Chapelle, the missionary, Louis Way, suggested the political independence of the Jews in Palestine as one means of their final reform. His disciples, especially those gathered around the London Society for the Promoting of Christianity amongst the Jews, preached this final political and religious solution with great fervor. In the 1840's, especially, the troubled situation in the Near East gave rise to a prolific publicist output, and to diplomatic negotiations for Jewish restoration. In 1845 Lt. Col. George Gawler, former governor of South Australia, published a pamphlet entitled *Tranquillisation of Syria and the East. Observations and Practical Suggestions in Furtherance of the Establishment of Jewish Colonies in Palestine; the Most Sober and Sensible Remedy for the Miseries of Asiatic Turkey.*

These British Protestants and missionaries found strange allies in a few eastern rabbis, rationalists as well as mystics. Rabbi Hirsch Zebi Kalischer, of Thorn, as far back as 1842 raised the question of a Jewish colonization in Palestine, in his correspondence with the leaders of European orthodoxy, Eiger and Schreiber. His ideas were soon supported by Elijah Guttmacher, a hasidic dreamer, who tried to prove that, according to the Kabbalah, the preparedness of the Jewish people must precede the advent of a redeemer. In the Balkans, Rabbi Judah Alkalai published, beginning in 1837, a series of volumes advocating the organization of a joint-stock company to finance the transplanting of thousands of European and oriental Jews to Palestine. Even the realistic banker, Moses Montefiore, was so impressed by the Palestinian opportunity that, after his visits to the country in 1829 and 1839, he opened negotiations with Mohammed Ali of Egypt for a charter for Jewish colonization, in return for a British loan to the Egyptian government. Montefiore was also instrumental in sending to the Foreign Office for consideration a detailed memorial by A. Benisch, subsequently the editor of the *Jewish Chronicle,* on how the British government might help to carry out such a project (published by Baron in *Kohut Mem. Vol.*) These disparate tendencies had a certain fruition after 1860. In those years, when French Jewry proceeded to found the Alliance israélite universelle, Joseph Salvador, the most celebrated Franco-Jewish scholar of the day, proclaimed, "Certainly the political importance of Jerusalem and of the land of Israel cannot but be reborn through the same human genius that will cut the Isthmus of Suez and mingle the waters of the Red Sea with those of the Mediterranean" (*Paris, Rome et Jérusalem*). About the same time, Kalischer convoked a rabbinical assembly at Thorn, out of which came the Society for the Colonization of the Holy Land, founded in Frankfort in 1861. Moses

Hess, a man of great social vision and almost prophetic intuition, laid down the fundamentals of Zionist ideology in his *Rome and Jerusalem,* published in 1862.

Once the ball was started rolling, it never came to rest. The remaining four decades of the nineteenth century witnessed the foundation of the agricultural school, *Mikveh Israel,* by the Alliance in 1870; the establishment of the first Jewish colonies in 1879-83 by the followers of Alkalai and the Russian pioneers, the *Bne Yaakob leku ve-nelka* (BILU); and the spread of the "Lovers of Zion" movement throughout eastern Europe. Through Smolenskin, Pinsker, Lilienblum and Ahad Ha-Am, the ideas expounded by Hess were further developed, and given a special coloring from the living national consciousness of Russian Jewry. It was, however, in the West that the movement reached its climax, in the Zionism of Herzl. In 1896 the latter published his *Jewish State,* and in 1897 two hundred delegates of various Jewish groups throughout the world gathered around him at the first Zionist Congress in Basel. There the Zionist Organization was founded, and its program definitely laid down, "to establish for the Jewish people a publicly and legally assured home in Palestine." It was out of obvious diplomatic considerations that the equivocal term "home" was substituted for "state," to describe the ultimate objective.[17]

SECULARIZATION OF JEWISH NATIONALISM

To many orthodox contemporaries the idea that the Jewish nation should become like the other nations was, paradoxically, nothing but assimilation in disguise. The logical trend of the new movement was in fact toward a more and more secular nationalism. To be like other nations, the Jewish nation had to give up the exclusively religious criteria of Jewishness. As there are Protestant Germans and Catholic Germans, so there might be, if logical reasoning were pushed to the extreme, also Jews who are national Jews while professing a non-Jewish creed. Quite in accordance with the teachings of both the Jewish secular nationalists and the racial anti-Semites, eleven citizens of Prague registered in the census of 1921 as of Jewish nationality and Roman Catholic religion. Many thousands more in Prague and elsewhere declared themselves ethnically Jewish, but recorded no religious affiliation. The number of Jews of these two categories in the Polish and Lithuanian censuses is still larger.

The responsible leaders of the nationalist movement, however, refrained from going to that extreme. With a certain deference to the convictions of the masses and with a half-conscious feeling that the Jewish nationality was, after all, a special kind of nationality, they insisted that whoever publicly deserts the Jewish faith is no longer to be regarded as a Jew, even in nationality. The fact that the majority of Jews converted to other creeds obviously had as a motive worldly advantage, such as governmental position, social career or marriage, gave these tendencies a semblance of logical justification. The man who leaves Judaism for such external reasons could be denounced as a renegade, deserting his army in the midst of the battle. Finally, experience had taught that, once Jews deserted Judaism as a religion, they or their descendants tended to be fully absorbed into Gentile society. Sooner or later they were lost, even to the Jewish ethnic group. No matter, therefore, how much discrimination baptized Jews and their offspring suffered through racial anti-Semitism, such converts to Christianity were no longer counted as Jewish conationals. On the other hand, religious beliefs and observances were no longer regarded as binding upon the Jews. A Jew may reject the teachings of both orthodoxy and Reform; he may refuse to believe in any of the "dogmas" of Judaism, and still be recognized as a national Jew. Ahad Ha-Am himself, in emphasizing the contrast between the oppressed, but intrinsically free, eastern Jew and the emancipated but therefore no less spiritually enslaved western Jew, boasted, "I can adopt even that scientific heresy which goes by the name Darwin without any danger to my Judaism" (*Selected Essays,* p. 194).

This secularization of Jewish nationalism had many far-reaching consequences. The more radical the break with tradition, the less essential seemed the choice of country in which to erect a Jewish state. Uganda or, in recent times, Crimea and Birobidjan, certainly have had the advantage of being slightly populated regions where Jewish newcomers would not encounter the resistance of a large non-Jewish population. Those groups, however, which leaned more on historical continuity than on logic, those for whom the traditional culture of Judaism represented values worthy of rejuvenation on the old soil, insisted upon Palestine. It, and no other country, was the scene of a glorious historical past which had generated a sentimental attachment for centuries. Furthermore, just as, in the days of early capitalism, the Jewish people had flocked into the rising lands of the West, so they now felt an unconscious drive toward the awakening Near East. At any rate, some Christian friends of Zionism, such as Sir Mark Sykes, saw its great mission for the world at large, "to be a bridge between Asia and Europe, to bring the spirituality of Asia to Europe, and the vitality of Europe to Asia" (in N. Sokolow's *History of Zionism,* II, 106).

Along with this dissension between the Zionists and the various types of territorialists, there also went the linguistic struggle between the Hebraists and the Yiddishists. For those interested in the preservation of Jewish culture, Palestine obviously was the country where the originality of the Jewish race could best be restored and the Hebrew language best used as a vehicle of rejuvenation. Hebrew, although but little spoken anywhere in the world, had been the sacred tongue of *all* Jews, and as such promised to be a means of unification of world Jewry. On the other hand, the Yiddishists could easily claim that, while Hebrew had not become the spoken language of any group of numerical importance, millions were actually speaking Yiddish. The western and Sephardic Jews must, therefore, learn Yiddish or regard themselves as cut off from the Jewish national body. The comparative success of the vast educational experiment in spoken Hebrew in Palestine was adduced by the Hebraists as proving the adequacy of a revived Hebrew as a medium of communication for all Israel. The relatively small number of Hebrew-speaking people outside of Palestine, however, continued to provide the Yiddishists with arguments. Ahad Ha-Am, the Hebraist, could finally invoke the testimony of history. "There is not a single nation," he wrote in 1902, "alive or dead, of which we can say that it existed before its national language was known to it" (*Selected Essays,* p. 281). To which argument the Yiddishists were able to reply only by pointing to their wholly novel experiment.

The impulses given by the nationalist and Zionist movements for the cultivation of the two languages resulted in an astounding renaissance of both—in the development of modern Hebrew and Yiddish literatures of great national and artistic merit. Gone was the anxiety permeating the entire Haskalah literature that Hebrew letters were doomed and that the Haskalah writers were the last in their illustrious story. A new optimism set in, which overcame innumerable obstacles. Eliezer ben Yehudah's limitless faith in the future of the language led to his fanatical insistence upon conversational Hebrew, even in the most trifling affairs. Hebrew periodicals, even dailies, and publishing houses for books, literary and scientific, sprang up in quick succession in the Diaspora and in Palestine, with utter disregard of financial conditions. The speech of the Sephardic Jews was adopted, not because it was scientifically more "correct"—the phonetics of the ancient, biblical language, with its numerous dialectical differences between Israel and Judah, is after all a highly controversial matter—but on account of its apparently more melodious and more truly oriental sound, as well as of its greater adaptability to the Arabic environment. A special committee, the *Vaad menihei ha-lashon* in Jerusalem was intrusted with supervising the development of new terms, artificially invented to fit the ancient tongue to the needs of modern civilization. In Palestine, moreover, Hebrew served as the most effective means of unification for the diverse elements of world Jewry who came to settle there. All attempts of Jewish socialists to introduce Yiddish as the predominant language of the country were frustrated by the opposition of the workers, and especially their children, who consistently spoke Hebrew. The renaissance of Hebrew poetry, under the leadership of Bialik and Tshernichovsky, has restored the glory of the Golden Age of Spain to the revived language. The Hebrew theater (after the memorable success of the Moscow *Habimah*), opera and even vaudeville in Palestine now contribute to the fullness of cultural life in that country.

The renaissance of Yiddish letters was equally amazing. The language, previously disparaged by intellectual Jews, often classified as a jargon and a "Mauscheln," developed a new literature, artistic and scientific, which could stand comparison with many a literature of the Western world. The Yiddish theater in Russia, Poland and America, at first appealing only to the unsophisticated masses, has risen in recent years to great heights of artistic endeavor. So impressed with the religious intensity of the audience was, for example, the historian Karl Lamprecht, during his visit in 1904 to a New York Yiddish theater, that he compared this experience with a visit to Cologne Cathedral. "In ancient Hellas, too," he concluded, "they must have played theater with such religious consecration" (*Americana*, p. 61). The Yiddish press, in particular, became a most influential factor in molding Jewish opinion and in the political and cultural development of the Jewish masses. Although dating back to the periodical *Kurant,* which appeared twice a week in Amsterdam in 1686-87, the Yiddish press did not become a potent force in Jewish life until the last half century. In the *Yidishes Folksblat,* a supplement to Zederbaum's Hebrew *Hamelis* in 1881-89, was created the first literary organ worthy of this designation. The *Yidishes Tageblat,* established by Sarasohn in New York in 1885; and *Der Freind,* the first Jewish daily in Russia from 1902 on, began spreading the gospel of Yiddish among the masses. In the peak year, 1928, there were appearing no less than 411 Yiddish journals, among them 52 daily papers. While Poland accounted for 45 percent of this total, the number of readers of the few American and Russian dailies was far in excess of the Polish. It has been estimated that, notwithstanding the progressive Americanization of the Jews in the United States, even today the entire Anglo-Jewish press, with a total circulation of approximately 300,000, runs behind the combined circulation of American Yiddish dailies. It can hardly be doubted, moreover, that a Yiddish paper appeals to more readers than its actual subscribers, while in the case of the Anglo-Jewish press the opposite is more likely to be true. However disquieting the future, this grandiose achievement of the last few decades in both the Hebraic and the Yiddish renaissance has few parallels in history.

One of the fundamental features of both literatures is their secular character. For the first time in Jewish history, "literature" assumed the meaning which it ordinarily has among western nations, namely *belles lettres.* Ahad Ha-Am, himself a creator of fine, modern Hebrew prose, protested in vain that Jewish literature should primarily continue its ancient tradition of a scholarly nature. Even Mendele Mocher Sefarim (Shalom Jacob Abramowitsch) one of the most famous modern Hebrew novelists, acknowledged in vain the superiority of the Talmud and Midrash over modern fiction. Strenuously objecting to an opinion which had gained wide circulation in his day, that Hebrew literature was poor in comparison with the Russian, German or French letters, he sarcastically remarked that apparently only Ivan Petrovitsh's amours with the wife of Peter Ivanovitsh constitute literature, while Talmud and Midrash do not. "Has anybody ever seen a Jew who would complain 'I have no book to read'?" he exclaimed. It was perhaps this conviction of the alien character of *belles lettres* to Hebrew thought that motivated his preference for writing novels in Yiddish, rather than in Hebrew. In spite of all this, the steady advance of *belles lettres* in both camps was another sign of the influence of western standards, even upon nationalist Jews.

The often sharp rivalry between the two groups has caused comparatively little damage. The Czernowitz Conference of 1908 and the periodical *Freistatt,* which appeared in 1913 under the editorship of Fritz Mordecai Kaufmann with the coöperation of Nathan Birnbaum, declared war upon Hebrew. In 1912 Ben Yehuda and Ussishkin reëchoed the ancient slogan of Judah the Patriarch in its modern adaptation: "Either Hebrew or Russian, why Yiddish?" But before the War these skirmishes caused no serious disturbances to the cultural activity of either group. The greatest poets and writers of the period, Bialik, Mendele, Perez, and Berditshevski, wrote in both languages. It was only the postwar persecution of the use of Hebrew in the Soviet Union that envenomed the relations of the two groups. As time went on, however, it was more and more clearly recognized that this persecution had as many general communistic and atheistic, as purely Yiddishist, antecedents.[18]

OPPOSING TRENDS IN ZIONISM

The somewhat chaotic condition of Jewish society has naturally resulted in the most varied theoretical reactions. There is, of course, the large mass of Jews who do not accept the nationalist teachings at all. Some cosmopolitan Jews, particularly among socialists and radicals, refuse to recognize the nationality principle as such, and even less the principle of Jewish nationality. During the Peace Conference in Paris, President Wilson received a petition signed by a number of American Jews led by Congressman Julius Kahn of California, "All Jews repudiate every suspicion of a double allegiance, but to our minds it is necessarily implied and cannot by any logic be eliminated from the establishment of a sovereign state for the Jews in Palestine" (*New York Times,* March 5, 1919). Still others declare Jewish nationalism a pernicious movement likely to destroy the religion they cherish. These are, characteristically, divided into two main groups, the partisans of extreme orthodoxy or of extreme Reform. Another substantial section of the Jewish people may be classified as indifferent. Especially those not politically minded, or who live in a society where politics appear to be of no vital importance, have hardly any definite view on the subject. Such people sometimes accidentally join one or the other group, but, as a rule, prefer to keep altogether aloof.

On the question of nationalism and Zionism, there can be detected four main positions of substantial Jewish groups. Apart from complete negation, there are the contending philosophies of Diaspora nationalism, Palestinophile antinationalism, and the usual combination of nationalism and Zionism. We have already spoken of the strong Diaspora nationalist movement, which is opposed to Zionism. It has had its chief protagonists in the radical wings of communists, Bundists, populists and others. All of them desired a broad national autonomy in the countries of the dispersion, but denounced the Palestine ideal and the Hebrew language as reactionary and bourgeois. Both Zionism and nationalism were extremely unpopular for a time within western Jewry, largely belonging to the upper-bourgeois stratum. In the last decade or two, however, Zionism has advanced rapidly. But even today, perhaps, the majority of Western European, and a large section of American, Jews seek the realization of the Zionist ideal without nationalism. Even some antinationalist movements, including early Reform, became increasingly reconciled to the project of reclaiming Palestine as a homeland for Jewry. In 1929 the Jewish Agency for Palestine was so reorganized as to include fully one-half "non-Zionist" members who were willing to take an active part in upbuilding the Jewish homeland. But the main stream has consisted in a synthesis of Zionism and nationalism as formulated by the Basel Program, which is at present backed by large masses of the Jewish lower middle class and the Jewish intelligentsia throughout the world.

Within this main stream, too, there have always existed minor currents. Political Zionism, which sought the main solution through the creation of a political organism in Palestine, thereby hoping to solve the Jewish problem everywhere, was opposed by cultural Zionism. The latter laid chief emphasis upon the erection of a cultural center in Palestine, whence the rejuvenated spirit of Judaism shall radiate to all corners of the Jewish dispersion. Again, some Zionists renounced Diaspora life altogether, declaring that Jewry is doomed to extinction, except for the remnant which is gathered in Zion. Some insisted upon the secularization of both nationalism and Zionism, in order to make the Jews a "normal" people. Others regarded the past religious history of the Jews as a very precious heritage, even for the secular culture of the future. Some emphasized the principle of social justice, not so much in the sense of prophetic and Reform Judaism, as in the sense of modern socialism, and consequently preached class war in Hebrew or Yiddish. Others would have liked to establish a reign of justice, in the name of a higher ethical ideal, through love and the mutual understanding of classes. Some wanted the Jewish people merely to attend to its own business and to try to become as strong, affluent and happy as it possibly can. Others insisted, under one guise or another, on the mission of Israel. Although this particular idea has been violently denounced by political and even cultural Zionists, it returned, as it were, through the back door, in the ideology of Buber, Chajes, Rosenzweig and others.[19]

The attitude of the Zionist organization as such has changed with circumstances. In the first Herzlian period, political Zionism was paramount. Herzl had a sincere belief in his own supreme power to unite the people and to obtain an international charter. Indeed, he and many of his followers had been so much detached from the living stream of Jewish ethnic life as to put their faith in a single international act, rather than in the slow inner growth of the people. In view of western conditions exclusively, they pessimistically abandoned the hope of the survival of the Jewish people anywhere outside the Jewish homeland. As a whole, this group did not go the entire length with Nordau when he denounced "all racial mysticism and historical or sociological teleology which are likewise a form of mysticism." But few were ready to accept his "firm conviction" that neither the amalgamation of the Jews with, nor their separation from the nations would have any serious effect upon the world and the processes of general evolution (Sombart *et al., Judentaufen,* p. 103). Equally few were those political extremists who, like Marmorek, advocated the suspension of all Zionist activities in Palestine and the setting aside of all its funds until such time as a charter would render their employment more immediately advantageous. Herzl and the majority of his followers rejected such extremes. But even they had set their hearts upon their charter idea, the realization of which they, like many other messianic dreamers, expected within a very short time. Reckoning on some twenty years in all, they considered lightly not only *Gegenwartsarbeit* (a term introduced in 1901 by Buber and Feiwel to connote work at the immediate tasks of Diaspora life), but even the slow colonization and reconstruction of Palestine.

Consistently this group was open to the ideas of non-Palestinian territorialism. Not springing from the main stream of Jewish messianism, they could easily disregard its irrational imponderables and envision settlement in any country offering natural and political advantages. Throughout the nineteenth century Jewish colonization in countries other than Palestine had been frequently proposed, on economic, political and philanthropic grounds. As far back as 1819, an Englishman, Robinson, suggested a Jewish colony in Mississippi, but his personal interest as owner of large tracts of land in that state lent an unsavory touch to his scheme. In 1832 Issachar ben Isaac of Hesse submitted to the Rothschilds a detailed plan for a Jewish agricultural settlement in North America, and issued a public appeal advocating the establishment of a colonization agency. In 1844 Jewish philanthropic societies in London, Paris, Berlin and Frankfort seriously considered transplanting the persecuted Russian Jews to Texas and other

North American territories. Two years later Ludwig Philippson's *Allgemeine Zeitung des Judentums,* the most influential Jewish organ of the time, advocated a great interterritorial Jewish society for this purpose. A quarter of a century earlier, Noah's fantastic project had found a responsive echo even among the Eastern European Maskilim. Others, such as the Decembrist, Perez (of Jewish origin), advocated the Crimea as the best place for a Jewish state. An anonymous writer of 1840 made it quite plain that, while the colonization should be of a national and not philanthropic character, Palestine would be too small and the financial resources of the Jews insufficient to acquire it. Herzl may never have paid much attention to the question of the Palestinian natives; as Weizman once remarked, there is not a single reference to it in his voluminous diaries. Others, such as Nordau, may have easily acquiesced in the argument that the Arabs would obviously derive such benefits from Jewish immigration that they could not possibly object to the erection of a Jewish state—a conception not quite so ridiculous before the war-time rise of modern Arab nationalism. But all readily recognized Palestine's geographic limitations and her comparative lack of natural resources, as compared to other extensive, still unexploited territories. Although Nordau grandiloquently announced that there is space in and around Palestine for a population of 12,000,000-15,000,000, he left the more detailed exposition of these possibilities to Davis Trietsch, a most imaginative statistician.

No wonder he and Herzl were inclined, in 1903, to accept the British offer to open a section of British East Africa to Jewish colonization. They yielded only to the pressure of the Eastern European Jews, who otherwise would have seceded from the Zionist organization. The secession of a minor western group under the leadership of Israel Zangwill, which soon formed the Jewish Territorial Organization (ITO), left the Zionist Organization under the complete control of the Palestinophiles. The Palestine ideal proved to be so firmly rooted in the Jewish people that even Zangwill increasingly emphasized the temporary character of every other territorial solution: to acclimatize the Jews to independent life on the soil, and thus to prepare them for their ultimate restoration to Palestine. It was Zangwill himself who, even before the War, found some of the most enthusiastic words in favor of a return of the Jews to Palestine. "Then the nations they quit," he declared, "will sustain an immense loss, politically, economically and spiritually, while the Jews themselves will lay the foundation of a State that will within a century or two recall 'the glory that was Greece and the grandeur that was Rome'" (Sombart *et al., Judentaufen,* p. 144). After the Balfour Declaration, territorialism vanished from the western countries, to reappear, under a new guise, in the Soviet projects of Jewish autonomous settlements along the Black Sea and in the Far East. The Diaspora nationalists' old opposition to Zionism, the expediencies of communist propaganda among World Jewry and the Arabs of western Asia, and the suspicions that the Palestine Mandate was nothing but a tool of British imperialism, all contributed to generate the scheme to build a rival Jewish homeland within the Soviet Union.

Recurrent frustrations in the negotiations for a charter, even in Herzl's own lifetime, and, more important, the discontinuation of negotiations after the nationalist Young Turk revolt of 1908, lent increasing force to cultural Zionism. Although its main protagonist in the pre-Herzlian movement, Ahad Ha-Am, remained outside the Zionist Organization, his voice found increasing response in the Zionist constituency. At first the majority of his adherents were Eastern European Jews, with their inner attachment to Jewish cultural values. Soon, however, his following included the most prominent Western European leaders, beginning with the profound, although inconsistent, thinker, Nathan Birnbaum, and culminating in Buber and his disciples. In Ahad Ha-Am, the best traditions of rabbinism were united with the teachings of modern positivist philosophy to form a new modern, secular synthesis of Jewish culture. In Buber, the realities of western assimilation were synthesized with the combination of enlightenment and Hasidism prevalent in Galicia, Buber's native land. Combining the metaphysical conception of a "national spirit" as introduced into Jewish thought by Krochmal, Luzzatto, Hess and Lilienblum, with a biological concept of nationality, Ahad Ha-Am stressed the positive will to survive as opposed to negative defense against anti-Semitism. It is for this living biological and cultural organism that Palestine is needed, as the liberation of Judaism must precede that of the Jews. A small percentage of Jews settled in Palestine, having the untrammeled opportunity to rejuvenate the creative Jewish spirit, would establish a cultural center for the entire dispersion. To be sure, this was a rationale for inescapable facts: the impossibility of transplanting a majority of Jews to Palestine, the futility of the expectation of building a Jewish state in the near future, and the reluctance of this group to abandon Diaspora Jewry to its fate. Ahad Ha-Am and his disciples refused to admit this negative foundation. Buber, fighting within the ranks, drew the line between the organization and the movement, which is so much greater in compass and in goal.

Zion is more than a territory in western Asia [he idealistically proclaimed, in an impressive address in 1918]. Zion is more than a Jewish commonwealth on that territory; Zion is reminiscence, admonition, promise; Zion is the new sanctuary in the image of the old; from Zion the Law shall once more go forth. It is the foundation-stone of the messianic structure of humanity. It is the endless task of the Jewish national soul. [*Die jüdische Bewegung,* II, 167.]

More realistically, he defined Zionism,

Not the improvement of the position of the Jews but the redemption of the nation is the content of our idea. . . . If we endeavor to focalize Jewish life in Palestine, we do it not because "the friction arising from the intensified struggle for subsistence serves as a spawning-ground of anti-Semitism" and we must give way, but because only out of the gathering of our people upon its own soil, out of the renewal of its historical continuity, out of the forces of the Palestinian soil can a healthy national organism arise, a Judaism regenerated in impulse and in action, a transformed Jewish spirit. [*Ibid.* I, 124 f.]

This neo-mystic interpretation of Zionism easily provoked opposition in the name of common sense. Even Birnbaum, himself no less mystical, derided it as a "rhapsodic, philosophic intermezzo of all kinds of intellectual moods and whimsies." Buber's ideas have, none the less, molded the minds of Zionist youth since 1910, just as much as those of Ahad Ha-Am did in the preceding generation.

A large body of young Zionists refused to accept the teachings of the two masters. Many others went beyond them in seeking new solutions. For the most part, they found their way into one or another of the socialist and "revisionist" movements. Even before the World War, socialist ideologies of some sort permeated the entire Zionist movement. Herzl himself, although by class position an upper bourgeois, by personal inclinations and contacts an aristocrat, could not escape the demands of social justice, so integral to any form of Judaism. His utopian state, the "Old Newland," combined in itself nationalist and socialist features. Hess, prominent in German socialist ranks, was naturally still less able to imagine a future Jewish commonwealth without full social justice. But it was in the special Zionist Labor parties that the socialist idea, in combination with Zionism, achieved its greatest fruition. In 1900-5, the Poale Zion movement took definite shape. In the period of the Russian Revolution, in 1905-6, it made great strides, even though it encountered the opposition of the newly organized Zionist Socialist (SS) party, which had a pronouncedly territorialist program. With the decline of territorialism, the Poale Zion long remained the only important group. Regardless of their relatively small following within the actual proletariat, the intellectuals who gathered under its flag have ever since exercised a considerable influence within and without Zionist ranks. The sponsorship of its national program by the great socialist parties of the neutral countries in 1918, and its own ultimate admission to the Fourth Socialist International in 1921, gave it external recognition in the international field. After the War, it was hopelessly split into many warring camps of communists and socialists. Nevertheless, it was the labor elements which now became most decisive in the reconstruction of Palestine under the Mandate. The organized labor unions, with a membership of almost 60,000, at present dominate the Palestinian scene, while at the elections to the Eighteenth Zionist Congress, the Labor party polled about 40 percent of the entire vote of the world organization. At the Nineteenth Congress, in 1935, it controlled 199 of the 455 elected delegates. During this process of growth, however, the radicalism of its early period was greatly modified, and compromises with Palestinian conditions have greatly weakened the consistency of its ideology.

Two major forces have striven for the control of this ideology: the Marxian socialism of Borochov and the national socialism of A. D. Gordon. For Borochov, Zionism was an intermediary step between the present and the future. Expressing in Marxian terms the desire of the Jews to acquire a territory, he declared, "The fact that the Jewish people possess no territory is the primary cause for the abnormality of the working *place* of the Jewish laborer and of the strategic basis of the fighting Jewish proletariat" ("Vos villen di Poale Zion?", 1906, in *Poale Zion Shriften,* I, 96). Even in 1917, when Palestine seemed nearest realization, Borochov thus defined the attitude of his party,

The class interests of the Jewish proletariat are our starting point; our final goal is socialism. Zionism is the maximum point in our minimum program. The way to realize our program is class struggle. ["Palestina in unser program un taktik," *ibid.,* II, 272.]

This Marxian basis, however, did not militate against the active participation of the Zionist workers in the reconstruction of Palestine. True, Birnbaum's earlier Marxist convictions made him suspect any preconceived idea which was to lead to mass action. He believed that the people itself, following the dialectic of its own position, was to evolve its own program. But the Poale Zion leaders, in formulating theoretical as well as practical aims for the unconscious strivings of the masses, were no less convinced Marxists. Marx himself had taught that the development inherent in a given social situation may be accelerated by human action. If anywhere, it was in Jewish socialism, and in the Poale Zion movement in particular, that the conscious formulations of the leaders had frequently to be substituted for the inner drive lacking in the masses.

Within Palestinian labor circles, the Marxist concept of class struggle found a powerful opponent in the idea of love and mutual aid. The prophetic preachments of social justice as a supreme ethical postulate were combined with Dostoievski's exaltation of manual labor as a means of physical and mental regeneration, in Gordon's philosophy of a new Hebraic socialism. Rejecting Marx as mechanistic, it preached the national struggle of the peoples against their parasites, bourgeois or proletarian, rather than class struggle against the capitalists. For Gordon, labor was elevated to a cosmic principle, and Palestine to a country of cosmic labor. The redemption would not come through statesmen or prophets (referring to the respective positions of Herzl and Ahad

Ha-Am), but through men of the soil whose chthonian strength is greater than that of their intellect. Although Gordon's socialism, focusing in his "cult of labor," was liable to create a religious sect rather than a political faction, his associates and sympathizers soon proceeded to organize a party. They called it the *Ha-Poel ha-Sair* (The Young Worker), and issued a periodical under the same name. They gained in strength with the progress of Palestinian colonization. Combined with the Zeire Zion (Zionist Youth) in the Diaspora lands, this group organized at the Prague Conference of 1920 the so-called *Hitahdut,* which immediately became a significant factor in shaping Zionist policies throughout the world.

In comparison with these great ideological trends, "revisionism" represented, from the outset, a practical, much more than a theoretical, innovation. There have always existed within the Zionist ranks countless dissensions, arising from questions of political strategy or tactics. The sharp conflict over the problem of whether preference should be given to slow economic reconstruction of Palestine or to international political action, almost wrecked the party before the World War, and in 1921 caused the eventful exodus of the Brandeis group. Jabotinsky's agitation, beginning with the organization of the Jewish legion in 1915 and 1917 on the side of the Allies, differed in method but not in fundamental idea from official Zionism. Just as during the World War the official Zionist party saw fit and, indeed, was bound by circumstances, to observe strict neutrality between the belligerent camps, so it proceeded after the establishment of the Mandate to build Jewish Palestine in a circumspect, gradual way. Jabotinsky favored direct action on the side of the Allies, and later forceful action of a legion backed by England against the Arab majority. To call revisionism Jewish fascism, is in so far a misnomer as its program is not based mainly upon an ultimate corporative society. Occasionally, the leaders of the movement doubtless flirt with fascism, the totalitarian state, the elimination of class struggle by "state socialism," etc., but their main strength and unity comes from their opposition to the diplomatic methods employed by the Zionist Organization in regard to Great Britain and the Palestinian Arabs.

It is characteristic that the oldest faction to be fully organized within the organization was its religious wing, the *Mizrahi*. Facing the increasingly secular accentuation of Zionism by Herzl and Nordau, and still more by a few eastern secular nationalists, the orthodox Jews, Eastern European and American, felt that certain religious safeguards were necessary. In 1902, following the discussions on Jewish cultural problems at the Fifth Congress, in 1901, and the subsequent Minsk Conference of the Russian Zionists, a group of religious leaders headed by Rabbi Jacob Reines of Lida constituted itself a special wing within the party. From that time on, a large and influential body stood for the synthesis of Zionism and orthodox Judaism. Compromises were frequently necessary. In 1911 the decision of the Tenth Congress to interest itself in cultural activities led almost to a complete break with the Mizrahi. Dr. Feuchtwanger, the president of the Mizrahi, advocated secession from the organization, but was overruled by the majority and had to resign. Many minor crises have been weathered since, the Mizrahi point of view generally prevailing, however.

Apart from these major movements within Zionism, there were innumerable shades and nuances of opinion. For some, such as the renowned economist Franz Oppenheimer, the western Jews possess a consciousness of Jewish tribal allegiance, while they also have a German, English, or American national consciousness (cf. his "Stammesbewusstsein und Volksbewusstsein," *Die Welt*, XIV). For the celebrated American jurist, Louis D. Brandeis, the meaning of Zionism was to "protect America and ourselves from demoralization which had already to some extent set in among American Jews." Contrasting the exceptionally high general standard of morals among the Jews during the previous centuries of persecution, with the spread of racketeering and prostitution among the emancipated American Jews, he saw in Zionism the most efficacious means of moral regeneration. For some the Jewish nation was a biological fact, pure and simple. The Jews should abandon their excessive evaluation of the life of the spirit, and appreciate even excesses of physical strength. Following the popular misinterpretation of Nietzsche, Berditshevski, for example, glorified the crude but colorful men of Jewish history, and condoned even crime and vulgarity as long as they testified to the superabundance of vitality. For many others, the Jewish nationality had a primarily spiritual meaning. The very rejuvenation of the Jewish physique was to serve only spiritual regeneration.

With respect to practical problems, there were numerous differences of opinion. Ussishkin, "the strong man" in the upbuilding of Palestine, defied even a majority of Zionist opinion when he declared in an unguarded moment, that

this land must be given to us and the Arabs must find land elsewhere. We have higher ideals than that of safeguarding the interests of a hundred thousand fellaheen. [Quoted by H. Bergmann, in *MJ*, XIX, 48.]

In comparison with him, even Jabotinsky appeared moderate. Labor has consistently championed the rights of the Arab worker along with those of the Jewish. It has occasionally tried to organize united labor unions of both nationalities and generally encouraged class struggle in the Arab camp. It was led by Palestinian conditions, however, to advocate the exclusive employment of Jewish labor in Jewish enterprises and was often ready to sacrifice class interests to those of nationality. The *Brith Shalom* organization, on the other hand, long preached *rapprochement* with the Arabs to the extreme of self-denial. The Jews should, under all circumstances, come to terms with the Arabic population, forever abandon the idea of a Jewish majority in Palestine, and be satisfied with its vast future cultural opportunities.

Despite these wide differences of opinion, Zionism was elastic enough to retain its unity. The experiences of ages of religious history have taught the Jews to preserve unity, regardless of profound doctrinal divergences. The Basel program, itself the result of numerous compromises, was as open to differing interpretations as any religious scripture. Its ambiguity did not escape the attention of contemporaries. At the very first congress a delegate argued in vain that an authoritative interpretation should appear with it, while soon thereafter Ahad Ha-Am heaped ridicule on this "monument of diplomacy." But it was this very ambiguity which enabled the organization to weather innumerable dissensions and to adapt its actions to constantly changing requirements. Characteristically, it was Weizman, long a leader of the cultural

Zionists, who in 1917-20 achieved the greatest victory of political Zionism.[20]

RELIGIOUS OPPOSITION TO ZIONISM

Above all these deviations in principle and tactics towered one problem: the reciprocal relation of religion to nationalism and Zionism. For a time nationalism was entirely secular, and religionists of all shades were opposed to it. The majority of orthodox leaders saw in the political aspirations of Zionism, and even more in secular nationalism, a denial of their own messianic doctrine. Even though Kalischer, Guttmacher, Mohilever, and later the Mizrahi rabbis, invoked Nahmanides' emphasis upon the commandment of settling in Palestine (*misvat yishub Eres Israel*) as well as the traditional pilgrimages and settlement in Palestine of both the Hasidim and their opponents, the irreconcilables in eastern and western orthodoxy insisted that redemption must come only through a miraculous advent of the Messiah. Ever since its foundation in 1912, the Agudat Israel, the orthodox world organization, has consistently combated Zionist policies. Zionism became for it, in the words of Breuer, "the most formidable enemy that ever arose to the Jewish nation" (*Das Judenproblem,* 1919, p. 62). The Agudah's dissociation from Zionist work in Palestine, its frequent alliance with Arab nationalists against the Zionist executive, its numerous protests before the League of Nations and the Mandatory Power, have so embittered the relations between the two groups that in 1924 Jacob I. de Haan, one of its Palestinian leaders, fell a victim to an apparently political assassination. Indirectly, the Agudah is deeply indebted to Zionism. Its organization on a worldwide scale was itself a reaction, and as such an imitation, of the Zionist movement. The impact of Zionism was so irresistible, that the Agudah itself embarked upon colonizing ventures in Palestine. Ironically, it was from its inception frequently accused of secret Zionist leanings on the part of the still more adamantly orthodox, such as the hasidic rabbi of Belz.

The opposition of Reform to Zionism was at first equally sharp. Rumors that Napoleon III contemplated a Jewish restoration under the reign of one of the Paris Rothschilds provoked, for example, the characteristic retort of Isaac M. Wise, "The thing is so absurd that none can believe it; for it is evident that European and American Israelites would not emigrate to Palestine and there fight half-savage Arabs, Druses and Turks and wild beasts in order to have a king of their own, the vast majority of enlightened Hebrews being republicans in principle" (*American Israelite,* VII,66). Oscar S. Strauss, in assuring the Porte in 1888 that the Jews did not intend to establish a Jewish kingdom in Palestine, spoke primarily as the American envoy. He was, however, voicing a sentiment current among his coreligionists in American Reform. As late as 1909, Martin Philippson, the historian, mentioned among the reasons of western Jewry's rejection of Zionism that "they could not bear the idea of exchanging life within the order and comfort of modern civilization, for a life in a country wholly lacking in culture and disorganized through Turkish misrule, and where, moreover, they would have to live side by side with hundreds of thousands intellectually and spiritually backward coreligionists from Poland and Russia" (*Neueste Geschichte des jüdischen Volkes,* 2d ed., II,163). Even Felix Adler, who had left the Reform camp, saw in the repugnance of the various Jewish groups to one another and in the heterogeneity of elements a prospective "clashing of uncongenialities that would prophesy disaster rather than prosperity to the enterprise of constructing a new state—a miniature tower of Babel rather than a new Jerusalem" (*The Standard,* V,164). More penetrating were the objections of Geiger, Kohler, and especially Hermann Cohen. Geiger's summary dismissal of Hess's ideas as "new reactionary views of an old romantic," is typical. It was Geiger, too, who, in an unguarded moment, voiced resentment over the international negotiations during the Damascus affair, which might impair the chances of Prussian Jewry's emancipation. Cohen, the German patriot and pious Jew, saw in Zionism a danger to both his patriotism and religion. The modern Jew, he declared, feels at home in the various countries of the dispersion and wishes to become more deeply rooted in them. He denied the existence of specific native characteristics of the Jews. "I would much rather accept the idea of a Jewish skull than that of a specifically Jewish logic." The Hebrew language should be cultivated as the language of Jewish scholarship and prayer. But, as a medium of general intellectual pursuits, it would mean only self-imposed contraction of the intellectual horizon, and the betrayal of cultural consciousness. Most of all, Zionism conflicts with Judaism as a world religion. "He who, as a matter of principle, reserves the fundamental teachings of Judaism for the Jewish people, denies the One God of messianic humanity" (H. Cohen, *Jüdische Schriften,* I,319-40). The American reformers, in formulating a declaration of Reform principles at the Pittsburgh Conference of 1885, succinctly stated, "We consider ourselves no longer a nation, but a religious community, and therefore expect neither a return to Palestine . . . nor the restoration of any of the laws concerning the Jewish state" (quoted by D. Philipson, *Reform Movement,* p. 356).

The Reform opposition was, however, gradually overcome. From the beginnings of the western, Herzlian brand of Zionism, certain pro-Zionist tendencies made themselves felt in German as well as American Reform. Gustav Gottheil, Bernhard Felsenthal and Stephen S. Wise, all Reform rabbis, became very prominent Zionist leaders at an early date. Of course, the majority was still hostile. Their opposition came clearly to the fore at various round-table conferences and incidental discussions, called by the Central Conference of American rabbis. The conference held aloof, even in the midst of the general enthusiastic affirmation of the Zionist ideal in the years 1917-20. But already voices were heard among its influential members that

Israel is greater than Zionism, and Palestine more important than parties. Let us unite for the common good! [H. G. Enelow in his "Palestine and the Jews," 1918, in *Selected Works,* III, 311.]

The gradual infiltration of younger rabbis brought up on Zionist teachings, moreover, combined with the growing moderation of Zionist propaganda, brought about an increasing reconciliation. The organization of the Jewish Agency for Palestine, with the participation of prominent non-Zionists, laymen and rabbis, silenced most of the opposition, with the exception of a few irreconcilables. The Central Conference, meeting in Providence in 1930, decided to include the Zionist anthem *Hatikvah* in the Union Hymnal, for use in Reform services. In Germany Reform opposition was somewhat more tenacious. It lasted, in fact, although with diminishing fervor, until 1933, when Palestine turned out to be a haven of refuge for a large sector of German Jewry. Under these circumstances, the decision, in 1930, of the World Union for Progressive Judaism, "to exclude the discussion of Zionism," was a profession of weakness rather than of earnest opposition.[21]

INTERNATIONAL RECOGNITION

To clinch all this, came great international developments. Even in the nineteenth century all thoughtful observers realized that a restitution of the Jews to Palestine could take place only with international coöperation, or at least with the support of some one of the great powers. It was natural that the Jewish and non-Jewish nationals of the various countries should look for support to their respective governments. In 1845 Noah thought that the United States, as the only country which had never persecuted the Jews, was called to pave the way for their restoration to Zion. Langallerie and Napoleon, Joseph Salvador and Hess looked to France, age-old protector of Latin Christians in the Near East and pioneer in Jewish emancipation, as the main agency for such a restoration. Occasionally Germany, with her "drive to the East," her schemes concerning the Bagdad railway, and her alliance with Turkey during the War, was considered as a possible supporter of such a policy. Herzl himself opened spectacular negotiations with William II. During the Great War the Zionists of Germany obtained the official declaration of the German government (signed by von Kuehlmann, then secretary of state) in favor of a Jewish homeland in Palestine. Russia alone, notwithstanding her perennial enmity with Turkey, could not be counted on. Alexander I, to be sure, supported the memorial submitted by Louis Way at Aix-la-Chapelle in 1818. But from the days of Nicholas I until the Revolution of 1917, Russia appeared as the arch-enemy of the Jews in all national and international affairs.

It was Great Britain to which most eyes turned when such a program was under consideration. Great Britain's offer of Uganda in 1903 was merely a prelude for a much more momentous undertaking as soon as the opportunity arose. It had long been interested in the affairs of the eastern Mediterranean. But while Russia and France found natural allies in their Greek orthodox or Latin coreligionists, England had no Protestants in the Near East whose cause it might properly espouse. Especially after the construction of the Suez Canal, its main trade route to India could be safeguarded only by some sort of control of Egypt and Palestine. As far back as the 1840's, various British consular officers stationed in the East, pointed out to their government this correlation of British and Jewish interests. In 1876 the Earl of Shaftesbury greatly stressed the point, "It would be a blow to England if either of her rivals got hold of Syria . . . her empire . . . would be cut in two" (Sokolow's *History of Zionism*, Vol. II, Appendix LXXI). Out of this combination of political and religious interests, Great Britain could be expected to favor the erection of a Jewish home in Palestine, first in coöperation with her traditional protégé Turkey, later with her allies against Turkey in the World War. All the financial and colonizing corporations, such as the Jewish National Fund and the Jewish Colonial Trust, founded by the Zionist Organization in its early years, were incorporated in London and from the outset enjoyed the protection of the British diplomatic and consular representatives in the Ottoman Empire.

Attempts to obtain an international solution prior to the War never went beyond publicist agitation. Even the memorial of leading clergymen, journalists and business men of Chicago, Boston, New York, Philadelphia, Baltimore and Washington submitted by William E. Blackstone to President Benjamin Harrison of the United States on March 5, 1891, was merely a pious wish. Referring to the unbearable situation of the Jews in Russia, the petitioners urged the President to use his good offices with the czar, Queen Victoria, William II, the pope and other European powers "to secure the holding, at an early date, of an international conference to consider the condition of the Israelites and their claims to Palestine as their ancient home." The furthest America was ready to go in those years was to intervene, when in 1887-88 the Porte attempted to close the gates of Palestine to Jewish tourists and immigrants.

During the Great War this prolonged agitation yielded positive results. Under the leadership of Weizman, the Zionist Organization obtained from the British government the so-called Balfour Declaration of November 2, 1917. Weizman's personal merits as chemist-inventor in the British military service, combined with Lloyd George's warm interest in the welfare of the Jewish people, Balfour's personal memories of the Uganda offer, which had been made under his premiership, and General Smuts' active sponsorship of a Jewish homeland as part of the new order to be established under the aegis of a league of nations, were a happy concatenation of circumstances. Behind the accidental personal factors loomed powerful political forces. Selfish interests of the Allies, seeking to win over Jewish world opinion, united with the widespread idealistic expectation that the "war to end war" would bring about a permanent settlement of all national disputes to gain favor for the idea of establishing a Jewish national homeland. As attested by Lloyd George in his speech before the House of Commons on November 17, 1930, the Declaration "was truly national in the sense that it represented the views of the three parties in the State, and was issued for a reason which was regarded by the Allies as paramount to the great conflict then going on" (*Parliamentary Debates,* CCXLV, 76). After successful diplomatic representations by Sokolow and others, the main prospective opponents, France and the papacy, indorsed the Balfour Declaration. A few months later President Wilson not only gave his approval, but added the expression of his satisfaction "in the progress of the Zionist movement in the United States and the Allied countries since the Declaration of Mr. Balfour" (Letter to Wise, August 31, 1918, in J. de Haas's *New Palestine,* p. 9). The indorsements of Greece, Holland, Italy, Siam, China and Japan were speedily obtained. The socialist International and other bodies of public opinion rallied behind the proposal.

The heroic fight of the Jewish legions on the side of the Allies at Gallipoli in 1915 and in Palestine in 1917-18 enhanced the responsibility assumed by the Entente. In 1918, in particular, almost every able-bodied Palestinian Jew responded to Jabotinsky's call and enlisted in the Palestinian battalion of the Jewish legion. Two other battalions, recruited in the United States, Great Britain and Canada, raised the number of Jewish combatants on the Palestinian front to 4,000—a considerable number, indeed, in comparison with the 6,000 British and 4,000 Italian regulars participating in the expedition. The older, Sykes-Picot Treaty of May, 1916—which had, in a preliminary fashion, contemplated the erection of an international state in Palestine—and the corresponding promise to the Arabs were, perhaps somewhat too informally, discarded. After all, the Treaty of 1916, which was, unlike the Balfour Declaration, concluded in strict secrecy, bound only the contracting parties: Britain, France and czarist Russia, and could easily be altered by unanimous agreement. On the Arabic side, King Hussein, officially informed of the Balfour Declaration in January, 1918, "took it philosophically." Somewhat later Emir Feisal expressed his sympathy with the Zionist undertaking in a message to Felix Frankfurter (March 1, 1918) and, less directly, in a letter to Sir Herbert Samuel, written as late as December 10, 1919. It was only at a later date that the Arabs began voicing their grievances against this alleged betrayal by Great Britain. The ultimate outcome of all these moves and countermoves was the well-known resolution of the Conference of San Remo in 1920. It was followed in 1922 by the establishment, through the League of Nations, of the Palestine Mandate in the A category of mandates, amplifying the Balfour Declaration by numerous specific provisions in favor of a Jewish homeland (cf. especially Sections 2, 6 and 7). The United States concurred through a convention with Great Britain, signed December 3, 1924.

From that time on, the upbuilding of the Jewish national home has made steady progress. To be sure, the Mandate's simultaneous second goal, "the development of self-governing institutions" in Palestine, inherently conflicted with the first, since a self-governing hostile majority of Arabs could issue regulations preventing Jewish immigration, and otherwise obstruct the realization of a Jewish homeland. This contradiction was clearly recognized by the Permanent Mandates Commission of the League of Nations, in its discussion on the first report of the Palestine Administration in 1924, in which it urged the Mandatory Power to hold the balance between the conflicting interests. As early as 1922, the White Paper issued by the Colonial Office (under Churchill) laid down a middle course. On the one hand, it expressly rejected "the imposition of a Jewish nationality upon the inhabitants of Palestine as a whole" and, on the other, it asserted that the Jewish people "is in Palestine as of right and not on sufferance." The Order in Council of the same year having, according to the Foreign Jurisdiction Act of 1811, the validity of an act of Parliament, established a compromise constitution for Palestine. In 1923, it had to be amended by another Order in Council, since the Arabs definitely declined to participate in the elections to the projected legislative council, in which government appointees were to maintain equilibrium. By 1934 the situation was so profoundly changed that the staunchest opposition to the establishment of the council has come from the Jews. Recurrent attempts to obtain some compromise on the question of the legislature have thus far failed.

In October, 1930, as a result of the riots of 1929 and subsequent inquiries by a British commission, the Colonial Office (under Lord Passfield) issued another White Paper. This was instantly denounced, even by neutral observers, as little short of an abandonment of the Balfour Declaration and a violation of the Mandate. Under the impact of widespread Jewish and non-Jewish protests, Prime Minister Ramsay MacDonald addressed on February 13, 1931, a letter to Dr. Weizman, which was to serve as an "authoritative interpretation of the White Paper"; he reaffirmed here the Balfour Declaration and the provisions of the Mandate. The equivocal position of the Mandatory Power at this critical juncture was officially censured by the Mandates Commission of the League. Since that time the British administration of Palestine has pursued a policy of greater impartiality. It reiterated its unflinching adherence to the terms of the Mandate, in the face of bloody demonstrations of the Palestinian Arabs in November, 1933, and the far more serious uprising of 1936, even though it made them a significant concession by ruthlessly deporting numerous Jewish tourists who had overstayed their term. It has also, through a much too conservative estimate of the "economic absorptive capacity" of the country, tried to stem the tide of Jewish immigration which had gathered great momentum in 1933-36.[22]

PALESTINE'S RECONSTRUCTION

The Jewish settlement in Palestine has in the meantime taken firm root. Jewish agricultural colonization, in particular, has become the backbone of the entire *Yishub* (settlement), culturally as well as economically. The initial difficulties were enormous. During the centuries of Arabic and Turkish rule, extensive deforestation had removed natural barriers against desert winds. The black soil was washed down from most of the once-flourishing hill slopes, and the country as a whole presented a barren appearance. The maladministration of Turkish officialdom, the lack of agriculturally trained Jews and their difficulties in adjusting themselves to a new climate and to unhygienic conditions in a country infested with malaria and trachoma, seemed almost insuperable obstacles. Nevertheless, the enthusiasm of the early settlers and the financial support of Baron Edmond de Rothschild, who invested some 50,000,000 francs in the enterprise, overcame these difficulties. The early period, ending in 1899, called by Ruppin the "patriarchal" period of Jewish colonization, led to the establishment of 25 Jewish colonies with some 4,500 inhabitants, engaged chiefly in the cultivation of vineyards. The shortcomings of pure philanthropy, however, the dependence of the colonists upon the support of the "Baron," and the corruption of the officials, became ever more obvious. Rothschild, therefore, transferred his Palestinian holdings to the Jewish Colonization Association, which had by that time a few years of colonizing experience in other countries. Between 1900 and 1907, in the period of the "philanthropic" colonization under the guidance of the ICA, and especially between 1908 and 1914, when the Zionist World Organization devoted its main attention to the practical work in the country, the colonies made great progress. The ICA's Palestinian branch, reorganized after the War as a special subsidiary, the Palestine Jewish Colonization Association (PICA), and the Zionistic Palestine Land Development Company (PLDD) planned more scientifically, adding grain growing and orange plantations to the grape industry. By 1913 the colonies had increased to 43 in number, with 11,600 inhabitants. During the sad interlude of the World War, the Turkish governor, Djemal Pasha, disregarding the intercessions of neutral governments, such as the United States in 1915, of Turkey's German-Austrian allies, and even of the sultan himself, suppressed all Zionist activities as treasonable. Under the British Mandate, however, the country began to recuperate speedily. Palestinian agriculture rapidly expanded under the impact of Jewish immigration and the investment of considerable PICA and Zionist funds, public as well as private.

The Jewish agricultural population, which by 1918 had decreased to some 7,000, amounted to some 40,000 in 1931, distributed in 145 colonies. By the end of 1935, 90,000 Jews lived in 175 rural settlements. The orange plantations, which as late as 1924 covered only 2,500 acres, increased sevenfold in the subsequent seven years. The recent annual exportation of oranges from Jewish groves has been in excess of 3,000,000 cases in 1933, of 4,000,000 in 1934, and of 7,500,000 in 1935. It has been estimated that the plantations already under cultivation should yield by 1939 an export surplus of 12,500,000 cases. Although the government assigned the Jews a very small share in the distribution of state-owned lands, Jewish landownership amounted in 1935 to more than 300,000 acres, or about 5 percent of the land, and 10 percent of the cultivable area of Palestine. Two-thirds are under the control of the PICA and the Jewish National Fund. The JNF has pursued the radical and generally effective policy of retaining perpetual title and granting long-term leaseholds over plots cultivable by a farmer and his family without hired aid. The Jewish colonies fall into three major categories: the *moshavah,* consisting of private landowners; the *moshav ovedim,* combining private ownership of produce with coöperative marketing, sanitation, etc.; and the *kvusah,* a strictly collectivistic settlement. During the last two or three years, Palestinian Jewish agriculture has grown by leaps and bounds, and especially large areas have been put under cultivation of citrous fruits.

Industry and commerce have likewise made rapid progress. The Anglo-Palestine Bank, for example, the leading Jewish bank, with head offices in London, had, as far back as 1930, a paid-up capital of over £300,000 and deposits totaling £1,865,000. The figures for Palestine's foreign trade tell the same story. In 1913 it amounted to 1,616,000 Egyptian pounds in imports, and £E1,093,000 in exports. This grew to £P7,924,000 and £P2,625,000 respectively, in 1932; to £P11,269,000 and 2,911,000, in 1933; £P15,426,000 and 3,502,000 in 1934; and to £P18,375,000 and 4,516,000 in 1935 (cf. *Palästina,* xix, 207). The unfavorable balance is evidently the result of the importation of capital goods and other prerequisites of a country's speedy upbuilding. Nevertheless, it has been estimated that even in 1934 Palestine herself could have produced some £P2,250,000 to £P2,500,000 worth of goods which she imported from abroad. The newly opened harbor of Haifa "can accommodate five times as much shipping as Beirut and nearly as much as Marseilles." It promises to become "the chief westward-looking port of the Near East for 46,-000,000 people." Industries of all kinds have been introduced by the Jews and are growing with increasing speed. In 1929 there existed 2,475 Jewish industrial enterprises, with 10,968 employees and working employers. In 1933 the figures were: 3,132 enterprises and 16,870 persons. In 1935 over 4,000 enterprises, employing more than 25,000 workers, produced £P6,500,000 worth of industrial goods. The consumption of electric current supplied by the Ruthenberg Company rose during 1933 alone by 60 percent. The first Palestinian steamship, "Tel-Aviv," employed 103 Jews in a crew of 130, at the end of the first year of operation (1935). No wonder government finances have been in excellent shape. Even after Palestine paid in full a proportionate share in the old Ottoman debt (no other succession state of Turkey did so) and paid £P1,500,000 to the British government as compensation for the Turkish railways and to cover the deficits of the early military administration, the public debt consisted in 1935 of a comparatively small loan of £P4,475,000, due in 1942-67. By the end of 1930 the government possessed an accumulated surplus of £P626,111. Since that time the revenue has increased further. In the fiscal year 1932-33, the excess of receipts over expenditures amounted to £P1,200,000; in 1933-34, to £P2,800,000. The treasury accumulations at the beginning of 1936 exceeded £P6,000,000, equivalent to a year's budgetary expenditure. To the grievance of the natives, these funds are invested in London, rather than in productive long-term undertakings in the country. This revenue comes chiefly from Jewish sources, which have paid some 40-50 percent of the total taxation. In 1931-35, the country thus presented the spectacle, so unusual during the world-wide depression, of a treasury surplus, an acute shortage of labor and a general rise of prices.

This prosperity was, of course, incidental to the large Jewish immigration. According to the census of 1931, the Jewish population of 175,000 constituted about 18 percent of the inhabitants. At the beginning of 1936, it has reached approximately 360,000, or nearly 30 percent of the population. The official estimates of 61,541 immigrants in 1935 are the highest on record. The let-up of both immigration and employment during the winter months of 1935-36, largely due to the war scare in the Mediterranean, has all the earmarks of a merely temporary retardation. Tel-Aviv, founded in 1909 and numbering ten years later no more than 3,600 inhabitants, now has over 135,000 Jewish residents. It has already surpassed the ancient metropolis in size. Led by the young pioneers, the Halutsim, many middle-class entrepreneurs have settled in the country. They brought with them the increasing pace of production and higher standards of life, but at the same time also all the vices of ruthless competition and speculation, so characteristic of our modern individualistic civilization. In short, Zionism, still a utopian dream at the beginning of this century, has become a hard and fast reality, with many of the imperfections of all human achievement, but also containing a definite promise of inaugurating a new era in Jewish history.[23]

ZIONISM'S PLACE IN JEWISH HISTORY

Behind all these diverse theories and practical accomplishments, mighty social forces were vibrating. The tremendous increase of the Jewish population and the settlement of the Jewish masses in the principal countries and cities of the world, lent to the Jewish problem an international import, which received general recognition during the World War. For a time at least the people won international victories, under the leadership of American and British Jewry. Mass entrance into western culture opened new avenues to both assimilation—with its recurrent frustrations—and reaffirmations of Jewish cultural values. The size and distribution of the people, its economic stratification, varying from land to land, were conducive to lack of unity and the development of multitudinous variations of opinion and attitude. The constant necessity of migration, on the other hand, and the relentless urge to economic diversification, helped shape rationalizations connected with one sort of national reconstruction or another. Under these circumstances, nationalism easily became the dominant factor in Jewish life, sometimes combined with religion, sometimes replacing it, itself becoming a new religion. As throughout Europe, nineteenth-century Jewish nationalism really constituted a great religious movement, with the fervor and spiritual elevation as well as the fanaticism and vagaries of any new creed.

Zionism has thus become one of the most significant movements in the history of Jewish society and religion; the most important, indeed, in many centuries. Hasidism has deeply affected Jewish life in eastern Europe and to some extent in Palestine, but its influence in other countries, notwithstanding the steady immigration of Eastern Europeans, has been of small consequence. The enlightenment also had geographical limitations. It suffered further from the lack of simultaneity, as it had become a matter of the past in Prussia before it reached Galicia. Neither did the Reform movement extend beyond the boundaries of a few countries. Both Enlightenment and Reform, moreover, failed to reach the masses to any considerable extent. Zionism, on the other hand, became a mass movement within a few years, spreading out to Yemen and Bokhara as well as to the most distant towns of Argentina and Australia. There are today forty-six provincial branch organizations and twenty-one smaller groups, covering every important country, with the exception of the Soviet Union and Turkey. Wherever Jews live, they have felt the impact of this new force, and have had to declare themselves for or against it. Zionism has also attracted the attention and finally won the recognition of the world at large far more than could these other, more internal, movements. Its compass, too, has been much larger, as it was intended to revolutionize the ideas and actions, and to transform the most inveterate habits, of every individual Jew.

But was this revolutionary movement not too sharp a break with all the previous history of the Jews? Were not the new emphases upon secular nationalism, upon state and territory, upon the return to nature and life on the soil, essentially contradictory to the main tendencies and achievements of preceding millennia of history, social as well as religious? It may be too early to give definite answers, but, as far as can be ascertained from the short historical perspective, it would seem that the stream of Jewish history has not been diverted into new channels. Perhaps it will eventually be found that its flow has been quickened and its bed widened.

Like traditional Judaism, Zionism was from the outset more practical than theoretical. Externally the constitution of the World Zionist Organization specified the admission of every Jew who was willing to *do* something, namely to pay the Shekel—a symbolic act, even more than a financial contribution. Of far greater significance was the fact that no questions were asked concerning one's *Weltanschauung*. The movement displayed a forbearance of opposing views and internal factions to a degree unparalleled by the other nationalistic currents of the day. Recently, as a consequence of the assassination of Arlosoroff, its brilliant young leader, the Poale Zion proposed the exclusion of the Revisionist Party. The Eighteenth Congress, however, refused to budge from the traditional policy of toleration. Although such exclusion has since been largely achieved by a technicality (the requirement of a declaration of loyalty on the part of each Shekel payer), this bears all the earmarks of a temporary solution, designed to appease excited passions. This largess might indicate weakness, were it not integral to the optimistic patience on an ancient people, which has learned to tolerate a multiplicity of opinions, confident that unity will be restored in time of crisis. There can be no more consummate contrast than the multitude of intramural divisions within Zionist labor ranks, on the one hand, and the unanimous reaction of the Jewish people (excepting a few peripheral groups) against the Palestine riots of 1929 and the White Paper of 1930!

Again there lies a world of difference between the state and territory as an actuality, and the state and territory as an idea or an ideal. We have mentioned that at no time were Palestine and the Temple exalted more than during the Babylonian Exile, when both were lacking. Perhaps in the final culmination of this movement, state and territory will again become "nature" and as such a danger to the "historical" aims of Judaism. But granted this possibility, it must obviously take a long time before Palestine becomes "as Jewish as England is English." Furthermore, no matter how successful the Zionist movement may be, only a minority of the Jewish people can find room to live in Palestine, even including Transjordan, and only a minority would contemplate leaving their present abode. At most, the Zionists may hope to duplicate the situation found toward the end of the Second Commonwealth. The grandiloquent exclamation of Herzl at the first Congress of Basel is certainly not the prevailing sentiment of the people, "There can be no contemplation of a complete exodus of the Jews from anywhere; those who wish assimilation and can achieve it may remain behind and become absorbed." The state and territory as a goal are therefore driving historical forces, rather than obstacles in the historic procession. Again, as in the time of Moses and of the Babylonian Exile, world Jewry must try to evolve a system of Judaism, applicable simultaneously to Palestine and to the Diaspora, and consequently reaching out beyond both.

The peculiar circumstances of present-day Jewry make the Zionist solution appear anything but "natural." Economically the Jewish people, in order to become "normal," must leave the towns and settle in villages, must give up commercial occupations and devote themselves to agriculture, at a time when the trends throughout the world are in precisely the opposite direction. The emigration to an old Mediterranean country, the erection of a small homeland in a period favoring larger and larger political combinations, the revival of a spoken tongue unused for centuries, are all artificial solutions for a perennial, artificial problem. As the Jewish religion in previous ages, so now Zionism was compelled perversely to direct Jewish life counter to the tidal waves of the age. But it was just such guidance by an idea to which Hegel referred when he spoke of history "standing, as it should stand, on its head." Once again the Jewish head was to support the whole body.

In this sense, there can be no vital conflict between Zionism and the Jewish religion. Secular nationalism laid stress on one essential component of the Jewish religion, just as early Reform had stressed exclusively the other. Abetted by the agnostic tendencies in western life, this extreme national movement could claim to be the rightful heir of religious Judaism, which was declared to be an earlier stage, now surmounted. Reform, justified by the first flush of emancipation, claimed that nationality was the earlier stage, now overcome. But nationalism was less hostile to religion than Reform had been to nationality. Not only did it purport to embrace all Jews, including the religious, but, congruent with the conditions of the age, it recognized religion as merely a private affair of the individual. The antireligious propaganda of the Russian Jewish communists is the outgrowth of general conditions in Russia, rather than a necessary corollary of Jewish national sentiment. For the rest, the secular nationalists of the left wings often eschewed religion as an element of nationality, but even they left it to the individual Jew to work the problem out for himself. In fact, the religious ingredients in Jewish nationalism have made themselves felt even more than the modicum of nationalism in the concept of the Jewish *people* adhered to by Reform. Under these circumstances the pronunciamento of Herzl, "Zionism is the homecoming to Judaism, before the return to the Jewish land," had a subtle religious connotation beyond his ken.

Thus Zionism and nationalism became another landmark in the historic progress of both Jews and Judaism. Whither? Even for the most secular Jewish nationalist, the answer given is not a matter of knowledge, but of faith.

EPILOGUE

HAVING noted the millennial flow of the broad streams of religious and social history, constantly intermingling in one living totality, from time to time separating to produce fateful discord, only to reunite in a new harmony, we might conveniently terminate our investigation at this point. Today discord appears most intense, and a new harmony far from discernible. From the vantage point of past experience, however, it may be possible not only to evaluate the present, but also to sketch rough outlines of the future. This epilogue will strive to do both within brief compass, and to discuss present actualities and future probabilities, as they appear to the present author.

The task has been approached with great diffidence, because of the realization that, leaving the firm ground of historical fact, ascertainable for the most part by objective methods of scholarly investigation, we enter a realm where partisan bias necessarily colors the analyses and prognoses of all who, by virtue of their position in the midst of the battle, are in some ways best able to furnish authentic data. This epilogue cannot hope altogether to escape the tinge of personal conviction.

The first section of this chapter, devoted to an analysis of the critical aspects of contemporary Judaism, permits an approximation of scientific objectivity. In subsequent suggestions for remedial counteraction, however, the author's personal opinions and attitudes must needs come to the fore, clearly and unequivocally. The sympathetic reader, even he who disagrees with most of these conclusions, will recognize the legitimacy of their underlying motivations, which, in the profoundest sense, present no contradiction: a quest for truth, and an interest in the preservation of the Jew for the common benefit of himself and all mankind.[1]

The Jewish people are passing through one of the greatest

of their historical crises. Not the upheavals of early modern times, nor the rise of Islam, nor, perhaps, even the simultaneous loss of national independence and the maturing of the great daughter religion in the first century, were fraught with more dangers for Jewish survival than are contemporary developments. One must go back perhaps to the First Exile to find a situation equally threatening. The fact that Jews and Judaism have so long survived against tremendous odds may help to reassure the present generation. Their vitality and persistence over more than three millennia have rooted them in the life of this globe with ever deeper permanence. Nevertheless, there has been heard for decades the unceasing question: will the Jews survive? That the question is most frequently heard on Jewish lips need not be in itself a sign of weakness, but it reveals the instinctive realization of increasingly large sections of Jewry that the day of nonreflective persistence along the path of well-established folk life has passed, and that a new rationale is needed for the approaching decisive struggle for existence. There are perhaps more fundamentalist Christians today, than Jews who are satisfied with the supernatural guarantees that Israel will last until the end of days. Nor are many Jews contented with an agnosticism which proclaims that the ways of history are altogether inscrutable, and that the Jews will probably manage to go on living somehow. Rejecting the passivity of fatalistic answers, most thoughtful Jews seek new, rational vistas into the future. Above all, they seek to know their rôle in the events which are to shape the destinies of their people.

BIOLOGICAL DANGERS

Among the many danger signs today, the biological is the most conspicuous. The great fecundity, which, together with the decreasing mortality rate, accounted for the astounding growth of Jewish population in the last three centuries, has been steadily declining during recent years. In many Western European communities, consisting largely of wealthy and thoroughly assimilated Jews, the birth rate has fallen below the level of reproduction. In Prussia, for example, there has been an almost uninterrupted natural diminution since 1905, compensated for solely by immigration. In 1911-24, when the general population showed a natural increase of 3,019,100, the Prussian Jews had 18,252 more deaths than births. In 1925-28 the remarkably favorable balance of 1,182,056 in the general population, contrasted sharply with the loss of 5,090 among Jews. Commenting on these figures, H. Silbergleit rightly remarks that "this is no longer a crisis, this is a complete internal breakdown in the development of Jewish population" (*Die Bevölkerungs-und Berufsverhältnisse der Juden im deutschen Reich*, I, 38*). In Vienna, where most of the 250,000 Austrian Jews reside, 2,744 Jews were born and 2,866 died in 1920, while in 1929 natality (1,343) lagged behind mortality (2,709) by more than 50 percent. This unfavorable balance of 1,366 was surpassed in Budapest, where it rose from 1,319 in 1931 to 1,588 in 1932. The two central European capitals have thus been losing from two-thirds to three-quarters of one percent annually, an unusually high ratio even for metropolitan areas today.

In eastern Europe, too, at least in the larger towns, the increase of the Jewish population has for years trailed behind that of Christians. In Warsaw, for example, in 1925-29, the Jewish population grew annually at the rate of only 4.4 for every 1,000 inhabitants (15.5 births against 11.1 deaths), while the Christian group showed an increase of 7.0 (22.4:15.4). In 1932 the general rate of increase of 13.7 for all Poland contrasted with a Jewish rate of 8.3 per thousand. In Rumania the Jewish rate in 1927 was 5.4, the general rate 12.3. Soviet Russia, which still shows astounding regenerative power, had a general increase of 23.3 per thousand in 1926, and a Jewish increase of only 14.97. In particular, the birth rate, which in the preceding three decades had diminished from 50.2 to 43.3 for every 1,000 of general population, dropped in the case of the Jews from 35.9 to 24.6, the lowest rate of all major ethnic groups in the Soviet Union.

Almost everywhere in western Europe natality gradually falls behind mortality, which, for many preceding decades, had shown an even greater decrease. Prussian Jewry, for example, with its mortality of 14.1 in 1928, and 15.4 in 1929, could not expect substantially to reduce the figure, although it has been in many countries as low as 8 or 9—9.1 among the Jews of the Soviet Union in 1926—and varied among the

Prussian Christians in 1926-29 between 11.7 and 12.9 per thousand. The protracted decline of the birth rate over a long period has swelled the ranks of the old and middle-aged, who naturally show a greater mortality than the younger groups. Of recent years Berlin Jewry has not only included numerous bachelors and unmarried women, but 40 percent of all Jewish marriages have been altogether childless, while the remaining couples frequently practiced a one-child system. In eastern Europe, too, the number both of marriages and children per family has been steadily declining. Quite apart from conscious birth control, the average marrying age of Jews has been so greatly advanced, under economic pressure, that traditional fecundity has sharply diminished. Even in Poland the number of youthful persons entering matrimony has shown a consistent retrogression. This is true not only in comparison with Jewish conditions in previous generations, but also with those among contemporary Christians. In Warsaw, for example, in 1925 only one-fifth of newly married male Jews were less than twenty-five years old, while the corresponding figure for non-Jews was nearly twice as high. In Budapest the respective figures were 15.5 per hundred for Jews, 42.4 for non-Jews.

The increase of mixed marriages has likewise long been a threatening symptom. To be sure, Trieste, where the number of mixed marriages in 1927 exceeded that of purely Jewish marriages, is an exception. In Germany, Austria, Hungary and the interior of Soviet Russia, however, in recent years between 10 and 22 of every 100 Jews married outside the fold. Unfortunately, no conclusive figures are available for other important countries, but there is little doubt that they, too, would show a slow upward trend in this category. That mixed marriages are detrimental not only to racial cohesiveness but also to the Jewish religion, is common knowledge. Occasionally, a Christian wife adopts Judaism for the sake of uniformity and greater family harmony. In the majority of cases (in Europe even more than in America), however, mixed marriages result in the abandonment of the Jewish creed by the Jewish partner. Even where an actual change in religious allegiance fails to materialize, mixed marriages are seldom prolific, and their offspring for the most part join a non-Jewish creed or at least become professed agnostics.

It is mainly for this reason that even Reform Judaism, its missionary ideals notwithstanding, combats intermarriage.

Suicide has likewise become a factor of biological significance in Jewish life. Effectively checked by rabbinic law for centuries, it has in recent years, with the weakening of religious sanctions, the nerve-racking complexity of modern life and economic instability, spread widely in many a Jewish community. In Berlin, in 1925, there were 13 suicides among 1,000 deceased Catholics, 27 among Protestants, and 53 among Jews. In the very citadel of orthodoxy, Poland, the suicidal wave has assumed dangerous proportions since 1928. There were, in 1928, days in which several Jewish suicides were recorded in the city of Warsaw alone, and that year's toll amounted to 891, or the staggering ratio of approximately 280 suicides to every 100,000 inhabitants. Throughout Poland the proportion of Jewish suicides, less than one-half the general figure in the prewar period, has in the cities become about twice as large.

In short, the Jews who, in the period of western expansion, led the world in numerical increase, now, in the period of general recession, show a more retarded growth than does any other people. Even France, so long stagnant, still shows 17 births annually for every 1,000 in population, but many a western Jewish community has only 10 or less.

Should these processes continue for another four or five decades, world Jewish population would become stationary. Even those eugenists who refuse to regard such an event as a misfortune in itself, deplore the concomitant result that the persons in the higher would speedily outnumber those in the lower age groups. This ancient people, hitherto steadily rejuvenated through the prevalent share of youth in every generation, has increasingly become old in the biological sense. In the long run, birth control would be unnecessary, since the high average age of the population would automatically check undue expansion. In 1930 Silbergleit, discussing Prussian conditions, predicted that in 1940 there were likely to be 24 percent fewer Jewish women of fifteen to forty years of age than there were in 1925. Should such a situation prevail throughout the Jewish world, there would not remain enough "mothers in Israel" to produce a numerical aggrandizement of the people, even if the situation were again to demand it.

These biological deficiencies, common in all western nations, are perhaps the most dangerous single factor threatening the survival of western and Jewish culture.

There remains not even the melancholy satisfaction that, with a stagnant population, the Jews would need no further outlets for emigration. The German experience, in particular, has taught that a relative decrease by no means remedies the anomalous position of the Jews. In Poland the existence of three million Jews, economically maldistributed, will remain a serious source of disturbance, even should the prolific Polish race go on reducing their proportionate strength. As to the major countries of immigration, the present stoppage has all the indications of permanency. Canada, South Africa, Australia, etc., to be sure, still possess vast open spaces which could be populated in the near future. With nationalism rampant, however, they are not likely to facilitate Jewish mass immigration. The only regions which still hold out great promise for Jewish settlement are western Asia, the Soviet Union and South America. Not only Palestine, but the adjoining territories of Transjordan, Syria, Iraq and Northern Arabia would greatly gain by an influx of Jews. For the time being, however, animosities aroused by Zionist undertakings serve as a deterrent. The Soviet Union, too, although severely discouraging emigration, has thus far refused to open her frontiers to any mass immigration. Technical "experts" (including some Jews) have been invited from abroad, and a few skilled artisans have been admitted, but the numbers involved are negligible. Even the much-heralded autonomous Jewish settlement in Birobidjan, which undoubtedly offers vast possibilities for the future, was not originally intended to attract more than an insignificant fraction of foreign Jews. Only recently did the Russian government, partly in answer to Japanese imperialist advances, declare its readiness to transplant thousands of German and Polish emigrants to the shores of the Amur. In May, 1935, it decreed that 4,500 picked settlers be admitted in the near future. Precisely these strategic considerations, however, militate against the influx of a mass of peace-loving *émigrés*. Even patriotic Russian Jewry sent but 7,700 colonists in 1928-32. These arrivals found living conditions so discouraging that more than 40 percent have left Birobidjan for more promising parts. All in all, the Jewish population of that "autonomous region," with its 28,000 square miles, has not yet reached 20,000 in a total of 60,000 inhabitants. It will take a few years before the required minimum of 50,000 Jewish settlers will enable the Soviet government to proclaim the promised "Jewish republic."

The pressure of Jewish metropolitanization shows no sign of abating. No organized attempt is being made to distribute the agglomerated Jewish masses of New York and other metropolitan centers over larger areas. After the collapse of Israel Zangwill's futile "dispersion committee," Jewish organizations have refrained from sponsoring similar projects. At the same time, many thoughtful Jews and non-Jews have pointed out the economic, social and intellectual dangers of concentration. Even its advocates on political grounds, who saw in the accumulation of Jewish voters in one or another district a safeguard for their equality of rights, have recently been shaken in their belief in the efficacy of parliamentary elections to secure the permanence of emancipation.

ECONOMIC CRISIS

The Jewish economic crisis is no less acute than the biological. Quite apart from the recent world-wide depression, which, because of the more exposed position of the Jews, has hit them especially severely, Jewish economic stratification has long been the subject of great concern. During the twentieth century, to be sure, there was not a little economic readjustment. A sizable group, by concerted voluntary action, returned to the soil, so that one in every twenty-five Jews now derives his livelihood from agriculture. Never before in modern times had this happened, but even now few of the 700,000 Jewish farmers may be classified as peasants in the full sense of the word. In America, especially, they devote themselves almost exclusively to dairy and truck farming, essentially semi-urban occupations. Even though, on the whole, the trend seems to foreshadow increased typicalness of suburban farming, the present status is still far from satisfactory.

Moreover, the agricultural problem, although ideologically and biologically of great importance, is not central to Jewish economics. True, we are now witnessing the revival of a sort of physiocratic school in many countries. The militarist and fascist régimes of Mussolini and Hitler, especially, lay increasing stress upon the farming population as the nation's backbone. As an independent survival of the physiocratic orientation, which had influenced the early struggle for emancipation, Jewish leaders today likewise emphasize agriculture as the main factor in Jewish economic regeneration. Judged on purely economic grounds, however, the national destiny during the next century or two will be determined much more decisively by developments in the industrial and commercial fields.

It is precisely in these two domains that we find many disquieting phenomena. Outside the Soviet Union and Palestine, one can hardly find a full-fledged Jewish industrial proletariat, except perhaps by somewhat stretching this term to include the masses of workers in the Lodz textile industry, the Galician and Rumanian oil fields, and the American needle trades. Whether the reason be Jewish individualism, supposed physical disqualification, or the force of tradition, it is evident that only in the atypical conditions of the communist upheaval in the Soviet Union, and in Palestine where Haluts enthusiasm knew no obstacles, have the Jews succeeded during the last decade or two in becoming factory and railway workers, road builders and even miners. On the other hand, the large artisan class, like that of all other nations, has constantly lost ground to mechanized large-scale industry. Even in the American needle trades, the Jewish rôle, formerly overwhelming, has declined steadily during the last decade.

In the International Ladies Garment Workers Union [said B. C. Vladeck in 1934], which numbers at present nearly 200,000 members, less than 40% are Jewish. . . . In the men's clothing industry the percentage of Jews is even lower, my last estimate . . . being around 15%. [*JSSQ*, XI, 15.]

Commerce, still the most important occupation of the Jews, likewise shows the effects of increasing concentration and formation of trusts. Large corporations with numerous stockholders and employees and small boards of directors, and various combines among them, increasingly replace independent shopkeepers and money lenders. Even where, as in central Europe, the Jews still hold prominent positions in the directorates of such corporations, their share among the employees is constantly diminishing. Whether it be due to political pressure, as in Nazi Germany today, or to a policy of discrimination on the part of the preponderantly Christian directors, or to the imagined or real decreased proclivity of Jews for the disciplined and organized routine work of minor employees, it is clear that, with the gradual elimination of the petty trader, the Jewish merchant class has been gravely imperiled. In the United States and England, the Jews have but a small share in the directorates of the large banking, industrial, and mercantile corporations, and they figure still less prominently on the pay rolls of minor employees.

Big business is not impersonal [rightly comments S. Pearlman on the American situation]. When business becomes consolidated in large units and big corporations, they develop an employment policy. Their leadership is always democratic. Economic organization is plebeian in character and has to be. [*JSSQ*, X, 18.]

Because of this plebeian character, it is naturally open to all popular prejudices and pursues a more rigid policy of racial and religious discrimination than is justified by its own economic interest.

These factors are of a more or less permanent nature, and the depression has merely accelerated the pace of an inherently unfavorable evolution. It has also considerably weakened the remedial measures. The credit coöperatives, for example, established throughout eastern and central Europe for the purpose of helping the small shopkeeper and artisan, and supported by the Joint Distribution Committee, the ICA, etc., had to curtail or even suspend activities. Of the 775 institutions still operating on January 1, 1933, 81 suspended all activities in the subsequent nine months.

The influx of Jewish youth into the liberal professions has assumed threatening proportions. Notwithstanding the rigid discrimination practiced at numerous universities, and especially medical schools, in Europe and America, the number of Jewish lawyers, physicians, etc., has been steadily increasing. Excluded from their home universities, many Jewish students have found refuge in more liberal schools of higher learning abroad. American students meet many of their coreligionists from Poland and Rumania, from Germany and Hungary, at the Sorbonne or the University of Aberdeen. Mussolini in the early years of fascism magnanimously invited all students, who had been refused admission at home on national and religious grounds, to the universities of Italy, where they were exempted from the customary tuition fees. The celebrated University of Padua, although situated in a town which harbors only some 700 Jews, has had in recent years a large Jewish enrollment. Liberal Czechoslovakia, having a Jewish population of 400,000, has recently admitted some 3,000 Czechoslovakian Jews and more than 2,000 foreign Jews to her schools of higher learning. Proportionately the native Jews, although only 2.72 percent of the total population, have supplied almost 9 percent of the student body, and, together with the foreign Jews, fully 15 percent. Notwithstanding numerous difficulties, legal and extralegal, many Jewish students, having obtained a diploma from a foreign university, succeed in establishing themselves in their chosen profession in their native land. As a result, even in eastern Europe, despite orthodox inhibitions, the number of Jews in the professions has grown disproportionately. In Poland, for example, in 1926-27, Jews, while only one-tenth of the population, constituted one-third of the medical profession. In the provinces, Lodz, Tarnopol and Stanislawow, their share rose to 55, 65, and 76 percent, respectively.

This top-heavy economic structure has often been deplored as the gravest danger to Jewish survival. The difficulties are further aggravated by increasingly antagonistic governmental policies. The more mankind seems to veer away from individualistic to planned economy, the greater becomes the government's share in the distribution of economic services and rewards. Were there no political discrimination, the Jews might hope to obtain a very large part of such governmental appointments. Being a highly urbanized, intellectually alert and generally well-educated group, they place on the market a disproportionate number of qualified candidates. Indeed, in the Soviet Union, where no discrimination is practiced, they constituted in 1926 fully one-twelfth of Russian officialdom. Even there, however, with the rising level of education and progressive urbanization, the availability of non-Jewish civil servants steadily increases, entailing a gradual decline of the

Jewish share. In the United States the recent more active participation of the Jews in public affairs has aroused exaggerated suspicions concerning the number of Jewish officials. The conspicuous positions occupied by the Secretary of the Treasury, three governors and two Supreme Court justices must not blind us to the fact that in the lower ranks the Jewish share is much smaller. Were statistics available, they would probably show that the total share of the Jews among the federal, state and municipal employees is less than 4 percent. Commenting on the problem of the Jew as a teacher, a careful observer remarks,

> There are some jobs which are appointive and some which are obtained as a result of civil service examinations. Wherever the latter is the case, Jews hold more than their proportionate share of good jobs; wherever the former, their numbers are insignificant. [S. Tenenbaum, in B. Lasker's *Jewish Experiences in America*, p. 78.]

These words were written in 1927, at a time when teaching positions in general were abundantly available for qualified candidates. With the growing scarcity of governmental jobs, other than federal, the Jew has still less chance of obtaining the appointment, if a non-Jewish candidate offers barely approximate qualifications.

In America governmental agencies, following democratic impulses, idealistic as well as opportunistic (the large Jewish vote in certain regions), are less discriminatory, on the whole, than private business. But in most other countries, state control becomes directly instrumental in the elimination of Jews from many branches of economic endeavor. In "etatist" Poland, for example, increasing nationalization of property and enterprise (state ownership of railroads and steamships, state management of post, telegraph, telephone and radio services, state monopoly of tobacco, liquor, etc.), as well as state supervision and regulation of agriculture, industry and commerce, have been determining factors in the gradual proletarization of the Jewish masses. The situation in the tobacco industry is particularly illuminating. Formerly 3,000 Jews were engaged in it as workers and clerical employees. After the establishment of the Polish monopoly in 1922, their number was reduced until by 1934 the total was 102, or 0.85 percent of the persons employed in the industry. Similar conditions prevail in the numerous other state monopolies, which, as far back as 1930-31, were estimated to control 22.5 percent of the country's industrial and commercial wealth. At the same time the 3,000,000 Jews must derive a livelihood from urban occupations alone, since there is not enough land available to satisfy even the Polish peasants. Under these circumstances, the placing of a Jew in, say, every fourth post in the state bureaucracy would evidently have an economic justification. More realistically, one might expect from an equitable government the appointment of one Jew to every nine non-Jews, in accordance with their numerical strength. As a matter of fact, however, in its present nationalistic mood, the Polish government is trying to build a strong Polish middle class and constantly reduces the number of Jews in public employ even in regions (such as the formerly Austrian Galicia), where they had previously enjoyed a greater equality of opportunity. According to data from the official Polish census of 1923, the Jewish share amounted to 2.6 percent in the civil service proper, and 1.39 percent in state industrial enterprises. Almost 88 percent of all Jewish officials, moreover, were stationed in the "southern provinces," largely taken over from the Hapsburgs, only 40 Jews (among 3,642 non-Jews) having been admitted to the main central offices in Warsaw. In the formerly Prussian provinces, where the spirit of Polish nationalism, repressed in the former, anti-Polish régime, was most rampant, not a single Jewish official appeared on the records. During the twelve subsequent years, the number of Jewish public employees has further declined, both absolutely and relatively. A similar situation also exists, with local variants, in the neighboring countries of Rumania, Hungary, Lithuania, etc. The habit of urban Rumanians to rely upon government support, reflected in Senator Karp's popular adage that "the Rumanian is born a stipendiary, lives as a functionary and dies a pensionary," has further decreased the slim prospects of governmental careers for the Jews. In Budapest the Jewish community of 208,000 constituted in 1925 21.6 percent of the population. Occupationally, however, they constituted 61.7 percent of the independent merchants and only 3.9 percent of the public employees. In short, the Jews, predestined to a leading rôle in government economic enterprise by virtue of their urbanization and exclusion from agriculture, as a rule obtain, for reasons irrelevant to pure economics, even less than is due their numerical strength.

THE MENACE TO JEWISH EQUALITY

This interlocking of politics and economics has also contributed greatly to the crisis in the political status of the Jews. Until 1919 the progress of Jewish emancipation was slow but steady. Nobody doubted that gains once achieved would be permanently maintained, possible temporary reversals notwithstanding. At the Peace Conference in 1919, the Jews seemed to have reached the climax of their political achievements. True, certain radical demands had to be toned down in the face of the staunch opposition on the part of the new or enlarged countries. The postulated, separate, national parliaments, to legislate on all matters pertinent to ethnic and cultural life in states of multiple nationality, were nowhere established. Not even separate national electoral bodies to guarantee the representation of the minorities were accepted. In fact, the temporary creation of such a national "curia" for the Jews in Salonica had a decidedly anti-Jewish tinge, and its abolition was vociferously demanded by Jewish public opinion in Greece and abroad. Neither did the League of Nations become a league of nationalities, representing the diverse ethnic groups; it became rather a league of states. The Jewish people, having no state of its own, were given no official representation at either the Assembly or Council. On the other hand, the minorities clauses of the peace treaties introduced a new principle into international law, full of promise of world pacification. Many hoped that, just as the Treaty of Westphalia, with its safeguards for religious minorities, had put an effective check upon violent outbursts of religious intolerance, the Paris treaties of 1919 would blunt the edge of national conflicts.

These hopes soon turned out to be premature, to say the least. In Rumania, the Bratianu government resigned, rather than accept a treaty which it regarded as infringing on national sovereignty. Rumania and the others signed eventually under compulsion and with ill-will. The tragic frustration of these international guarantees has disheartened Eastern European Jewry and dampened its militant buoyancy of the first postwar years. Jewish initiative, which more than any other single factor may have quickened the pulse of economic and political enterprise, so urgently needed in these new states, was unnerved by an increasingly despondent feeling which has for years prevailed over a vast area from the Baltic to the Dardanelles. This feeling was well summarized by Sir Stuart Samuel, the head of the British commission to investigate the condition of Jews in Poland, when he reported that "the Jewish soldiers do their duty to their country in the certainty that their country will not do its duty by them." It is futile to argue that anti-Jewish policies must result in permanent injury, economic as well as political, to these countries, and that the very existence of a large, totally ruined section of the population necessarily weakens the entire body politic. In the haze of nationalist enthusiasm, it is left to an outsider to realize, for example, that "Germany might vanquish a Poland without Jews, but she never could overcome a Poland with a thriving Jewish population." Since 1925, moreover, when these words were written, Germany has made her peace (however dubious in point of duration) with Poland, and the Jewries of both countries are increasingly victimized to meet political exigencies at home. In Poland, especially, the "etatist" policies of the government bear the main responsibility for the reduction of the Jewish masses to a state of extreme poverty. No less than 1,000,000 are now dependent on charity. In Warsaw alone the applications for Passover relief, supplied by the Jewish community, have risen from 22.3 percent in 1934, to some 60 percent in 1935. More dramatically, a wave of pogroms swept over Poland at the beginning of 1936, which has marred the relatively clean record of the Polish nation. Until recently the provinces inhabited by ethnic Poles (which excludes Ukraine, White Russia, etc.) could claim to have spilled less Jewish blood than any other European country of large Jewish settlement, with the exception of Italy. But now nationalist agitators, in the district of Warsaw particularly, have resuscitated this medieval and czarist method of settling the differences between the Jews and their Christian neighbors.

While these difficulties have consisted primarily in what may be styled imperfect emancipation, whose perfectibility in the course of time few disputed, many doubted whether the Jewish people could at all survive complete and universal emancipation. The experiences even of America and France, with century-old emancipated Jewries effectively resisting extinction, appeared inconclusive. As long as there was a permanent influx of nonemancipated Jews from Russia, Poland, Rumania and Turkey, the forces of assimilation were greatly weakened. But since the enfranchisement of 1917-19, Eastern European Jewry was likewise seized by the maelstrom of assimilation, and the very spring of revitalizing energies seemed to be running dry. It appeared that, with emancipation affecting the bulk of the people rather than one or another of its minority groups, a final answer to the haunting question concerning its effects on the survival of Jewry might be at hand.

Long before this fairly universal emancipation (frequently only a paper emancipation) had a chance to become fully operative, however, it was suddenly checked by events in Germany. There was no longer a crisis caused by emancipation, but a crisis in the process of emancipation itself. Countries have before revoked or curtailed emancipation, but recent legislative enactments of the German government, quite apart from the well-attested early "atrocities," far overshadow the Napoleonic decree of 1808, and even the restoration of the prerevolutionary status in Germany and Italy after 1815. Napoleon's "infamous" decree was a temporary and "educational" measure, and even most legitimists of the Holy Alliance professed the hope that Jewish disabilities would be removed some day under more propitious circumstances. Only a few theorists defended the principle of Jewish inequality as such. Some of them, such as the philosopher Fries and the historian Ruehs, may, indeed, be classified as forerunners of modern anti-Semitism. Contemporary Germany preaches permanent denial, to Jews, of full-fledged citizenship.

It is too early now to foretell fully to what extent the preemancipatory disabilities will be restored. More likely, there will emerge from the present confusion a wholly unprecedented legal status. During the previous elections to the German diet the Jewish voters were not only allowed, but positively encouraged, to vote, in order to swell the number of the participants in the "plebiscite"; but during the March,

1936, election, Jews, at the moment still entitled to exercise their electoral rights, were threatened with severe reprisals. Apart from its fear that the constitution, in legal form, of a Jewish national minority might facilitate the interference of the League of Nations—indeed, von Keller, the German delegate, took pains to convince the League's Assembly in October, 1933, that "the Jews of Germany are neither a linguistic nor a national minority"—the Nazi party long seemed to have cherished the hope that the Jews, through mass exodus, would relieve it of the responsibility for devising new constitutional methods of dealing with a minority. One of its official spokesmen, Achim Gercke, the expert on race questions in the Reich ministry of the interior, summed up his discussion of "the solution of the Jewish question" by stating, "In short, there can and shall be only one sort of governmental regulation—an orderly exit of the Jews, their emigration" (*Nationalsozialistische Monatshefte,* 38, pp. 3-5). Many wild schemes for transplanting the Jews to a far-off colony, such as Madagascar (Palestine was thought too near), were presented and often seriously discussed. Seeing these expectations frustrated, mainly through world-wide unemployment and anti-immigration laws, the ministry undertook in the autumn of 1933 to draw up a new statute. That it did not immediately execute the Nazi platform of the opposition years 1921-32, which had demanded a sort of "law of aliens" (persons without rights of citizenship anywhere else) for the Jews, may have been due to the difficulty of working out such a statute in detail, to international considerations, or to the counsels of responsible business leaders. The government was frequently reminded that Jewish business firms still furnished employment to some five million German wage earners and had a large share in the German export trade. On the other hand, the representatives of the German Jewish community vainly attempted to negotiate with the government over the projected legislation.

German Jewry faces the destiny [these leaders helplessly wrote in May, 1933], of becoming a disinherited people in their German fatherland. Their honor is impugned and, as a minority, they are unable to defend themselves. [*Jüdische Rundschau,* June 9, 1933.]

The progressive repudiation of the League of Nations (Germany's withdrawal became fully effective in the autumn of 1935) and of sincere international coöperation, however, has since paved the way for the adoption of rigid citizenship laws. In April, 1935, an official announcement stated that

> for the National Socialist State citizens are not simply those who more or less by chance live inside the Reich's borders, but they are those who bear in them the State viewpoint and philosophy. . . . Among other things it will be necessary for a citizen to belong to the Aryan race. [*New York Times*, April 28, 1935, Sect. I, p. 9.]

The Nuremberg decrees of September 15, 1935, finally stated succinctly: "Only subjects of the state [Staatsangehörige] who are of German or kindred blood and have proved by their attitude that they are both willing and adapted to serve the German people and the Reich loyally, are classed as citizens of the Reich [Reichsbürger]" (Section 2a). Thus was established the unprecedented distinction between "subjects of the state" and Reich citizens, who alone are invested with full political rights. Although supplemented by the legal exclusion of Jews from the fighting forces of the newly created German army; the prohibition of mixed marriages and extramarital relations, and of the display of Reich colors by Jews; and by numerous detailed regulations concerning the Jews in public service, professions, labor unions, agriculture, etc., there still are many juridical problems to be solved by legislation and judicial interpretation. But, however controversial certain practical aspects may seem to be—and this is amply attested by the large monographic literature appearing on the subject since September, 1935—the main purport of the law is not subject to doubt. To quote two of its semi-official expounders, who otherwise try to minimize its effects upon the life of German Jewry: "it will henceforth and for all future times be impossible for the Jews to mix with the German people and to meddle in the political, economic and cultural management of the Reich" (W. Stuckart and H. Globke in *Kommentare zur deutschen Rassengesetzgebung*, I,15).

The anti-Semitic movement has entered a decisive phase. Having achieved such a conspicuous victory in Germany, it threatens to spread to other countries. A philosophy "scientifically" justifying the undisciplined appetite of race hatred, naturally encourages its satisfaction everywhere. Even the early, purely theoretical discussions of the 1870's and 1880's had strong reverberations in the neighboring lands. In Russia and Rumania they were in part responsible for the pogroms and riots of the ensuing decades, since they seemed to remove the stigma of barbarity from the assailants and their governmental wirepullers. Today it is the German government which bends its energies to develop a world-wide anti-Jewish agitation. Its propaganda organization, with headquarters in Hamburg, is said to have established more than 350 national and provincial units all over the globe. It finds attentive listeners, especially among men and women of German descent. Should this propaganda, cunningly and ruthlessly conducted, prove successful, it would in the first place align more than 100,000,000 Germans or persons of German parentage against the 16,000,000 Jews. Although the "purge" of June 30, 1934, seems to have had a sobering effect abroad and decidedly cooled off the religious fervor of Nazism's foreign missionaries, its German exponents continue looking forward to the universal spread of anti-Semitism as the best safeguard for their own future.

ZIONIST PERPLEXITIES

The political side of the Zionist solution likewise reveals numerous perplexities. The crisis of 1929-30 has largely passed, and Palestine long resembled a prosperous island in the midst of a sea of depression. The startling contrast between the rapid rate of progress in Palestine and the stagnant, indeed, miserable conditions in neighboring Transjordan has necessarily brought home to many thoughtful Arabs the great gains accruing to them from Jewish immigration. The negotiations with Emir Abdallah concerning the settlement of Jews east of the Jordan, may have been frustrated by the nationalist reaction west of the river. They clearly mirrored, nevertheless, the growing desire of the Transjordan Arabs to partake in the benefits of Jewish colonization. Similarly the French administration of Syria has recently granted a far-reaching concession to a group of French Jews, to acquire 10,000 *dunam* of land for a Jewish colony. It seems that the original condition, that this land must not be in the vicinity of Palestine, has been dropped, Arab suspicions notwithstanding. These negotiations merely mark the beginning of a historical revolution which cannot be permanently checked by nationalist fanaticism. It is, at the present moment, too early to foresee the ultimate outcome of the Arab uprising, which has gripped the country since April, 1936. But it does not seem likely that Great Britain, not only in defiance of the terms of the Mandate, but against her own imperial interests and prestige, should yield to the Arab demands, stop all Jewish immigration and prohibit land sales to Jews. For the time being, the British administration of Palestine, for many years friendlier to the Arabs than to the Jews, has become the main target. Palestine Jewry, moreover, all partisan divisions notwithstanding, has shown such remarkable discipline and self-control, that one cannot but acknowledge its intrinsic vitality.

Under these circumstances, the assertion, so frequently reiterated in recent years, that the Zionist experiment rests solely upon British bayonets, becomes less and less true, the more the Jews are able to take care of their own defense. A Jewish community of over 360,000, as it is today, with an all-Jewish city of 135,000, is no longer a negligible quantity. If they should grow, as it appears they might within a few years, to two-fifths of the population, they undoubtedly would be able, with their superior cultural and economic power, to resist the pressure of the majority, even without British assistance. As to the much-debated ultimate absorptive capacity of the country, it suffices to refer to our estimates in the preceding chapters, according to which Palestine in the days of David and Solomon, and again in the first century A.D., had a population density of more than 250 souls per square mile. There is no reason to doubt that, with modern technological improvements, the 9,000 square miles of western Palestine could be made to support twice as many in the course of one or two generations. Even this hypothetical 5,000,000 population would still lag far behind that of present-day Egypt, the population in the settled area of which averages as much as 1,100 per square mile. The possibility, for example, that Haifa, with a harbor as good as that of Marseilles, and a hinterland larger and more populous, should reach in a few decades the French city's figure of 550,000 inhabitants cannot easily be ruled out on logical grounds. In fact, the recent growth of its Jewish community, although less conspicuous than that of Tel-Aviv, has been relatively speedier.

Should all that come to pass—whether it actually will, is still a matter of belief rather than pure, logical reasoning—the Zionists would have accomplished two great historical "miracles": a dispersed minority everywhere would have recaptured, through voluntary nongovernmental colonization, its own mother land, and this extraordinary evolution would ultimately have obtained "the consent of the natives." That this can be realized only in a binational state which will be neither as Arab nor as Jewish as "England is English," and which will be built on wholly unprecedented forms of social as well as ethnic justice, need hardly deter a people which, for two millennia, have been thinking in categories other than those of political power and domination.

This optimistic picture, however, has also serious drawbacks. The Arab opposition to Zionism, led by a coalition of jingoistic intellectuals, fanatical priests and profiteering landowners (who see in the anti-Zionist agitation, though not in its real success, the best means of further raising skyrocketing land prices) is still very potent. It will take many years before the bulk of the Arabs, with the spread of education and class consciousness, will effectively reject this leadership. The British Palestine administration, moreover, increasingly realizing the perplexing contradictions of the Mandate, has reduced its part in the upbuilding of the Jewish homeland to the absolute minimum of maintaining public order. Only an insignificant fraction of the budget goes to the excellent Jewish educational and health institutions, while the expenditure of almost the entire Arab school and sanitation systems is defrayed from the public treasury. This, at a time when the astonishingly favorable budgetary situation is due wholly to the revenue from the Jewish sector, which in 1930 contributed, according to official estimates, 36.6 percent, and according to the Zionist, 43 percent, of all taxes. It may readily be assumed that the Jewish portion has since risen to over one-half. In the most decisive fields of its land and immigration policies, the administration has become a positively retarding factor. Ever since Sir John Simpson's report in 1930, it has lavished all its solicitous concern upon the landless fellaheen (whose number has not yet been ascertained, although it probably does not exceed 1,000), and made no move whatever to promote the Jewish agricultural colonization. In regard to immigration it has, in violation of the spirit of the Mandate, refused to grant 24,000 certificates each for the two six-month periods from October 1, 1933, to April 1, 1934, and from April 1, to October 1, 1934, as demanded by the Jewish Agency; and allowed only 5,500 each, raising it to 7,500 in the following half year, although the *"economic* absorptive capacity" of the country would now favor the admission of at least 50,000 Jews of the noncapitalist class annually. Inasmuch as the great achievements of Zionist colonization have come about not only without the backing of a colonizing mother land, but in the face of considerable governmental obstacles, they constitute an even more reassuring sign of Zionism's elemental vitality. Nevertheless, the menacing combination of Arab and governmental opposition cannot be lightly dismissed. Should the administration carry out its plan of establishing a legislative council in the face of unanimous Jewish rejection, mild Arab resentment and considerable opposition in the British Parliament, the upbuilding of the Jewish homeland would be gravely imperiled. The Jews controlling 3 elective and 4 appointive seats, would be permanently outnumbered by 11 Muslim (8 elective and 3 appointive) and 3 Christian (1 and 2) members, 2 economic advisers and 5 government officials. Although the right to fix the immigration schedule is to be reserved for the high commissioner, the opportunity for making "suggestions" in this matter and passing regulations on many other vital phases of the country's reconstruction, would enable the majority of the Council effectively to obstruct Zionist efforts. Worst of all, it would basically perpetuate the minority position of the Jews, regardless of the present dynamic speed of transformation. The progressive weakening of the authority of the League of Nations, finally, may impair its supervisory control of mandated territories, and thus remove the ultimate check to the arbitrariness of the British civil service in Palestine.

The growth of Palestine Jewry, on the other hand, must not blind the observer to the constant decline of the Zionist organization outside the country until 1933, and in many aspects also thereafter. Decrease in the support given by world

Jewry has caused considerable difficulty to all central and local institutions financed from abroad. The National Fund, whose income, in contrast to that of the other Zionist bodies, reached in 5694 (1933-34) predepression heights (£P283,000, as against approximately £P288,000 in 5686 and 5687) and increased to the record figure of £P348,450 in 5695, has been handicapped by rising land prices and colonization costs. During the five years, 1930-34, it has acquired altogether 60,000 *dunam* of new land, to which were added some 17,000 in 1935. Even considering the Huleh concession, which during the last two years has redeemed about 33,000 *dunam* for cultivation, these acquisitions, though favorably contrasting with private purchases, are wholly incommensurate with the needs of the present mass immigration. Other Zionist funds have been greatly depleted. Indeed, they still are burdened with debts from which they must extricate themselves before they can resume in full their beneficial services. Many of their functions have already been taken over by the local settlement. One of the most momentous developments of the last few years has been the transfer of the educational system from the province of the Jewish Agency to that of the Palestinian National Council. All lines of development thus point toward the progressive emancipation of Palestinian Jewry from the tutelage of outside bodies. This emancipation, although in itself highly welcome and absolutely indispensable at some future date, appears rather premature. At any rate, by largely removing the burden of responsibility from Diaspora Jewry, it saps the vitality of the Zionist movement the world over.

The idea of coöperation with non-Zionists, as expressed in the Jewish Agency, has admittedly been a failure thus far. The expected large funds from non-Zionist quarters have not been forthcoming, while the Zionist group had to surrender much of its former militancy, thereby losing its hold upon Jewish youth in Europe and America. Where only fifteen years ago the overwhelming majority enthusiastically affirmed its messianic hope, one now finds lukewarm participation, inactive sympathy, or even positive antagonism. The defections from Zionist ranks in Poland, Lithuania, etc., are much more serious than the decline in the financial contributions during the economic crisis. The successive biennial Zionist congresses graphically demonstrate the change in the movement.

The average age of the non-Palestinian delegates is so high as to present Diaspora Zionism in the light of a middle-aged as well as a middle-class movement. Symbolically, the congresses of 1931 and 1933 elected to the presidency their venerable "old man," not so much through the active support of a large following as owing to the absence of any vigorous opposition. Apart from the ensuing ideological reverses and the questions arising therefrom as to the survival of the movement after two or three more decades, the threatening defection of Zionist youth may adversely affect the very basis of the Palestine colonization, *i.e.*, man power. For the moment, the Nazi upheaval has more than replenished the ranks of the youthful pioneers in Germany and elsewhere. But in the long run, the task of securing vigorous groups of *Halutsim,* so much more vital than that of obtaining large contributions, can only be fulfilled, if the spirit of "sober ebriety" with the Zionist ideal is kept alive for another generation or two. It is perhaps intrinsically impossible to evolve a positive ideal, as well as a practical course of action, which would simultaneously appeal to conservative, half-assimilated, often philistine benefactors, and to radical, nationalistic, often revolutionary youth.

The frequent, perhaps unavoidable, inefficiency of Zionist bureaucracy and the favoritism of Zionist politicians have been exposed to even more severe criticism than, for example, the analogous leadership in the labor unions. The critics have aired their grievances the more freely, the more Zionism, basically an idealistic, noneconomic movement, seems to call for wholly disinterested leaders. The very machinery of the organization, copied from the prevalent semidemocratic systems of the Herzlian age, has greatly suffered from the universal decline of parliamentary institutions in our time. The last two or three congresses, in particular, lacking the grandiose eloquence of the "heroic" age of Herzl and Nordau, have presented to the world a most unedifying spectacle of an ineffectual "debating society," and of petty party politics, usually ending in political deadlocks. Much outstanding oratory and fine constructive talent is wasted. It is perhaps fortunate that the time limit of the sessions and the physical exhaustion of the delegates, after a fortnight of incessant maneuvering, force them to adopt some resolutions and to proceed to final elections, both usually along the line of least resistance. Little wonder that perusal of the congress minutes is one of the least gratifying of tasks, and that many a reader has echoed the malevolent exclamation of Otto Pohl concerning "the protocols of the Unwise Men of Zion."

The situation is vastly complicated through communist antagonism. Even though originating from a twofold historical accident, international and domestic, this antagonism has had many adverse effects upon the Zionist movement in and outside the Soviet Union. Russian Jewry, which had long been the mainstay of Zionist thought and practice, and which, even on the eve of the Communist Revolution, had cast 90 percent of its total vote for Zionist candidates, can now cherish its Zionist ideal only in strict secrecy. The majority of Russian Jewish youth is positively anti-Zionist. Even outside Russia, many socially minded young Jews are discouraged from participating in an experiment which is denounced by the leading socialist power in the world as a tool of British imperialism, an attempt of the Jewish bourgeoisie to exploit the Arab fellah and a reactionary utopia, diverting the energies of the workers from the fundamental class struggle. One may feel that the conflict between communism and Zionism is not quite as irreconcilable as it now appears, and that, having its origin in accidental rather than essential discrepancies, it will sooner or later give way to mutual understanding. For many years to come, one must, nevertheless, reckon with it as a most critical force in Jewish life.

COMMUNAL AND RELIGIOUS TRANSFORMATIONS

The communal, cultural and religious life of the Jews likewise faces a profound crisis, generated by emancipation and assimilation. It may be worth repeating here that it is only today, half a generation after 1917-19, that one may feel less diffident in drawing empirical conclusions in regard to the fateful question: whether and under what form Judaism can survive emancipation. The experiment has, of course, been far from scientifically correct. The millions of Jews, residing in Poland, Rumania, etc., have enjoyed during these years theoretical rather than actual equality. The widespread anti-Jewish sentiment of the postwar years, and especially the

German events, have generated counteremancipatory and dissimilatory forces which have counteracted, if not positively reversed, the basic effects of legal equality. With the checking of the flow of mass immigration from nonemancipated to emancipated communities, however, the effects of emancipation upon the latter can be watched more closely. A most casual scrutiny of the situation throughout the world necessarily reveals alarming phenomena.

In the western countries, where emancipation has been effective to a greater or lesser extent for several generations, the disintegration of Jewish cultural and religious life has progressed very far. Even in eastern Europe and among the recent Eastern European immigrants in the West, who had themselves been born under preëmancipatory conditions, the forces of Jewish religious and cultural decadence become more and more obvious. The general intellectual and religious unrest in the Western world is inordinately magnified in the case of the Jews, through the perennial conflict between their necessary adaptation to western life and thought and the equally inescapable preservation of their Jewishness; between some sort of unavoidable assimilation and the apparently impossible, wholesale absorption. The necessity of a compromise between the two extremes has long been sensed by perspicacious thinkers in the Jewish and non-Jewish camp. Heinrich Mann, for example, having in masterly fashion described the deterioration of the assimilated Jewish bourgeoisie in the metropolitan *Schlaraffenland* of the Hohenzollern age, wrote the following remarkable lines in 1913,

> I regard assimilation as desirable, as long as it does not mean evanescence, but *rapprochement* and mutual influence. The Jews must not embrace the ideal of becoming Teutons. Not only that Jew is lost who commits suicide, because he failed to secure a commission as lieutenant-in-reserve, but also the one who has obtained it. He is through with the compulsion of possessing intellectual prowess. . . . The effects of both complete assimilation and water-tight separation would be equally frightful. [In Sombart *et al., Judentaufen,* p. 69.]

From another angle, Edmond Fleg, addressing the Second Conference of the World Union for Progressive Judaism, declared, with the evident approval of most of his listeners, that "assimilation is indispensable for the spread of the Jewish truth and to incorporate it with reality, while for preserving and fortifying the soul of Israel, Zionism and orthodoxy are no less indispensable" ("The Mission of the Jews," *Second Conference of the World Union for Progressive Judaism,* p. 120).

To say that religion no longer holds uncontested sway over the minds of Jews is to repeat an evident truism. Orthodoxy in its old form has been constantly losing ground, even in eastern Europe. The degeneration of orthodox Jewish life in America has gone so far as to enable officers of orthodox congregations openly to pursue their business on Sabbath— a mortal sin indeed, in the eyes of the orthodox of a previous generation. To an increasing extent, orthodox persons throughout the world make compromises of their own with the antireligious forces from outside. One man carries money and purchases food, but refrains from writing on Sabbath. Another regards writing as a smaller transgression than purchasing necessaries. Still another abstains from either kind of work, but drives a car or rides in a public conveyance, trying to pacify his conscience by arguing that he thus comes much closer to complying with the spirit of the Sabbath-rest commandment than if he walked many miles. One consumes all ritually prohibited food, but does not eat pork; another draws a distinction between roast pork, of which he cannot think without nausea, and ham or bacon in which he willingly and regularly indulges. In short, everyone composes a new unwritten Shulhan Aruk for his private benefit, and whimsically acknowledges or repudiates its authority thereafter. The decline in social control and the growing individualism of the modern period, the full or partial separation of church and state and the collapse of the Jewish communal organization, have given rise to so many varieties of orthodox conformity that one can hardly distinguish any more the basic standards of conformity. The orthodox rabbis themselves follow the inescapable trend and evolve compromises of all sorts, to meet halfway the necessities of the new environment. Israel Meir Kahan published, half a century ago, his *Stray Children of Israel,* in order to ease the burden of the Law for pious immigrants in America. But he frowned on all attempts to adopt the very same regulations in the Old World!

Quite apart from ritualistic nonconformity, old type orthodoxy is confronted by the evident exhaustion of its truly creative forces. Hasidism, long absorbed in the great fold of talmudic Judaism, has lost its original creative *élan* and degenerated into petty regional sectarianism with fewer and fewer original contributions. The Mussar movement of the last half century has not only lost some of its strongholds in the Soviet Union, but one would search in vain for a novel independent contribution or any other sign of true vitality among the contemporary adepts of this celebrated ethical school. In the United States, particularly, the achievements of orthodoxy, though backed by several generations of pious Jews, have been external and organizational rather than enriching the substance of Jewish life. Its creative contributions to Jewish culture can hardly stand comparison with those (none too great) of the numerically so much weaker Reform movement.

At the same time there has always persisted some sort of sentimental attachment to the orthodox mode of life. Gone is the iconoclastic zest of the *Haskalah*. Even among indifferent youth there exists an undeniable, romantic longing for the glories of the past, for the ideal Sabbath rest and holiday observance, for the "Paradise Lost" of the beautiful ghetto folk ways. The witty suggestion, once made, to found in New York orthodox congregations for atheist Jews, is not quite so paradoxical, as it first appears. Nevertheless, there have been few full-fledged "conversions." Nathan Birnbaum's religious experience,

I have not searched after God. . . . He has announced himself within me and then suddenly entered into my consciousness,

reminding us of some of the great conversions of former ages, has been a singular occurrence in contemporary Jewish life.

Neither is the situation in the Reform camp more encouraging. Not only is Reform Judaism still limited to a few countries, but it has lost much of its former intensity as a movement. All attempts of the World Union for Progressive Judaism to spread its gospel in other lands have proved unsuccessful against the staunch resistance of the Eastern European block. Neither has Reform ever made more than abortive attempts at becoming a mass movement. Here and there a small Jewish congregation in Poland or Rumania has adopted the Reform ritual, but its influence upon the whole of Jewish life has been negligible. In Germany and America, the two lands of classical Reform, little progress has been made since prewar days. Although as a result of the expansion of American Jewish life after the War, many new Reform congregations were founded and magnificent synagogues erected, their entire membership in the United States never exceeded 55,000, according to the official estimates of the Union of American Hebrew Congregations. Even multiplying this number by four, which seems rather high in the case of most Reform families, this total of about 220,000 would represent no more than 5 percent of American Jewry. Even more important is the diminution of Reform's missionary enthusiasm. For many years the movement has rested upon its laurels, satisfied with maintaining its previous achievement. Not even the sad experiences of a whole generation have cured its leaders of the dangerous illusion that the progressive Americanization of the immigrant masses will *automatically* bring a new host of recruits into the Reform camp. Ideologically too, Reform does not manifest the resiliency of a self-rejuvenating movement, but it threatens to develop an incrustated philosophy which would, of course, prove even more detrimental to a reforming trend than to true orthodoxy. The manifold complaints about the lack of appeal exercised by Reform upon Jewish youth are not without foundation and augur ominously for the future of the movement.

    The social and historical background of Reform explains many of these difficulties, but also enhances the insecurity of its position. From the outset, it has fully appealed only to the western upper-middle class, whose economic and intellectual emancipation postulated the loosening of the shackles of orthodox ritual and social control. Like Protestantism, it was, at the beginning, an iconoclastic, revolutionary trend. Coming two hundred years later, it also absorbed the prevalent liberalistic currents of the nineteenth century. Even more than Protestantism, however, it is now identified with the existing social order whose preservation seems essential to the maintenance of the chief class of its supporters. With the overwhelming majority of its membership steadfastly conservative in politics, economics and daily habits, it has lost almost all its reforming zeal. The Reform rabbis (mostly recruited from the poorer, Eastern European immigrant circles) on the whole keep their fingers more closely on the pulse of time and frequently invoke the prophetic ideal of social justice; but the lay members of their congregations, at best, smilingly tolerate these "nice" utterances, as appropriate to ministers of religion. Whenever a rabbi takes his own words more seriously, and pedantically insists upon their application to life, a clash is well-nigh unavoidable. With the present distribution of power, the outcome in ninety-nine out of a hundred congregations is not subject to doubt, and insult is added to injury when the losing rabbi is scornfully dismissed as an impractical and unsuccessful visionary.

The shortcomings of the Reform ritual and theology have likewise increasingly become manifest. Even in Protestant ranks, the view has become more and more articulate that it is a grave mistake to assign to the sermon such a central position at the expense of worship (cf., for instance, L. G. Leary, *Problems of Protestantism*). For Reform Judaism, which has in essence maintained the continuity of Judaism as an activist creed, this adoption of Protestant models has proved to be even more disturbing. The congregants, thus greatly relieved from active participation in worship, have frequently availed themselves of the opportunity, stimulated by the pressure of other interests, to exercise their religious duty "by proxy." The rabbi, the main proxy, has suffered both from the lack of active response and from the frequent necessity, under these circumstances, of substituting rhetoric for thinking.

Theological thinking, consequently, although not without vigor, has often been lacking in clarity and consistency. One of its major drawbacks was also its erratic discontinuity. Even though largely confronted by the same theological problems as discussed and rediscussed in the rabbinical assemblies in Germany in the 1840's and 1860's, in the half century of deliberations of the Central Conference of American Rabbis, and in the recent meetings of the World Union, Reform theologians have tried to solve them time and again by a fresh start, rather than by beginning where their predecessors had left off. Steinheim, Formstecher, Samuel Hirsch, Einhorn and Hermann Cohen, each represents a new unrelated endeavor. Only Geiger, Holdheim, the two Wises, Kohler and Baeck have impressed their outlook upon many of their disciples and successors. But this was wholly due to the fact that their emphasis was activist, rather than metaphysical. An anecdote, told of Hermann Cohen, illustrates the ineffectiveness of his lofty speculative structures better than many a critical tractate. The great philosopher, the saga reports, once tried to expound the place of God in his ethical system to an old Jew of Marburg. The old Jew listened attentively and reverently. When Cohen finished, he put the simple question, "But where is there room left for the *Boreh Olam* (Creator of the World)?" To which Cohen, bursting into tears, gave no reply.

The intermediate religious currents, such as the neo-orthodoxy of Samson Raphael Hirsch, and conservative Judaism as represented by the Breslau Seminary in the Old World and the Jewish Theological Seminary in America, although facing a less severe immediate crisis, have no reason to boast of considerable gains. Frankfort orthodoxy, while still appealing to a limited circle of persons, particularly in Germany, has had little effect upon the life of world Jewry. Its chief contribution, the organization of Agudat Israel with the participation of eastern orthodoxy, can hardly be classified as truly beneficial. The inclusion of the inert eastern masses in some sort of organization—doubtless in itself a highly meritorious task—might have been accomplished without the injection of the intolerant spirit of Frankfort into its fundamental policies. Eastern orthodoxy, left alone, would have developed a modern organized movement at a much slower pace, but it would also have shown many more positive attitudes and achievements.

The separatist tendencies of old German orthodoxy have communicated themselves, even to the Palestinian sector. Neither the latter's recurrent defeats at the League of Nations, nor the reorientation of its chief German spokesmen, Isaac Breuer and Jacob Rosenheim, as a result of the Nazi upheaval have as yet mitigated the ardor of this most extreme *Trennungsorthodoxie* of our day. Against the intention of its founder, moreover, Frankfort orthodoxy has tended to crystallize Judaism in contrast to the living flow of orthodox life in the East. S. R. Hirsch began by trying to find a new rationale for the "yoke" of the law, whose severity was doubly burdensome to the western Jew; and stressed philosophy and ethics and especially the emotional element in religion. His followers, for the most part, paid lip service to this rationale, but insisted the more stringently upon the observance of each and every detail of the Jewish code. It was not without some justification that their enemies began denouncing them as a neo-Sadducean group, adhering to the literal interpretation of Scripture, the only difference being that their Scriptures included also the Talmud and the Shulhan Aruk. And it was they who had gone out to defend the living flow of tradition against the purported Sadduceo-Karaite reversion to the Bible on the part of modern Reform!

Pharisaism is very fashionable today. Reversing the age-old prejudice in the Christian camp, modern scholarship has revealed so many of its basic virtues, that it became endeared to every group of Jews. Eastern orthodoxy naturally feels that it is the offshoot of Pharisaism in the direct line of continuity. Western orthodoxy regards its own conservative adaptation of Judaism to western life as truly Pharisaic. Reform argues that these ancient progressives, the Pharisees, would now have embarked upon the road of speedy transformation, in the light of modern needs and advanced ideas. The very Zionists, notwithstanding their rather Sadducean attachment to a Palestinian political commonwealth, identify themselves with these ancient nationalists. But it is conservative Judaism which seems to show the greatest similarities with the method and substance of teaching of the popular leaders during the declining Second Commonwealth, inasmuch as, clinging to the traditional mode of life, it nevertheless allows for the adaptation of basic theological concepts to the changing social and environmental needs. Perhaps also, like early Pharisaism, it has thus far failed to develop a new comprehensive and uniform philosophy of Judaism.

Much more than Pharisaism, however, conservative Judaism seems to labor under the compromise character of its doctrines. It has as yet satisfied neither the traditionalist nor the one who looks for a fuller synthesis between the Judaism of tradition and western culture. More significantly, the formal principle of distinguishing between Judaism's dogmatic and historical side, which is open to free investigation, and Jewish actional life, which must conform with the Halakah, only externally resembles the basic Pharisaic approach. It overlooks the fundamental historical difference between ancient Pharisaic law, then still in the making, and the Halakah's comparative finality in our own day. Pharisaism, moreover, is really known to us in detail only from the days of Hillel down. By that time, it had lost some of its revolutionary zeal and merely followed in the footsteps of the exilic and postexilic prophets, priests and scribes. It was these early leaders, long before Hillel, who had radically transformed the system of Jewish creeds and observances, by offering creative solutions to the complex problems which had arisen out of the crisis of the Exile. It is with these early leaders that we ought to compare Jewish leadership during the present crisis—a comparison, which can but accentuate the latter's timidity in taking decisive steps.

It is only fair to state that, unlike the First Exile, the Jewish religion today faces most dangerous enemies in agnosticism and atheism. There are some who draw comfort from the fact that religion in general and Judaism in particular have successfully weathered the storm of enlightenment and empiricism, of extreme individualism and liberalism, and of the various other "isms" in modern life. The worst has already come to pass, they argue, and religion has survived, but they forget that there is no absolute bad by which this worst might properly be measured. One may agree that religion, as such, cannot be endangered by science and liberal thought, since they operate primarily on such different planes as the emotional and the reasoning parts of man. No matter what "religious" fervor did accompany modern scientific discoveries and agitation for political panaceas, it was either limited to a small circle of intellectuals or was too shortlived to constitute a serious danger. Only now, when social planning in Russia and emphasis on race in Germany have been elevated to religious idols, the menace of the rise of rival creeds appears more immediate.

However, the greatest danger to Judaism comes not from the professed atheists, but from some of its official devotees. Those lukewarm Jews who feel that religion, though superfluous for themselves, is necessary for the people, necessary, in particular, for the maintenance of public order and the security of their own position, are religion's true enemies, boring from within. The increase in economic independence has often led to a shallow "rationalist" explanation of the "supernatural" phenomena and to the observance of a minimum of ritual as a matter of external piety; to a comfortable mode of existence, weak-kneed and cowardly, and total incapacity for boundless sacrifice; to yawning saturation and deep boredom, at best finding expression in esthetic Epicureanism or philanthropy. In other cases, a purely individualistic form of religion is preached as a "private affair" of the individual, unmindful of historic experience which teaches that each and every great religion has speedily grown into an intrinsically social, thoroughly institutionalized trend. Some "liberals" look forward to one great humanitarian religion embracing all mankind. Perhaps under the impact of early postwar humanitarianism, Emil G. Hirsch expressed in 1920 the fantastic hope, "Ten more years and there will be no difference between Reform Judaism and liberal Christianity." One need not take issue with such utterances on the ground of religious exclusiveness, such as found expression in the recent papal encyclicals or in the characteristic pronunciamento of Harnack,

There is only one religion, which was revealed from God. Mohammedanism, Confucianism, Judaism, Brahmanism, and other so-called religions are the inventions of men. [Quoted by C. Manshardt, in *JR,* XII, 529.]

But one must admit that such exclusiveness, if sincere, is at least a sign of living and profound belief; whereas the more attractive oratory on mutual tolerance and good will frequently springs from simple lack of conviction. Can a really and deeply religious person believe in the relativity of truth and the perfect equality of all creeds not only before the law—which kind of equality is absolutely indispensable for peace among men—but also before God?

Out of this chaos within religious Judaism were steadily nourished the nonreligious Jewish forces. Few Jews, outside of the Russian *bezbozhniki,* actually hate the Jewish religion today. But in ever-swelling numbers they join the ranks of the professedly indifferent, while acknowledging that racially or through an indescribable something they still regard themselves as Jews. But atheists and indifferent alike have so far failed to develop a convincing and satisfactory brand of secular Judaism; satisfactory, moreover, not only in its logical cogency but also in its enduring application to life. Religion can never be replaced by scientific theories, however intellectually alluring, unless they are supplemented by some sort of secular mysticism and ritual, the one to satisfy emotional yearnings, the other to furnish an outlet for activist energies and to become socially rooted through communal worship. Secular Zionists have long preached the erection of a non-religious Jewish civilization in Palestine, but the futility of this experiment has become ever clearer in recent years, and one can now perceive a definite reaction even within the Zionist camp. On the whole, secularism thrives on indifference and negation, rather than on the truly creative forces of Jewish life. Should it succeed, however, in the course of time, in formulating a new positive philosophy, creating for it a legend and a ritual, and finding devoted self-sacrificing adherents, the rise of a new Jewish schism and the rending asunder of the Jewish national body into warring camps of believers would appear imminent.

Can the Jewish people survive such an overturn in all its traditional patterns of existence? Are the contemporary Jews condemned to be merely passive bystanders, witnessing this gradual dissolution, or is it in their hands to direct their collective and individual destinies? If so, what practical measures could and should be taken to stem the process of disintegration and to fortify the reconstructive factors?

ANTIDOTES

The attentive reader doubtless has already noticed that even in the above presentation, where all the threatening symptoms have been marshaled to show the severity of the crisis, rays of hope were not altogether lacking. In the following he will find a discussion of the various antidotes inherent in the very elements of destruction or in the newly emerging forces of preservation, and a few suggestions for remedial counteraction. The latter, in so far as they can be included in this brief general analysis, belong by their very nature to the political and cultural, rather than the economic and biological, fields. Even in economics, undoubtedly, human energy bent upon certain aims, can substantially alter the course of events. Many modern Jews, especially Marxists, who, misunderstanding their master's "astronomic" predictions of economic developments and his "determinism," fatalistically accepted given conditions, confident that the future *must* change them in their favor, have dearly paid for their underestimate of the unexpected, irrational human impulses. However, action to be taken to remedy the purely economic evils will, in the face of the overwhelming power of the general economic trends, whether world-wide or confined to the individual states, be primarily political and ideological. The validity of these suggestions, it is needless to say, is largely conditioned on the degree to which the assumed general tendencies will actually be realized, although some may prove applicable also to a new, as yet unpredictable order.

The deep crisis in all domains of Jewish life would really threaten the people's survival, were not many of its phases so contradictory as to efface one another's effects. The trend toward a more stationary population, for example, doubtless mitigates the manifold handicaps of migration and facilitates the process of economic readjustment. It also makes the concentration of the Jews in certain professions and in commerce less conspicuous, and consequently less objectionable from the political standpoint. Neither does the spread of anti-Semitism, no matter how prejudicial it may be to the individual Jew, endanger the survival of the entire group. On the contrary, it has long been recognized that complete assimilation has more frequently resulted from perfect equality than from persecution. It actually appears, says J. Blau, "as if anti-Semitism were an International Benevolent Society for the Preservation of Semitism." Those who deplore this negative force of preservation and find therein a confirmation for the now fashionable assertion that the Jews have been objects rather than subjects of history, forget that all nations are deeply influenced by trends and events outside their own boundaries. It is needless to dwell here on the merits of the "primacy of the foreign over the domestic policies," as taught by great historians such as Ranke, because no one will deny that many interior developments in every nation are positive or negative reflections of foreign influence. The Jews in the dispersion, even more intimately woven into the fabric of their environmental life, necessarily react instantly to pertinent developments outside their own life. Anti-Semitism has certainly occupied a focal position in all Jewish "foreign" relations throughout the ages. The urbanization of the Jewish people, while lending unnatural prominence to urban occupations and coresponsible for many phases of physical and cultural degeneration, often enables the Jews to live a fuller Jewish life than when they are distributed in sparse and scattered settlements. Especially in emancipated Jewries, communal life and communal institutions thrive only where there is a considerable agglomeration of Jews. Many valuable endeavors require a metropolitan Jewish community counting scores or hundreds of thousands. The partisan divisions along religious, social and political lines doubtless weaken the unity of Jewish effort, but they also help to maintain an active interest in Jewish affairs. Indifference, rather than extreme partisanship, has been the real menace to Jewish survival. On extraordinary occasions, moreover, such as the Palestine riots, the White Paper of 1930 and the rise of Hitler to power, one finds practically the entire people united in sentiment, if not in action. On such rare occasions the much heralded solidarity of the Jews becomes a reality—a negative reality though it be.

POPULATION POLICY

For the time being, at any rate, the biological force of the Jewish people is far from exhausted. The actual decrease in a few Western European countries is more than made up by the permanent increase in the Jewish mass settlements. This increase itself may now be diminishing in eastern Europe, in the more backward regions of northern Africa, western Asia, etc., it does not yet show any signs of recession. With the spread of modern sanitary improvements in those countries, mortality falls off much more rapidly than natality. We now witness there a repetition of those phenomena which so beneficially operated in eastern Europe during the second half of the nineteenth century. On the whole, we may still conservatively assume that world Jewry grows by some 120,-000 persons a year. J. Lestshinsky has recently estimated the increase during the last decade at 1,300,000, averaging 140,000 annually in 1926-30, and 120,000 in 1931-35 (cf. especially his latest statistical studies on the Jewish world population, published in *JB*, IX). Under these circumstances the fear of race extinction, which has superseded the Malthusian specter of overpopulation in the minds of modern men, has but relative justification in Jewish reality. As far as one can see, it will take several more decades before the Jewish population will actually become stationary. Much can happen in the meantime to reverse the present unfavorable trend.

There are Jews who, after the fashion of certain western sociologists, are apprehensive lest recent biological developments affect quality even more than numbers, in coming generations. Since birth control operates more strongly among wealthy and educated western Jews, they feel that their offspring will necessarily be increasingly outnumbered by the children of the poor and backward eastern Jews. To them it is cold comfort that the function of numerical preservation may shift from northeastern Europe to the Balkans, Asia and northern Africa, to those Sephardic and oriental Jews who, in recent centuries, have assimilated so many unsavory "Levantine" traits.

These apprehensions have seldom been aired in the open, however. Generally, the conviction prevails that in the Jewish people there exists no qualitative difference in hereditary substance between the offspring of notables and that of "average" Jews. The absence of hereditary nobility (descent from a famous scholar created temporary social, but not permanent legal privileges), the insecurity and the comparatively short duration of wealth in any one family, constant migrations and extensive intermarriage between the various groups, have obliterated all incipient marks of differentiation. The environmental distinctions are wholly accidental and can often be removed in one lifetime. It may be doubted whether Emil Meyerson, the distinguished French philosopher, would have achieved equal fame and "attracted European interest in Polish philosophy" (Chwistek), if he had remained in Lublin. Nahman Krochmal, at least, the profoundest thinker in Polish lands during the nineteenth century, perhaps on account of his Jewish subject matter and use of Hebrew, has not become widely known even in Polish philosophic and literary circles. But Meyerson, his still more celebrated confrere, Henri Bergson (son of a Warsaw Jew), and many others, have demonstrated that, once given full western educational opportunities and an influential public, the eastern Jew can climb the ladder to high achievement in the West. As to specific Jewish services, one may leisurely speculate on what might have happened, if Chaim Weizman had remained in Pinsk or moved to Vilna or Kovno. Most likely he would now be one of the abject Russian *émigrés,* or else wasting his extraordinary abilities on a futile fight in or outside parliament against the oppressive measures of the Polish or Lithuanian government. As a professor of chemistry in Manchester, however, he had during the World War and afterwards a unique opportunity, which he so splendidly utilized that—in the words of Lloyd George—"his name will rank with that of Nehemiah in the fascinating and inspiring story of the children of Israel" (*War Memoirs,* I, 587).

All this applies likewise to the Sephardic and oriental Jews. In their mass settlements on the Mediterranean shores they have retained much of the vigor and vitality of their renowned ancestors, a vitality lost (perhaps through prolonged prosperity and over-civilization) by many of the western Sephardim. In fact, one may speak today of a Sephardic renaissance with many cultural and religious, as well as biological facets. The impulses of Zionism and the Hebrew revival, coupled with the rejuvenation of Islam, with which the Sephardic world has always been closely knit, have infused new lifeblood into its veins. Like Islam, it may look forward to a new era of great achievement, reminiscent of the past glories of Bagdad and Andalusia.

Recent changes in Jewish fecundity have had social, rather than strictly biological causes. In the midst of greatest nineteenth-century expansion, perspicacious thinkers rightly contended that the so-called Malthusian law of over-population was a historical, rather than a natural category. Today, the threatening under-population has no less definitely historical, *i.e.,* temporary, reasons. Any change in the social and economic order would immediately affect the rate of procreation. Even purely psychological transformations, such as a different attitude of the modern emancipated woman to motherhood, a revitalization of the family, and a reintensification of the personal relationships between parents and children, would go a long way to blunt the edge of the hitherto prevalent antagonistic forces.

A sentimental reaction among Jewish women is gaining in strength. The zeal of the suffragettes, who several decades ago saw woman's participation in public affairs as the only road to salvation, has been dampened by the manifestly indifferent results of their political emancipation. Growing technological unemployment among men militates against a continued disproportionate increase in the number of working women, such as took place during the World War and in periods of rapid industrial expansion. For a long time to come, the majority of women will be free to devote their undivided attention to the family and the raising of children. Progressive social legislation insures greater protection for maternity and better care for the child during the working hours of the mother. The heroic stage of feminism having passed, the disadvantages, mental as well as physical, of the childless state for a young and healthy woman have become more and more obvious. The zest of those eugenists who have associated extensive birth control with the immediate improvement of the race, has also been tempered by the growing recognition that one child in a family is "a crime rather than a child." Such lonely children, moreover, upon reaching maturity frequently wish to avoid the "mistake" of their parents. Fundamentally, the reversal of previous individualistic trends now enhances the social responsibility of the parents, gradually displacing the exclusive emphasis upon their personal comfort.

These general trends affect the Jews in an even higher degree, since so many of them have been placed, through metropolitan life and economic stratification, in the vanguard of civilization. Where birth control is not practiced, the basic fecundity of the race is undeniable. Lagarde once seriously suggested that Jewish fertility was due to the Jews' preference for a fish diet, which they must have acquired during their sojourn in ancient Egypt. Whatever the merits of this contention, there are many Jews today who see in the Jewish cuisine, and especially in fish prepared in the Jewish manner, the essence of their Jewishness. The much-debated rationalization of sexual life through medieval rabbinic law, as we have seen, has not weakened the religious sanctions which promoted the growth of the people. Only when this rationalization entered an unholy alliance with the profit and saving motive in the capitalistic age, did the "gospel of abnegation," as Marx said, begin to be taken seriously. It was further emphasized in the liberalistic age, when individual comfort, pleasure and the avoidance of pain assumed undue prominence in the pursuit of happiness. The most Epicurean age has thus approximated the results of the most ascetic generations. Recent secular rationales, however, once more favor procreation. Although the Jews cannot share Mussolini's or Hitler's enthusiasm for boundless propagation as the mainspring of economic and military power, they are aware of the vital importance of this source of ethnic self-preservation and cultural rejuvenation. Among nationally minded Jewish youth, especially among the Palestinian pioneers, this sense of responsibility has been clearly awakened.

The anti-Jewish persecutions appear to perform, in this respect, too, a conservatory function—not only in the ironic sense of impeding the accumulation of wealth by Jews, and thereby removing one of the chief causes of birth control, but also by direct reënforcement of ties linking the individual to his family and people. The information thus far available shows that a considerably larger number of young German Jews entered the state of matrimony in 1933-34, than in the preceding years, the great economic uncertainties notwithstanding. The Nazi propaganda for procreation, enforced abandonment of free relationships with non-Jews, and gradual exclusion from public amusements, have all made the previously extremely individualistic German Jew more family-minded. Most decisively, the reconstituted ghetto necessarily again focalizes Jewish life in the family. For the time being, economic instability and the mental agonies of the Jewish children attending German schools, still militate against more rapid propagation. "I shall not give birth to another Jew-child," is frequently heard from the lips of young German-Jewish mothers today. In the long run, however, the growing number of youthful couples cannot fail to increase natality, especially if economic conditions are stabilized and a specifically Jewish school system mitigates the sufferings of Jewish pupils. The process of dissimilation, moreover, diminishes defections through baptism and intermarriage. Treitschke once deplored the effects of emancipation, which absolved many Jews from the necessity of giving up their religion; but his more radical disciples have made conversion to Christianity altogether unremunerative. Since September, 1935, intermarriage is not only legally void, but also subject to severe punishment. With world Jewry's attention focused on the German scene, the results of these biological experiments in the German laboratory will doubtless also have an effect upon communities in which these extraneous influences make themselves felt in a lesser degree.

Jewish communal leaders will also once again have to pay much more attention to the family. It will not do to go about rhapsodizing on the sweetness and purity of medieval family life. As in other periods of retarded growth (the declining Roman Empire and the later Middle Ages) positive measures will have to be adopted. But now, with the weakening of the legislative and religious sanctions of the community, it will not suffice to reiterate the old rabbinical injunctions concerning the advisability of early marriages, procreation as their only purpose and the great sin of self-imposed abstention from either. Orthodox rabbis, such as J. J. Z. Horowitz, may still neatly reproduce the halakic outlawry of birth control, except when indispensable to the health of the mother; they preach to deaf ears, even among their own congregants. It is a matter of common knowledge that birth control is widely practiced in the orthodox strongholds of eastern Europe. Jewish, as well as non-Jewish, leaders will have to reckon with voluntary parenthood, rather than that by compulsion or accident. The exaltation of the eugenic values of birth control, on the other hand, on the part of some Reform rabbis who, whenever they can synthesize Judaism with the "latest" social fad, compliment themselves upon their modernity, does more harm than good. Birth control, the Jewish people is to be constantly reminded, is neither avoidable nor reprehensible, if practiced for medical or really urgent socio-economic reasons. Otherwise it is prejudicial not only to society, but to the parents themselves and to the single child previously born.

Apart from these preachments of dubious influence, positive measures may be taken to encourage marriage and procreation. All western states will necessarily, for the sake of self-preservation, allow certain premiums to fathers of families in the form of preference in public employment, raises in salaries and substantial tax reductions; establish better and less expensive maternity hospitals, and so forth. Jewish charitable institutions will likewise turn once more from mere maintenance of life, to the question of reproduction of life. As in the ghetto *haknasat kallah,* aid to young women about to enter matrimony, and other subsidies may be necessary to counteract the economic handicaps in the constantly narrowing employment market of capitalistic countries. As long as thoroughgoing economic planning, or a socialist order, does not guarantee employment to parents and minimum of care to children—the only really permanent solution—so long will it rest with the religious groups to share with the state the burden of responsibility. Only thus is it conceivable that the average Jewish family should raise three, and in some countries four children, the absolute minimum necessary, even in our period of relative longevity, to replenish the ranks and to maintain the people on its present numerical level. E. Kahn estimated in the Germany of 1930 that, in view of the numerous mixed marriages and the large total abstention from marriage, an average of seven children would be indispensable.

NEW AVENUES FOR MIGRATION

The opening of new avenues of Jewish migration undoubtedly is an even more urgent task of the day. The 80,000 German-Jewish refugees have dramatized it before Jewish and world opinion, but they are only a fraction of a vast mass of actual or potential expatriates for whom a place must be found somewhere on this globe. The millions of Polish Jewry, in particular, must find an outlet, if they are not to be totally pauperized. In the meantime Poland has admitted about 20,000 German refugees, becoming, after Palestine and France, their largest recipient. This reflux has suddenly nullified the results of many years of Polish-Jewish emigration to the once hospitable Reich. In 1931, moreover, even before the rise of Hitler to power, only 14 Jews left Poland for German destinations.

Where are the Jews to turn at present? In Europe there are only three potential hosts: France, the Iberian Peninsula, and especially the Soviet Union. It is not universally known that since the Great War France has become the foremost country of immigration and that in the decade of 1921-31 the number of foreign residents increased by 1,470,000. In contrast to prewar America, however, there were no more than 35,000 Jews among the new arrivals. Poland sent in 1931, 28,396 *émigrés* to her western ally, but there were no more than 646 Jews among them, or only one-fourth of their ratio in the Polish population. The reason is evident: France needed mainly agricultural and industrial laborers, and the Jews could furnish but few of these. More recently, it is estimated, some 25,000 German refugees have entered the country. Unfortunately, the world-wide depression affected France later than other countries; with increasing unemployment and civil unrest she could not be expected to continue her liberal immigration policy. Spain and Portugal are at present willing to accommodate larger numbers of Jewish sufferers, especially among the Sephardim. This receptive mood, fortified by the desire widespread in Spain to expiate for the wrongs once inflicted upon Spanish Jewry, persisted even through changes of government and was still strong at the outbreak (1936) of the rebellion under Franco. But Spain and Portugal now have a very limited economic absorptive capacity. The Soviet Union, on the other hand, has had untold possibilities for assimilating immigrants during the second Five Year Plan, but the wish has been lacking. The very low standard of life of the Russian population and the aversion to admit masses of immigrants, accustomed to a different mode of living and hence often quickly disillusioned, may be advanced as the main explanation, although suspicions have been voiced that this reluctance is due, in part, also to considerations bearing upon the world revolution. The waves of discontented prospective emigrants held back in their native lands can but swell the ranks of potential revolutionaries. In the case of Jews, in particular, there is the additional safeguard that few would be likely to enlist in fascist armies, which in most countries bear a distinctly anti-Semitic tinge. On the other hand, the Third International certainly realizes that an excess of Jewish members in any particular communist party is liable to offer a special target for attacks and seriously jeopardize the effectiveness of communist propaganda. The primary difficulty, moreover, being alleviated through the steady rise in the standard of life of the Russian masses, persistent effort of

Jewish leadership may break down this reluctance of the Soviets.

Neither should efforts be spared to throw wide open the harbors of Palestine to Jewish mass immigration, especially of the noncapitalist type. Even now it is still true—to quote the Memorandum of the Zionist Organization, to the Peace Conference of February, 1919—that the country "is sparsely populated; 40 [now 140] persons per square mile as contrasted with Lebanon to the North with 400 persons per square mile and Egypt to the South with double that [number]." A substantial increase of certificates for pioneers is also necessary, to mitigate the evils of a purely middle-class influx, to help maintain the beneficial hold of labor on the Palestine community, and to enable it to carry on its experiment of establishing a new social equilibrium. Only such a well-balanced immigration on a large scale would justify the great sacrifices of world Jewry, and be in line with the early exalted aspirations.

The handling of the delicate Arab problem, on the other hand, calls for particular care, not only with respect to the upbuilding of Palestine, but also in regard to the large potentialities for Jewish immigration into Transjordan, Syria and Iraq. The peculiar problems of Australia and New Zealand, South Africa and Canada, Argentina and Brazil, must likewise be thoroughly considered before favorable action on the part of these governments can be obtained. Jewish leadership certainly must not allow itself to be taken by surprise, as it did when Brazil adopted, in February, 1935, a stringent immigration bill, amplifying the provisions of the Constitution of 1934. According to newspaper reports, "immigration is to be limited to two percent of the number of aliens of each nationality already in the country, and only restricted citizenship is conferred by naturalization" (*New York Times*, April 28, 1935, Sec. I, p. 20).

The discussions of the League of Nations on the refugee problem and the creation of an intergovernmental body under a high commissioner appointed by the League, have opened the road for world-wide negotiations. The forceful memorandum of James Macdonald, the resigning high commissioner in December, 1935, has added stimulus to far-reaching action, and may bear fruit as soon as the League regains its composure after the Ethiopian and the Rhineland crises. If Jewish leadership the world over will focus its attention somewhat less upon the spectacular, but not very fruitful, boycott agitation against Germany; the equally unproductive, incessant apologias; or even the collection of funds for sheer relief —however meritorious all these undertakings may be in themselves—and concentrate, instead, on the task of transplanting large Jewish groups into more hospitable regions, such concerted effort will doubtless yield more permanent and beneficial results. The action initiated by the spectacular visit of Sir Herbert Samuel and two associates to America, which led to the organization of the "Council for German Jewry," is a step in the right direction. But the scope must be considerably broadened and must include the vast Eastern European masses. Many years of persistent negotiations, backed by large funds for purposes of colonization and vocational training of prospective settlers, will be needed, before the aversion of the respective governments toward mass immigration may be overcome. One must realistically reckon with the fact that the dangerous, but frequently useful, myth of Jewish world domination has been largely exploded through the recent Jewish financial reverses, and that simultaneously the tie-up in the international flow of credit has tempered the interest of debtor countries in the good will of Jewish financiers. Nevertheless, really united, well-considered action by responsible Jewish leaders, proceeding along a detailed and farsighted plan, backed by a powerful Jewish and non-Jewish public opinion, should even today be able to duplicate the achievements of the Jewish delegations at the Paris Peace Conference. Only instead of dazzling victories on paper, the new leadership may try to obtain less spectacular, but more substantial and enduring gains.

DIMINISHING ABNORMALITY OF ECONOMIC STATUS

Neither are the economic trends in the long run really as unfavorable as they first appear. Economic restratification, to be sure, can make only very slow progress. One may, perhaps, expect a further increase of the Jewish agricultural population to one million in the course of a decade or two, but this would be a unique achievement, in the face of the contradictory general trends, pointing to progressive further urbanization and industrialization of the world. The temporary reflux of urbanites to farms, in the United States, Germany and England, since 1930, may be regarded as a passing retardation, rather than a reversal of these trends. Indeed, in recent years the process of agricultural colonization has been slowed down in both the Soviet Union and Palestine on account of the shortage of labor, accompanying the rapid industrialization in the former, and the predominantly urban middle-class immigration in the latter country. In 1933 fully 17 percent of the population of the Palestine "collectives" (*kvusot*) flocked to the city. Although they were speedily replaced by more recent immigrants, the proportion of the Jewish rural population in the country sank from 25.6 percent in November, 1931, to 21.7 percent in September, 1934. To expect, under these circumstances, that within a generation or two the Jewish people as a whole will include a farming population of, say, 30 percent, seems futile. Nevertheless, one may look forward hopefully to increasing "normalcy" of the Jewish economic status. The outstanding feature in the recent evolution toward normalcy has been that it occurred, not because the Jewish structure has greatly adapted itself to that of the other nations, but because the world has become, so to speak, increasingly "Jewish." Once more the Jews may have merely anticipated general developments.

Most fundamental, of course, is the question of the numerical participation of Jews, outside the Soviet Union, in the heavy and basic, rather than the light industries. The ultimate answer to this haunting question seems to be given by recent trends in industrial production. Most western nations now show a gradual decrease of industrial workers, strictly speaking, and a corresponding increase of employees of the white-collar class. The changes in the relative strength of the two groups in Germany from 1907 to 1925, have been mentioned already. The occupational statistics of the United States for the last sixty years may serve as another illustration. The agricultural population has declined from 52.8 percent in 1870, to 25.8 percent in 1920, and to 21.3 percent in 1930. At the same time the manufacturing and mechanical industries employed 22 percent in 1870, 30.5 percent in 1920, but only

28.6 percent in 1930. On the other hand, those gainfully occupied in trade and transportation steadily rose from 9.1 percent in 1870, to 18 percent in 1920, and 20.7 percent in 1930. Similarly, clerical service rose from 1.7 percent to 7.2 percent and 8.2 percent, while professional service advanced from 2.7 percent to 5.4 percent and 6.5 percent respectively, on these dates. The trend is equally pronounced, if one considers that

in 1870 about 75% of gainfully employed engaged in production of physical goods in agriculture, mining, manufacturing and construction. In 1930 only about 50% of the labor supply was so required. [*Recent Social Trends,* I, 281-84.]

In short, although the recent heated controversies on the merits of technocracy have discredited prophecies of this type, everyone seems to agree that the potentialities of the machine have vastly outstripped the pace of domestic consumption and the absorptive capacities of markets, in the newer and less-developed countries. With the progressive industrialization of all countries, moreover, quite apart from the nationalist doctrines of self-containment, new markets, that great savior during the sustained British industrial evolution of the last two centuries, will hardly be available much longer. There is scarcely any other acceptable alternative, but progressive reduction of hours of labor, combined with a constant diminution of the number of people employed in the actual process of mechanical production. This means a corresponding numerical increase of those engaged in its organization as well as in the transportation and distribution of the various products. In such a case, what is now an anomaly of Jewish structure, would become the more or less normal occupational division of western society.

Let us assume, for the sake of illustration, that about 2000 A.D., 20 percent of the working population, laboring for twenty hours a week, will suffice to obtain the entire agricultural and industrial output of both capital and consumers' goods, necessary at that time. The remaining 80 percent would chiefly belong to the employees' group in industry and farming, or to those classes of professional men, civil servants and others who provide for the satisfaction of other wants of man. Of course, the efficiency of physicians, teachers, etc., cannot be so greatly increased through mechanical inventions. With the evident progressive reduction of working hours also in these nonmechanical occupations, and the growing needs of all kinds during the vastly expanded leisure time, one can easily visualize a society in which the overwhelming majority would consist of white-collar employees, professional men and women, and public officials. Even if disproportionately few Jews were to be found then among the industrial and agricultural workers, and almost all of them continued to crowd the other occupations, their economic maldistribution would be much less conspicuous. It is one thing to belong, in an overwhelming majority, to classes which are now in a minority of less than one-fifth, and another thing to partake in the life of a majority of four-fifths.

Decreasing Jewish "abnormality," owing to general economic factors, may also be observed in a highly disturbing phase of contemporary life. During the last few decades, anti-Semites, Jewish social reformers, Zionist ideologists and general philanthropists concentrated their combined attacks upon the Jewish *Luftmenschen,* who in Eastern European censuses have often officially figured as high as one-sixth of the entire Jewish population. As a matter of fact, their proportion was frequently much higher, since many of those registered under one trade or another actually had no permanent occupation, but lived on accidental income from haphazard jobs and, temporarily, on public or private charity. Unfortunately, the recent economic upheavals have rendered that Jewish anomaly much less exceptional. Now almost every western country has for years had millions of unemployed, often far in excess of the ratio of one-sixth of the working population. What is even more deplorable, we must reckon with considerable permanent unemployment in all countries, without strictly planned economy. The millions of these forcible, often well-trained, unemployed in England, Germany and America have demonstrated, even to the superficial critic, that this by-product of early Jewish urban and commercial civilization has been due much less to national characteristics than to purely economic causes.

A new type of *Luftmensch,* in particular, becomes a growing menace to western civilization: the unemployed intellectual. The enormous multiplication of these individuals during the present generation, especially among Jews, and the apparent tendency to further growth by geometric progression, are truly disquieting. Not only does the higher level of education make the intellectual more sensitive and perhaps also less resistant to sordid reality, but his disillusionment grows ever deeper, as he compares his own status with the hitherto traditional superior standing of a man in the professions. The calculation that great sacrifices, self-imposed by families to see their children through many years in school, warrant also larger financial returns, and the lingering insistence of society that the intelligentsia continue displaying its middle-class façade add to the bitterness of the disappointment. Western and especially Jewish youth will have to reëvaluate the function of general and vocational education in a better-planned world, in which few skilled or unskilled laborers, running an efficient machine, will ultimately command decent wages for short working days, will be insured against unemployment, disability and old age, and will increasingly assert themselves in public life. A higher social appreciation would automatically follow. Even now one frequently hears comparisons between the standard of life of the average workingman and that of the average professional, which pretend that the lot of the former is little short of enviable. In capitalistic countries this still is a gross exaggeration, reflecting the pretentious demands of the hitherto-fastidious professional class, rather than actual facts. But all modern trends unmistakably point in this direction, and it is not without socio-economic justification that many level-headed thinkers see in the industrial proletariat the harbinger of a new age, notwithstanding the present middle-class revolt under the mantle of fascism.

Does this mean that Jewish youth is now to check or to keep in abeyance its natural propensities for higher education? By no means! It must only learn the lesson which its forefathers learned for centuries, that higher education is of value in itself, to be appreciated in total disregard of the economic opportunities it may offer. The talmudic or medieval rabbis, or the orthodox students in modern times, never were an economic class apart. Dependent on their particular circumstances, they were wealthy or poor, patricians or proletarians, but all of them shared the deep veneration of the entire people for learning per se. In fact, they always denounced, as a profanation of wisdom, the commercialization of expert knowledge, which in our mercantile age has become self-explanatory. Sometimes they went to the length of affirming, "It is a good sign for a scholar, if he devotes much time to study and little to earning a meagre sustenance" (*Seder Eliyahu Rabba,* chap. III). It is perhaps the greatest task of the new economic regulation, by securing to every individual work, bread and leisure, to liberate learning once again from the clutches of commercial exploitation. That such a development would not run counter to the "materialistic" conception of history, is perfectly clear to every student of Marxism, which is, in more than one respect—as Frederick Engels himself once characterized it—"the child and heir of German idealistic philosophy." In the long run, it certainly hopes to emancipate human culture from all class determination, and to free it for a fully autonomous development in a measure achieved perhaps only once before, namely in Jewish history. Fascism, too, has found inner justification in its reassertion of the national totalitarian culture as opposed to the present materialistic abuses of cultural accomplishments. Jewish youth, in particular, will have to understand that in a well-ordered society, everyone may enjoy the benefits of school education until the age of eighteen and of adult education for the rest of his life, and that the differences in formal training should mean little in regard to one's economic status. On the other hand, it must learn to appreciate the opportunity of obtaining higher education for its own sake as a privilege and as a road to a richer, though not more "abundant," life; richer undoubtedly in both happiness and sorrow, but hence really worth living.

A certain measure of Jewish economic restratification will, nevertheless, remain imperative. Here again Jewish communal leadership is confronted with grave responsibility. It must give up its perennial policy of "muddling through," lay down a farsighted program for a period of years, and provide the means necessary for its realization. Such a program is particularly needed to combat anti-Jewish discrimination, public as well as private. As far as the Jewish share in the steadily expanding civil service is concerned, the measures taken must be primarily political. While perfectly aware of the dangers of overactive participation in high official functions, Jewish leaders will nevertheless try to protect the rights of their coreligionists in the lower ranks of bureaucracy. To what extent and how, prominent Jewish individuals, called to serve in an exposed position, may reconcile their duty toward the state with apprehensions of provoking anti-Jewish demonstrations, must be left to special consideration in each particular case. The oft-cited example of Germany is inconclusive, since German anti-Semitism was the cause rather than the effect of the agitation against the high Jewish government officials, whose number was by no means excessive. One might also adduce the contrary, more plausible evidence of Soviet Russia, England and Italy, where the distinguished services rendered by Jews to the state have, at least thus far, not been rewarded by wholesale condemnation. But self-imposed moderation and restriction of Jewish pugnacity and careerism in public life will doubtless accrue to the benefit of all. Wherever governmental discrimination is in evidence, however, it is to be publicly combated. The use of the "Jewish vote," as a means of self-defense, is not to be shunned on account of possible aspersions. At any rate, incidents such as occurred in the Kings County Hospital in New York, in 1927, where three Jewish internes were steadily abused by their fellow physicians ("once they were dragged out in the middle of the night, bound, gagged, ducked in a bath-tub of ice-cold water and otherwise maltreated") must be resisted to the utmost.

Much more difficult is the struggle against discrimination in private corporations. So-called education of public opinion, reiterated apologias and fostering of "good-will" are not likely to have lasting effects. Really promising is only such vocational and character education of Jewish youth that the technical and personal qualifications of Jewish candidates should strongly appeal to the self-interest of the employers. True, it may require long and intensive efforts to enable the average Jew to attain such superior qualifications as an employee, *i.e.*, as a part of a large organizational body, as those which he had attained as an independent merchant. Psychologically, the individualistic and collectivistic springs of the Jewish personality, nurtured from Judaism's checkered career, are about evenly divided. The conviction that the Jew has a native disposition for commerce, is derived from the limited historical experience of Slavonic and German-speaking countries, where the bulk of Jewry has resided for centuries. There, for absolute self-preservation, the Jews had to cultivate their mercantile talents, and the "hereditary" superiority of the Jewish merchant is, by and large, undeniable even today. In the Near East, however, where the Jews always had other than commercial opportunities, the old adage that it takes two Jews to beat one Greek, and two Greeks to beat one Armenian, is to be supplemented by the frequent observation that the individual Arab merchant is no less shrewd than the Jewish. Neither has Jewish commercial hegemony or predisposition been proved in the Anglo-Saxon or Latin countries. The only exception is medieval Spain, where the Jewish mass settlement and special historical and social circumstances (Spain's mediating position between Christendom and Islam, the long lack of a powerful Christian middle class, etc.) operated in favor of Jewish commercial predominance. With increasing state control, on the one hand, and the tendency to create ever-more-powerful trusts in private business on the other, the adaptation of the Jew to the subordinate, but no less important, functions of an employee, becomes a matter of life and death. And "therefore choose life" (Deut. 30:19), is the old divine injunction which the Jewish people has always found it possible to obey.

It is proof of this amazing vitality that German Jewry in the very first months of the Hitler régime embarked upon the ambitious venture of economic readjustment of its youth. Such an impressive program of *Berufsumschichtung* in the face of tremendous odds should be emulated, under more propitious circumstances, in other countries. In Germany everyone is aware that the main emphasis must be laid upon men and women below thirty and, in particular, upon those between fifteen and twenty. In America and elsewhere, however, more attention may be paid to children below fifteen, since the pressure is less immediate. The generally easier transition from one occupation to another in the younger countries makes also the case of men over thirty less hopeless, especially since the suspicions against middle-aged and older men, so rampant in the reckless 1920's, have in part given way to a juster appreciation of their steadiness and conservative expertness.

However, is not economic normalization in itself a danger to Jewish survival? There are, indeed, prophets who predict the disappearance of the Jewish people soon after its loss of those economic peculiarities which have maintained its separation from the rest of the world. The Marxian conception of history, especially, furnishes many arguments for such a conclusion. Did not Marx himself foretell that with the disappearance of the "civil society," the Jew will likewise disappear? Many Marxist writers have gone beyond their master in trying to prove that the Jew has always been merely the outgrowth of a society built upon vendibility (production and exchange of "merchandise") and that, with the establishment of a socialist order, no room would be left for either Jews or Judaism. Otto Heller's shallow distortions in *Der Untergang des Judentums* may be cited as an extreme illustration of this school of thought. Every serious student of the Jewish past, however, will recognize the futility of such facile generalizations; in fact, will repudiate the reduction of the vast and complicated Jewish question to any single issue. The Jewish people existed long before vendibility became the basic characteristic of ancient or modern society, and, all dogmatic beliefs apart, it should easily outlive that society. Economic normalization would doubtless remove much friction with the outside world, and improve the lot of the individual Jew. It might thus weaken the undesirable negative forces of preservation. But it would leave untouched the positive, ethnic and cultural springs of Jewish endurance. The developments in the Soviet Union may already be cited as an instance of how, in contrast to certain irresponsible publicists, the official builders of a new socialist order necessarily reckon with the incontestable ethnic reality of the Jews. The Trotskyite groups abroad include in their program even more comprehensive plans for Jewish reconstruction.

COMMUNISM OR FASCISM

From the political point of view, however, the communist policy does not justify the belief that generally the proletariat as a class is necessarily friendly to Jews. The revolutionary Fourth Estate, in the early stages of its struggle against the existing social order, happens to cherish humanitarian ideals and to champion equality for all men. But the Third Estate, in its own heroic revolutionary stage, also indulged in such lofty messianic hopes, although it tried to realize them in a different manner. A proletariat in opposition staunchly supports civil and political liberties, and becomes the chief protagonist of the rights of the disinherited and oppressed peoples. A proletariat in power is easily persuaded to abandon political liberty and national equality for the sake of general economic equality. The Russian experience has been too short to allow for legitimate generalizations. The Soviet leaders themselves readily admit that the present order is still far from communistic. They tenaciously cling to the hope that the dictatorship of the proletariat which, with the imperfectibility of all human institutions, strongly tends to become a dictatorship of bureaucracy over the proletariat and a dictatorship of an upper clique over the rest of officialdom, will ultimately become unnecessary. With respect to the Jews, one may perhaps discount their active antagonism to traditional Judaism and to the Zionist and Hebrew renaissance as both part of a general antireligious policy and as the result of an accidental concatenation of international developments. But so are the Jewish minority rights largely due to the specific historical circumstances and to the peculiar ethnic composition of the Soviet Union. What may appear indispensable to the internal peace in a country in which the largest single ethnic group, the Russians, forms only 50.6 percent of the population, and the other half consists of a conglomeration of most diverse races and nationalities (the Jews, with 1.7 percent in 1930, were the sixth largest nationality), may be superfluous, or even prejudicial to the best interests of a more homogeneous proletarian state.

The peculiar national psychology of the Russians, moreover, makes every generalization as to the behavior of the rest of the world extremely hazardous. In no other powerful nation is the humanitarian and cosmopolitan dream so profoundly intermingled with the national yearnings, a blending which offers some striking parallels to the Jewish reconciliation of universalism and nationalism. Very unjewishly, however, Russia, in her entire orthodox tradition, in her very Panslavism, has always preached a violent brand of messianism. She was ready to sacrifice herself for the benefit of mankind, but was also prepared to subjugate it, if it should refuse to accept that sacrifice. This idealistic streak in the Russian national character, explaining so many perplexing antinomies, must not be overlooked in any attempt to dismiss lightly the historical experience of centuries, that peasants and urban workers have more often than not been hostile to their Jewish neighbors. Furthermore, notwithstanding its violent explosions during the last century, anti-Semitism has never sunk as deeply into the consciousness of the Russian masses as it did, for instance, into that of the German farmers and employees. Senator Henry Bérenger is quite right in asserting that "national socialism is not a mushroom born through spontaneous generation upon the disorder of the post-war period, but a new, most violent explosion of a very old sentiment, a mass explosion against Semitism" (In W. Simon's *La Question juive*, p. 201). In the Russia of 1917, on the contrary, the almost total absence of Jews before 1772, and thereafter their small number and sporadic appearance outside the Pale of Settlement, rendered them imaginary rather than real persons in the eyes of the devout but kindly peasants of the interior. It has yet to be proved that had Germany become communistic in 1919, it would, for any length of time, have pursued with respect to Jews a course similar to that of the Soviet Union.

Neither is, on the other hand, the fascist state, as such, necessarily antagonistic to the survival of Jewry. The anti-Jewish preachment of German national socialism must not conceal the fact that it is not necessarily the new social order sought by the Nazis that is overtly hostile to the Jewish people. This revolt of the German petty bourgeoisie would have had an animus against the large Jewish upper middle class, even if anti-Semitism had not had such deep roots in the tragic past of German-Jewish relations. Ironically, it raged against the Jews much more because they had furnished a number of distinguished leaders to the proletarian groups (to the social-democrats, rather than to the communists) than in their capacity of capitalists. But this is more in the nature of a historical accident, emanating from the rivalry between national socialism and communism, in the bloody struggle for succession after the long-expected downfall of the Weimar republic. In this struggle the Hitlerites have long drawn their major financial support from capitalist circles, and reciprocated by constantly toning down their anticapitalistic exhortations. Even Jewish capitalists have been treated with comparative mildness. Thus a movement which started out to destroy "Jewish" finance capital and "interest servitude," has concentrated all its implacable ire upon middle-class Jewish doctors, lawyers and shopkeepers.

Italy furnishes a classical illustration of a tolerant brand of fascism, as far as Jews are concerned. Their very small number (some 50,000 in a population of over 40,000,000) may help to explain the relative insignificance of the Jewish question on the Apennine Peninsula. However, the high position, in society and government, held by the Jews in the liberal era could have aroused widespread resentment. Not only were Jews of Italian birth found among the prominent statesmen, scholars and business men (to mention only the statesmen, Isacco Artom, Luigi Luzzatti, Giorgio Sonnino; the mayor of Rome, Ernesto Natan; the generals Giuseppe Ottolenghi, once minister of war, and Segré, the head of the allied armies in Vienna in 1919; the scientist, Cesare Lombroso; and the historian, Guglielmo Ferrero), but even comparatively recent immigrants had unquestioned opportunity to win distinction in all walks of life. A few of them obtained high-sounding noble titles; others became members of parliament; and one, Schanzer, served as minister of foreign affairs. There have been at least 5 Jewish counts and 15 barons among the Italian nobility. Even the fascist Senate has included 14 Jewish senators; the army, a few years ago, 11 Jewish generals. General Rodolfo Graziani, second in command of the Italian armies invading Ethiopia, and now, as viceroy, in charge of the reconstruction of that vast colonial empire, is— if we are to believe recurrent newspaper dispatches—a professing Jew. A recently compiled incomplete list enumerates over 200 Jewish professors and lecturers at Italian universities. The concentration of almost one-half of Italian Jewry in the two cities of Rome and Trieste, their disproportionate share in the liberal professions, and their comparative well-being, could not pass unnoticed. The observation that almost every tenth Jew, according to the census of 1910, lived on unearned income, as against only 2½ percent of such "rentiers" in the general population, were likewise conducive to anti-Jewish envy. An undercurrent of hostility against the *ebreo,* moreover, has always existed among the populace, which is still deeply imbued with the religious atavisms of sixteen centuries of Catholicism. Anti-Jewish sentiments have become quite articulate in modern *belles lettres,* where Jewish types are often depicted in a very unsympathetic manner. Nevertheless, the temperamental Italian masses have refrained from public anti-Jewish demonstrations, and the fascist state has enacted no discriminatory legislation. The promulgation of the Jewish community law in 1931 has, on the contrary, reëstablished the Jewish community as a body of public law with the right of taxation, and has thus ended a long period of anarchy and disintegration (cf. M. Falco, "Lo spirito della nuova legge," *Israel,* VI, 3-22). Some Jews actually hold positions of trust and confidence in the fascist party and government.

Neither have the semifascist states of Yugoslavia, Turkey and Poland pursued a uniform policy. Yugoslavia, like Italy, has constantly maintained full Jewish equality of rights, adding to it, through the reorganization of the communal system in 1929, considerable religious self-government. Kemal Pasha's radicalism in totally recasting Turkish social and cultural life has played havoc with all traditional Turkish institutions. One could not expect too much consideration for the hereditary usages of the national minorities, or even for their internationally guaranteed minority rights. But at least the principle of equality has, by and large, remained intact.

The Polish administration under Pilsudski, facing a much vaster and more complex Jewish question than those of Mussolini, King Alexander and Kemal Pasha, adhered in principle to Jewish equality, reëstablished the Jewish community as an effective organ of religious autonomy, and even championed in international gatherings the Jewish right to Palestine, and to fair treatment in all lands. If the new community law of 1931 appears in many respects reactionary and prejudicial to Jewish unity, this is due to the influence of the ultra-orthodox groups, rather than to the dictator's anti-Jewish animus. There is, however, a great deal of governmental discrimination in employment, taxation, the granting of public licenses and concessions, the apportionment of cultural and educational subventions, etc. While these administrative chicaneries have been the cause of many just complaints, one must bear in mind that the government has been subjected to constant pressure from the fanatically anti-Semitic Right parties, buttressed by the generally anti-Jewish sentiment of the Polish middle class. Its own deal with Germany has likewise weakened the anti-

Nazi forces in Polish society, and opened the country to a large influx of Nazi agitators. All attacks on Hitler, as the head of a friendly state, are being suppressed, while rabidly anti-Semitic pamphlets imported from Germany obtain free circulation. With Pilsudski's death, moreover, the government feels much less secure and is more readily prepared to sacrifice the Jews to the untrammeled hatred of their nationalist enemies. Its lukewarm suppression of the widespread acts of violence and its sponsorship in 1936 of an anti-slaughtering law, overtly aimed at a further reduction of Jewish economic opportunities, have revealed its inner weakness. On the other hand, apparently the only alternative given under present conditions, viz., a national democratic victory and the formation of an "Endek" government, would make the life of the three million Polish Jews even more unbearable.

These contradictory attitudes, especially the diametrical opposition in the two full-fledged fascist countries, Italy and Germany, merely reflect the contradictions inherent in fascism. Having originated in overpopulated countries with too narrow economic bases, it offers ample room for domestic economic rivalries; but the totalitarian state insists upon the elimination of class struggle. Being placed in a position which calls for wise restrictions of further population growth, it cherishes the ideal of military and economic expansion for which increasing masses of soldiers and producers seem indispensable. With respect to the Jews, Germany chooses the narrower path of ousting them from their few but coveted economic posts to make room for their Aryan rivals. Italy takes the longer view, buttressed by centuries of experience in the state capitalism of the mercantilist age, that the Jews are valuable accessions to the national productive power and, consequently, to the real strength of the nation. Perhaps Mussolini, who preaches war, but, at least in Europe, will always prefer diplomatic and economic conquests, recognizes the value of a pacific and industrious minority more than Hitler, whose constant professions of peace, although not necessarily altogether insincere, cannot hide the inherent militarism of Nazi government. The thirty odd thousand Jews, who won decorations for distinguished service during the World War, have not sufficiently placated the suspicions concerning the pacifist and internationalist heritage of the Jews. Economic realities, however, reassert themselves, even in overzealous Germany, and various decrees of the cabinet ministers for Economics and the Interior, Schmitt, Schacht and Frick, were issued to preserve, at least temporarily, Jewish big business. Whether and how soon these economic and expansionist considerations will put an end to the excesses of racial and nationalist frenzy, it is too early to judge.

Communism and fascism contain one common element of danger, however. Both stress the power of the state over the individual in a way which cannot but be prejudicial to the millennial nonpolitical people. Concentrated state power, to be sure, has not always been detrimental to the Jews. Quite apart from the ancient autocrats, Cyrus and Darius, the Ptolemies, Caesar and Augustus, who dealt mildly with their Jewish subjects, the princes and statesmen of the western absolute monarchies were the prime movers in attracting Jews into their territories and in offering them new and vast opportunities. The "enlightened" despots of the seventeenth century knew how to utilize the ingenuity and the resources of their "court-Jews" for the task of erecting the modern state, against the stiff resistance of medieval corporations. The emphasis upon state power in the twentieth century, however, has many ominous aspects. Enlightened absolutism coincided with the individualistic commercial revolution and the Reformation, which benefited also the Jewish individual. Contemporary trends are all essentially anti-individualistic. In the period of the rising bourgeoisie, the Jews shared in the general emancipation of the middle class, and the princes appreciated their services and rewarded them with a certain measure of protection. We now witness a general decline of the middle class and its growing and inescapable proletarization, while no class nor government seems actually interested in the preservation of Jewry. Communism, with its messianic dream of the ultimate disappearance of all states, is at least theoretically less inimical to the stateless ideals of Judaism. But fascism, glorifying the state above all human institutions, well-nigh apotheosizing it as the absolute being, eternal and omnipotent, seems hardly reconcilable with the Judaism of the last two millennia. This holds true not so much, as some rhetoricians assert, because the Jewish people are intrinsically sworn friends of democracy and parliamentarism. It existed long before these systems became the fetishes of civilization, and will exist long after civilization may have adjusted itself to their absence. If fascism were nothing but "order, hierarchy, discipline," which Mussolini has contrasted with the ideal of liberty, the Jewish people, with its living memories of a successful medieval synthesis of authority and liberty, would have little reason for anxiety. Neither is the erection of the corporative state in itself so gravely prejudicial to the best interests of Jewry. Although it is a far cry from the long and slowly growing medieval estates, those truly fraternal communities of blood, faith and destiny, to the artificial vocational estates of fascism, the Jewish people might stand to gain just as much as to lose, were it to be reconstituted as one of the new corporations. But it would have to be once more a corporate body *on a par* with all other corporations, not an extraneous part of a totalitarian intolerant entity. The Jewish people suffered persecution and martyrdom for two thousand years, because they tried to maintain their identity outside of state and territory. They neither could nor would lose themselves now in the many hostile and mutually exclusive jingo-patriotisms, and sacrifice themselves on the altar of the new type of "imperial worship." Despite the Italian Jewish fascists, the Zionist Revisionists, the orthodox supporters of the Pilsudski régime, the German *Vortrupp* or Naumann, one cannot view, without the gravest misgivings, the prospect of reconciliation between Jewish ethics and the glorification of *sacro egoismo,* between Jewish messianism and relentless militarism, between the Jewish affirmation of "powerlessness" and the fascist deification of power.

At this juncture there arises another menacing question: Will not the age-old intolerance of the national state toward the Jews reassert itself once more? The nineteenth-century attempt to reduce Judaism to a creed only, and to allow the ruling ethnic groups completely to absorb the Jews in all other respects, without the crudity of enforced baptism, appears to have definitely failed. Are the outbursts of anti-Semitism in Germany, which has elevated ethnic homogeneity to the place of an all-pervading social and political philosophy, merely a beginning of a long chain of developments toward dissimilation and disfranchisement? Will other states, similarly nationalistic, likewise despair of the feasibility of absorption, and insist on peremptory dissimilation, and, perhaps, ultimate elimination?

The answer to these perplexing questions evidently depends on one's general convictions concerning the future of nationalism and internationalism in the Western World. It has long been recognized that abandonment of assimilation logically leads to Jewish minority rights, except in that extreme Zionist view which looks forward to Jewish survival exclusively in Palestine. But minority rights can hardly be expected in a national state, where the Jews are the only minority. In England, France and Italy, and even in the United States, that vast national state in the making, the Jews neither could, nor in their overwhelming majority would, claim constitutional safeguards along the lines of the minority clauses in the peace treaties. If Germany, on the other hand, ultimately recognizes the Jewish minority as a legally constituted corporate body, the Jews will dearly pay for that privilege with the permanent loss of constitutional equality. Even the states of multiple nationality, we have seen, have for the most part defeated the purpose of these international guarantees.

The only power which has thus far prevented their complete breakdown is the League of Nations. However timid and ineffectual have been its attempted interventions, however openly defiant are the most serious transgressors, Germany and Poland, the League has held on steadfastly to that new international principle of mutual ethnic-cultural toleration. This is not accidental, and one may, indeed, find therein merely another instance of the operation of the historical law, often referred to in this work. Just as in the early Roman Empire a measure of equality could be combined with extensive Jewish autonomy only through the strenuous efforts of the supernational power of Rome, so also today only a League of Nations or another such international body may insist upon a similar equilibrium between equality and minority rights. Even the short postwar perspective permits the conclusion that international intervention alone may sustain this great positive achievement of the peace treaties and, through the gradual extension of the minority rights to all ethnic-cultural groups in the world, eliminate a constant source of friction in our civilization.

EPILOGUE

The idea of an international solution in this avidly nationalistic age may seem futile and visionary. Nevertheless, so many world-wide issues, political, economic and social, confront mankind, issues which can never be solved on a purely national basis, that human reason is bound sooner or later to renew its coöperative endeavors. One may also frankly believe that, after this period of extreme nationalism, the inherently international forces fostered by technological discoveries and growing facilities in transportation, will obtain the upper hand. We are perhaps now witnessing the climax of nationalism, its last excessive flare-up, which may leave behind a trail of ruin and disaster, but which will eventually give way to a new, superior human unity. (There may be some intermediary stages. One may easily visualize at first "ultra-imperialistic" rivalries between large economic and political areas, such as the British Empire, the Soviet Union, the United States of America, possibly the United States of Europe, etc. Such a rearrangement of forces would still be prejudicial to world peace, but it would nevertheless mitigate the raging nationalist conflicts of our day.) Of course, such internationalism would foster rather than destroy healthy and positive nationalism, and merely eliminate its present destructive aspect, the nationalism run amuck, which has distorted one of the most beautiful loyalties of the human soul into a contagious mass madness. It is an international body such as the future League of Nations, a League much more perfect in its composition and efficacious in its operations than that which bears this name today, which would be able to deal also with the complex Jewish problem and to devise for it a satisfactory international solution. Apparently, equality combined with autonomy of a sort, will remain the best method of mitigating at least the political difficulties arising from an extraordinary historical phenomenon, in regard to which "many sagacious minds have doubted whether it can at all be explained in a purely human way" (Wilhelm von Humboldt, *G.S.*, X, 97).

The affirmation of internationalism by the Jews is thus dictated by sheer selfish interest. But it is also deeply ingrained in their psyche through the millennia of their peculiar and, on the whole, successful reconciliation of ethnic allegiance and international aspiration. Neither the anti-Semitic denunciations of Jewish humanitarianism and of the supposedly implied lack of patriotism, nor the still more ludicrous insinuation that the Jews try, by controlling the main international agencies, to reach out for world domination, will deter the people from continuing the historic procession toward their messianic goal. Fearful Jews will bend their heads in silence, when national chauvinism renders the profession of a universalist credo little short of treason. Courageous and upright Jews will openly cling to their ancient ideals of peace and the brotherhood of man. They will soon find out that the humanitarian hope, though suppressed and almost outlawed at times, is, like patriotism, deeply rooted in the human soul, and will always reassert itself after periods of repression. And if there ever will be a moment propitious for a truly universal internationalism, it is most likely to come in the historic era now dawning upon us, notwithstanding, and perhaps because of, the present outbursts of the nationalist mania.

From this point of view, an interterritorial Jewish representation also appears to be a historical necessity. The din of controversy over the merits of convening a World Jewish Congress at the present time and over the programmatic or tactical shortcomings of its sponsorship, must not blind us to the indispensability of an organ entitled to speak with authority in the name of world Jewry. One may not believe in Jewish unity in action; one may, in particular, doubt the wisdom of organizing such a body at a time when other international organizations face their hardest struggle in years. But that preparations must soon be made for creating a mouthpiece to render articulate the wishes of the masses, however dissonant these may be, and pave the way for an ultimate international solution, appears unavoidable, unless the present analysis is grievously mistaken.

Still more controversial is the Jewish attitude to the communist movement. One often hears, even from the lips of non-communist youth, that since the world now must choose between fascism and communism, the Jewish people as a whole ought to align itself with the forces of the radical Left. These summary counsels appear both rash and impractical. Quite apart from the question of individual conviction, which would make it difficult for many religious Jews to choose the least of several evils, anti-Semitism, totalitarian absorption, or "godless" suppression of Judaism; apart from the serious, immediate dangers which would threaten the Jewries of the capitalistic countries, such an alliance would be unnatural, and consequently dangerously insincere. A people, consisting in its overwhelming majority of members of the middle class, with practically no sickle to match the hammer, with the very hammer swung mainly by master artisans and would-be capitalists, with legions of unproductive beggars and "lumpen" proletarians (the "great unwashed"), such a people identifying itself in its totality with the mortal enemy of the bourgeoisie, *i.e.,* its own most destructive class enemy, would be an unheard-of paradox. Not even the Hegelian-Marxian-Leninist masterly reconciliation of antitheses, nor the history and theology of the Jewish people, however rich in polarity of coëxisting antinomies, would allow for any more than a temporary tactical understanding, to be followed by rupture of truly tragic dimensions.

Of course, many Jewish individuals will continue flocking into the communist ranks. Workers and intellectuals, disinherited and idealists, will furnish ever-new recruits for the revolutionary army, despite all anti-Semitic denunciations and all warnings of Jewish leaders. The present social order has become so untenable that the term "revolution," formerly uttered in a whisper and almost cause for criminal prosecution, has become the fashionable watchword of statesmen and rulers. Revolutionary change will appeal especially to Jewish youth, filled with hereditary passion for social justice and deeply discontented with the existing conditions. The progressive proletarization of the Jewish middle class, in particular, constantly broadens the revolutionary base, and may ultimately create conditions in which communism will find its positive economic justification. For the time being, however, it would merely serve as an afterthought, an escape or dialectical toy for parlor communists, or, at best, as a supplementary weapon or secondary line of defense with other main issues at stake.

All signs seem, nevertheless, to point in the direction of an ultimate victory of socialism, although it will probably be socialism of a new, as-yet-unpredictable kind, greatly differing from its present Russian models. The Jewish leaders will do well to lay the ground for the necessary political and economic readjustment of their people to such a new social order. Those who cherish democratic and liberal ideals may hope for a compromise along the lines of social democracy or the American National Recovery Act (N.R.A.). But unfortunately the downfall of the Austrian socialist party has once more demonstrated that a liberal and democratic socialism is well-nigh unachievable in a class-ridden society, and that social democracy at its very best, as it actually was in Vienna, will go down to defeat before the combined attack of "patriotic," nationalist, capitalist and middle-class forces, swelled by discontented intellectuals, racketeers, scabs and other mercenaries. The Jews have no reason to be ashamed of those prominent socialist leaders in Vienna who, through their constructive theoretical as well as practical contributions, have enhanced the prestige of European socialism and, in their heroic defeat, have saved its much-damaged honor. As to fascism, one cannot help feeling that notwithstanding its great temporary successes, it will sooner or later go down in the insoluble contradictions of its capitalistic and nationalistic doctrines. Germany, for example, has not sincerely attempted to cure the inherent economic evils, and has simply glossed them over temporarily with the veneer of patriotic slogans and parades. Many Germans, indeed, have prophesied, both before and since June 30, 1934, the coming of a new, the "real" Nazi revolution. What is more important, Germany's nationalist spirit draws the country irresistibly into military adventures. Should it win and conquer large territories in Lithuania, the Baltic states and the Ukraine, it would lose its national homogeneity and become a state of multiple nationality, which, incidentally, might cool its anti-Semitic zest. The road of conquest thus obviously leads to imperialism and ultra-imperialism, and to the abandonment of true nationalism. If Germany lost, it would become ripe for another internal upheaval, which, under the present circumstances, could hardly be anything but communistic. That is why, among other things, there is no reason to despair, even of the survival of German Jewry, if it stands the strain, which is likely, until the country will have either reverted to its prewar imperialistic expansion or else joined the phalanxes of the communist world revolution.

In the intervening decades, the Jewish people must be prepared for a hard struggle, not only in Germany and not only against the anti-Semitic front. No matter in what form the new social order will eventually emerge from the chaos of the first half of this century, the anti-individualistic strains of planned economy and the authoritarian state will find the Jews at a disadvantage. Just as the antagonistic medieval developments placed them in a strategic position at the advent of the early capitalistic and individualistic era, so have emancipation, free competition and liberalism, in our age, although in themselves favorable to Jewish enterprise and achievement, weakened their position in the new era of regulation and control, the new "medievalism" which seems to be dawning. It is futile to shed tears over the "Paradise Lost" of the liberalistic age, over the individual liberties which have disappeared in both the fascist and the communistic countries, and which threaten to vanish everywhere. The Jewish people and their leaders must lose no time in fruitless lamentations, but rather should turn to a realistic and farsighted policy of adjustment. One must not, under any circumstances, allow emancipation, or theoretical equality, to become a fetish, and to spend all available energies in its defense. The frequently heard identification of the German governmental discrimination with the Dark Ages, is highly misleading. It has been pointed out here in various connections that during the European Middle Ages, the Jews belonged to the privileged minority of each country and that consequently, in comparison with the majority of Christians, modern equality was for them a relative (though by no means absolute) loss. The recent policy of the German government making the Jews alone subject to numerous disabilities, presents a considerable new lowering of status, rather than a repetition of medievalism. "A mere perusal of the basic privileges of medieval Jewry (enacted by Henry IV, Frederick I, Frederick II, etc.) and of the recent Nazi laws reveals the difference between a primarily positive and constructive and a purely negative type of legislation" (S. W. Baron, "Germany's Ghetto," *The Independent Journal of Columbia University,* Nov. 15, 1935). In short, not emancipation versus medieval status, but emancipation versus an unprecedented, exceptional status has become the paramount issue.

It is an altogether different question, whether or not the fascist or socialist state will eventually break up into corporate estates, with specific social and economic functions and with complementary special politicolegal rights and duties.

Should this occur, the national minorities may likewise perform peculiar functions of their own, and obtain a peculiar standing in public law. The Jewish group, preserving its religioracial integrity, in that strictly corporate society, may, in this hypothetical case, also be placed in a peculiar legal position. Such an arrangement need not violate the fundamental equality of all citizens; it merely would interpret equality in a less mechanical fashion. A repetition of the Middle Ages on a higher plane, with the Jews having their own corporate status, not necessarily inferior to that of the other corporations, might then become imperative. In other words, a revocation of emancipation for the sake of corporate reconstruction, with the Jews reasonably well treated, could hardly be rejected. A revocation of emancipation, with the sole aim of degrading the Jews and of satisfying the appetites of competitors or sadists, is an aberration of the human mind which is to be deplored and vigorously combated.

This evolution is, of course, by no means certain. Should the Marxian dream of classless society actually come true, full democratic equality might coëxist peacefully, with a rigidly socialized economy. The extension of the franchise and the introduction of the secret ballot by the Soviet government in 1934-35 undoubtedly were steps in that direction. The new Soviet constitution of 1936 has the earmarks of one of the greatest constitutional experiments in history. State capitalism on an international basis, with the formation of international trusts and with international settlement of internal disputes, may likewise lead to the retention of democratic liberties in a regimented system of production and distribution. In either of these events, which many would dismiss as little short of utopian, the Jewish people would have to undergo no less radical adaptations. The concentration of all energies upon the maintenance of the present form of equality, even if successful, would secure purely imaginary rights, to be discarded on the slightest provocation. After all, it was primarily the new equalitarian structure of the modern state which had irresistibly postulated emancipation in the last two centuries. The merit of Jewish leadership largely consisted in accelerating its pace, and in reducing to a minimum the unavoidable difficulties of adjustment. Similarly, the task of leaders today is not simply to cling to the cherished achievements and ideals of the past, but to explore the nature and the implications of the coming type of society and state, and to find ways and means to diminish the sharpness of the inescapable collision between the new forces and the present Jewish community.

At any rate, Jewish leaders must not allow the growth of anti-Semitism to place them wholly on the defensive. A few years ago the struggle for emancipation, even though devoid of its original messianic enthusiasm, still offered a worthwhile objective for Jewish activists. In nonemancipated communities they fought desperately to obtain such equal footing as their conception of justice and the economic pressure of the Jewish masses imperatively demanded. In other lands, much ingenuity and considerable material resources were spent on aiding these warriors, politically and financially. The later struggle for minority rights, although much more controversial, likewise released powerful energies. So did Zionism in its heroic attempt to transform Jewish life from within and to regain through colonization a motherland for the entire people. The gravest danger today is that sheer defense against anti-Semitism, increasingly absorbing the attention of the people, may foster negative rather than creative forces. One must also bear in mind that anti-Semitism is essentially a disease of Gentile peoples, and only non-Jews acting on their own unsolicited initiative may effectively eradicate it. A sufficiently large non-Jewish group of upright and intelligent citizens, seeing in anti-Semitism a threat to their own interests and ideals, may muster sufficient strength and persistence to cut off the hydralike heads of the anti-Semitic monster, nourished from the self-replenishing springs of racial and religious, social and economic bias. But the Jews may in vain spend all available communal energies in conducting a campaign in which, although the main objects, they would play but a secondary rôle. If anything, the fruitless efforts of the German Centralverein and, for that matter also, of the non-Jewish German League for Combating Anti-Semitism, should serve as a warning, while Zola, Picquart and their associates in the Dreyfus affair may be cited as shining examples of the effectiveness of an intrinsically non-Jewish crusade.

JEWISH COMMUNAL PLANNING

The main emphasis of Jewish leadership must shift toward a deliberate and detailed constructive program of action. Reference has already been made to the categoric necessity of Jewish economic planning. Even more important are the more peculiarly Jewish aspects of communal and religious reconstruction. Mankind at large can offer merely external solutions, whereas the inner developments of the Jewish spirit, the continued preservation of a separate Jewish ethnic and religious entity, on positive rather than negative grounds, will largely depend upon the Jews themselves. The great crisis of emancipation must be met with extraordinary measures. The present process of transformation of Jewish life being speedier and further-reaching than any other since the days of the First Exile, the necessary adaptations will have to be as profound as were those after the first fall of Jerusalem.

A novel compromise will have to be reached between assimilation and ethnic preservation. Today both appear absolutely inevitable and, for the majority of Jews, also perfectly reconcilable. By assimilation is not meant here that type of opportunistic self-alienation, often contrasted with Zionism, which allows one's life to be determined by "utilitarian rather than ideal motives." Neither is it the equivalent of the visionary idea that the Jewish people will disappear in the near future because they will have fulfilled their religious mission. It is much rather the constant and inescapable absorption of outside ideas and the adaptation of outside patterns, which, if illumined by conscious approval, lose much of their incidental harmfulness. It may also be called a new synthesis between Judaism and humanitarianism, or else between Judaism and the various western cultures. The insincerity and obnoxiousness of much of the old type self-negating assimilation has now been widely recognized. The friendly counsel of Otto Flake to his German Jewish friends, written several years ago, deserves to be heeded also by Jews of other lands.

One must not try to be German at all costs, if after all one is not a German—one must courageously step over the boundary. The primary task is to fashion the future and not to entertain an unreciprocated love to the dominant nationality. It is enough to realize that much of what appears so very important today is not so important; do not imitate, nor court, nor hide. The use of the German language is a utility and nothing else.

One may disagree with this low estimate of language, but the fact that the American Jews speak English, indeed increasingly speak nothing but English, clearly reveals both the strength and the limitations of their progressive "Americanization." Gone is the optimistic naïveté of the early 1900's, which led to the belief that, were mass immigration to cease and the immigrants to learn English, the Jewish question would resolve itself in the general brotherhood of the nascent American nationality. "Americanization" in the old sense is speedily nearing completion. More and more Jews are actually American-born and have thoroughly grown into the American atmosphere. Now begins their much more arduous task of synthesizing American (and not Americanized) culture with their own Jewish heritage. American Jewry has a great opportunity, implying also a great obligation, to continue along the line of their ancestors in Hellenistic Egypt and the caliphate, in Spain, Italy and Holland and more recently in Germany, and to build on solid foundations the new and spacious edifice of American Jewish culture. It may not be too rash to hope that this new amalgam will prove more enduring, and exercise more lasting and beneficial effects, than any of the earlier attempts. All the aspersions cast at so-called double allegiance by narrow-minded provincials cannot prevent the Jews from feeling that in their innermost being they simultaneously belong to two worlds, to the vast American nation as well as to the interterritorial Jewish people. Judaism has long ago demonstrated to the world that a national and a universal religion may be happily blended into one living ethnic reality. It is perhaps its greatest mission today—if one may call mission, the setting of an example through the sheer force of circumstances rather than deliberate preachment—to vindicate the general validity of its experience and to prove that internationalism and nationalism are truly and profoundly complementary. No one suspects incompatibility between the love of one's family and that of one's country. So shall we learn to appreciate the legitimacy of "dual cultural allegiance" in a civilization in which fragments of various ethnic groups are thrown together through the growing interpenetration of world-wide political and economic forces. International public law has already come to recognize the existence of numerous *sujets mixtes,* who owe political allegiance to two countries simultaneously, an allegiance which in the case of armed conflicts must lead to embarrassing and even tragic complications. How much more justified is a general recognition of dual nationality in the ethnic and cultural sense, which, in its very essence a positive and constructive force, leaves no room for serious discord! In short, the universal approval of concentric loyalties (family, community, county, province, state, federation of states) must be extended to include also many intersecting loyalties in a vast and complex world, with its shrinking distances and its growing necessity of mutual toleration.

If this vital reconciliation of assimilation and separation proceed in an orderly and least harmful way, it presupposes vigorous communal leadership. Under the impact of individualism, the decline of autonomy and the withdrawal of state support for the enforcement of its will, the Jewish community has suffered severe losses both in outward prestige and inner authority. The few rays of glory that remained after the legal emancipation, were dimmed in the general metamorphosis of Jewish life, concomitant with its concentration in metropolitan areas. In some countries, such as France and Belgium, the Jewish denomination was converted, through consistories under rigid state supervision, into a sort of state-church. It was a paradoxical combination, indeed, for non-political Judaism, and it accrued to the benefit of the state, rather than of the Jewish community, which obviously was the weaker partner. To some extent these shortcomings came to the fore in all other modern communal systems under the sanction of public law. In the preëmancipatory community, public law compulsion had greatly strengthened the natural ties of that true confraternity of blood, religion and economic interest. Some of the most beautiful flowers of Jewish autonomy (the Council of Four Lands, for example) blossomed in the rough clime of external enforcement, springing from the ruthless fiscal policies of the state. But the modern community, although profiting from its status as an agency of public law with respect to its budgetary situation and its vastly expanded range of activity, has not required constant coöperation with its membership. In the large cities, especially, thousands of Jews became mere communal "taxpayers," whose only interest in the community often seemed to consist in schemes of tax evasion. Some, especially very wealthy, members officially seceded from the community for no other reason than to save expense—a procedure which, after the liberalization of the community laws in Prussia, became so obnoxious as to provoke the ire of Bismarck and his conservative associates. In the United States, on the other hand, as well as in prefascist Italy, in France since 1906, etc., the full independence of each congregation, although undoubtedly conducive to keeping alive the members' interest in congregational affairs, became coresponsible for a state of anarchy not to be found in any other sector of Jewry. The four million American Jews have only slightly more than three thousand organized congregations, embracing in their aggregate membership but a minority of the people. More, only about one-fifth of these congregations belongs to one of the three central unions of the orthodox, reform and conservative groups, although (or rather because) these unions exercise merely a minimum of authority over the constituent organizations.

Radical change now appears to be facilitated by the rise of the universalist tide, even more than by the anti-Semitic onslaught. The community, to be sure, cannot expect to become an authoritarian body, since it necessarily lacks the state's power of enforcement and even its religious sanctions have lost much of their former vigor. In contrast to the monarchical forms under Islam, it has maintained its essentially democratic (or, at its worst, oligarchic) character throughout the European Middle Ages, and it is hardly going to submit to dictatorship today. Even limited autocracy, exercised by a few powerful and wealthy chiefs, would be just as harmful today as it was in eighteenth-century Holland or Poland. Party politics, on the other hand, which have in recent decades envenomed Jewish public life, especially in Palestine, Germany and Poland, have clearly demonstrated the unreasonableness of blindly imitating the forms of democratic or parliamentary government in totally different religious and ethno-cultural domains. (Cf. also Baron's "Historical Critique of the Jewish Community," *JSSQ,* XI.)

The resolution of these difficulties seems to lie in the restoration, under a novel and appropriate form, of the medieval equilibrium of freedom and authority and of central and local organization. Authority may perhaps best be restored by reassigning the position of leadership to rabbis and teachers, which largely depends, however, upon the transformation of the rabbinate from a purely "religious" into an all-embracing communal institution. Such transformation can only take place in conjunction with the other structural changes in Jewish religious life which will be discussed presently. As to centralization, the time seems speedily approaching when the deep antagonisms between the older and newer immigrants, between the Sephardic, German, Russian, Polish and Galician Jews, and even between orthodox, conservative and reform Judaism will give way to a new superior unity of "American Israel." More and more Jews are born and bred in America, more and more of them associate in business and pleasure and intermarry; increasingly also, do they face common hostility and discrimination. The edge of conflicts carried over from the Old World and the halcyon days of early Reform becomes blunter from day to day. Soon communal ventures, such as a renewed agitation for a unified New York *Kehillah,* will encounter much less resistance than they did only a few years ago.

In centralizing a metropolitan community or an entire country, one must leave to the individual "cells" their independent and characteristic life. Even if it should be proved beyond peradventure that a federation of charities, for example, actually succeeds in collecting more contributions than the sum total of all previous, disorganized donations, one must not disdain the great communal and cultural value of decentralized bodies which foster the active interest of numerous honorary officers and sometimes even of the much-harassed individual contributors. There is a great deal of truth in the old Jewish saying that he who gives a thousand shekels to a thousand recipients has fulfilled the commandment of charity in a higher degree than one who gives the same amount at one time. A somewhat novel constitutional experiment will have to be made, to allow for both the uncurtailed vitality of even the smallest association, and for strong, though self-restrained, powers of supervision, coördination and consultation of the central agencies. The relations between the various types of communities and the National Council in Palestine and, partly, between the communities and the Board of Deputies in England, approximate perhaps more closely than any other in contemporary Jewish life such an ideal equilibrium.

Charity and social work have been used here as classical examples because, especially in America, they have long focalized most of the communal endeavor. The various factions in American Jewry found in the struggle against misery and disease a common ground, where their differences in religious and social attitudes were less disturbing. Charity and social work undoubtedly will also in the future remain, to reëcho a popular apophthegm of two millennia, one of the three pillars upon which the Jewish world is built. While in essence, like the struggle against anti-Semitism, a defense against social (and natural) evils, it positively fosters human devotion and loving-kindness, and ennobles many personal relationships. Of course, this presupposes more intimate and discreet contacts between donor and recipient than is possible in our mechanical civilization, where most human relations have been dehumanized and replaced by an effective, but often cold and impersonal, organizational machine. Neither are the frequently harmful effects upon the recipients to be lightly dismissed.

You cultivate beggars [thundered Herzl, in addressing the great benefactor, Baron Maurice de Hirsch], it is characteristic that in no other people do we find both so much charity and so many paupers as in the Jewish people. . . . It is charity which pauperizes our national character. [*Tagebücher*, I, 22.]

The growing realization, moreover, that society as a whole is coresponsible for its disinherited, shifts the emphasis from individual and denominational relief to public social work of state and municipality. Nevertheless, numerous functions of a more constructive nature will have to be left to denominational agencies. As far as the Jews are concerned, even the few fields of communal endeavor previously mentioned, such as regulated migration, farsighted population policy and, especially, vast economic planning and restratification, will tax all the capacities of their existing and future social-service agencies.

438   EPILOGUE

Equally constructive efforts are needed to uphold the two other traditional pillars of Judaism: study and worship. Jewish education once again looms large in all programs of communal activity. Apart from vocational instruction and guidance in preparation for agricultural and industrial work, much greater stress must be laid upon character building, a major phase of which will consist in making Jewish pupils conscious of the worth of their heritage. To reduce the number of "inverted Marranos" and to eliminate many tragic conflicts in western Jewish youth, which necessarily affect their general morale, it is imperative to instill in them the feeling that, through both knowledge and emotional yearning, they wholeheartedly affirm their Jewishness. The educational goal must accommodate itself to the growing universalist demands. From exclusive emphasis on the development of personality, it must be shifted toward fuller integration of the individual in the group and in society at large. An effective Jewish educational system, taking care of children, adolescents and adults, thus increasingly becomes a categoric necessity. Conditions, as they now prevail, for instance, in the United States, are truly deplorable. According to a survey of 1926, only 138,658 pupils attended any kind of Jewish school, the majority being enrolled only in so-called Sabbath schools. "To deceive Jews into believing," pointedly writes Rabbi Solomon Goldman, "that their children are being educated at the Sunday School, or that the Sunday School is in any way adequate as a solution of the problem of Jewish education is to be downright dishonest" (*A Rabbi Takes Stock*, p. 18). The average attendance of these pupils, moreover, was only two years. Adult education, outside of the orthodox group, notwithstanding its encouraging developments during the last few years, is still in its infancy.

Let no one contend that intensive instruction in Jewish history and literature, added to the general course of studies in primary and secondary schools, would place too heavy a burden upon Jewish youth. Granted that the demands of western education may be further increased, most Jewish pupils under proper guidance and with an intense desire to preserve their intellectual and emotional integrity, ought to be able to do justice to both. Such an all-inclusive educational program may even become instrumental in shaping certain new pedagogic methods. That this hope is not to be relegated to the realm of fancy, is borne out by one of the most extended and successful experiments in educational history, the two thousand years of Jewish communal education. Judaism has once before, under the stress of its peculiar needs, performed a great pioneering service in popularizing education, making it accessible to and obligatory for every person, and in elevating it to a focal position in all matters of public policy. The new type of Jewish education, evolved to meet the new emergency, may also incidentally become a significant contribution to human civilization.

Of course, the nature of the new educational system is as yet unpredictable. It may, however, achieve its aims much more effectively, if it continues along the historical line and tries to impart sound knowledge of Judaism and its historical sources, in the light of really basic trends in western civilization, rather than if it presents superficial syntheses with ephemeral fads, or adopts the "newest" pedagogic methods propagated by sanguine "up-to-date" educators. In order to duplicate the millennial achievement, moreover, adult education must once more become a matter of principal concern. The general economic and intellectual trends of our age greatly facilitate the task, inasmuch as they secure also to Jewish adults the enjoyment of prolonged periods of leisure. The progressive transformation of masses of Jewish shopkeepers and artisans into employees and wage earners, however harmful in other respects, gives them the benefit of steady reduction of working hours. What appeared in the talmudic and medieval legislation as a semi-utopian postulate, namely that each and every adult Jew devote one-third of his day to study, may easily be realized now, when the weekly hours of labor are being reduced to forty or less. The Jewish community must wake up to this new opportunity and task, and devise ways of utilizing the mighty energies so released, to its own and its members' best advantage.

To adult education in our age belongs also the dissemination of good Jewish books, journals and newspapers. Hebrew and Yiddish publications, in particular, ought to be much more intensively supported by the community at large than is now the case. The efflorescence of the Hebrew renaissance in Palestine must not be allowed to wither in the oppressive provincial atmosphere of an island in a sea of indifferent non-Hebraic Jewry. The Diaspora needs the light which emanates from Zion; but Palestine, too, though increasingly independent, will always profoundly react to the intellectual response of the millions in dispersion. The prophets now composing advance obituaries for Yiddish, may for a long time prove as wrong as those "clear-sighted" matter-of-fact men of the last generation who discounted all possibilities of resurrecting Hebrew, the "dead" language. The Yiddish press, in particular, a mighty organ of Jewish public opinion in the United States, Poland and Russia, shows no signs of the approaching doom which has been so frequently foretold in recent years. No one will deny that the progressive Americanization, Polonization and Russification constantly diminish the use of spoken Yiddish. However, the Yiddish press may for a long time to come replenish its ranks from the growing mass of newspaper readers, and from those who get into the habit of reading more than one paper a day. In the din of controversy, it often appears as if Hebrew and Yiddish were deeply inimical forces, and one had to choose one, to the exclusion of the other. If such a sad choice were really indispensable, one might certainly argue in favor of Hebrew, not only on account of its more glorious past, but also of the greater promise it seems to hold out for the future, and perhaps even of its present more universal function in world Jewry. Fortunately such a decision appears unavoidable only to the chauvinist Hebraists and Yiddishists, of whose mutual hostility the central organs of the community at large must needs steer clear.

The increase both in number and quality of the newly appearing books of Jewish interest in the vernacular, and the rising circulation of Jewish weeklies and dailies, though not devoid of the well-known modern danger of overproduction of literary mediocrities, is a sign of greater vitality. Through proper guidance and the support of serious-minded scholarly, literary and artistic societies and publishing houses, communal leadership might help raise the standards and stimulate the interest of the public. Only such a very broad program of adult education would prepare the ground for that great new synthesis of Judaism and western culture, whereby to meet the unprecedented intellectual and religious crisis. This task, of course, will be accomplished primarily by a few creative men of genius. But such men do not arise in a vacuum. They spring out of the living consciousness of the people, to whose inarticulate yearnings they lend definite form and substance, and whose intensive response, favorable or unfavorable, they in turn need, like oxygen for breathing.

Education, and especially adult education, becomes more than ever before also the major task of Zionism. With the progressive shift of its center of gravity to Palestine, the movement must undergo a thorough reorientation in the Diaspora. It need no longer appeal to Jews to go to Palestine; there are more candidates available than the country can possibly admit. Neither is the collection of funds, however necessary, more than of incidental consequence in a movement which went out to rebuild Jewish life on new foundations. Besides, investing capital in Palestine now has a sufficient appeal to the profit motive, and consequently loses its previous attraction as a means toward the realization of a great national and social ideal. It is, indeed, too easy nowadays to be a Zionist.

Zionism which began as a passion of the poor [says Buber], now sometimes appears as if it were to become a hobby of the rich. Woe unto it, if it so becomes! [*Kampf um Israel,* p. 402.]

In order to regain its hold on Jewish youth, it must fill itself with new meaning. While it evidently cannot give up colonizing activities and intrust them to the (much too indolent) non-Zionist half of the Jewish Agency, it must justify them to Jewish youth by unflinchingly upholding the universal social import of the Palestinian venture. It cannot give up its political negotiations with the Mandatory Power, but it must seek to refute the lingering suspicions of aiding British imperialism by sincerely trying to reach an understanding with the Arabs, however tremendous the odds. A thorough familiarity with the life and culture of the Arab neighbor, hitherto sadly neglected, is undoubtedly a preliminary to such an understanding. The courses in Arabic, Panislamism, etc., recently opened by the workers' council in Jerusalem, and the work of the Oriental Department of the Hebrew University, certainly are steps in the right direction. Apart from these two primarily political functions, however, until recently the alpha and omega of the Zionist Organization, it must concentrate upon really constructive cultural work in the Diaspora. After the establishment of the Jewish Agency, Chaim Weizman, once leader of the "cultural" Zionists, encouraged the hope that, the tasks of realizing "practical" and "political" Zionism being transferred to the new body, the old organization would turn primarily to promoting Diaspora culture and to propagating the pure Zionist ideal. Regardless of the failure of the Agency to fulfill this expectation, the world organization must add a bold program of this kind to its older aims; it must do so, one feels, if it wants to survive its present incontestable crisis. A broad educational program, with the main accent on Jewish history and Hebrew letters, would not only implant in Jewish youth that love of their people and appreciation of their heritage which seem so indispensable to true Zionist allegiance, but also promote close intellectual coöperation between the Diaspora and Palestine, which alone can save the unity of world Jewry. By attracting ever new recruits, it would also fill the gaps left in the ranks of Zionist youth by the departure of its most active, gifted and devoted members, who hasten to join their fellow pioneers in one of the collectivistic settlements in Palestine.

This recurrent sapping of the Diaspora's best energies, on the other hand, is most vital to Zionist accomplishment in Palestine. It is comparatively easy to win a war or even a revolution through superhuman but brief exertion. But the upbuilding of a homeland over a period of many decades, calls for such relentless perseverance of the entire people and such indefatigable effort of its leaders and pioneers, that only generations born and bred in the conviction of its inevitability can achieve this goal. Strong reverberations of Jewish and world opinion, moreover, are indispensable for maintaining the necessary good will of the League of Nations and the Mandatory Power. All flirtations with alliances with either the Panislamic movement or the Soviets against Great Britain, are, under the present circumstances, little short of suicidal. The mere insistence upon the British pledges, on the other hand, leads nowhere. In the long run, only Great Britain's self-interest, buttressed by the pressure of a powerful and sincere public opinion, will determine the British course out of the present difficulties. Diaspora Zionism, especially of the propagandist and "cultural" brand, is now, if ever, an absolute necessity.

THE FUTURE OF RELIGION

The great structural changes in the synagogue must likewise include a gradual return to its educational rather than its devotional functions. Outwardly, this focal institution of traditional Judaism has shown an astounding tenacity, even in the midst of the great crisis. The very depression of the last few years has affected it, externally at least, to a smaller extent than perhaps any other vital organ of the community, not only in countries where it enjoys the protection of public law, but also in the United States. Although no statistics are available, it seems that Jewish congregational losses did not exceed those of the Christian churches, which, in the years 1929-33, amounted only to one in 2,344. This, compared with one American bank in five, and one private hospital in forty-five, which were forced to shut their doors. The income of the individual congregation may have dropped considerably (on an average probably somewhat more than the 40-50 percent, in most Protestant churches), but they have carried on. In fact, from the purely religious point of view, the cessation of the previous trend toward overexpansion is not wholly regrettable. While entailing much temporary hardship, it may have helped check the more serious dangers of the progressive externalization of worship. If the excessive synagogue construction of the 1920's had at least fostered the development of Jewish architectural and decorative arts, if it had contributed certain new elements to the creation of the oft-postulated specific Jewish style, or else if it had, by enhancing the beauty of the ceremonial, evoked a greater religious response among the congregants, one would have no quarrel with it. In fact, however, it merely diverted the attention of lay and ecclesiastical leaders from more important congregational tasks, to contributing and collecting money for the benefit of builders and bankers. This overemphasis on money, incidentally, lent undue prominence to the wealthy members, and completely shut out the poor from exercising influence on congregational affairs. Some congregations resembled plutocratic clubs, rather than humble and equalitarian houses of worship, and outside class divisions were paradoxically carried over into the domain of a religion which still publicly prided itself of its millennial preachment concerning the equality of all Jews before God. That is why today congregations defaulting in their interest payments on mortgages and those (one hears that such exist) which are run by their Jewish or even Christian mortgagees, interested in their carrying on until times improve, certainly are a sad, but not altogether deplorable, spectacle.

The externalization of the synagogue's functions has many other aspects. The recent tendency to convert it into a kind of community center to satisfy most social and communal needs of its membership, although fully in line with the medieval and perhaps ancient tradition, tends, under modern conditions, to emphasize its external to the detriment of its intrinsic values. It is one thing to serve as a "house of the people" (Jer. 39:8) in a Jewish commonwealth or a medieval ghetto, and quite another to do it in a modern emancipated and more or less assimilated community. Wherever religion, law and life are so profoundly welded together as in medieval Judaism or Islam, the synagogue or mosque can easily be opened to every activity, no matter how individual or private, because each act of man is placed under the sanction of religious law. The secular interests of the modern Jew, however, which he shares with the other citizens, irrespective of faith and nationality, have no bearing whatever upon his Jewishness. That is why a business contract between two Jews, written in Hebrew and with a view to settlement of all litigations before a Jewish court, could properly be concluded on the premises of the synagogue. A modern swimming pool or dance hall remain wholly extraneous, however, except, perhaps, in Palestine or in the case of an associated specifically Jewish sports organization. Whether or not the inclusion of such otherwise innocuous diversions among congregational activities commends itself because they incidentally attract young folk to the other, more religious functions, is to be decided in each particular case on grounds of congregational policy. However, they must never be allowed as a substitute, in any sense whatsoever, for the two really vital tasks of the modern synagogue: worship and education.

Traditionally, education ought even to surpass worship.

One ancient teacher, paraphrasing the words of the Psalmist, proclaimed that "the Lord loves the 'gates' of houses distinguished in learning more than those of synagogues and school houses"; and another declared, with the obvious assent of his audience, that "from the day that the Temple was destroyed the Holy One, blessed be He, has nothing in his world, but the four ells of the Halakah" (Ber. 8 a). The abandonment of Hebrew prayers by Reform temples has removed one of the means of imparting knowledge of the original sources, and the incentive to acquire more such knowledge. Even in the orthodox congregations, the wholesale omission, often on puristic grounds, of *piyyutim,* those didactic poems which had expressly been composed for the purpose of conveying pertinent information, has considerably weakened the educational import of the Jewish prayer book. The general tendency to shift the responsibility for the divine services from the congregation to the rabbi, as unnatural in Judaism as it is in Protestantism, both of which reject the Catholic distinction between laity and clergy, has even more substantially diminished the instructional value of worship. A new reform of the Jewish ritual will have to explore carefully all the possibilities of restoring its old intellectual, as well as emotional appeal. Beautiful and touching prayers, in their daily repetition, undoubtedly strike a responsive chord in the heart of those who recite them. But their power is greatly enhanced if their full significance is first to be assimilated through intellectual exertion, and if they evoke ever-new associations with other texts or theological doctrines acquired in the course of prolonged study. The sermon of a great rabbi may stir the emotions of his audience to religious frenzy (although such is rarely the case with the overcritical modern Jewish audiences, which are more frequently entertained than moved), but the effect will quickly evaporate in the cold atmosphere of our mechanical civilization if no more lasting intellectual curiosity is simultaneously awakened. Only such curiosity might induce a part of the worshipers to endeavor to digest what they have heard, by the process of paraphrastic rethinking, and to obtain further clarification. The "enlightened" critics of the nineteenth century made a grievous error in underestimating the emotional value of the Halakah. Law and mysticism, rationality and irrationality, never seriously clashed in the living texture of

Judaism. If the synagogue is to regain part of its lost ground, it will once more have to cultivate both, and to detect a new harmonious blending for intellect and emotion, for piety and enlightenment.

The modern rabbinate must accommodate itself to that transformation. The preacher must increasingly become a teacher. The wider the circle of educated laymen, the maturer and more sophisticated their tastes, the less will they be impressed by oratorical fireworks. Great oratory, forensic, parliamentary and ecclesiastic, is generally on the decline. The rabbi's great chance is now in teaching and leading. It has often been noticed that among the representative Jews of our age, one will find few rabbis and a majority of "unsynagogued." Inasmuch as representation was entrusted, especially in America, to the wealthy lay leader through the sheer magnetism of his wealth, the rabbi was powerless. But it looks as if the economic depression had rudely, but deeply, stirred the mass of success worshipers from their hypnotic trance. The Jewish intellectual, especially the rabbi, teacher and social worker, may now really be called upon to replace the financier in guiding the destinies of the people. A rabbi, particularly, an intellectual specifically trained to understand the import of the major issues in Jewish life, if personally endowed with a modicum of creative *élan* and awake to the needs of the age, might once again become the true leader. Particularly in countries where religion appears permanently to remain in the focus of Jewish life, the odds seem to favor the religious expert. Undoubtedly, the possibility is not to be lightly dismissed that, as a result of the present crisis, the rabbi and the scribe will follow the ancient priest (whom they themselves had forced out through their Pharisaic solution of the postexilic crisis) into oblivion, and be replaced by a new type of communal leader. But it appears more likely that, in the generations needed even in our fast-moving age for such a transformation, the rabbinate will be able to make the necessary adjustments and synthesize the new, with its old, functions. After all, the rabbinical, unlike the priestly, office has not been identified with one particular type of communal service, but has shown great adaptability to changing environments since the days of Ezra.

Of course, the crucial question remains: what is the future

of religion generally and of the Jewish religion in particular? It is not science and the new discoveries, we have seen, nor even religious indifference which appear as the main enemy, but rival "religious" trends. Among these, the proletarian "godless" creed of the Russian communists, and the resurrected paganism, especially of Germany, threaten all established denominations; while secularism, under the guise of nationalism, beclouds particularly the future outlook of religious Judaism. Since secularism, however, has thus far shown little vitality outside the proletarian parties, it may properly be discussed in conjunction with the general communist menace to the traditional forms of religion.

Students of the new Russian mentality are amazed at the persistence of the old religious springs of Russian sectarianism. Dostoievski, Tolstoy, and the more strictly "orthodox" writers of the czarist past, may be relegated by the Soviet government, in part or in full, to limbo. The identity in style (though not in content) of Bolshevism and the former official, as well as heterodox, religious currents appears undeniable. The parallel with primitive Christianity is perhaps even more striking. Should the communistic world revolution prove ultimately victorious, the future historian might easily compare the struggle of the rich and multicolored liberalistic civilization of our day against the onslaught of the Russians, with the losing battle of the advanced, philosophical and tolerant individualistic Graeco-Roman world against the poor and bigoted eastern "barbarians." With the Marxian "gospel" and Lenin's "epistles," the adepts of the new creed threaten to submerge the variegated pattern of western artistic, literary and scientific achievement in a maze of homilies and exegetical controversies. The contrast between the technically crude, often downright primitive, art of the Soviets (as shown at the biennial international exhibitions in Venice, as presented in the music of Shostakovich, and the fine mass scenes of the Russian motion picture), and the sophisticated, elaborate, often technically perfect, but increasingly artificial and inane western creations, offers striking comparisons with the victorious march of primitive Christian art through the centers of exhausted Hellenistic civilization. The endless anathemas of the warring factions outside Russia, where alone the new church-state is able to suppress the Trotskyist and other "heresies"; the deposition and banishment of some of the most prominent leaders of yesterday, frequently in the name of the only "true" interpretation of a passage in Marx or Lenin, are too obvious parallels to have remained unnoticed. When the editors of a scholarly organ, such as the *Zeitshrift* (issued by the Jewish department of the White Russian Academy of Science) express in the foreword to the fourth volume their regret for the "opportunistic mistakes" and the "pure academism" in which they had indulged in the previous issues, one cannot help seeing therein the replica of an ancient recantation. Voltaire may be right in saying that in his day men "ceased to speculate on the nature of free grace and began to speculate on the price of grain"; but in the intensity of their factional strife over theoretical economic issues, they have often shown "religious" fanaticism equal to any of the partisans of Arius or Athanasius. Did not Marx himself, in *The Poverty of Philosophy,* poignantly describe the economists as a new brand of theologians,

who also establish two kinds of religion. Every religion but their own is an invention of man, while their own religion is an emanation from God. [Page 191.]

To speak, under the circumstances, of a permanent contrast between socialism and religion appears decidedly unwarranted. One may easily argue, on the contrary, that a victory of workers and peasants would secure the supremacy of a social class which had for millennia belonged to the staunchest supporters of organized religion. The recent professed atheism of the proletarian parties, even if accepted at its face value, is explicable in the light of the historic alliance of the official churches with the socially conservatory forces. But in essence religion has often been as revolutionary a force as any. The proletariat undoubtedly has more deep-rooted religious leanings, it has learned more humility and courageous acknowledgment of life's tragic burden, it has developed a deeper sense of social solidarity, and recognized more readily the value of authority and discipline, than the individualistic, free-thinking, often unnerved bourgeoisie of our time. There was a profounder justification for the antireligious upheaval in middle-class Enlightenment and religion of Reason than for the godlessness of contemporary communism. If these historical parallels are at all instructive, the conclusion seems not altogether unwarranted that the present atheist outburst in Russia is by no means the last word in the checkered history of Russian sectarianism.

The Jewish religion, especially, bears all the earmarks of potential adaptability to a new socialist order. To be sure, Jewish *bezbozhniki* belong to the most radical opponents of their inherited religion. Throughout the world, Jewish atheists, middle-class as well as proletarian, have been quite vociferous for decades. As far back as 1878, Aaron Liberman, the first Hebrew-writing socialist, on being asked in court for his religion, replied, "I am a socialist." Fritz Mauthner, even before the World War, suggested that the main task of the "chosen people" today appears to be the setting of an example for life without a god. Less flippantly, a few Christian critics have accused the modern Jew of aligning himself with either Spinoza or Marx. They were all misled by a small, but articulate, minority. The profoundly religious Jewish masses of eastern Europe and the Near East and even the considerable group of pious Jews in the West, either wholly escaped their attention or were dismissed as mere relics of the past. The inherent strength of an ancient ethnic religion, buttressed by traditions of social justice and communal solidarity, easily detachable from the present social order which it has not created, and with proved elasticity in adjusting itself to changing wants, has been much too readily overlooked. The religion of a minority, in many countries lowly and oppressed and everywhere powerless, has also much less to fear from the transfer of power from one class to another, than other, more power-approving and state-dependent churches. The moral passion, moreover, so characteristic of both Judaism and the new social revolution, has been so deeply ingrained in the Jewish soul that it permeates with equal intensity the sermons of generations of devout rabbis, Katzenellenbogen by name, and the *Capital* of their "atheistic" descendant Marx; the writings and addresses of Trotsky and Max Adler, who recriminate against each other's "talmudistic arguments"; and of Disraeli or Durkheim, who "has rewritten the Talmud in sociological terms." A "this-worldly" religion which has not relegated salvation to the Hereafter, but has constantly striven for the betterment of the human race in this world, appears quite likely to reëmerge, after a period of confusion and groping, in a new synthesis with the forces of humanity, whatever they may turn out to be. Jellinek once rightly compared Judaism's millennial growth to the geological formations of the earth, in which every new stratum merely covers, but does not remove, the older layers. It is consequently to be expected that the new "tertiary" stratum will retain its unmistakable identity with the "primary" biblical, and "secondary" Pharisaic-rabbinic, religion. Of course, in many ways, it may as profoundly differ from Pharisaic Judaism as the latter differed from the ancient Israelitic creed.

The specter of a recrudescent heathen Germanic religion, on the other hand, need not trouble the Jews too seriously. They undoubtedly would suffer from it indirectly. The abandonment of Christianity by a great people might initiate a more general reversion to pagan standards. Such a relapse would then gravely jeopardize the harmony between the non-Jewish world and the professing Jews, no matter in what stage of evolution their own religion might find itself by that time. Even a Christianity purified of the Old Testament, a resurrected Marcionism, might reduce the Jewish God in the eyes of their neo-gnostic neighbors to a mere *demiourgos,* to an artificer of this imperfect and wretched world. There are enough signs that polytheistic as well as dualistic forces are again operative against the prevalence of "Jewish" monotheism. The new extreme worship of power and the search, to quote Professor Ernst Bergmann, for an "antidote to the effeminate demoralizing ethics of Christianity, which like some sugared poison has eaten into the hearts of men" (*New York Times,* March 11, 1934), cannot but be prejudicial to the equally "effeminate" ethics of Judaism. The very idea of *Schöpfungsordnungen,* widely adopted now even in Protestant circles in Germany, preaching eternal inequality between man and man as willed by God, greatly enhances the belief in the irremediable inferiority of the "non-Aryan" races. Judaism, however, seems on the whole to be safe against the incursion of such doctrines. Just as, two thousand years ago it staved off all attacks of prepotent paganism and successfully resisted the influx of gnostic and dualistic conceptions, so also in our day this menace appears comparatively slight. The much-debated elimination of the Old Testament would thus be harmful to Jews rather than to Judaism, and to Jews much less than to Christianity.

The repudiation of the Old Testament [wrote the prominent theologian, R. Seeberg, in the early years of the Nazi agitation], ultimately turns against the God of Jesus Christ. It is the uprooting of all Christianity. [*Antisemitismus, Judentum und Kirche,* p. 30.]

That is why the Jews may largely leave the combating of these tendencies to Christian leaders. Their problem is their own atheism, rather than polytheistic or dualistic nonconformity. Should this atheism, however, help them to search their innermost hearts and induce them to make a fresh start toward a reformulation of their old religion, then the beautiful words of Franz Rosenzweig might really come true, "To him who invokes God with the double prayer of the believer and the unbeliever God will not deny himself."

HISTORICAL-HALAKIC REFORMULATION

A thoroughgoing reformulation it certainly must be. Judaism has often been praised for its great adaptability to the needs of every age. The gradual modification of Jewish thought and mode of life frequently had so strong a cumulative effect as to alter completely the physiognomy of the Halakah. One need merely compare the Law of the Pentateuch with that of the Mishnah to realize how revolutionary the transformation had been. A comparison of the Mishnah with the Babylonian Talmud, on the other hand, instantly reveals to what extent Diaspora Jewry had divested itself of Palestinian traditions and supplanted them with new institutions growing out of the life in Exile. A superficial glance at Maimonides' enumeration of the 613 commandments, suffices to convince the reader of how far the Jewish religion had traveled since the biblical period. In this list, rendering the talmudic reinterpretation of biblical law, about one-half appears so obsolete as to claim practical attention only after the coming of the Messiah. The other half is for the most part either so thoroughly revised, as to appear wholly unrecognizable from the standpoint of an ancient Israelite; or else it represents certain general religio-ethical teachings (such as most of the Ten Commandments) common to many human creeds and by no means characteristic of Judaism. A large bulk of talmudic law, moreover, professedly has no biblical foundation at all. While Maimonides admitted, in his *Book of Precepts,* that an ordinary Jew may have no occasion at all to comply with more than 60 of the 248 positive commandments; that a woman may be satisfied with the fulfillment of but 46 of them; and that many laws have become altogether obsolete, I. S. Reggio could, from the standpoint of nineteenth-century orthodoxy, speak of 10,000 valid commandments. Of course, even this archopponent of Reform could not possibly prove the origin of most of these laws in the Bible without confusing the hermeneutic interpretation of the rabbis with the simple meaning of Scripture. (Cf. also the very pertinent remarks in the introduction to Aaron ha-Levi's thirteenth-century code, the *Sepher ha-Hinnuk*). From a historical point of view, the most important religious institutions of talmudic and medieval Jewry are, in the main, creative innovations of the postexilic age—to mention only the synagogue, the public school, the rabbinate, the type of holiday observance, and many kinds of prohibited food. They may all have precedents in the Old Testament, but their focal importance in Jewish life was due exclusively to the Pharisaic and rabbinical restatement of the entire body of Jewish observance. Even the difference between the Babylonian Halakah and that of the sixteenth-century Shulhan Aruk are much more extensive than one would be inclined to believe, in the face of the medieval rabbis' recurrent professions of unlimited adherence to every word of the Talmud. That these differences are not larger still, is mainly due to the analogous social background of both, which necessitated but minor adjustments.

In modern Jewish life, however, orthodoxy has not demonstrated the same elasticity. The tempo of change during the emancipation era has been decidedly too fast. Orthodox Jewry's mass concentration in eastern Europe, where more or less stable social conditions, reminiscent of ghetto life, have long prevailed, likewise accounted for its resistance to radical adjustments. But now that emancipation has begun to make inroads also into eastern Jewish life, the conviction rapidly spreads throughout the Jewish world that major changes are unavoidable. Gradually the rhythm of adjustment may be quickened, as leaders realize better the profundity of the crisis and its historical significance. Everybody agrees that practically the entire civil law, once a foremost component of the Halakah, is rapidly becoming obsolescent, at a time when Jewish courts of justice have been reduced to little more than occasional courts of arbitration. One may readily assert that should an orthodox Shulhan Aruk be composed in the twenty-second century, it would necessarily differ from that of the sixteenth in an even higher degree than did Joseph Karo's code from the compilation of Judah the Patriarch. These differences would have to be as far-reaching as were those between Pharisaic Judaism and the preëxilic Israelitic religion.

This is nevertheless not a restatement of the ideology of Reform. The return to prophetic, as against talmudic, Judaism, long proclaimed by Reform as its main goal, would be an impossible turning back of the wheels of history. Indeed, as we have seen, perspicacious reformers themselves soon recognized that the continuity of Jewish evolution must be maintained. More important are the shortcomings of the basic conception of religion, as preached by the classical reformers; its reduction to a system of creeds and observances, nowadays recognized by Christian society and state as belonging to the domain of religion; the abandonment of Jewish ethnic values and the concentration upon a missionary form of ethical monotheism. All these teachings might have been necessary correlatives to the emancipation movement, but now they seem to have no future. The present recession of liberalistic and individualistic forces has considerably weakened the foundations upon which the Reform structure was originally erected. The divergence between its democratic teachings and its conservative, undemocratic practice, has served to accentuate its minority character. With the growing conviction, therefore, that a totalitarian ethnic assimilation can no longer be expected, the Reform movement has itself been searching for new ways of adjustment. There is an undeniable sentiment abroad that the time is ripe for the "reforming of the Reformation." The discussions in the 1935 session of the Central Conference of American Rabbis clearly revealed the wide gap between the theological thinking of our day and that embodied in the Pittsburgh platform of half a century ago. Indeed the distinctions between the advanced groups of western orthodoxy and conservative Judaism, and the right wing of Reform, have increasingly been obliterated in point of ideology, under the impact of the unifying forces released by both Zionism and anti-Semitism. Differences in ritual are constantly diminishing. More and more Jews see themselves bound to disregard orthodox law, but are unwilling to give up their emotional and intellectual allegiance to Jewish tradition. At any rate, the nineteenth-century struggle between orthodoxy and Reform has long passed its heroic stage, and is now carried on by force of inertia rather than out of vital necessity. To think today of a reunification of all religious forces of Jewry on a common basis, is certainly no longer as utopian a dream as it was half a century ago. In America, for example, the trend toward the reëstablishment of catholic Israel, to use Schechter's well-known term, becomes more and more irresistible.

This does not mean that Judaism is likely to develop, in the near future, such a uniform and all-embracing philosophy of life as that which it possessed in the Middle Ages. The geographic, political, economic and social divergences in world Jewry must find their counterpart in a variety of cultural and religious patterns. The major cause for divisions, however, lies not so much in the disparate views on religion as in the struggle between the religious and nonreligious forces. If a permanent schism is to be prevented, the official Jewish religion must possess as vast a latitude as is consistent with that minimum of loyalty without which no organized religion may persist. It must also meticulously avoid laying down any dogmatic credo which would instantly crowd out all who cherish different convictions. Judaism has for centuries succeeded in dispensing with an accepted system of dogmas, and maintaining its integrity without a *Dogmatik* (to use Rosenzweig's distinction), if not necessarily without a number of dogmas. This is still more imperative today when, with Jewish life changing so rapidly, Judaism can ill afford the luxury of sectarian strife. Reflecting the transitions in Jewish society, the Jewish religion will necessarily long remain in flux. In the meantime, the major adaptations will have to be left primarily to the "creative genius of the masses." Only after several generations will the people be ready for that new definitive formulation, the new Shulhan Aruk of the twenty-first or twenty-second century, which we have hypothetically postulated.

Even then it may again be a real Shulhan Aruk, a new *halakic* code. Those who, witnessing the generations of progressive decline of religious observance, pronounced the Halakah dead and buried, mistook individual laws for the legal system as such. Even if most existing commandments and prohibitions were to be discarded, the Halakah as a "way" of Jewish life would still remain intact. All attempts of Reform to "spiritualize" Judaism, merely tended to blur the distinctions between the Jewish and the Christian religions, and thus to estrange the masses who had always been attracted to Judaism as a mode of living, rather than a religious philosophy. No amount of philosophic preaching or historical instruction can substitute for the elaborate system of folk ways and traditional observances which has heretofore maintained the identity of this religio-ethnic group. Halakah, taken in this widest sense, can easily adapt itself to a new theology. Should Judaism decide to discard its present superannuated conception of God and change it, as it has done on previous occasions, to one more suitable to the philosophic tastes of the coming generation, it could still cling to many of its folk ways, after modifying some of them. One may venture, perhaps, the paradoxical assertion that a reconstituted legal ghetto community, consisting exclusively of atheists, may still adhere to most regulations of Karo's Shulhan Aruk, while expurgating those few passages which refer directly to belief in a personal God, a thorough reformulation of which is undoubtedly demanded by a machine age. If fear really were the foremost creator of gods, it would no longer be the animistic fear of personal beings, but that of the impersonal crises, such as result from business cycles, inflation, wars and other "inescapable" social developments, which would now call for a theology centered around an impersonal "Cause of causes." Folk ways, however, the slow growth of centuries, generally reveal a greater tenacity and more easily adapt themselves to the changing conditions than do metaphysical ideas.

The restoration of an authoritative Halakah is evidently going to be stimulated by the rise of the new "authoritarian" social forces. The acids of philosophical relativism in the past, the counterpart to the abstract representation of relative values through money in the capitalist era, have long undermined the validity of all social regulations, unsupported by state power. So will the forthcoming, apparently more strictly regimented, social order tend to reintroduce absolute evaluations and to strengthen the long-neglected human proclivities to discipline and voluntary obedience. Together with the Halakah, medieval Jewish scholasticism, as well as mysticism, is likely to assume a new living significance, as does, for example, Neo-Thomism in the Catholic world today. Just as Catholicism today, preaching in the main the gospel of the medieval authoritative Church, is everywhere on the offensive against the receding individualistic and liberalistic forces of later Protestantism, so one may expect a further resurgence of the halakic (combined with the scholastic-kabbalistic) type of Judaism against the hitherto prevalent individualistic reformatory trends.

The new Halakah, however, will have to differ from the old not only in details, but in its fundamental methods. The terrific pace of modern transformations and the depth and extent of the present crisis in Judaism, preclude the possibility of another successful application of the traditional way of reinterpreting older scriptural authorities. No midrashic reinterpretation of this type would be able to retain the identity, however superficial, of the older and the newer meaning. For example, it is one thing to extend, over a period of centuries, the significance of the three biblical injunctions: "Thou shalt not seethe a kid in its mother's milk" (Exod. 23:19, etc.), to include cooking, eating and all other uses of any kind of meat and milk, and then to amplify this prohibition by innumerable casuistic regulations; and another thing to interpret it away altogether, for a generation which balks at this particular restraint. We would have to turn back to the early Diaspora rabbis of the Pharisaic age, who invalidated entire sections in biblical and even pharisaic law by declaring them applicable exclusively to Jewry in Palestine, in order to find prototypes for such leadership. To understand the far-reaching significance of this distinction, one need only imagine a modern parallel and assume that a synod of contemporary rabbis, working *within* the framework of the Talmud, should decree that a large body of law was valid only under preëmancipatory conditions, but might now be discarded in countries with full legal equality. The Reform rabbis who attempted such a twofold interpretation saw themselves speedily forced to reject altogether the authority of tradition. A new experiment along the lines of scriptural reinterpretation, moreover, would be immediately frustrated through the widespread basic disbelief in the revealed character of biblical law. Less and less are Jews inclined to accept a regulation simply because it is a "decree from heaven," when their reason revolts against it.

The methods of readjustment, found adequate for more than two millennia, thus no longer appear satisfactory. We have to go back to that first great crisis in early postexilic times and revise the methods then adopted. While it is too early to judge as to which novel ways will eventually be followed, the bare contours of a new road seem to emerge from the mist of present uncertainties. To put it in a nutshell: the interpretation and reinterpretation of the history of the people, a kind of *historic Midrash,* is now to serve as a guidance for the future. A new divine book has opened itself before the eyes of the faithful: the book of human and Jewish destinies, guided by some unknown and unknowable ultimate Power. This book, if properly understood, would seem to answer the most perplexing questions of the present and the future. It is over the exposition of this historical "Scripture" that sectarian controversies are already raging, and are likely to grow more intense and sweeping. The historical study of Judaism has long cut across all factional divisions. If anywhere, it is to the satisfaction of this growing interest in the Jewish past, that all parties, conservative and Reform, Zionist and communist, diaspora-nationalistic and assimilationist, have contributed their share. The very orthodoxy, although soon sensing a dangerous rival, could not resist the overwhelming trend of the "historical" age. It is in this field that the unity of Israel is still well preserved. The sectional and factional strife affects primarily the application of the findings to the present, but much less the method of historical exegesis and interpretation, and least of all the mere ascertaining of facts.

Study and research in Jewish history, to be sure, have not yet formed their own specific method. They still follow too slavishly the general historical trends in the outside world, not paying sufficient attention to the peculiar subject matter, which calls for a peculiar kind of investigation. Even though western historiography has long passed the stage of Freeman's once famous definition, "History is past politics and politics is present history," it cannot yet do justice to this unique type of ethno-religious, nonpolitical history. A profounder familiarity with the workings of the Jewish mind in the past, with the logical categories, and the psychology underlying its halakic and exegetical type of thinking, would help reëstablish a sort of historical continuity in this field likewise, and would open the way for a truer understanding of the Jewish past. It will perhaps be one of the major tasks of the growing circle of scholars attached to the Hebrew University creatively to reformulate, in the course of time, the methods of the science of Judaism. (It is needless to say that this is not a nationalistic denial of the universality of science, nor even of historical science. It is merely a contention that within the general frame of scientific method, there is room for ample variations to meet the specific needs of particular subject matters).

Let no one raise the objection that the scientific, historical study of religion has often militated against true and intensive religious feeling. The comparative study of religion, and especially the investigation into the origin and development of primitive creeds, has undoubtedly tended to unravel the crude, chthonian origins of some of the most "advanced" religious conceptions. A more detached research into creeds other than one's own has frequently demonstrated to the student the untenability of many preconceived notions fostered by centuries of polemics and apologetics. It simply proved that, were, for example, Pharisaic Judaism as deadly legalistic as has often been asserted, it would have been a religion of corpses rather than of men of flesh and blood. Religious relativism and skepticism were thus fostered, to the detriment of the naïve belief in the revealed basis of one's own acceptances and rejections. Through sheer contrasting of various attitudes, of the "on the one hands" and "on the other hands," man often lost all power of decision and affirmation.

These and similar other objections are superficially true, but contain the basic fallacy of overestimating the corrosive influence of science and mistaking effects for causes. As a rule, skepticism and relativism have been ingrained in the investigator or reader long before he reaches his scientific conclusions. The relativistic trends of the modern age have been much too overwhelming to allow the historical sciences to cling to absolute values. The same scientific inquisitiveness in a less relativistic age may lead to opposite results, and to the support, by scholarly argument, of certain absolute beliefs. Medieval scholasticism evidently was one case in point. Even today, the moment men's emotions are really stirred, their minds really bent upon a particular political, social or religious aim, they readily place the increased power given by knowledge at the service of these specific biases. Thus Marxist, nationalist-romantic and Catholic conceptions of history are just such modern reconciliations of absolute dogmatic standards with the scientific ascertainment of facts and the critical examination of sources. All of them doubtless may appear prejudicial to scientific "objectivity," as postulated by the relativistic historiography of the modern "liberal" period. But, even granted that the prevalent standards of liberal historiography, whose most rigid application the present author personally accepts, are more apt to satisfy pure scientific curiosity, one may view *absolute* objectivity as an unrealizable dream. Pragmatic history, the utilization of historical knowledge as a handmaid or, if one wishes, a "mother" of life, possesses an independent justification.

The Jewish religion has little to lose and much to gain from a thorough knowledge of the past. In the first chapter of this book an attempt has been made to demonstrate, in complete independence of the present discussion, how much the peculiar Jewish theism has always hinged on the contrast of history and nature. To a "historical monotheism" the buttresses of history must appear the more welcome, the weaker the traditional theistic sanctions become in the modern environment. In their subconscious, as well as conscious, historical feeling, modern Jews have much in common, both with one another and with their ancestors. Through it, steeped in their religious heritage, even agnostic Jews cannot escape its transcending power. The description of Jacob Wassermann's work, in a recent obituary, has more general validity, not only for Jewish writers and scholars, but also for the inarticulate majority. "He comprehended his work," writes the *Frankfurter Zeitung*, "as historiography in the deepest sense, as the illumination of our time; he aimed at one's identification with the destiny of the period and demanded that everyone should place himself squarely behind the truth which he had found." Such agnosticism approaches very closely, indeed, to the theism of the ancient prophets. It is only through history that Jewish atheists may learn the significance and power of historical continuity. Like natively unmusical persons before the beauty of music, these irreligious Jews may bow before the historic function of organized religion. They may thus resign themselves to a community of life with their other, perhaps more fortunate, compatriots, to whom the solaces of religion are open through a native or acquired emotional capacity. In short, it may not be presumptuous to hope that such an authoritative unity of historical reinterpretation, coupled with the persistence of historically rooted folk ways (a resanctified Sabbath, for example), may yet save the Jewish people from internecine, schismatic warfare. In any event, however, a larger or smaller "remnant" of Jewry would thus be safeguarded to continue its historic procession toward its final historic, *i.e.*, messianic, goal.

However that may be, and whatever one thinks of the ultimate value of "history" for Jewish preservation, the road of the Jew will long remain a thorny road. Our modern civilization, with its overemphasis upon comfort and the general amenities of life, has made Jews and non-Jews alike a rather easy-going lot. Especially in the boom years of prosperity, life's tragic implications were much too easily forgotten. The present generation, however, seems better prepared to face the grandeur of profound joy and profound sorrow. Young Jews, in particular, realize with growing intensity that, to quote a popular proverb, "it is difficult to be a Jew"; but that, at the same time, being a Jew may really have compensations. Only a Judaism worthy of great sacrifice, and if necessary hallowed by great sacrifice, now appeals not only to the active pioneers on Palestinian soil, but to the myriads in dispersion. "Every commandment," said an ancient rabbi, "for which Israel have suffered martyrdom in a period of persecution (e.g., idolatry and circumcision) is still strictly adhered to, whereas every commandment for which Israel have not suffered martyrdom (phylacteries, for example) has remained of dubious observance" (Shabbat 130a). The positive principle underlying the animal (and human) sacrifices of the ancient religions still holds true for every full-fledged religious allegiance, although their outward form has been rejected by subsequent more "humane" generations. Just as every true human love grows into permanence by unlimited mutual sacrifice, so only one who is ready to sacrifice all for the sake of his conviction, religious or secular, has truly taken hold of his ideal in perpetuity. This is not a philosophy of ascetic abnegation nor a glorification of suffering as such. But the readiness for suffering, wherever necessary and the joyous affirmation on all other occasions—this is perhaps the very kernel of Jewish religious and ethnic survival.

"A NEW SONG"

If the preceding analysis is not altogether erroneous, the answer to the searching question of our time is evidently given: The Jewish people and their religion *are* going to survive the present extraordinary crisis. The unique interlocking of Jewish religion and nationality, in fact, offers even greater impregnability than the purely religious safeguards of the other denominations. Just as, in the former religious-minded ages, the Jewish faith has often saved the Jewish nation from imminent extinction, so will, in the present nationalist period, the Jewish ethnos rescue the Jewish religion. Before our very eyes, the neo-messianic hope, surging higher and higher toward Zion, has tremendously fortified Judaism also in its momentous struggle for survival in the dispersion. It is, nevertheless, the first duty of leaders to try to alleviate the sufferings incidental to the new adjustments and to shorten the period of trial and error. Through extensive economic planning, they must help to restratify and redistribute the people on a sounder basis, and to prepare them for the likely advent of the new, regimented social order. Although trying to retain the precious heritage of the nineteenth century, they must take a more critical view of the effects of emancipation, and think much more in postemancipatory terms. Through their entire history inescapably linked with the ideals of social justice, peace and the brotherhood of men, the Jewish people must none the less work out their essentially nonpolitical destinies in independence of prevalent political trends, liberal or conservative, communist or fascist. But they must never surrender their humanitarian aspiration to any kind of jingoistic nationalism, no matter how great the temptation within or the pressure without. They must also rebuild their ethnic, communal and religious life on new foundations. Western Judaism, especially, must be revitalized, through culture and education, as a value worthy of affirmation, rather than be allowed to vegetate as a sort of "inverted Marranism." Jewish unity, in so far as it is at all possible in such a dispersed and diversified people, must be built around these positive principles, much more than around negative and purely defensive aims.

The religious Jews, in particular, must follow the line of their own "historical monotheism" as well as the true, though now long forgotten, meaning of the word "religion," and give back to Judaism that double function of *relegere* and *religari* of which the ancients spoke. They must reread their profession of faith in the light of both past history and present needs, thus retaining historical continuity in the midst of most radical adaptations; and they must reëstablish that firm *link* between the individual and the community which alone can reawaken in each Jew the sense of discipline and spontaneous obedience to the supreme postulates of his people's historic destiny. Like Deutero-Isaiah and his disciples among the psalmists during Israel's emergence from the crisis of Exile, the religious leaders of our postemancipatory age must be ready to "sing unto the Lord a new song" (Isa. 42:10; Ps. 96:1; 98:1, etc.), new and appropriate to the great historical epoch which has just begun. But even more than at that juncture, the "new things" and the "former things" (*hadashot* and *rishonot*), so often vividly contrasted by the exalted poet-prophet, must now subtly intermingle in the great stream of Jewish social and religous history.